MARGARET
LAURENCE

For Judith

MARGARET LAURENCE

The Making of a Writer

Donez Xiques

DUNDURN PRESS
TORONTO

Copy-editor: Patricia Kennedy
Designer: Jennifer Scott
Printer: University of Toronto Press

Library and Archives Canada Cataloguing in Publication

Xiques, Donez
    Margaret Laurence : the making of a writer / Donez Xiques.

Includes bibliographical references and index.
ISBN 1-55002-579-1

1. Laurence, Margaret, 1926-1987. 2. Novelists, Canadian

(English)--20th century--Biography. I. Title.

PS8523.A86Z994 2005   C813'.54   C2005-904877-8

1   2   3   4   5   09   08   07   06   05

We acknowledge the support of the **Canada Council for the Arts** and the **Ontario Arts Council** for our publishing program. We also acknowledge the financial support of the **Government of Canada** through the **Book Publishing Industry Development Program** and **The Association for the Export of Canadian Books**, and the **Government of Ontario** through the **Ontario Book Publishers Tax Credit program**, and the **Ontario Media Development Corporation**.

Care has been taken to trace the ownership of copyright material used in this book. The author and the publisher welcome any information enabling them to rectify any references or credit in subsequent editions.

J. Kirk Howard, President

Printed and bound in Canada.
Printed on recycled paper.

www.dundurn.com

Dundurn Press
3 Church Street, Suite 500
Toronto, Ontario, Canada
M5E 1M2

Gazelle Book Services Limited
White Cross Mills
Hightown, Lancaster, England
LA1 4X5

Dundurn Press
2250 Military Road
Tonawanda NY
U.S.A. 14150

BOOKS BY
MARGARET LAURENCE

FICTION
This Side Jordan (1960)
The Tomorrow-Tamer (1963)
The Stone Angel (1964)
A Jest of God (1966)
The Fire-Dwellers (1969)
A Bird in the House (1970)
The Diviners (1974)

NON-FICTION
The Prophet's Camel Bell (1963)
Long Drums and Cannons: Nigerian Dramatists and Novelists (1968)
Heart of a Stranger (1976)
Dance on the Earth (1989)

FICTION FOR YOUNG ADULTS
Jason's Quest (1970)
Six Darn Cows (1979)
The Olden Days Coat (1979)
The Christmas Birthday Story (1980)

TRANSLATIONS
A Tree for Poverty: Somali Poetry and Prose (1954)

TABLE OF CONTENTS

PREFACE

Margaret Laurence in Africa. The phrase is unfamiliar; yet it was *The Prophet's Camel Bell*, a remarkable travel memoir recounting a two-year residence in East Africa, that first brought Laurence's writing to my attention the year after her death at the age of sixty. I was spending the summer of 1988 in Canada, but I had never met Laurence and was then unaware of her passing and of her enormous impact on Canadian letters during the mid-twentieth century.

I found the narrative voice in *The Prophet's Camel Bell* remarkable, and then began researching her subsequent five-year sojourn in the Gold Coast (Ghana). Eager for more of her writing, I read *The Tomorrow-Tamer and Other Stories*, a collection of ten stories with West African settings and characters. It was only after these "African" works that I read her "Manawaka" fiction — books with Canadian characters and settings.

Over time my engagement with Margaret Laurence's books led me to ask: how did this woman, born Peggy Wemyss in the Canadian prairies in 1926 and raised there during the years of the Great Depression, become such an accomplished professional writer? It was the trajectory of Margaret Laurence's apprenticeship that I wanted to discover, for it was her writing that drew me, and for which she will be remembered.

In search of clues about the period of her apprenticeship, I embarked on my research. At that time other scholars had published analyses of her major fiction, but little attention had been paid to her beginnings. I was fortunate in my quest, because I was able to locate and interview more than one hundred people who had known her (former teachers, classmates, neighbours, and professional associates), and who were scattered across Canada from Vancouver to Winnipeg, Toronto, Montreal, and Nova Scotia, as well as those living in England and Scotland. These interviews, augmented by extensive archival research in North America and England, form the background of this study and made it possible to chart the course of Margaret Laurence's development as a writer, one of the most important of her generation. I wanted as much as possible to narrate the story of that development from her perspective — and from a time when she had no idea what the future might hold or what results her efforts to become a writer might yield.

The notion of following Margaret Laurence at the peak of her career was less interesting to me than tracing the path of her literary growth. She was an ambitious young woman, who, after graduating from college, worked as a journalist, married, and then set out to accompany her husband during his quest for challenging engineering work in remote areas. While doing so, she found her literary voice in the high desert plateau of the British Somaliland Protectorate and in the semi-tropical regions of the African Gold Coast. This young woman, who lived abroad as Peggy Laurence, returned to Canada, where she became, as Margaret Laurence, one of the most respected and beloved writers of her day.

In tracing her experiences as a young writer during the months following her graduation from college, I read more than a hundred columns that carried her byline in two Winnipeg newspapers. Although material exists from that period and from her school years, as it sometimes does for other writers, we might not have known much about the many years of her slow apprenticeship prior to her literary successes had it not been for her voluminous correspondence while abroad. Hundreds of letters provide information about this period and supplement the information in her memoirs, *Dance on the Earth*. There are letters to her literary agent, and to editors at three major publishing houses: McClelland & Stewart, Canada; Macmillan, London; and Alfred A. Knopf, New York. In addition, there is an extensive and unique body of correspondence with another Manitoban, Adele Wiseman, who became a lifelong friend and a significant author in her own right.

These letters make clear that Margaret Laurence's efforts to develop her talent as a writer extended over a long period, even though interviews much later in her life tend to convey the impression that her writing was "inspired," a concept that she seemed to endorse.

The Margaret Laurence who emerged from my research is not the middle-aged woman who is shown casually walking to the post office in the National Film Board's presentation *First Lady of Manawaka*, nor is she the woman, whom some people recall, anxiously arriving hours ahead of time for appointments and cautiously waiting for a light to change before crossing a street. I discovered rather the younger writer who slept in the back of a Land Rover in the desert plateau of Somalia while accompanying her husband as he directed a project to make water available to the semi-nomadic herdsmen and their camels. Margaret Laurence in her twenties was intrepid and eager for adventure. She endured sandstorms, sudden *kharif* winds, and monsoon rains. She sat around campfires under the stunning African night sky, undertook a study of the Koran, learned to drive, and was cool-headed in emergencies. More importantly, Laurence was also a singularly dedicated writer, with perseverance and strong determination, who worked assiduously to develop her literary talents.

In presenting this study of Margaret Laurence's apprenticeship years, I put forward a portrait of an ambitious writer, who time and again ripped up pages of manuscript when her novels were not working out well. Here is a writer, weary of rejection slips, pouring out her insecurities and anger in letters to her good friend Adele Wiseman. Here is the younger Laurence, sparring on the page with her publisher Jack McClelland and prodding her agent to secure a contract for a collection of her short stories.

Others will write of Margaret Laurence's decency as a human being, of her great compassion, of her attentive listening as she encouraged fellow writers, and of her personal failings. She drank heavily in her later years, but that was a private matter, known to friends and family; it was not manifest outside the private sphere. Conscious of her own shortcomings, Margaret Laurence struggled with feelings of guilt during most of her adult years. And she never resolved the tensions that arose from being a writer, a wife, and a mother. Overcoming a natural shyness, she would speak out against injustice and the evils of the nuclear arms race. Taking time from her own work, she would reply to letters from children and petitioners. Writing was the air she breathed, and it is difficult for us, as readers, to fully grasp the agony Margaret Laurence suffered when she felt that gift had been taken from her. She was ambitious but not self-centred, and if, in her later years, she could be stubborn and impatient, that was chiefly the result of principle, feelings of anxiety, or the sense of a moral imperative.

Today, the forms of biography are undergoing change and experimentation. As a result, I believe it is important to clarify my own approach to narrating the story of Margaret Laurence's literary apprenticeship. Much of the evidence in this book, documented from various archives, contemporary newspapers, and the many interviews I conducted, has not been used by previous biographers. Those studies have not focused exclusively on telling the remarkable story of Margaret Laurence's efforts to develop her voice as a writer and of her dedication to the craft of writing, as this one does. I have not appropriated scenes or characters from Laurence's novels. I do not attempt to construct the story of her life from the fragments of her fiction, as if that were some sort of semi-transparent account of her personal life. Although it is a truism that all literature is in some sense autobiographical, in my opinion, searching for a one-to-one correspondence is merely a distraction. I believe that with creative people, such as artists, writers, and composers, the source of their creativity, whether inspired by real events or persons, frequently transcends and transforms any purely personal material.

As my endnotes demonstrate, a decade has passed since I first embarked on this work. Nevertheless, my interest in Margaret Laurence has not abated. I hope this story of her growth and development as a writer, told as much as possible from her perspective and not from hindsight, will lead more readers to her books and serve to encourage a new generation of writers.

Donez Xiques

ACKNOWLEDGEMENTS

This book is the result of many years of research and travel, during which I have been privileged to meet and be welcomed by numerous people. I am grateful to all, and, in particular, to the following individuals, for interviews and conversations: Chinua Achebe; Mary Adachi; Madge (Hetherington) Allen; Ruby Amor; William Atkinson; Margaret Atwood; Douglas Barnaby; A.G. Bedford; John Bell; Dan and Audrey Billings; Joanne (Blondal) Bishoprick; Jeanette (Grosney) Black; Ken Black; Kay Bolton; Remi Bouchard; Laura Bowman; Dorothy (Batchelor) Brown; Ann Cameron; Robert Carter; Greta Coger; Doreen and Neil Cohen; Max Cohen; Jean Murray Cole; Gerald and Marie Colwell; Jack Coutts; Jane Cushman; Jan De Bruyn; Jessie-Marie Deplissey; Miriam Wiseman Distler; Mary McAlpine Dobbs; Kay (Mrs. George) Douglas; Shirley Douglas; Gordon Elliott; Marjory (Osborn) English; Timothy Findley; Rev.Charles Forsyth; Noreen Foster; Doris (Peterson) Franklin; Ursula Franklin; Joyce Friesen; Margaret Fulton; Priscilla Galloway; Rosemary Ganley; Jean Gartlan; Rev. Mark Gibson; Kenneth Goldstein; Dorothy Goresky; Eileen (Goodrich) Graham; Bea Guinn; Anne (Mrs. Robert) Hallstead; Ann (Phelps) Hamilton; Vern Hamilton; John Handford; Robert Harlow; Rev. Phillip Hewett; Alan Hockin; Jack Hodgins; Don C. Humphrey; Margaret Hutchison; Percy Janes; Hans Jewinski; Doris (Blondal) Johnson; Nadine Asante Jones; Frances (Bolton) Jones; Judith Jones; Jim Julius; John Kerr;

G.D. Killam; Hilda Kirkwood; Kate and Kim Krenz; Louise (Alguire) Kubik; Christine Kurata; Nick Lalani; Dorothy Lawson of the Bowen Island Historians; Dorothie (Neil) Lindquist; Jack (John Fergus) Laurence; Karen Laurence; Peggy (Mrs. Robert) Laurence; Robin Laurence; Delza Lakey Longman; Helen Lucas; Jack Ludwig; Nonie Lyon; Charles Meighen, QC; Alan Maclean; Lino Magagna; Patricia Morley; Margaret (Main) Schoenberg; John Marshall; Joyce Marshall; Wes McAmmond; Jack McClelland; Carol McIver McConnell; William McConnell; Senator Heath Macquarrie; Capt. M.R. Miller; Patricia Morley; Alice Munro; Mildred Musgrove; Rev. Bruce Mutch; Brenda Neill; William H. New; Rev. Jack Patterson; Roland Penner; Elizabeth Pennie; Harry Penny; Muriel (Laurence) Peterson; Eric Pettit; John S. Pink; Cecil Pittman; Helen Porter; Al Purdy; Laurie Ricou; François Ricard; Earl Robinson; Anne Ross; Julie Ross; Malcolm Ross; Jane Rule; Enid Rutland; Said S. Samatar; Doris Saunders; Rev. Thomas Saunders; Rev. David Shearman; Fred and June Schulof; Norman Seymour; Shirley (Lev) Sharzer; Annabel Smith; Meg Stainsby; Helen (Warkentin) Stanley; Walter Swayze; Connie (Offen) Sword and J.H. Sword; Eve and René Temple; Mary Thomson; Shelia Thompson; Leona Thwaites; Ivan Traill; Margaret Tunney; Mary (Mindus) Turnbull; Steven Turtell; Alan Twigg; Evelyn Vivian; Frauke Voss; Miriam Waddington; Laurence Wall; Rev. Ron Ward; J.A. Wainwright; Robert Weaver; Michael Welton; Pat (Mrs. Robert) Wemyss; William F. Whitehead; Marjory Whitelaw; Leone Wilcox; Alice Olsen Williams; Budge Wilson; Jean (Kerr) Williams; Lois (Freeman) Wilson; Michael Wilson; Adele Wiseman; Peggy Woods; J.C. Woodbury; Dorothy (Beales) Wyman and Rev. Harold Wyman; David Zieroth.

I am grateful to Jocelyn Laurence and David Laurence for their interest in this project. They granted permission to quote from Margaret Laurence's books and letters, and generously allowed access to various archives that contained relevant material.

I wish to extend very special thanks to the following persons who gave me valuable information and comments: Asabea Acquaah-Harrison; B.W. (Goosh) Andrzejewski and his wife, Sheila; Silver Donald Cameron; Victoria Ofosu-Appiah; Connie Offen Sword and the late Jack Sword; Clara Thomas; and Marjory Whitelaw. I am also grateful to the following members of the Anglo-Somali Society, who knew the Laurences in the British Somaliland Protectorate and shared their recollections with me in the early 1990s: C.R.V. Bell, OBE; J.J. Lawrie; Michael Wilson; and especially C.J. ("Bob") Martin, whose hospitality, interest, and unfailing kindness were of great assistance. In addition, I extend thanks to many citizens of Neepawa and the several presidents of the Margaret Laurence Home Committee, particularly Dorothy Campbell Henderson, whose assistance and enthusiasm have been invaluable over the years.

It is a pleasure to thank Clara Thomas (*Margaret Laurence*, and *The Manawaka World of Margaret Laurence*), Margaret Laurence's first biographer, who has written extensively on her work and who encouraged my research into Laurence's early career. I am also indebted to the following scholars, whose work is significant for all subsequent Laurence biographers: John Lennox, editor of *Margaret Laurence — Al Purdy : A Friendship in Letters*; John Lennox and Ruth Panofsky, editors of *Selected Letters of Margaret Laurence and Adele Wiseman*; Patricia Morley for *Margaret Laurence: The Long Journey Home*; Susan J. Warwick, who compiled the first comprehensive annotated bibliography of Margaret Laurence's work; and to J.A. Wainwright for *A Very Large Soul*, an important edition of Margaret Laurence's letters to selected Canadian writers. Although two biographies of Margaret Laurence have been published in the past decade, my own research was completed prior to those publications. In addition, this book provides a unique focus, in that it presents a detailed examination of the significant years of Laurence's early literary development.

I have been fortunate to have access to relevant holdings in the following libraries and am grateful to all there who gave assistance, especially to: the National Archives of Canada (Anne Goddard); the National Library of Canada; Columbia University Library; Dalhousie University; Georgetown University Library; the Harry Ransom Humanities Research Center (Cathy Henderson); William Ready Division of Archives at McMaster University (Carl Spadoni); the Provincial Archives of Manitoba; the Provincial Archives of Nova Scotia; the Public Records Office, Kew, England; Queen's University Library, Kingston; the Schomburg Center for Research in Black Culture; the University of British Columbia (George Brandak, Chris Hives); the University of Calgary (Apollonia L. Steele); the University College of Cape Breton; the

Thomas Fisher Rare Book Library of the University of Toronto; the University of Trent (John Wadland); the University of Waterloo; York University (Barbara Craig, Suzanne Dubeau, Phyllis Platnick, the late Kent Haworth); the Library of Congress, Washington, D.C. My thanks also to Sally Keefe-Cohen of Marian Hebb and Associate; Jane Buss of the Writers' Federation of Nova Scotia; and to the staffs of the *Vancouver Sun*; the *Winnipeg Free Press*, and the *Neepawa Press*.

I acknowledge and appreciate the interest and assistance of: Shareen B. Brysac; Barbara Heyman; Park Honan; Stuart Hughes; Jennifer Longobardi; Lindsey Petersheim; Mhari Mackintosh; Barbara McManus; Victoria Ridout; Marilyn Rose; Joan Johnston; David Stouck; Lewis St. George Stubbs; and Robert Thacker. I appreciate as well the interest shown by the chairs of the English department at Brooklyn College of the City University of New York over the past decade.

I wish to thank in particular the following persons who read and commented on all or part of various versions of this book: Janet Baker, Kathy Chamberlain, Mona Spratt Meredith, Elizabeth Peirce, Jack Pink, Dorothy Coutts Shields, Connie Offen Sword, and Budge Wilson. I appreciate the careful attention and comments of my editor, Patricia Kennedy, as well as the assistance of my editor at Dundurn, Barry Jowett.

As a participant in the following groups, I wish to express my gratitude: to Ken Silverman and the members of the New York University Biography Group and to the members of the Women Writing Women's Lives Seminar in New York City.

The assistance and interest of the following Canadian booksellers is acknowledged with gratitude and pleasure: Hugh Anson-Cartright, David Mason, Richard Spoffard, and Steven Temple.

This work would not have been completed without the invaluable assistance of Steven Siebert of Nota Bene, and grants from the following: the Canadian Embassy; the Fulbright Foundation; the Professional Staff Congress of the City University of New York; and Wolfe Institute of Brooklyn College.

Finally, I am indebted to: Sandra Barry, Julia Hirsch, Robert Viscusi, Judith Walter, and my sisters, Nadine Yurko and Adrienne Caldwell. I am deeply grateful to Beth Bruder of the Dundurn Group, and to Julie P.

Gardinier, and Robert E. Svenson for their insights and personal support. This project would not have been completed without them. I owe a special debt of gratitude to my partner, Judith Chelius Stark, for her encouragement, generous help, and steady good humour during the long process of completing *Margaret Laurence: The Making of a Writer.*

CHAPTER ONE

Landscape of the Heart

SEPTEMBER 1986
PETERBOROUGH, ONTARIO

The elevator door opened quietly on the third floor as the wail of a siren pierced the September air and an ambulance quickly turned into the drive below. Margaret Laurence's friend Joan Johnston stepped from the elevator and walked down the corridor of St. Joseph's Hospital, Peterborough. A smile crossed her anxious face when she heard the steady clackety-clack of a typewriter growing louder as she passed the nurses' station and approached the door of Room 351.

"Margaret, how are you?"

The writer paused. "Hello, Kiddo."

Across the bedsheets, Margaret Laurence had spread out the photographs that she planned to use in her memoirs, *Dance on the Earth*.

To the friends and family of this distinguished Canadian writer, it seemed unbelievable that, at the age of sixty, Margaret, a robust and independent woman, was terminally ill with cancer. The trajectory of her literary career had brought Margaret Laurence two Governor General's Awards. She had written a landmark translation of Somali tales and poems, important fiction and non-fiction about Africa, several children's books, a collection of essays, and a memorable group of novels set in Canada — a total of sixteen books.

Now, in St. Joseph's Hospital, Joan Johnston set down her packages and moved to admire the photos that were spread out across the sheets. The two women talked over the details of Margaret's memoirs, and chuckled together as she recounted an incident from that morning. Margaret still had a quirky sense of humour, but her hearty laugh was muffled, because the pain in her chest had become severe.

Later, as Joan walked from the hospital into the afternoon sunshine towards her car, an anxious look settled again on her face. She wondered whether Margaret Laurence would be able to finish writing her memoirs.

In a matter of days, the typing in Room 351 stopped. The task was too difficult. Although Margaret wanted so much to complete the book, she no longer had the strength to type. Joan Johnston offered a solution. If Margaret could dictate the rest of her memoirs into a tape recorder, Joan would type them up. That plan was put into action after Margaret was discharged and returned to her home in Lakefield, Ontario. At first things went well, and she was pleased to focus once more on her writing; but within a short time even that effort became too taxing. As the cancer took its toll and Margaret Laurence realized there would be no cure, she confided one day to Budge Wilson, fellow writer and friend, "Oh, Budge, I'm going to miss the fun things."[1]

Margaret Laurence was worried that she would not be able to complete the revisions. Nevertheless, she managed to make frequent entries in a very personal journal that she had begun earlier that summer at the urging of her close friend Professor Clara Thomas.[2]

Although at first glance Margaret Laurence seemed to be hardy, she had not been in good health for a number of years. In the 1970s she had been diagnosed with diabetes. In the 1980s issues with her eyesight necessitated cataract surgery. Furthermore, she had suffered from bouts of carpal tunnel syndrome, exacerbated by typing, and may also have suffered long-term health issues from taking diet pills years before.

As the summer days gave way to autumn, Margaret's strength diminished and the pain increased, although her voice remained strong over the telephone, concealing that pain from friends and family. She had always been very independent, but now, despite the urgency she felt to complete her memoirs, Margaret found it tiring even to use the tape recorder. Nevertheless, as her friend Joan transcribed the audiotapes, Margaret made the effort to edit them. Writing was then, as it always had been, Margaret's life-support system. Joan Johnston was eager to assist, but she continued to worry, thinking that, if Margaret's writing stopped, her life might end as well.[3] After the publication of *The Diviners* in 1974, Laurence had struggled with several drafts of a new novel, but she was not satisfied with its progress and seemed unable to wrestle the new material into shape. Now, Margaret herself felt that her work as a writer was completed. She told friends and family that she had completed what she "had been given" to write.

As the weeks passed, her physical condition rapidly worsened. Margaret was weak and in more pain than others realized. Her health was further compromised in early December when she fell and broke a leg. The fracture necessitated wearing a heavy cast that extended along the leg to well above her knee. The need to use crutches complicated matters, and Margaret became increasingly dependent on family and friends for daily care. However, she worried about being a burden to others, and remembered all too well her beloved stepmother's lengthy illness from cancer in 1957, when Margaret herself had been about the same age as her daughter, Jocelyn, now was. Margaret was very reluctant to have Jocelyn and her brother, David, endure what she had experienced at her stepmother's death many years earlier.[4]

At that time, Margaret had returned to Canada in haste with her two young children from Africa's Gold Coast, where her husband was completing an engineering project, in order to be with her stepmother, whom she always called Mum, and who was dying in Vancouver. As the months passed and Mum grew weaker, experiencing intense pain, Margaret's anguish and worry increased. Nine long months after Margaret's return to Canada, Mum died in September 1957.

Now, as Margaret realized her own condition was terminal and would only worsen, she gradually came to the decision to end her own life. That decision was exceedingly difficult, and she struggled with it over a period of several months as she pondered, prayed, and sought counsel.[5] As November and December passed, she did manage to edit the third draft of her memoirs. Then, on the morning of January 5, 1987, Margaret Laurence took an overdose of pills and died in her home on Regent Street in Lakefield, Ontario, where she had lived for the past twelve years. Her pen lay on the table nearby, where it had fallen from her hand and now rested beside her journal. Margaret had composed a message to her children and loved ones. To the very end, she had been writing.

As the news of Margaret Laurence's death reached the public, tributes to one of Canada's most loved writers began to pour in over radio, on television, and even from parliament in Ottawa. Her friend, the poet Al Purdy, in his poem "To Margaret," has captured the effect that she had on her friends. He wrote:

> . . . .
> remembering how alive
> she lit up the rooms she occupied
> like flowers do sometimes and the sun always
> in a way visible only to friends
> and she had nothing else.

After her funeral in Lakefield, hundreds of mourners attended a public memorial service at Bloor Street United Church in Toronto. Memorials were held in other provinces, too — gestures of respect for this woman from the prairies whose books had touched so many and whose generosity to fellow writers had become legendary.

How had Margaret Laurence become so accomplished? How had Peggy Wemyss, born in a small prairie town during the 1920s and raised there during the Great Depression, managed to develop her literary gifts and become a writer whose books were published not only in Canada, but also in England and the United States? To those questions there is no single or easy answer. The making of a writer, an artist, or a musician is a mysterious and complex process. In the case of Margaret Laurence, she had a profound belief that she had been blessed with the gift to be a writer. And in addition to a strong desire to write, she felt a deep responsibility to nurture and develop that gift. The gift may have been given, but it was Margaret's ardour and ambition that endowed it with shape and form. Over the years her self-discipline and diligence enabled her abilities to develop, even though there were many times as an adult when she felt torn between her responsibilities as wife and parent and her need to write.

The development of Margaret Laurence's talent as a writer was influenced not only by her character and temperament, but also by situations and people in her life. Before that talent could flourish, however, she had to set herself on a long, arduous, exacting, and at times exciting, period of apprenticeship. And for those who know something of Margaret Laurence's childhood, it will come as no surprise that those childhood years had a profound impact of the unfolding and development of her literary talent.

Neepawa, Manitoba
1926

Born on July 18, 1926, in Neepawa, Manitoba, Margaret Laurence was christened Jean Margaret Wemyss, although she was known as Peggy. She was the only child of Verna Simpson and Robert Wemyss, a lawyer. Margaret Laurence once described her ancestry as follows: "a Celt of sorts, being Irish on my mother's side and Scots on my father's, with a slight admixture of Sassenach blood through one of my grandmothers, who came from United Empire Loyalist stock." She went on to add that "The sense of sorrow (and laughter as well) is in me, also, I believe."[6]

Margaret's parents, Verna and Bob, had grown up in Neepawa. The town's name, according to local history, was derived from the Cree language and means "land of plenty" or "beautiful land." Even today, the description seems apt. Situated about 125 miles northwest of Winnipeg, the capital of the province of Manitoba, Neepawa was then and remains today a very stable and relatively prosperous town. Peggy's father, Robert, the eldest son of a prominent town lawyer, completed his education at St. Andrew's College in Toronto.[7] Then, with the Great War raging in Europe, Bob and his younger brother, Jack, enlisted in the army. Assigned to the Canadian Field Artillery, 60th Battery, the Wemyss brothers saw action during four years of bitter fighting in Europe, Bob as a gunner, Jack as a driver.[8] Margaret Laurence retained her father's copy of *The 60th C.F.A.*

Battery Book, published in 1919, and in a strongly cadenced prose passage in her memoirs she poignantly describes the situation of those veterans, her father and uncle: "They will not talk, later on, of what they have seen, of what they had to do, in the blood and mud, in the trenches of France, amongst the wounded and dying, amongst the dead, in the gunfire. They have become old men at twenty-one and twenty-four."[9]

After surviving the horrors of trench warfare overseas, the brothers returned to Canada. Robert Wemyss joined his father's law firm in Neepawa, and, in the summer of 1924, he married Verna Simpson. Their daughter, Jean Margaret, was born two years later.

From all indications Verna and Bob were very much in love. They were active socially in Neepawa and had a close circle of friends. A photo taken of them when Peggy was two years old shows her parents at a Fancy Dress Ball. Wearing Spanish costumes, Verna and Bob Wemyss look very happy as they pose for that photo with about fifty guests, including their friends the Kerrs, the Spratts, the Crawfords, the Alguires, Dr. Cleave, and Dr. Martin.[10]

Margaret Laurence's mother, Verna, was the second-youngest of seven surviving children of John and Jane (née Bailey) Simpson. John Simpson's ancestors had come to Canada from Ireland in the mid-nine-teenth century. John, born in Ontario in 1856, was a cabinetmaker by trade and had come west to Manitoba as a young man. A family story relates that he walked the impressive distance from Winnipeg to Portage la Prairie. There he worked with a cousin and met his future wife, Jane Bailey. Her family were United Empire Loyalists, who had come to Canada from the United States during the American Revolution. Several years after Jane Bailey married John Simpson, they moved to Neepawa, where he went into the furniture and hardware business and later became a local funeral director. Their daughter Verna, who became Margaret Laurence's mother, was said to be more lighthearted and spontaneous than her three older sisters. She also had genuine talent for the piano, and in 1907, Verna, at the age of eleven, played in a recital held in Neepawa's new Opera House.[11] The program from that recital was treasured by Margaret Laurence until her death.[12]

As Verna matured, she continued to study piano under several fine teachers, among whom was Eva Clare, a Neepawan who had enjoyed a celebrated career as a pianist. Eva Clare had studied in New York and Berlin, and her concert performances in several European countries had met with acclaim.[13] The *Vienna Tagblatt* reported that Eva Clare's technique was "brilliant."[14] Studying under such an accomplished pianist must have been exciting and exacting for Verna Simpson. However, a career in music was out of the question, because her father would not permit it. Verna did, however, manage to pursue advanced piano studies in Winnipeg for several months. After returning to Neepawa, she taught piano there and played occasionally in local concerts.

Within two years of Verna's marriage to Bob Wemyss, the couple moved into a bungalow on Vivian Street. Although their home was small, it was located at the south end of town, close to Park Lake, an area where many of Neepawa's most distinguished families lived.[15] Verna had two miscarriages before Peggy's birth, and the young couple were relieved when their healthy, active little daughter was born.[16] There were doting relatives, too, for baby Peggy had become the youngest Neepawa member of the Simpson family, displacing her teenaged cousin Catherine Simpson, who lived nearby. During the next three years, Peggy's mother proudly made entries in a "Baby Book": "At thirteen months trying to say everything; at two years telling us she was crazy about beet greens; has a great imagination; speaks a lot about her 'funny' house, where Paper Slim, and Mr. and Mrs. Slim live."[17] Verna notes her little daughter's "accomplishments," and mentions Peggy's large vocabulary and talent with words, her response to music, and her early interest in making up stories. Her mother's comments describe a child who is curious and imaginative.[18]

The future Margaret Laurence spent her childhood and adolescence amidst the familiar and secure surroundings of Neepawa. The town was proud of its Opera House, and the citizens valued musical and theatrical talent. In her parents' day, performances of light opera and various concerts were popular, as were large parties and dances.[19] The town was surrounded by fertile prairie farmland with its distinctive rich, black soil. Neepawa, which was also a commercial centre for the area, had a population of approximately twenty-five hundred, and was remarkably self-sufficient for a town of that size.[20] It could boast of being the nexus of two major railway lines, the Canadian Pacific and Canadian National railways, and had a roundhouse as well. The town also had several well-attended churches, three auto dealerships, a brick factory, and a large salt plant. Its citizens were justifiably proud of Neepawa's hospital and nursing school.

Everyone in that small town knew the Wemyss and Simpson families; everyone knew little Peggy. She could wander freely about the tree-lined streets or be invited in for a cookie at a neighbour's home. If anything seemed seriously amiss in town, people were quickly alerted by telephone. In fact, the party lines and central operator made it hard to have a truly private phone conversation. On July 20, 1930, two days after Peggy's fourth birthday, those phone lines began to ring. Her mother, Verna Simpson Wemyss, had succumbed to an acute kidney infection and died in the Neepawa hospital after a brief illness. The town was shocked. Sixty years later a neighbour still recalls how devastated her own mother had been over Verna Wemyss's death at the age of thirty-four.[21]

Little Peggy thought her mother was in the hospital, and was not immediately informed about her death. She learned of it while playing outside one day with a playmate who accidentally blurted out the shocking news. Stunned, Peggy ran inside, where adults told her that her friend had not lied. It was true. Her mother was dead. "After that," she said in her memoirs, "I have no conscious memories for about a year."[22]

Overwhelmed by her mother's death, four-year-old Peggy was comforted and supported to some extent by the familiar surroundings of her home and by the reassuring presence of her father and Aunt Marg, her mother's sister. Aunt Marg had come home from Calgary for a holiday that summer and, after her sister's sudden death in July, she had remained to take care of her young niece and keep house for her brother-in-law. A year later, Bob Wemyss and his sister-in-law, Marg Simpson, decided to marry and, in August 1931, went to Brandon for a quiet wedding.

This was Marg's first marriage. After completing Normal School, she had taught in Calgary for a number of years, but now as a married woman she was no longer eligible to teach. Perhaps Marg missed the classroom and her old friends in Calgary, but as Mrs. Robert Wemyss she was well-liked in Neepawa, became active in local circles, held the customary afternoon teas at their home, and was instrumental in helping inaugurate the first public library in Neepawa.[23]

Peggy was fortunate in the love of her father and of Aunt Marg, who did not hesitate to talk to Peggy about her biological mother, Verna, referring to her as "your other mother."[24] Nevertheless, Margaret Laurence frankly states, "I cannot say that Mum [Aunt Margaret] stepped into the vacuum left by my mother's death." It is clear, however, from the many incidents in which she recounts her aunt's goodness, that Peggy's love for Aunt Marg was deep, and she later dedicated her first novel, *This Side Jordan*, to her. However, as a young child Peggy was profoundly affected by her mother's sudden death and the loss of her cheerful, loving presence. Laurence states several times: "A measure of my own pain and bewilderment is that total gap in my memory of at least one year."[25] Peggy also had nightmares, walked in her sleep, and recalls being "difficult in many ways." She later interpreted that behaviour as a way of expressing her emotional loss and her inability to absorb "the enormity" of what had happened.[26]

Nonetheless, in many ways life in their home on Vivian Street resumed a comfortable routine after the marriage of Bob and Aunt Marg. There were playmates Peggy's age who lived nearby, and during the week Peggy's father came home each day at noon for dinner, walking the few blocks from his law office on Hamilton Street. Since it was then the custom for school children to return home for their midday meal, Peggy would have been home, too. In a snapshot included in *Dance on the Earth*, Bob Wemyss has the look of a successful businessman. Dressed in a dark three-piece suit, with a neatly folded handkerchief in his breast pocket, he is wearing spats and reading a newspaper. On his left hand he wears a seal ring with the family crest, "Je pense."

On Sunday, after services at the United Church, the family typically went for dinner with the Simpson grandparents who lived in "the Big House" on First Avenue. In addition to that family routine, there were, for Peggy, recurring seasonal events in Neepawa: fall fowl suppers, Thanksgiving, skating parties, hockey games, fireworks on Victoria Day, and agricultural fairs at harvest time. All these gave the youngster a sense of permanence and continuity.

Her home, fondly referred to as "the Little House," was a small white bungalow on the corner of Vivian Street and Mountain Avenue, an area known as Coutts's Corner. Peggy's dormer room on the second floor had a window facing west, and the afternoon sun poured in. The Little

House was surrounded by flowers in spring and summer. At the front, facing Vivian Street, there was a screened-in veranda, where Peggy "sometimes slept in hot weather," and at the back a large garden, where her father enjoyed tending his flowers.[27] Although he was a lawyer by profession, Bob Wemyss probably had very little business during those years of the Great Depression. He was active in Neepawa's Horticultural Society, served on the school board, belonged to several fraternal organizations, and enjoyed playing tennis. He was also an avid photographer, who took many pictures of his family.[28] Laurence also mentions that her father was "a good amateur carpenter and painter." He did much of the interior work in their home: "built-in kitchen cupboards, painted apple green; built-in china cupboard in the living-dining room." Such features were then considered "very modern and innovative."[29]

On the west side of Mountain Avenue, opposite Peggy's home, there was an impressive brick house (which still stands), where Blake Dunlop, publisher and editor of the *Neepawa Press*, lived with his mother. On another corner was the Coutts's family home, hence the name "Coutts's corner." Wallace Coutts and Bob Wemyss served together on the Public School Board and Mrs. Coutts often came to tea at their home. The couples were good friends and played bridge together. Dorothy, the youngest of the Coutts's five children, was one of Peggy's childhood playmates. Another friend, Jean Kerr, who was several years older than Peggy, remembers feeling a tinge of envy when she played with the toys and inventive games that Peggy's doting aunts and parents had given her, but she also recalls Peggy as "a lonely, difficult child" after her mother's death.[30]

Dorothy Coutts, on the other hand, remembers Peggy as friendly, outgoing, and imaginative. She recalls frequent meals and occasional "sleep-overs" at their "cozy little house" as well as vacation times with the family at Clear Lake in Riding Mountain, where Bob Wemyss taught Dorothy how to swim, as he had taught his own daughter and another of her childhood friends, Mona Spratt.[31] Because Dorothy Coutts was close in age to Peggy and lived across the street, the girls played together frequently in Peggy's room upstairs or in "the wonderful playhouse outside" that her father had built. The playhouse, tall enough that adults did not need to stoop, was the perfect setting for "let's pretend." The girls also rehearsed little concerts and plays, mainly instigated by Peggy's active imagination.[32] "Then," recalls Dorothy, "Peggy's stepmother would ask my mother over for our performance. At the end, Marg Wemyss would serve tea and delicious orange bread to us all." Once, when Japanese kimonos were "all the rage," Peggy and Dorothy performed an oriental dance for their parents and friends.[33] Other playmates recall that Peggy was "a great fantasizer. Pretend this, pretend that."[34]

One summer, after Dorothy Coutts had vacationed with the Wemyss family at Clear Lake, Peggy wanted to write a story about their holiday and turned to Dorothy, who was a year older, "to help with the spelling." Peggy dictated the story, and then she and Dorothy went up and down the street, "asking neighbours if they would like us to read our story for a penny. Many of them cooperated and we even got a piece of chocolate cake from one dear lady."[35]

Margaret Laurence herself mentions in interviews that she was a "sort of solitary child," who told stories even before she could write.[36] Her early interest in telling stories and making up plays was fostered by the atmosphere at home and by the encouragement of her father and stepmother. Within a few years, writing stories and poems was to become an indispensable part of young Peggy's life.

School Years: 1932-1939

In September 1932, Peggy, now six years old, began Grade One at Neepawa Public School, three blocks from her own home and across from the United Church. Little mention is made of her introduction to school except for a family story that Peggy was disappointed because she had expected to read after her first day in school.

When winter loosened its grip on the prairie, Peggy and her young friends could not resist the adventure of testing the "rubber ice" that had formed on the roadside ditches. When the children arrived home with wet feet, scoldings inevitably followed. As winter began its slow retreat, the youngsters challenged one another to find, amidst the remaining patches of snow, the first pale-mauve prairie crocuses with their "greengray featherstems."[37] A college classmate of Peggy's recalls the sweet smell of the thawing earth when, as a child, he and his siblings gathered prairie crocuses in large basins, often bringing them in baskets to church for the Easter service.[38]

Another welcomed harbinger of spring is the western meadowlark whose flute-like song from fence posts and fields announces the end of winter. The Manitoba prairies then resemble a vast lake, as water from melting snow and spring rains fills the fields and roadside ditches, forming knee-deep sloughs that attract migrating waterfowl on their northward journey. In early April, skeins of blue geese and lesser snow geese fill the skies, reaching all the way to the horizon.[39] In towns across the prairie, adults as well as children rush outdoors to watch as tens of thousands of geese pass overhead, their glad cries signalling the end of winter, though patches of snow may still lie in the fields. During springtime Peggy and Dorothy sometimes played at "boating," using a neighbour's duck-hunting boat to paddle in the water-filled ditches beside the road.[40]

In late spring 1933, Peggy's father and stepmother adopted an infant boy, whom they named Robert Morrison Wemyss.[41] They probably felt it would be good for Peggy to have a sibling. Peggy, who had turned seven that summer and had been the only child, was pleased and excited at the prospect of having a baby brother, but she remembered feeling some jealousy after the new baby actually arrived.[42] Although adoption was not unusual in Neepawa, Laurence does not state in her memoirs that Bobby was adopted. She saw no reason to call attention to it, and putting that fact into her memoirs would have seemed insensitive. She felt, in fact, that Bobby was "just her brother" and that Marg Wemyss, while not their biological mother, was always "our mother."[43]

In the summer, Peggy's father would take his family on holiday to Riding Mountain, a great escarpment fifty miles northwest of Neepawa. There a park of twelve hundred square miles encompassed a native forest teeming with moose, deer, elk, and other varieties of wildlife. And there Bob Wemyss and his brother-in-law, Stuart Simpson, had built a cottage near the shores of Clear Lake.[44] When Riding Mountain became a National Park in 1933 (the second-oldest in Canada after Banff), the town site at Clear Lake was renamed *Wasagaming*, from the Cree language, meaning literally: "the water is so clear that the sun shines on the bottom."[45]

The family's one-storey frame cottage with its large stone fireplace was a place that Peggy loved. She cherished memories of Clear Lake throughout her life, and from time to time found pleasure living and writing in similar rustic surroundings, such as Point Roberts, near Vancouver, and later at her "shack" on the Otonabee River, near Lakefield.

The cottage at Riding Mountain was situated in a wooded area surrounded by poplar, birch, and fragrant evergreen trees. From the living room there was an unobstructed view of Clear Lake, its waters lapping the shore at the foot of a steep hill about a hundred feet from the front of their cottage. Years later, when asked to name her "most loved place in Canada," Laurence replied that it had been "many places," and added that, although she no longer inhabited those places, they continued to inhabit her: "portions of memory, presences in the mind." Then she identified one such place as her family's summer cottage at Clear Lake in Riding Mountain National Park.[46] In a passage that conveys her childhood excitement and the sense of delight associated with those summer holidays at Riding Mountain, she wrote:

> Before the government piers and the sturdy log staircases down to shore were put in, we used to slither with an exhilarating sense of peril down the steep homemade branch and dirt shelf-steps, through the stands of thin tall spruce and birch trees slender and graceful as girls, passing moss-hairy fallen logs and the white promise of wild strawberry blossoms, until we reached the sand and the hard bright pebbles of the beach at the edge of the cold spring-fed lake where at nights the loons still cried eerily.[47]

In the summer when her family was not at Clear Lake, there were other activities for Peggy to enjoy in Neepawa: concerts and picnics in River Bend Park; the agricultural fair near Scotty Burnett's farm; trains to watch as they arrived to load wheat or take on passengers for Brandon and points west; swimming in the White Mud River, which meandered across the prairies from Saskatchewan through Neepawa's River Bend Park and eastward towards Winnipeg. While the summer heat could be cruel and punishing to farmers, it was less oppressive under the magnificent tall elm trees that lined the town's streets.[48] However, in August "dust devils" rolled about, and during periods of drought the dust seemed to be everywhere.

The year after Bobby was adopted, Marg and Bob decided to move into the Wemyss's family home on Second Avenue in order to have more room. In fact, there were three houses in Neepawa where Margaret Laurence lived during her childhood: her own home on Vivian Street, which she refers to as "the Little House;" the Wemyss's house on Second Avenue known as "the big red-brick house"; and the Simpson family residence on First Avenue, "the Big House" that belonged to her maternal grandparents.[49]

Peggy's second home, the Wemyss's big red-brick house, had been the home of her father's people. At the rear, there was a large garden. The façade of the house was covered with Virginia creeper, and attractive details distinguished the Wemyss's family home from others. Coloured glass was set into its front door and, on the landing of the second floor, there was a distinctive rose window, also with coloured panes of glass.[50] The large house had plenty of cupboards and "hidey holes" that appealed to Peggy's imagination. In addition, there were many formal features that had been absent in Peggy's first home, the cozy bungalow on Vivian Street. Peggy remembered that, while Grandmother Wemyss had lived in the red-brick house, visits had been rather uncomfortable, because certain rooms were off limits. She had to be very careful of her manners and avoid making noise or spilling things on the Chinese carpet.

Although Peggy had never known Grandfather Wemyss, who had died a few weeks after her birth in 1926, she held him in high esteem. John Wemyss, born in Scotland and educated at Glasgow Academy, could read the Greek tragedies and comedies in their original language, a fact that Margaret Laurence always noted with pride.[51] She also remarked that Grandfather Wemyss's letters and journals revealed his sense of humour, another fact that pleased her.[52] As Neepawa's first lawyer, he had had the distinction of drawing up the papers that incorporated the town.

From Grandfather's den, where a bronze curved sword hung over the fireplace and the bookshelves held dozens of copies of *National Geographic*, foreign destinations seemed to beckon. The sword had been handed down from a distant relative, and had been sent from India to Scotland and from there to Canada. Looking at it, Peggy could invent any number of fantastic stories. For her there was also mystery and possibly intrigue in the Scottish background of the Wemyss family, for they had a crest and a motto. John Wemyss's wife, Margaret (née Harrison), who had been born in Upper Canada, seems to have had certain "airs," and one Neepawan recalls that Mrs. Wemyss was the only person in town to have calling cards. The couple's three children were born in Neepawa.[53] Sometime after her husband's death in 1926, Margaret Harrison Wemyss moved to Winnipeg and later to Ontario, where her daughter Norma lived.

The "big red-brick house" was closer to the Neepawa Public School, and Peggy once again had playmates who lived nearby. Her first few years at school seem to have been uneventful. Margaret Laurence remembered the milkman, Bert Batchelor, who lived with his wife and daughter a short distance to the west of Neepawa, where he operated a small dairy. Mr. Batchelor delivered milk to the townsfolk by horse-drawn wagon or by sleigh in winter. On weekends he invited his daughter Dorothy, along with other Neepawa children, to ride with him for part of the route.[54] Margaret Laurence remembered those times: "In winter, we used to hitch rides on the back of the milk sleigh, our moccasins squeaking and slithering on the hard rutted snow of the roads, our hands in ice-bubbled mitts hanging onto the box edge of the sleigh for dear life, while Bert [the milkman] grinned at us through his great frosted moustache and shouted the horse into speed, daring us to stay put."[55]

Christmas 1934 in the Wemyss's house on Second Avenue, was full of excitement for her and her little brother.[56] On Christmas Eve the family always went to the carol service at the United Church. Afterward there was the marvellous winter walk home with carols "Hark the Herald Angels Sing," "Once in Royal David's City," and Peggy's favourite, "It Came Upon a Midnight Clear," lingering in her heart. On such a night the tingling winter air was dry and sharp, and the stunning night sky was completely filled with bright stars. Suddenly the dark-shadowed snow would be transformed, looking "like sprinkled rainbows around the sparse street lights."[57] The Christmas season was still magical for young Peggy.

On Christmas morning, her family gathered in the study after breakfast to hear the Christmas Empire Broadcast over the radio. The children began to fidget as they listened to King George's speech, which always ended the broadcast. Then, at last, they could "have the Tree," Peggy and Bobby opening presents with great glee while their parents looked on.

The gifts that Margaret Laurence later recalled from that memorable Christmas in 1934 were the ones that her father had made. For Bobby there was a cream-coloured wooden rocking horse with a seat in the middle; for Peggy a small desk — her first. "It had chains on either side to let down the writing board and pigeon holes to hold important stuff." She remembered it as "possibly the most beloved desk I have ever owned." Those were the years of the Great Depression, and her father, having found the desk in the attic, had repaired and painted it turquoise blue.[58]

On that Christmas afternoon the family went for dinner to the Simpson grandparents at the Big House on First Avenue. There, more than a dozen relatives would enjoy the Christmas meal at the big oak table in the dining room, carefully set with the best Limoges china, edged in gold with tinymoss roses forming the bridal-wreath pattern that Margaret Laurence later remembered.[59] And they had another ceremony of "the Tree," with a whole congregation of aunts and uncles and cousins. Aunt Ruby, who was head of the nursing division in Saskatchewan's public-health department, had brought from Regina "an astounding assortment of rare and wonderful things": tiny packages of Swiss cheese wrapped in silver paper; chocolate Santas in red and gold paper; and chocolate coins contained in heavy gold foil, looking for all the world like Spanish doubloons and pieces of eight from *Treasure Island*.[60] It was a wonderful Christmas.

After the holidays, Neepawa Public School reopened on January 3, a cold and windy day, with temperatures hovering at -30° F. Heavy snow continued to fall during the week that followed. On the morning of January 16, eight-year-old Peggy, with her face pressed to the window-pane, could feel the penetrating cold. As her dark brown eyes searched the familiar landscape, all seemed changed and ominous. She could hear the opening and closing of the front door and the hushed voices of adults whispering in the parlour below.

Outside, the streets were empty. No children on sleds or snowshoes could be seen. The relentless snow concealed the front steps and smothered the caragana hedges. The winter silence remained unbroken. Already huge drifts made travel treacherous, even for adults.[61] Across the street and in the yards the muffled air was thick with flakes.

That afternoon the silence was shattered by the tolling of the church bell. Then, men filed from the Wemyss red-brick house and from the Legion rooms: veterans, neighbours, Oddfellows, Masons — their chins hidden in wool scarves, collars turned up against the piercing cold. They moved slowly toward the pealing bell and the doors of the United Church. The funeral of Bob Wemyss, husband of Marg Simpson and father of Peggy and Bobby, was about to begin.

Robert Harrison Wemyss had died of pneumonia at 7 p.m. on Sunday, January 13, 1935, in the red-brick house on Second Avenue where he had been born. He was forty years old.[62]

As the funeral service took place, the bitter pain of Bob Wemyss's death was deepened by increasing anxiety about Mum's brother, Uncle Stuart, who had been stricken with double pneumonia. His condition rapidly worsened and, on January 20, exactly one week after Bob Wemyss's death, Uncle Stuart Simpson died.

In the days that followed, little Peggy felt "very helpless." She wanted to protect Mum and was "angry at the minister who came to give his condolences and support. . . . [He] really couldn't comfort Mum."[63] As a grief beyond words enveloped the family, Peggy's anguish and anxiety deepened.

Now, Peggy's memories of her mother's death four years earlier crowded into her mind. She remembered playing outdoors with a friend, tramping around in rubber boots in a few inches of rain water in a weed-filled ditch. "Your mother's dead," blurts out Dorothy Coutts. Peggy stares at Dorothy and then shouts back at her bewildered playmate: "She is not! You're telling a lie! Liar! Liar!"[64]

Several days before her mother's death in 1930, Peggy had celebrated her fourth birthday and, with Aunt Marg's help, she had pushed and pulled her new tricycle up the back staircase to the second floor of the Simpson house, where her mother lay sick in bed. Peggy wanted to show her the "splendid green-and-silver" tricycle she had received for her birthday. Margaret Laurence remembers this: "My mother, lying in the grey-painted double bed, smiles at me. Her face is white and her dark hair is spread out across the white pillowcase. She touches my face, my hair. . . . I have no memory of anything more complicated than her look of love for me. I never saw her again."[65]

That last glimpse of Verna was to remain Peggy's only distinct memory of her mother.[66] Now her father, too, was dead. This time the terrible fact could not be concealed. This time there could be no delaying the news, no evasion. This time neither a new step-parent nor a nearby uncle would be there to ease the pain. Reluctant to return to school, "desperately afraid of crying," unwilling to let Mum out of her sight, young Peggy was devastated. "I remember the two of us together. I don't remember very much about anybody else," she wrote.[67] Her world had changed forever during that cold January in 1935 when she was only eight and a half.[68]

Many years later, while writing her memoirs, *Dance on the Earth*, Margaret Laurence related how she had mourned the death in 1981 of a dear friend, Anne Bailey. The similarity between the circumstances of her friend's death and those of her own mother struck a deep cord in Margaret. After learning of Anne's death, Margaret, who was fifty-five at the time, suddenly put her head down and cried as though she "could never stop." She realized later that, not only was she grieving for Anne, who like her own mother, Verna, had left behind a husband and a five-year-old child, but, more than she "could ever have believed possible," Margaret became aware that she was grieving for her own mother, "who also died at just about the same age." She then adds this poignant note: "I mourn that young mother of mine still, and always will."[69]

While Margaret Laurence was writing her memoirs, she looked intently at many family photographs — some were reproduced in *Dance on the Earth*, others were simply described or referred to in the text. By gazing for a long time at those photos, she tried to recall early memories of the childhood years when the family was together and her mother and father were still alive. As a musician, Verna must have sung to her baby, rocked her daughter to sleep, and danced around the room with Peggy in her arms, but Margaret Laurence could not remember that. Sometimes, as an adult, she reread her mother's comments in the "Baby Book." In doing so she may have hoped to summon other memories of her young mother. But Verna was to remain a sepia image, a mother whose photo Margaret could gaze at, a mother whose words could be reread, but whose voice would never again be heard.

Marg Simpson had married Bob Wemyss after Verna's death. Now she was widowed at forty-seven. Like a figure in a Greek tragedy, she found herself buffeted by a series of sudden deaths and unexpected changes: deprived of her lively younger sister Verna; shifted from a secure and respected teaching position in Calgary back to her hometown of Neepawa; finding herself in an unexpected marriage to her brother-in-law that ended abruptly with his death three and a half years later; dealing with the nightmare of her brother Stuart's death only a week after her husband's death. All those losses occurred within a five-year period. The emotional blows left Marg Wemyss reeling. Alone. The stepmother of two young children: Bobby, one and a half years old, and Peggy, eight and a half.

Somehow Marg Wemyss was able to hold things together through the rest of 1935. She and the children moved from the Wemyss's place back to their own little home on Vivian Street. The playhouse that Peggy's father had built was moved back with them, and Peggy returned to her familiar dormer room, putting the cherished blue desk back in "the corner where it had always belonged. Things could never be the same, though, even in this beloved house."[70]

The following January (1936) was the coldest since the town had started keeping records. In places where the cattle usually went for water, the ice was three feet deep.[71] On January 18, Rudyard Kipling died in England and was buried in Westminster Abbey. That news was overshadowed, however, by the death of King George V. All of Neepawa was talking about it. Schools and businesses were closed in observance of the monarch's death, and the town's carnival was postponed. A solemn, well-attended memorial service was held in Neepawa's Opera House. During those cold January days, only a year after her father and uncle had died, Peggy had vivid reminders of the sudden, unexpected changes wrought by death — whether it struck kings, famous writers, or parents.

In her memoirs, Laurence makes an interesting shift after relating the fact of her father's death. She then describes the panic in Neepawa over an outbreak of polio that raged during the following year. The situation was so serious that a stiff fine of fifty dollars was set for any Neepawan caught in the nearby town of Minnedosa. Polio, although frequently referred to as infantile paralysis, affected adults as well as children. Some were crippled for life; others died. Although Laurence interrupts her account to state that her childhood was "not all death and gloom," she seems to protest too much, especially in light of the fact that the next incident she recalls does focus on death. The incident took place during the polio epidemic and involved two neighbourhood boys. Laurence's account reveals the way a child's mind, which lacks the understanding of an adult's, may connect things.

As Peggy sat reading a book in a tree near the Wemyss's house on Second Avenue, two boys who lived across the yard called out and teased her. She remembers being afraid of them. After all she was younger and a girl. She realized she was powerless to stop their teasing. Finally, in a fury, she shouted at them "and managed to drive them off." When she learned later that one of boys had died from polio, she was horrified. "I had scared Gavin away and he had died. It was a great shock."[72] To young Peggy it was a profound experience of the power of the word.

Written words, too, began to have an impact for Peggy. By the time she was in Grade Five her own words on the page had taken on importance and power. In the following passage from *Dance on the Earth*, she describes the sort of writing she did in elementary school: "I was writing, too, all the time. Clumsy, sentimental poetry, funny verses, stories, and once a highly uninformed but jubilantly imaginative journal of Captain John Ball and his voyages to exotic lands, complete with maps made by me of strange, mythical places."[73] Perhaps looking at her father's copies of *National Geographic* had provided an impetus for her imagination. Composing childhood stories of voyages and adventures in faraway lands may somehow have become a part of Laurence's psyche, preparing the way for her later travels. Who can say? But her need to write undoubtedly took hold while she was still a youngster.

Two of Peggy's former classmates clearly recalled a day when the teacher took their class for a nature walk near Park Lake. At one point, the teacher dispatched those girls to find Peggy Wemyss, who was "missing." When they rounded a bend in the road, they spotted Peggy sitting beneath a tree, oblivious to her surroundings, writing in a scribbler. They remember that it was hard for them to convince Peggy to put down her pencil so they could hurry to catch up with the rest of the class.[74] At this early stage, writing was becoming a comfort for her. It was one way of bringing order out of the upheavals in her life.

In the weeks after Bob Wemyss's death, Mum had tried her best to establish a place of serenity and safety for Peggy, but she had her hands full with Bobby, still a toddler, and with worries about their future. Now there were times when Marg herself became volatile, anxious, and fearful. She fretted and she could lose her temper, sometimes yelling "with vigour" when Peggy and Bobby were "difficult."[75]

The following year, as spring approached, Peggy, now nine, was again spun into emotional turmoil when her favourite grandmother, Jane Bailey Simpson, died suddenly in the Big House on First Avenue on May 3, 1936.[76] One by one, the deeply personal relationships of Peggy's childhood years, the relationships that are so significant in a child's development, were rapidly disappearing. Moreover, the death of Peggy's father the year before had triggered a series of chain reactions which were propelled by financial constraints. Subsequent changes, which might have been taken in stride under ordinary circumstances, were now to have a profound effect on the sensitive and imaginative youngster.

Because the death of Grandmother Simpson left her husband, John, alone in the Big House without his wife's calm, comforting presence, their adult offspring seem to have decided that their sister, Marg, was the natural choice among them to move into the Big House — to take care of their eighty-two-year-old father, to oversee the household, and there to raise her two young children. Financial necessity and family responsibility would have made it impossible for Marg Wemyss to refuse. For her, there were no viable alternatives.

So, once again, Peggy had to move. The family left their Little House on Vivian Street and moved into the Simpson place, the Big House on First Avenue. Her beloved playhouse was moved again and placed in the backyard, which was then quite deep, running past the wood pile and the vegetable garden at the rear of the house to the former barn where Grandpa Simpson's old McLaughlin Buick was stored. The CNR station was only a few blocks away, and the frequent whistle of the trains became a familiar sound as the railway cars rolled into town, letting off passengers or loading grain.

From across the street, the Big House on First Avenue looked solid and comfortable behind its neatly trimmed caragana hedges. After walking up the path and the front steps, one crossed the veranda, and then entered the front hallway, where a staircase on the left led to the second floor. On the first floor there was a front parlour, a music room, a dining room, and, at the rear, a large kitchen, from which a set of stairs led up to the second floor and a room for a hired girl. The second floor also had bedrooms for family members and a complete bath.

Peggy had liked the Big House, of its warm associations with Sunday visits, holiday dinners, and afternoon chats with her grandmother when the delicious aroma of freshly baked bread or cookies filled the air, but she soon came to realize that living in the house after Grandma Simpson's death was an entirely different matter.

In an effort to make Peggy feel more at home, Mum gave her the best and largest room in the Big House. Formerly Grandma Simpson's bedroom, it also had a small dressing room, which held a Toronto couch, a dresser, and a cupboard full of old books. Mum and Peggy chose new wallpaper, "a soft green patterned with apple blossoms."[77] The colours may have reminded her of the apple-green kitchen cupboards that her father had painted in the Little House. Peggy's bright, cheerful bedroom had a large bay window facing directly east. In the winter, the morning sun sparkled on the feathery traceries of frost on the panes. Eventually that bedroom became her "refuge," and she recalled many hours spent sitting at a table in front of the bay window, writing.[78]

Despite the bright bedroom and the familiar playhouse, where she could crawl up onto the roof and write stories and poems beneath the sheltering branches of the tall evergreen trees, the atmosphere inside the Big House was often desperately uncomfortable. It was profoundly affected by Grandfather Simpson, who set the rules to suit himself and made demands on Marg and the children. As he stomped moodily through the house, uttering harsh remarks, Grandpa Simpson was a man to be avoided.

Peggy lived in that house with her grandfather from the age of ten until she left Neepawa at eighteen to attend university. Those years in the Simpson house were crucial in her development. Kipling's line, "When I was in my father's house, I was in a better place," may well have echoed in her heart, for Peggy had never really been comfortable around her grandfather.[79] Now she felt an increasing dislike of him and continued to long for her father's return. Impossible.

Thrust out of her familiar and beloved Little House, deprived of her father's good humour and easygoing personality, Peggy was forced to accommodate herself to the wishes and whims of an elderly and domineering grandfather.[80] The depth of her distress may be seen in later remarks when she admitted that she hated Grandfather Simpson for a long time, even after his death in 1953, when he was ninety-six and she was a married adult. In her unpublished journal she noted, "His own temperament worked against a celebration of anything."[81]

When Margaret Laurence returned to Neepawa in 1976 for a reception following the publication of *A Jest of God*, she was met at the airport in Winnipeg and driven to Neepawa by her former Grade Seven teacher. She asked him to drive by her first home, the little bungalow on Vivian Street, but she instructed him not to drive past the former Simpson house on First Avenue.[82] She had turned away from connections to John Simpson and the Irish side of her family. Instead Scotland, home of her father's people, the Wemysses, held a special place in Margaret Laurence's imagination and heart.

As a child she heard Scottish songs, and later she read Scottish history and listened to recordings of bagpipe music. As an adult, Margaret Laurence visited Scotland several times. She met the poet Douglas Young, explored the area from which her father's people had emigrated, visited the home of the bard James Macpherson, and viewed the battlefields of Culloden, where many Scots, betrayed by their chiefs, had been slaughtered. These personal experiences in the land of her ancestors provided Laurence with much of the Scottish material that she later incorporated into her final novel, *The Diviners*. Her immersion in the Wemyss ancestry and history also gave rise to her essay "Road from the Isles" (1966).[83]

In that essay, using emotionally charged language, she refers to the Scots who arrived in Canada as a people "bereft, who had been wounded psychically in ways they could not have possibly comprehended." Ostensibly about the betrayed Scots, her essay may well provide a clue to Margaret Laurence's own feelings of deep loss, and shed light on how she tried to cope with the death of her beloved father and mother:

I had known, of course, as every person schooled in Canada knows, of the external difficulties of the early Scottish settlers, the people of Glengarry and Red River. What I had never seen before was a glimpse of their inner terrors, a sense of the bereavement they must have carried with them like a weight of lead in the soul. What appeared to be their greatest trouble in a new land — the grappling with an unyielding environment — was in fact probably their salvation. I believe they survived not in spite of physical hardships, but *because* of them, for all their attention and thought *had* to be focused outwards. They could not brood. If they had been able to do so, it might have killed them.[84]

Here she presents the paradoxical view that the Scottish settlers may have been saved by the harsh physical reality of trying to survive in a new land. She suggests that their strenuous struggle to survive the harsh physical reality of creating a new life in Canada may actually have saved them from dying of broken hearts — from brooding over their betrayal by their own chiefs.

As a way of dealing with her own sense of bereavement, Laurence may have put much of her attention and thought into her writing. That struggle may paradoxically have helped her to bear the full impact of the loss of both parents — a loss still sharply felt as an adult.

When Laurence reflected on her Scots heritage in "Road from the Isles," she explained that she had come to the realization that her own roots were in Canada rather than in Scotland. She then understood, however, why the landscape of Scotland had seemed so familiar when she had first visited there. The trees — spruce and pine and birch, with moss around their roots — and the colours of the earth had brought back her memories of Clear Lake in Manitoba's Riding Mountain National Park. Recognizing the significant impact of those early memories, she then pointed to another kind of history — "one that has the most powerful hold over us in unsuspected ways, the names or tunes or trees that can recall a thousand images, and this almost-family history can be related only to one's first home."[85]

A keen sense of paradox also became attached to Margaret's memories of Neepawa: a place where she had experienced great joy, profound loss, and overwhelming anger. There is no doubt that, as a youngster, Peggy's feelings of rage and resentment at Grandfather Simpson were compounded by the losses and changes that followed inevitably upon her own father's death. Nevertheless, it is obvious that John Simpson's demanding disposition within the household left its mark on every family member who lived there. His first-born son, Stuart, felt obliged to assume the family's undertaking business rather than pursue a career in law.[86] Verna (Peggy's natural mother) was restricted in the development of her musical talent and interests, and Verna's older sister, Margaret (Marg), who in high school had attained the highest grades in the entire province of Manitoba, was not permitted to enrol at university, although John Simpson, for practical reasons, did allow his daughter to attend Normal School, because he felt that teacher training was acceptable.[87]

In *Dance on the Earth*, Margaret Laurence makes little reference to her uncles, but she proudly refers to her mother and her aunts, the "Simpson girls," as accomplished women who were professionals. Her assessment, however, glosses over the fact that such achievement came at a price. Most of John Simpson's children, even as adults, had to accede to their father's demands, and his control over them in their youth had caused resentment. Moreover, outside the family circle, many Neepawa citizens found Simpson to be tight-fisted, difficult, and autocratic.

A tenant recalls that, despite strained financial conditions during the Depression, John Simpson, warmly wrapped in his bearskin coat during the winter months, would come in person to collect the rent; no excuses for late payments were accepted. Once a neighbour of the Simpsons was obliged to work at the relief camp in Riding Mountain, where the typical pay was five dollars a month.[88] His daughter relates that her father offered to do odd jobs around the house and barn for Mr. Simpson. However, when it was time for the man to collect his pay, Simpson offered him not cash, but a pine box — the type that would be used to enclose a coffin. Since Simpson had been in the funeral business, he had some of these boxes on hand. The astonished worker, worried about feeding his family, asked what he was supposed to do with the coffin. "Use it as a wardrobe for clothes," John brusquely replied.[89] Today that narrow, unadorned pine box, donated by the man's family, sits in the museum in Neepawa, as a reminder of the unforgettable "Dirty Thirties."[90]

After Marg and the children were settled in the Big House with Grandpa Simpson, things continued to be difficult for each of them. The death of Peggy's father left her with deep feelings of loss and uncertainty: "There must have been a lot of suppressed unhappiness and bewilderment in my mind," she writes: "I used to walk in my sleep sometimes. . . . I've never forgotten that feeling of panic as I wakened and thought that perhaps I was going mad. We had very little money, and Mum was constantly worried. . . . I felt helpless and sad, or silently angry a great deal of the time."[91]

Despite the external stability and familiarity of Neepawa, her hometown now held palpable uncertainties for Peggy. Her anxious inner world was profoundly insecure; it was a place of pain too deep for words, where cataclysmic shifts had followed close upon the sudden eruptions of death. Peggy felt bereft in ways only those who have known the loss of parents in early childhood may fully understand.

In trying to convey her sense of the complexity of the world, as she experienced it in Neepawa, Laurence penned this description: "A strange place it was, that place where the world began. A place of incredible happenings, splendours and revelations, despairs like multitudinous pits of isolated hells. A place of shadow-spookiness, inhabited by the unknowable dead. A place of jubilation and of mourning, horrible and beautiful."[92]

This passage underscores how profoundly Margaret Laurence as a child was struck by the paradoxical nature of life in Neepawa. As the years passed, a keen awareness of paradox was to become an established feature of her world view as a novelist. She mentioned this in several interviews and it is reflected in many passages of her work — from her first book, *A Tree for Poverty* (a translation of Somali oral literature), to her final novel, *The Diviners*.

In a personal essay, "Where the World Began," Laurence again referred to the impact of her childhood and youth in Neepawa: "This was my territory in the time of my youth, and in a sense my life since then has been an attempt to look at it, to come to terms with it. Stultifying to the mind it certainly could be, and sometimes was, but not to the imagination. It was many things, but it was never dull."[93]

In an effort to garner a more specific sense of Margaret Laurence's "territory" in the time of her youth, one may turn to her memoirs, *Dance on the Earth*. That work, however, like all memoir, is selective, providing only a partial account of her life. In *Dance on the Earth* Laurence has forgotten or omitted many details about her early years, and she provides scant autobiographical information about the crucial period between her father's death in 1935 and her entrance into high school in 1939. It may be possible, nevertheless, to discover something of the emotional tone of that period in the stories which comprise her collection, *A Bird in the House*. That is the book which Margaret Laurence referred to as her "most autobiographical work."[94] But she also cautioned that the stories in it were "highly fictionalized."[95] No doubt both statements are true, and an examination of *A Bird in the House* may yield important insights into the emotional timbre of Margaret Laurence's own childhood as a strong desire to write gathered momentum within her.

CHAPTER TWO

A Bird in the House

A Bird in the House is a collection of eight interconnected stories set in a small prairie town during the Great Depression, the "Dirty Thirties."[96] In these stories Margaret Laurence creates a compelling fictional portrait of a young girl for whom writing has become very important amidst the many unpredictable events in her life.[97] The stories are told by Vanessa, now a young adult and writer, who is recalling significant events in her childhood. In calling them to mind, Vanessa captures something of herself at a much younger age and adds new meaning to those experiences as she reflects on them and writes about them.

Since Margaret Laurence described these stories as semi-autobiographical, it is appropriate to examine them more closely. She noted:

> [They] are based on myself & my family, when I was
> growing up in Neepawa, but are highly fictionalized.
> Manawaka, as is all my Canadian fiction, is partly based
> on my memories of my home town, but is also a town
> of the imagination, a fictional place not to be found on
> any maps except the maps of the mind. Vanessa is part-
> ly myself & partly a fictional person & the "brick house"
> is based on my memories of the old Simpson house but
> is also its own place.[98]

In what sense does Laurence consider the stories to be autobiographical? The following remarks about childhood provide some insight. The novelist Graham Greene has indicated one of the ways in which a writer may use material from his or her youth. Since Laurence quoted this passage from Greene in one of her own essays, his remarks provide one avenue by which to approach Peggy Wemyss's early interest in fashioning stories: "The creative writer perceives his world once and for all in childhood and adolescence, and his whole career is an effort to illustrate his private world in terms of the great public world we all share."[99]

After quoting Greene, Margaret Laurence added the following remarks:

> I believe that Graham Greene is right in this statement. It does not mean that the individual does not change after adolescence. On the contrary, it underlines the necessity for change. For the writer, one way of discovering oneself, of changing from the patterns of childhood and adolescence to those of adulthood, is through the explorations inherent in the writing itself. In the case of a great many writers, this exploration . . . involves an attempt to understand one's background and one's past, sometimes even a more distant past which one has not personally experienced.[100]

Although the fictional Vanessa MacLeod is depicted in some situations which parallel those in the life of young Peggy Wemyss, trying to establish a one-to-one correspondence between the details of Peggy's life and Vanessa's would be an unfortunate distraction. It would also diminish an appreciation of how Margaret Laurence's creative imagination functioned. Her comments in several letters about the semi-autobiographical quality of *A Bird in the House*, suggest that it resides not in the facts, but in the remarkable emotional resonance that exists between what is known of Peggy's youth and that of the fictional Vanessa. An indication of such an emotional correspondence was related by Helen Porter, who has performed dramatizations of several works by Margaret Laurence. She recalls meeting with Laurence on at least four occasions in order to review material in *A Bird in the House*. After Margaret attended Porter's performance, she sent Helen a note saying, "I could not bear to hear it."[101] Evidently those earlier emotions could still be keenly felt by Laurence. An examination of *A Bird in the House* may well contribute to a fuller understanding of Laurence's childhood years than can be gathered solely from her own descriptions in *Dance on the Earth*.

The principal characters in *A Bird in the House* are: Vanessa MacLeod (who is about ten years old in the opening story), her father, Ewen, a dedicated town doctor, and his wife, Beth. When Ewen dies, Vanessa, her baby brother, and her mother move into the home of Grandfather Connor. Several older relatives of Vanessa also have noteworthy roles in these short stories.[102]

A Bird in the House presents Vanessa's childhood world — one in which she experiences great loss: the death of her father; the illness of her mother; the absence of warmth and concern from her grandparents; and the torments of a neighbourhood bully. In these situations, which are also haunted by death and illness, neither Vanessa's mother nor her aunt can be relaxed or spontaneous. These women also suffer the consequences of financial problems that have made it necessary for them to return as adults to the family home, where their father, Timothy Connor, a stern authoritarian, exercises rigid control over life in his domain.

Various issues recur and bind the stories thematically. One of the most obvious is an unrelenting concern about money that permeates *A Bird in the House*. The Great Depression, which caused massive job losses throughout Canada's prairie provinces, forces Vanessa's Aunt Edna out of her job in Winnipeg and back into the family home in Manawaka. It pushes Uncle Dan to petition his brother Timothy Connor for money, prevents cousin Chris from enrolling at university, causes Grandfather Connor to worry about the taxes on his houses, and indirectly affects the health of Vanessa's mother and the new baby, since the family cannot afford either a nurse or a hired girl. Although no one loses his home or has to stand on a bread line, in contrast to situations that James Gray vividly recounts in *The Winter Years*, nevertheless, in *A Bird in the House*, plans are thwarted and lives irreversibly altered over and over again due to fiscal constraints and difficulties within the family.

Laurence's character, Vanessa, has a healthy curiosity and a strong imaginative gift, but she is reduced to silence and powerlessness in the despotic household of her grandfather, whose characteristic manner of speaking is described as "bludgeoning words."[103] When Grandfather Connor persists in criticizing her cousin Chris, Vanessa feels "the old rage of helplessness." She hopes Chris will speak up for himself and his family, but he remains passive and strangely unaffected. Chris carries on as if he has not heard the old man's harsh remarks. Vanessa, on the other hand, is overwhelmed with anger and can barely refrain from delivering a sassy retort. She bites her tongue and remains silent, but that silence is achieved at a price. She holds back "with a terrible strained force for fear of letting go and speaking out and having the known world unimaginably fall to pieces" as a consequence of her *words*, as the result of *speaking out*.[104] The youngster is torn between her desire to challenge Grandfather Connor and a great fear that doing so would have dreadful consequences.

In these stories Vanessa is enraged at various injustices within the family and keenly disappointed when relatives fail to defend a person or to correct a harsh misinterpretation of events. For instance, when her grandmother unfairly criticizes Aunt Edna, Vanessa expects her father to defend his sister-in-law, whom he likes, but he remains silent. Vanessa can barely control her rage at such an injustice.[105]

One Sunday, when Dr. MacLeod has to make a house call, Grandfather Connor is annoyed because his son-in-law will be late for dinner. Vanessa staunchly defends her father, insisting, "It's not his fault." She then relates imaginary details about the sick man her father is attending, informing her grandfather that the patient is dying of pneumonia: "I'll bet you he's spitting up blood this very second."[106] Although Vanessa has imagined that scenario, her own description of that patient affects her so powerfully that she begins to react as if she herself had the same symptoms: "All at once, I could not swallow, feeling as though that gushing crimson were constricting my own throat."[107] Her response to the powers of her own imagination, however, is held in check as Vanessa-the-author intellectualizes about how such a situation might work out in fiction. She wonders whether "something like that would go well" in the story she is currently making up: "'Sick to death in the freezing log cabin, with only the beautiful halfbreed lady (no, woman) to look after him. Old Jebb suddenly clutched his throat.'"[108]

At this point, Vanessa, who had felt helplessly enraged, begins to discover that she has achieved some power as an author. Her feelings of helplessness gradually dissipate. As time passes, she continues to use her imagination, creating stories when she is supposed to be listening to sermons at church or while walking home from skating. The stories she invents often contain feats of "spectacular heroism."

In "The Half-Husky," Vanessa cannot prevent the paperboy, Harvey, from cruelly taunting her dog, Nanuk. She becomes frustrated and furious over her helplessness. Unable to express that rage, she uses her imagination to alter the reality that confronts her. Although she is a child, Vanessa as an author is no longer powerless. She is able to exercise an exhilarating control over life and death. When she later recalls this situation as an adult, she reflects on how her imagination functioned creatively at that time: "My rage would spin me into fantasy — Harvey fallen into the deepest part of Wachakwa River, unable to swim, and Nanuk, capable of rescue but waiting for a signal from me. Would I speak or not? Sometimes I let Harvey drown. Sometimes at the last minute I spared him." She then reflects, "but none of this was much use except momentarily, and when the flamboyant theatre of my mind grew empty again, I still did not know what to do in reality."[109] The emotional tenor of "The Half-Husky" may well mirror that of young Peggy Wemyss, who also had come to the realization that she could neither change nor prevent the inexorable unfolding of painful events and situations in her own life.

Another interesting story about coping with difficult situations by using the resources of the imagination occurs in "The Sound of the Singing." Vanessa is making costumes for her clothespin dolls, but when the dolls do not turn out as she had visualized them in her imagination, she becomes very upset. Her wrath is evident in the passage's strong verbs and adverbs: "[The doll's] wooden face, on which I had already pencilled eyes and mouth, grinned stupidly at me, and I leered viciously back. You'll be beautiful whether you like it or not, I told her."[110]

Here the child-artist is determined to use her imagination and the power of words to transform reality — to create a better outcome than the one which actually confronts her. Laurence seems to be using the process of writing about such events, as another writer once noted, in order to feel less acutely things that would otherwise irritate beyond endurance, transform them into artistic experiences, and thereby soften their application to herself.[111]

In "The Half-Husky," creating and shaping a fictional world is a survival mechanism for Vanessa, even though at times the power of real events is felt so strongly that her creative impulse can become blocked. Then Vanessa is unable to transform people and situations through writing about them. For example, she finds it impossible to continue writing a story about pioneers when she learns that her grandfather, whose behaviour and control she deeply resents, had himself been a pioneer. On another day, Vanessa becomes frightened when she hears Aunt Edna crying painfully. The youngster then races "home quickly" in order to destroy a story she had been writing based on Aunt Edna.[112]

Margaret Laurence's presentation of childhood is conveyed with a sense of immediacy and a terrible poignancy. One of the arresting features of *A Bird in the House* is the profound sense of Vanessa's isolation. Vanessa, unlike Emily, in Lucy Maud Montgomery's Canadian classic, *Emily of New Moon*, is not depicted as having a close friend or friends, nor does she have an adult such as Dean Priest or Father Cassidy who understands Emily's writing and shows a sincere interest in it. Margaret Laurence's adults in *A Bird in the House* are so absorbed with their own problems that they are oblivious to Vanessa's presence, even when she is in the same room. Emily of New Moon, on the other hand, not only has support and friendship, but she also speaks her mind with an honesty and frankness that would never have been tolerated in Vanessa's fictional "world" or, in the case of Peggy, in Grandfather Simpson's house.

Alone in a world of adults, Vanessa MacLeod listens, observes, and remains almost invisible. She realizes that, in Grandfather's household, her mother and aunt must be secretive. They seek refuge in the kitchen or in an upstairs bedroom where, between whispers, they sneak a cigarette and try to comfort each other. Vanessa, in turn, becomes adept at watching and listening. Although she registers her aunt's and mother's conversations and gestures, as a child, she does not fully grasp what is taking place.

The events and people in *A Bird in the House* are seen through the eyes of a sensitive and observant youngster. When Vanessa recounts the conversations and behaviour of adults, she often refers to physical features that reveal their emotional states. Her awareness of the suffering of adults creates in her powerful feelings of sadness and anxiety. Vanessa recalls a look of "desolation" on her father's face.[113] When she later hears sadness in his voice, she realizes he is worried. She also notices that her mother's face is rigid and apprehensive, and the "intricate lines of tiredness" that she sees there alarm her.[114] Vanessa also remembers a sadness in both her mother and aunt: "I felt it as bodily hurt, like skinning a knee, a sharp, stinging pain. But I felt as well an obscure sense of loss. Some comfort had been taken from me, but I did not know what it was."[115] After Aunt Edna's beau is driven out of the house by Grandfather Connor's rude and controlling behaviour, Vanessa watches her aunt put her head down on the table and cry "in a way I had never heard any person cry before, as though there were no end to it anywhere."[116] Here, the words "never," "any," "no end," and "anywhere" convey a deep, unalterable sense of loss. In other stories fear is almost palpable.

One of the most poignant episodes occurs in "To Set Our House in Order." Vanessa's world is shattered when she is awakened at night by the sound of her mother crying: "I stood lest there be some sight more *terrifying* than I could bear [emphasis added]."[117] In another story, Vanessa is spending the night at her grandparents' house. She awakens with an uneasy feeling and goes for comfort to Aunt Edna. However, when she reaches Edna's bedroom door, Vanessa halts. She hears her favourite aunt crying painfully and becomes frightened. Then, "like some *terrified* poltergeist I flitted back to the spare room and whipped into bed. I wanted only to forget that I had heard anything, but I knew I would not forget [emphasis added]."[118]

The difficulties that her mother and aunt experience stem in large measure from the death of Dr. MacLeod and its consequences. Before her father died, Vanessa had a loving relationship with him. And because there is very little joy in her world after his death, the remembered scenes of closeness between father and daughter are all the more significant. In one story, Vanessa and her father go down to the lake at night to listen to the loons calling across the water. It is a magical moment. On another occasion, they go snowshoeing on a Sunday morning, and in the evening attend the church services they had missed earlier that day. Walking home afterwards, Vanessa wants to hold her father's hand, but she thinks she is too old for that. She decides instead to take long strides so they can walk side by side and her father will not have to adjust his pace to hers. Along the way, Vanessa asks her father about heaven and the afterlife. His reflective, honest responses comfort her, and Vanessa then reaches for his hand; father and daughter walk home together along the snow-covered streets.[119]

One night after her father has come down with pneumonia, Vanessa is permitted to sleep with her mother. The child awakens in darkness. At first it seems as if she is in her own bed and everything is as usual. Then she becomes aware of her mother weeping, and instinctively realizes that her father has died:

> Then in the total night around me, I heard a sound. It was my mother, and she was crying, not loudly at all, but from somewhere very deep inside her. I sat up in bed. Everything seemed to have stopped, not only in time but my own heart and blood as well. Then my mother noticed that I was awake.
>
> I did not ask her and she did not tell me anything. There was no need. She held me in her arms, or I held her, I am not certain which.[120]

Vanessa's memories of adults weeping are connected to profound feelings of anxiety, loss and grief. She cannot be sure that these adults, from whom children ordinarily expect comfort and reassurance, will be able to serve as her protectors against unknown elements in the wider world. To what extent can young Vanessa now count on her mother or aunts to be a bulwark of strength and security for her? The answer to that question is neither hopeful nor reassuring.

The fictional Vanessa recalls, "After my father died, the whole order of life was torn. Nothing was known or predictable any longer. For months, I lived almost entirely within myself."[121] In the days that followed, she remained near her mother, both to console herself and because she felt that her mother needed her protection, "I did not know from what, nor what I could possibly do, but something held me there [close beside my mother]."[122]

There are significant parallels between the wording in this story and Margaret Laurence's own account in her memoirs. There she states that one night she awakened to the sound of Mum crying and realized immediately that her father had died. She remembers feeling very helpless in the days that followed. She was not yet nine, but she wanted "to protect Mum." As an adult, Margaret Laurence could recall very few memories from that time "apart from not wanting to let Mum out of my sight. I remember the two of us together. I don't remember much about anybody else."[123]

If one looks at the fictional narratives in *A Bird in the House* and at Laurence's own memoirs, *Dance on the Earth*, the emotional correspondence between Vanessa MacLeod and Peggy Wemyss is clear and compelling. The narrative unfolding of these stories is so convincing that one feels the fiction must have been fashioned from the very fabric of Margaret Laurence's own emotional experiences in childhood. Laurence's comments in her memoirs underscore that link: "our father Robert Wemyss died of pneumonia. I have written about this in a story called 'A Bird in the House.' The story is fiction, but in that particular story, fiction follows facts pretty closely."[124]

If these stories are, as Margaret Laurence asserts, her most autobiographical work, they offer a significant insight into those important and impressionable years of early childhood. She was a youngster who lived chiefly in a world of adults; she saw their pain and was helpless to alter or improve situations. However, a strong desire to write and a talent for writing developed during those same years and, over time, as will be shown in more detail, that desire and talent came to provide her with some degree of control and escape from the pain and frustration that threatened her well-being. Later, Laurence would draw on the emotional tenor of those experiences to create the stories in *A Bird in the House*.

Although Vanessa and Peggy's lives certainly differ in significant details, the fact that Margaret Laurence created a character who was also a young writer, and had the story unfold when Vanessa is at approximately the same age that Laurence herself was when she faced similar situations, invites a close reading of these stories. There is a strong emotional congruence between the two girls. As children, Peggy and Vanessa experience a profound sadness that is often accompanied by feelings of isolation, loss, powerlessness, and rage.[125] Subtle references to such emotions also occur frequently in Laurence's memoirs. After such terribly bleak childhood years, however, an unexpected turn of events was to prove fortunate for young Peggy Wemyss. In the autumn of 1938, three years after the death of her father, a wondrous year at school began to unfold.

CHAPTER THREE

The Magic of Writing

1938-1940

The boys and girls of Grade Seven stopped fidgeting and cocked their heads, listening to their teacher's footsteps echo in the corridor. As Wes McAmmond approached the classroom, his strong tenor voice rose and he entered, reciting:

> The goldenrod is yellow,
> The corn is turning brown.
> The trees in apple orchards
> With fruit are bending down.
> . . . .
> By all these lovely tokens
> September's days are here.
> With summer's best of weather
> And autumn's best of cheer.[126]

As Peggy sat in Wes McAmmond's class that September morning, her life was about to undergo a sea change. Her Grade Seven teacher was a man who loved literature and his pupils.[127] Still in his twenties, Wes McAmmond's blue eyes twinkled as he recited poems from memory. He exuded energy and good humour. He was unfazed by things. He was Peggy's first male teacher, an extraordinary gift, a refreshing change from the maiden ladies and widows who had taught her up to that point. McAmmond's concern for his students and his ability to enjoy things made him an exhilarating and comforting presence in Peggy's life. He was a teacher she never forgot.

Wes McAmmond had grown up in Winnipeg. At the age of eighteen he went to teacher-training and then taught in country schools, where his annual salary was five hundred dollars. When he came to Neepawa, McAmmond was young, but experienced, and within a few years, in 1941, he was appointed principal of the elementary school. His abilities became well-known, and later McAmmond joined the faculty of Manitoba Teachers' College.

Wes McAmmond's influence on Peggy was deep and lasting. His class changed her life. She remarked: "Grade seven, when I was twelve, was an exciting year. Our teacher was a man who actually cracked jokes in class. We adored him. He was our hero."[128] Peggy showed him some stories she had written, and he gave her "kindly criticism." He encouraged both her writing and her interest in reading, and he listened to her enthusiastic outpourings about some of the books she had read, including, that year, Arthur Conan Doyle's *The White Company*, which she recalled borrowing from the school library "at least half a dozen times."[129] Wes McAmmond remembers that Peggy "was keen on Kipling, and enjoyed *Kim*."[130]

In Grade Seven, the curriculum required pupils to study an abridged version of a Shakespearian play: either *The Tempest*, *Julius Caesar*, or *As You Like It*. According to McAmmond, that year it was *The Tempest*. Mr. McAmmond liked to stage plays with his students up in the "attic," the top floor of the school. Once, Peggy showed him a play she had written, based on *The White Company*: "It was filled with knights and lords and ladies." They also studied the songs from Shakespeare, and McAmmond warmly recalls students memorizing speeches such as "Sweet Are the Uses of Adversity" from *As You Like It*.

Because he was fond of reciting poetry, McAmmond encouraged his pupils to commit poems to memory. Many of his former students quickly attest to the success of his efforts. On one occasion a lad who had become a truck driver was so delighted years later to see his former teacher that he rushed up to McAmmond at a gas station and began reciting lines from Shakespeare.[131] Memorization of poetry, of course, was also a requirement in schools in the province of Manitoba.

During Grade Seven, Peggy's class used an edition of the *The Canada Book of Prose and Verse, Book Three* that included works by British authors, a few Americans, and many Canadians — poets such as Charles G.D. Roberts, Marjorie Pickthall, Bliss Carman, Robert Service, and Duncan Campbell Scott. *The Canada Book of Prose and Verse* also had a wide-ranging selection of prose, with excerpts from fiction, biography, and essays. It did not take long for Peggy to finish that book on her own. There never seemed to be enough material for her to read.

During much of Peggy's childhood there was no public library in Neepawa or the nearby communities. In fact, one of Peggy's high-school teachers recalls that, when she arrived in Neepawa during the 1930s, the "library shelves were empty, not even a set of encyclopedias."[132] Aside from borrowing books from friends or from the very limited Sunday-school library, there were few avenues for obtaining good books or new books during the Great Depression. Available cash was reserved for essentials. However, Peggy's family enjoyed reading, and her home had more books than most others in Neepawa.[133] Nevertheless, she quickly read through the books at home, including a set of Kipling's works, and she remembers, as do several other writers of her generation, awaiting the arrival of the Eaton's catalogue — something new to read.[134] Marg Wemyss, herself an avid reader, worked diligently for months with a small group of citizens, including Wes McAmmond, Mildred Musgrove, Bill Spratt, and Principal Herb Ray to establish the town's first lending library, membership by subscription.[135]

Once that subscription library was established, Peggy continued to read omnivorously. Now current best-sellers were available, in addition to the older classics that her family owned. By the time Peggy was in Grade Seven, the library, staffed by volunteers, was open twice a week. Among the new titles that year were books of travel and adventure set in far-off countries and other centuries: *Northwest Passage*, *Khyber Caravan*, *Henry of Navarre*, *A Japanese Lady in Europe*, as well as *Gone with the Wind*, *The Citadel*, and *Ordeal in England*.

At school Peggy's interest in books was furthered by Wes McAmmond, who frequently read to his class because he "liked to and because they enjoyed it."[136] In addition to Arthur Conan Doyle's *The White Company*, he read them *Three Times and Out*, a war-protest book published in 1918 and edited by Nellie McClung, an older Manitoba writer and social activist. The hero of *Three Times and Out* is Private Simmons, a young lad from Manitoba. After many remarkable efforts, he finally escapes from a prisoner-of-war camp and returns to Canada. Peggy, with her active imagination, may have thought of the young Manitoba soldier as a comrade-in-arms to her own father and his younger brother, Jack, both of whom had seen action in Europe during the Great War.

According to Wes McAmmond, Peggy's friends were from the professional class and comfortable financially. Mona Spratt was the ringleader of their group, and McAmmond recalls thinking at the time that Peggy and her friends belonged to a snobbish sort of clique and were rather gossipy. But since McAmmond considered his own background to be working-class (his father worked for the railroad), he would have been sensitive to small-town exclusionary social circles. Nevertheless, Mr. McAmmond liked Peggy, called her "a fine girl," and was helpful to her.

In fact, when she returned to Neepawa in 1975 for the first time since becoming a successful novelist, Wes McAmmond met her at the airport. On the way back from Neepawa, they talked about Louis Riel, the Métis leader of the Northwest Rebellion (1885). As they drove along Portage Avenue in Winnipeg, McAmmond decided to surprise Margaret by continuing on to St. Boniface because she had never seen Riel's final resting place or his monument there.[137]

The summer after Grade Seven was critical in Peggy's development. "My childhood could be said to have ended in the summer and autumn of 1939," she wrote in her memoirs.[138] There were two major events for her during those months. The first was a visit to a "much-loved" older cousin, Bud Bailey, and his family on their farm, north of Riding Mountain. Laurence included a poem to Bud in *Dance on the Earth*. It seems that as a youngster she felt a romantic interest in her cousin; something fairly typical for a girl of thirteen. She knew Bud well, because he had been attending school in Neepawa, but she did not know the rest of his family. When Peggy reached their farm that summer, she felt shy and lonely. She was also upset. What she saw at the farm was markedly different from the description Bud had painted for her, one drawn in part from his imagination. That disturbing visit was a landmark for Peggy, as she saw in full measure how reality can play havoc with one's dreams. She also realized how Bud's future would be determined by his family's meagre resources. As things turned out, his life was marked by sadness. Although he very much wanted to attend university, there was no money for that. So, in the autumn of 1939, Bud Bailey enlisted in the army. He subsequently suffered a nervous breakdown while overseas, and was sent back to Canada, where he had to be hospitalized. He never completely recovered and over the years had many subsequent hospitalizations. For Peggy, Cousin Bud was a grim reminder of war's other casualties.[139]

The second major event for Peggy in 1939 occurred in September, when Canada entered the Second World War. She had been visiting in the home of other relatives, Bob and Elizabeth Pennie, when the news was broadcast over the radio. The recruiting officers soon arrived in Neepawa. Her cousin Bob enlisted and served in France, where he perished in a burning tank in 1944.

"We didn't know what war would mean," she later noted. "In a vague way, we felt tremendously excited."[140] Adults, however, were more apprehensive than the teenagers. Within days of Canada's entry into the war, forty young men from Neepawa and the surrounding area had gone to Winnipeg by truck to be examined "for a soldier." One citizen remarked, "It was awful to send our boys away like cattle."[141] Among the enlistees were several from the same family, including the three oldest Pasquill brothers.[142] Nevertheless, it would require time for the impact of war's reality to be felt by Peggy and her teenaged friends.

Grade Eight seems to have been unremarkable in terms of her schooling. Peggy was now spending more time on her writing, and in her memoirs she recounts a crucial decision that she made after her fourteenth birthday in the summer of 1940. As she was walking up the stairs at the Big House, the thought suddenly came to her with enormous strength: "I have to be a writer."[143] Although she had written poems, plays, and stories since childhood, the idea of actually becoming a writer seems suddenly to have become very clear to her. And being of a practical as well as an imaginative bent, Peggy began saving her earnings from babysitting so that she could help pay for her first typewriter, a second-hand Remington that her Aunt Ruby had found for her. Now she intended to prepare for her career by taking a typing course when she began high school in the fall.

READING AND WRITING: THE EARLIER YEARS

In *Dance on the Earth* and her essay "Books That Mattered to Me," Margaret Laurence mentions a number of books that had an impact on her during her youth. Among them she cites *Sowing Seeds in Danny* by Nellie McClung as "a real influence." Laurence reports that she had admired "the indomitable Pearlie, holding the family together against vast difficulties."[144] Other novels that influenced her then were: *Kidnapped*, *The White Company*, *Kim*, *Anne of Green Gables*, and *Emily of New Moon*. Should one consider these novels as an indication of a youngster's typical interest in gripping narrative and heroic tales of adventure or did their appeal for young Peggy lie in something she may not have been consciously aware of: the main character in each book is an orphan.

The central character in each of these novels yearns to be reunited somehow with family. As the fictional orphans strive heroically to overcome daunting situations and find a safe haven in their world, they grow in resourcefulness and moral character. Their personal strengths may well have attracted Peggy Wemyss as a youngster — more, perhaps, than the adult Margaret Laurence would later remember.

Although the stirring adventures of the clever and intrepid fictional orphans in *Kidnapped* (R.L. Stevenson); *The White Company* (Arthur Conan Doyle); and *Kim* (Rudyard Kipling) appealed to Peggy, she may have been more excited and also a bit overwhelmed by reading Lucy Maud Montgomery's *Emily of New Moon*. In that novel, Peggy Wemyss discovered uncanny resemblances between her own life and that of the fictional Emily Starr, a Canadian girl about her own age and from a background very similar to hers, although the setting is different. In the life of Emily, as in Peggy's life, the mother dies after a brief illness when the child is only four. Then, each father dies when his daughter is about nine. Peggy would have been moved by an early scene in *Emily of New Moon* when Emily's father, aware of his imminent death, tells his daughter: "Death isn't terrible. The universe is full of love — and spring comes everywhere — and in death you open and shut a door. There are beautiful things on the other side of the door. I'll find your mother there . . . I've never doubted that."[145]

Those were words Peggy would have wanted to hear from her own father, and they made the novel very personal to her. Perhaps, like Emily Starr, she too wrote poems or letters to her deceased father.

Among other similarities between the fictional Emily from Prince Edward Island and Peggy Wemyss from Neepawa are these: both have two unmarried aunts who figure prominently in their lives. Emily and Peggy also share a vivid, compelling, and imaginative gift, by which, as Emily said, "anything might happen and everything might come true." Both girls are determined to become writers, and they find special places away from the family where they can write, taking pains to conceal their notebooks.

Emily Starr turned to writing under circumstances that would have resonated with Peggy, who had not found in Neepawa other children as interested in language, poetry, and literature as she was.[146] Reading about the life of the fictional Emily must have been a real comfort to Peggy.

Emily Starr, like Peggy, takes her writing very seriously. When Emily feels close to tears, she pulls out her stubby pencil and the old yellow account book and begins to write. As she does, Emily forgets her relatives, the Murrays, although she is writing about them, and she forgets her humiliation, even though she is describing what had happened. She is content while she is writing and searching for the right word, and gives a happy sigh when she finds it.[147] In *Emily of New Moon*, Peggy read about a girl of her own age who, much like herself, yearned to write, to express her feelings, and to dramatize.

It would be a mistake, however, to assume that, in terms of Peggy's development as a writer, extensive reading was sufficient, or that she learned to write as an eager pupil in Wes McAmmond's Grade Seven class and while working her solitary way toward success the next year by crafting a story about pioneers. One important factor in Laurence's literary development (which has hitherto been overlooked) is the impact of the *Winnipeg Free Press*. In her memoirs she states that as an adolescent she entered writing contests which the newspaper sponsored. These two brief references in *Dance on the Earth* fail to convey any sense of the enormous impact that the *Winnipeg Free Press* had on her literary development when she was submitting her writing to them during her teenage years.

The *Winnipeg Free Press* was an influential daily paper, with a wide circulation that extended well beyond the province. During the Second World War, for example, sections were routinely sent to Canadian troops overseas. On Saturdays, it also had had a magazine supplement. During 1940-1941, while Peggy was in Grade Eight, it carried these features: a weekly column by Manitoban writer-activist Nellie McClung; serialized fiction (Sinclair Lewis's *Bethel Merriday* appeared for several months); and comic strips such as "Little Orphan Annie," "Charlie Chan," "Moon Mullins," "Li'l Abner," "Blondie," "Mickey Mouse," "Little Hiawatha," "Jane Arden," and "Off the Record." It also had a remarkable "Young Authors' Section," which usually appeared on page six.

While other Canadian papers did have a "Children's Page," the "Young Authors' Section" of the *Winnipeg Free Press* was directed primarily to advanced amateur writers. Seven columns wide, the "Young Authors' Section" was not a typical children's page. Although two columns were reserved for those under thirteen, the rest of the page was devoted to the work of writers between the ages of thirteen and thirty. Very young writers could find pen pals there, receive advice, and see some of their letters or poems in print. It should be noted that several children in the under-thirteen group wrote very maturely. A boy of ten, for example, defended his grammar in an interesting exchange of letters with the editor. He explained his idea and then told the editor that the verb he had used ("will lay") was transitive and hence he had used it correctly.[148]

The "Young Authors' Section" received submissions and letters from all over the English-speaking world: England, Scotland, Wales, Australia, New Zealand, India, and Hong Kong, as well as Canada and the United States. From those letters and from the editor's remarks, it is clear that people older than thirty regularly read the page. During 1940-41, among the frequent contributors were two Canadian servicemen: James Baker and Alfred Purdy. Al Purdy, then twenty-two, was in the RCAF. Many years later he became one of Margaret's close friends and an acclaimed poet.[149]

Reading the *Winnipeg Free Press* enabled Peggy to overcome the geographic and social isolation that often surrounds youngsters who hope to become writers. Each Saturday, she avidly read the "Young Authors' Section" and found in it literary companionship as well as reassurance about her own work. There she discovered real literary challenges, and there in 1940, at the age of fourteen, she hoped to be published. Not only did Peggy submit work to the "Young Authors' Section," but she also wrote to the editor. Contact with the *Winnipeg Free Press* played a very significant role in her literary apprenticeship. It was a place to learn from the work of others, as well as from the editor's advice. Having one's writing treated with seriousness and respect was a great encouragement to an aspiring young writer such as Peggy.

Although she lived in the safety and familiarity of her grandfather's house and her hometown, when Peggy read Saturday's *Winnipeg Free Press*, she became a citizen of the world. She was made aware of countries and events far beyond Manitoba or Canada. In the "Young Authors' Section," people from the English-speaking world joined one another on the page in their shared love of literature and an earnest pursuit of excellence in writing.

Aspiring authors sent in essays and science fiction, romance, mystery, travel, and adventure stories, as well as poetry. Encouragement and constructive criticism were heaped on those reader-contributors by a dedicated editor, who not only showed an interest in the writer's submission, but frequently made reference to a previous contribution by that person. The editor's attention and responsiveness were most encouraging, particularly for younger writers whose peer group often reacted with indifference or intolerance to their love of literature and their desire to write.[150]

The "Young Authors' Section" set very high standards for its readers and contributors, and writers were urged to improve their skills. The editor, for example, advised them: "Try and imagine *David Copperfield* written in the third person instead of the first." Referring to another book, the editor pointed out sophisticated elements in the entry: "the vivid fourth paragraph introduces an element of dread and suspense, then there is the strangeness of the climax, and the simile of the machine."[151] One young contributor's four-stanza poem was commended for its "Herrick-like smoothness and spontaneity," an allusion to Robert Herrick, a major seventeenth-century poet. All in all, the "Young Authors' Section" of the *Winnipeg Free Press* was unusually sophisticated. The talented efforts of many young writers were fostered through the personal attention given to their work and the editor's responses to their letters. Contributors were reminded: "Writing is a gift, but it also requires hard, severe labour."

Each week during the early years of the war this section also featured a photograph, often of well-known English sites that had been ravaged by bombs, among them Westminster Abbey, London's Parliament buildings, Manchester Cathedral, and the BBC offices. The captions and related articles expressed pride in being part of the British Empire and the importance of loyalty to Britain. However, on a number of occasions, Canadian contributors addressed matters that were quite specific to Canada. R.H. Grenville asked "When are we going to get a poem about a wheat field that is as truly representative of its subject, and at the same time as sincerely a work of art as Wordsworth's 'Little Celandine'?"[152] Grenville also commented: "Never will there be a lack of prairie or country color — firsthand, native color. None of your palms and magnolia, but the prairie crocus, the goldenrod, the flower on the flax."[153] A Manitoban contributor made a passionate plea for attention to Canadian subject matter and concluded with the statement: "We are struggling to become craftsmen, to smithy our language in a common fire."[154]

Editorials in this section often mentioned the importance of respecting the diversity of the cultures that made up Canada in the mid-twentieth century. That concern was also emphasized in an article, "Banishing the 'Beau Hunk' from the Canadian Vocabulary." The young contributor emphasized the dignity of immigrants, their contributions to life in North America, and the way in which their many languages had enriched the English vocabulary. The article closed with an appeal that derogatory terms such as "bohunk" be banished from Canadian speech.[155]

On Saturday, the "Young Authors' Section," following Matthew Arnold's dictum about literary "touchstones," also published and discussed the work of well-known authors, particularly poets. During Peggy's first year of high school (1940-1941), it featured work by D.H. Lawrence, John Drinkwater, John Milton, Alfred Noyes, Vita Sackville-West, Walter de la Mare, Emily Dickinson, A.E. Housman, James Stephens, and Rabindranath Tagore. The section's editor, in turn, challenged the young contributors and responded frankly to their inquiries:

> Since you want criticism we will say frankly that your poems showed the influence of moralistic commonplace versifying rather than of the distillations of the supreme poets. Wordsworth was a moralizer but still more he was a poet; and he was great despite, not because of his moralizing. . . .
>
> Our advice is to take the master poets, including Tennyson and Keats, the Shakespeare sonnets, and some of the moderns such as Walter de la Mare, to form your standards on. Let us hear from you again.[156]

These remarks, obviously, were directed to young adults who were serious about writing, who had read broadly and worked diligently to improve their work. It was assumed that these contributors would want to familiarize themselves with the work of famous predecessors. The editor called attention not only to the great names of the past but also to more recent writers such as Wilfred Owen, Edna St.Vincent Millay, Rudyard Kipling, Richard Llewellyn, W.H. Davis, Henry Sidel Canby (biographer and critic), and Clement Wood, who had recently published a handbook for poets.

The editor took for granted that these aspiring writers, as well as the readers, were genuinely interested in words, and used a dictionary that gave Latin or Greek roots, as well as suffixes and prefixes. "You enjoy understanding the build of a word," the editor advised, instructing them also to develop keen ears for diction, "for how clean-cut and well-voiced words can be uttered." Errors in pronunciations heard over the radio were pointed out: for example, that Anthony Eden's first name had been pronounced with a "th," and that "Sofia" had been incorrectly accented on the first syllable.

For aspiring writers, one of the most exciting and challenging features of Saturday's *Winnipeg Free Press* was the writing contests. Not only were readers encouraged to submit work, but they also were reminded of the achievements of others their age — for example, that Laura Goodman Salverson of Manitoba, winner of a 1939 Governor General's award, had begun her short-story career at the age of *twelve* with a story printed in an American magazine, and that recently a young contributor from Flin Flon, Manitoba, had been published in the prestigious *Christian Science Monitor*.[157]

In the summer of 1940, following Peggy's graduation from Grade Eight, the *Winnipeg Free Press* once again announced its annual short-story contest. The contest required a six-chapter serial on any subject; each chapter had to contain from 1,200 to 1,800 words (the total number of words, therefore, would fall between 7,200 and 10,800). Winners were to be announced in September.

Peggy Wemyss entered that contest. After her fourteenth birthday in July, she had felt a calling to be "a writer."[158] Now, if she won the writing contest, she would have the opportunity of seeing her work in print for the first time. Entering that contest was a very ambitious step for her. In doing so, Peggy left a sheltered situation in which she had shown her writing only to a respected Grade Seven teacher and entered a more challenging and uncertain world, one in which, at the age of fourteen, she would be competing with some of the best young writers, not only from the province, but also from other parts of the English-speaking world.

"I desperately needed my manuscript typed so I could enter [the contest]," Laurence recalled.[159] Her story about Canadian pioneers, "The Land of Our Fathers," would have totalled about thirty-five typed pages. With an entry of that length, no wonder she sought the help of Aunt Ruby's secretary to meet the deadline. However when Margaret Laurence later talked about this early effort, she was dismissive of it. She treated it off-handedly and mentioned casually that her story had filled "two or three scribblers." Such comments give the erroneous impression that her youthful effort was rather insignificant and ephemeral. Those who interviewed Margaret Laurence in later years probably were not aware of the calibre of writing in the "Young Authors' Section," or of the challenge that such a contest presented to a young, aspiring writer. In reality, Peggy must have worked very hard on her entry, because she certainly was aware that the short-story contests sponsored by the *Winnipeg Free Press* were very competitive and judged by exacting standards.[160]

Did Peggy relish time spent shaping her submission or did she agonize over her efforts? Did she think her entry would stand a chance? At least she would know the outcome of the contest by Thanksgiving.

CHAPTER FOUR

Hitler in Manitoba: The High School Years

In early September 1940, Peggy walked a few blocks from her grandfather's house on First Avenue to the local high school, Neepawa Collegiate Institute (NCI). An attractive brick building built in 1928, it could easily accommodate its student body of about 120. Under the leadership of principal, J.E. Sigurjonsson, the high school enjoyed a reputation for good teaching.

Peggy was to spend four formative years at Neepawa Collegiate Institute. There, among classmates who were friends, she participated in important school activities: playing violin in the orchestra, serving as convenor of the debating team, participating in various war-relief efforts, and working hard for two years as editor of the school's paper: *Annals of the Black and Gold*. At NCI, Peggy demonstrated team spirit as well as leadership ability.[161]

Although the faculty was small, those men and women made up in energy and dedication for lack of numbers. In high school, Peggy found teachers who encouraged her writing and took an interest in her personal development. Among that staff, Connie Offen and Mildred Musgrove were to figure in significant ways in Peggy's life. Over the years, she sustained her connections to both women, staying in touch by mail, sending news of her children and her publications, and, when the opportunity arose, visiting each of them.

Mildred Musgrove, from Boissevain, was adviser to *Annals of the Black and Gold*. She also taught English Literature, as well as typing and short-hand. While Miss Musgrove could be strict in class, she was devoted to the students' welfare and lent her support to many extracurricular activities, such as the drama club, girls' gymnastic events, and track meets.[162] A keen golfer and excellent curler, Mildred Musgrove was sometimes asked by students to serve as their team's "skip" during a bonspiel competition.[163]

Connie Offen, born in Rivers, Manitoba, was the daughter of a master-printer who had emigrated from England and founded the weekly *Rivers' Gazette*. She had grown up in a household where books were a staple of life.[164] Upon joining the faculty at NCI, Miss Offen taught Latin, French, and English Composition. She also coached drama and directed the school's small orchestra. She excelled at curling and was also an outstanding tennis player, competing frequently in provincial and Western tournaments.

Marjorie Osborn, the youngest female member of the NCI staff, taught Home Economics as well as English and Music. The vice-principal, Herb Ray, taught Science and Maths. When he had moved with his family to Neepawa in the 1930s, he had been an avid tennis player. However, not long after that move, he contracted a bad case of polio. Although Herb Ray eventually regained the ability to walk, he did so with some difficulty. Former students recall his determination and patriotism during the war years, when Mr. Ray, despite his disability and attendant pain, frequently drilled with the Neepawa Air Cadets.[165]

In the 1930s, years of the Great Depression, pupils often left high school after Grade Ten in order to join the labour force and help support the family. After Canada joined England in 1939 to fight the Axis powers, young boys left school to enlist in the armed services. The remaining students who did complete Grade Twelve at a collegiate, which was the equivalent of first year college, were admitted to university as sophomores. This was later to be Peggy's experience.

When she entered NCI in September 1940, Peggy was one of twenty-nine pupils in Grade Nine. There were a few students from surrounding areas, whom Peggy did not know, but most of the faces were familiar to her. A former neighbour, Jack Coutts, was then editor of the school's paper; David Rabinovitch was president of the student body; and the vice-president, Louceil Crawford, was the older sister of Peggy's friend Margie.[166]

For Freshman Day, Grade Nine students were obliged to dress in silly outfits and perform embarrassing pranks. In the evening, Laurence recalls, there was a Sadie Hawkins dance. Before beginning high school, Peggy had taken lessons in ballroom dancing at Mum's behest, but she was embarrassed by the whole idea and soon stopped going. Nevertheless, in time Peggy did become a fine dancer. She had a keen sense of rhythm and a love of music, and throughout her life would enjoy dancing. The title of her memoirs, *Dance on the Earth*, applies both to Margaret Laurence's enduring delight in dancing as well as a spiritual approach to her life's work.

When Peggy and her friends began their high-school studies, radio reports and newspaper headlines carried ominous news of the Second World War's escalation. That September, the *Winnipeg Free Press* headlines were sombre and unsettling: "Huge Attack on London Fails," "U-Boat Torpedoes Shipload of Children," "Japanese Fliers Bomb Canadian Liner." While England tightened its coastal defences against a possible invasion, Nazi bombers attacked London. When Peggy scanned the Saturday newspaper, she saw photos of the destruction caused by bombing raids and read articles about life in wartime England and stories about combat, such as "My Thirty Days in Hell." Little by little, the war was beginning to invade her consciousness.

On September 28, eager to find out the contest results, Peggy opened the *Winnipeg Free Press* and learned that she had not won the short-fiction contest. First prize went to a contestant whose entry dealt with the present war. His story was praised for a good plot and "a Canadian setting faithfully presented." Another contestant, however, was chided because her entry repeated a pattern she had used "with previous heroines" and because it had a "certain theatricality and anachronism."[167] Clearly, the standards were high, and it would not be easy to satisfy such attentive editors. Peggy's disappointment over her failure to win was lessened, however, when she noticed her name in the very first sentence of a column headed, "Specially Good." Her entry, "The Land of Our Fathers," was singled out for praise.[168] In addition to offering favourable comments, the editors said that they hoped to print Peggy's story in a future issue![169]

Ambitious to succeed, Peggy continued to work at her writing whenever she could. Later that autumn, she submitted a detective story to another *Winnipeg Free Press* contest. Once again she waited for the results. She was learning, as good writers must, that rejections should not signal the end of their efforts. Peggy had begun to develop a resolve, a determination, that would later come into play during the years of her serious apprenticeship.

During December, she was asked by Miss Offen to write a Christmas play for her Sunday-school class — a play with enough parts for each child. Perhaps that was not a great challenge for Peggy, but she was interested in drama and this was an opportunity to try her hand. She soon produced the required script.[170] That month she also wrote a long, enthusiastic review of a play and six skits performed by fellow NCI students. Published in *Annals of the Black and Gold*, the review marks her first appearance in the school paper. It was an encouraging accomplishment for a Grade Nine student who hoped to become a writer.

On Saturdays, when Peggy scanned the *Winnipeg Free Press* for news about the contest winners, she would have seen lengthy film reviews and photos promoting two new movies: "The Great Dictator," starring Charlie Chaplin as Hitler — a film destined to become a classic — and "The Thief of Baghdad," based on a well-known tale from *The Arabian Nights*. The producers of this action-packed movie had managed to create for the screen "a living, moving, 200-foot-high Djinn." When these films came to Neepawa, everyone in town flocked to the Roxy to see them. Peggy and her friends probably went too. The film would have been a dramatic visual introduction to the Middle East.

The Christmas 1940 issue of the *Annals of the Black and Gold* featured a story by Peggy, "The Case of the Golden Spaniel," which has not been noted before.[171] Written in diary format by a character named Nancy Grayson, "The Case of the Golden Spaniel," is very similar to another of her efforts, "The Case of the Blond Butcher." Both show the influence of *Emily of New Moon*, one of Peggy's favourite books. A few days after Christmas, Grandmother Margaret Harrison Wemyss died in Ontario. Although she had left Neepawa some years before to join her daughter there, Peggy had visited with her and the family in Ontario. Now, another death in the immediate family would have been upsetting to the sensitive teenager.

At NCI, Peggy was now in charge of the War Savings Drive for Grade Nine. She also worked on the school paper, and although she had stopped taking music lessons, she continued to play violin in the school's small orchestra. That year, the orchestra, using handsome new black-and-gold music stands made by the boys in shop class, played at Knox Presbyterian Church's "fall fowl supper," the Red Cross Tea, and various school functions. Peggy considered herself merely competent as a violinist, and later downplayed her musical interests and ability. This may have been due to the knowledge that her own mother had been a very fine musician — a significant accomplishment in a town that had many excellent musicians and singers and was justly proud of its musical traditions.

During the winter months, the younger Neepawans enjoyed snowshoeing, skating, musical gatherings, and the weekly feature at the picture show. The farmers used that time to sharpen fence posts, take care of harnesses, and tend to a host of chores around the barn and house. Many of the women darned, baked, quilted, looked after the poultry, and undertook seasonal household chores. From time to time Peggy, too, enjoyed baking thimble cookies with "Mum." Then she would don a thimble, put a dint in the cookie, and fill it with jam. Such familiar aspects of life on the prairie were later to appear in Laurence's Manawaka fiction.

On January 18 Peggy was excited to see that her detective story, "The Case of the Blond Butcher: A Wanted Man," Part I, had been published in the magazine section of the *Winnipeg Free Press*.[172] There, too, in a prominent position on the Young Authors' page she read with amazement:

> To Jean Margaret Wemyss: Thank you for what you say about our corrections in the stories and poems. You didn't give us much work on "The Case of the Blond Butcher." You do not need after this to be shy about sending in anything you like, Jean, "The Case of the Blond Butcher," for the effort of a fourteen-year old author, does you great credit.[173]

She reread that last sentence. "You do not need after this to be shy about sending in anything you like, Jean, 'The Case of the Blond Butcher' . . . does you great credit."

Could it be true that she had actually entered the ranks of published authors? Last summer's decision to become a writer now began to seem less like a dream and more like a reality. As Peggy held the newspaper in her hands, she was elated by this tangible recognition and by the editor's encouragement — something for which all young writers yearn. Not long after, she received her first fan letter. It was from a boy in Winnipeg. Peggy's reaction to his letter seems extreme, but it signals the kind of ambivalence about being recognized as a writer that was to persist for a number of years. "I was so embarrassed," she recalls, "I didn't know what to do, so I threw it in the kitchen wood stove before Mum could see it and I never told a living soul."[174] Peggy's world now had shifted. She had become a newly published and praised young writer; but life in Neepawa continued to move according to its usual and predictable rhythms. Externally, nothing had changed.

The plot of "The Case of the Blond Butcher" revolves around a suspected theft that, in fact, was not a theft at all. While this early effort at fiction is not in itself remarkable, Peggy does manage to create some suspense and generate interest along a secondary plot line that deals with minor personality conflicts among the young characters in the story. Despite stereotypical adolescent phrases such as "a darling housecoat," "simply sweet," and "I was perfectly frantic," Peggy writes dialogue well for her age and shows an interest in capturing colloquial speech.

Winter sports events continued at Neepawa Collegiate. Early in February, curling, a popular and challenging ice sport, required extra rinks for NCI's bonspiel against nearby high schools in Minnedosa and Gladstone. While Peggy liked curling, and the main rink was near her home, in Neepawa curling was chiefly the sport of adults.[175] Moreover, Peggy was never athletically inclined, a situation that was partially the consequence of her poor eyesight (a fact she had concealed during her earlier school years). However, she did enjoy skating with her friends.

One Saturday in mid-March, a blizzard began, stranding the shoppers in town. Prairie folks were used to winter storms, however, and Neepawans opened their homes on such occasions. Peggy's experience with prairie winters was to affect her attitude toward winter all her life. Years later, living in Lakefield, Ontario, Margaret Laurence complained when the snow quickly turned to slush. She told a friend that she yearned for a "real winter," when the snow would remain on the ground and people were accustomed to dealing with it. Friends in Ontario occasionally offered to take her for a drive during the winter. Then, Margaret, accustomed to prairie winters, would emerge from her home on Regent Street with a thermos, a snack, something to read, a candle, a book of matches, and a wool rug — in case the car and passengers might become stranded.[176]

In the autumn, NCI increased the number of debating teams, and the school's first debate, with Peggy as convenor, was held. These debates at NCI were followed with great interest, and the topics frequently challenged students to deal with pressing contemporary issues. NCI students, at least during the debate season, were expected to have an awareness of conditions in the wider world and to ponder alternate approaches to government and foreign policy. The following were among the topics debated while Peggy was a student: "Resolved: Co-operation has done more for the world than has competition"; "Resolved: that the war situation would have been better for the allies if the United States had not become involved"; "Resolved: that in the best interests of Canada there should be conscription of manpower, money, and industry"; and "Resolved: that ambition has brought more harm than good to mankind." The latter topic was for the first debate of the school year, and Peggy and a classmate upheld the negative, arguing for the benefits of ambition. Her class won the debating shield that year, a distinct honour for Grade Nine. At one debate, the presence of Mrs. R.F. McWilliams, an author and wife of the lieutenant-governor of Manitoba, added to the significance of the occasion. That day Mrs. McWilliams announced a forthcoming essay contest "for the fullest and most authentic account of an historical episode prior to 1900 in the history of the town of Neepawa or the surrounding district." The winner would receive a copy of her book, *Manitoba Milestones*. Since Peggy had been published in the *Winnipeg Free Press* and had twice received words of commendation from the editor of the newspaper's "Young Authors' Section," she may have submitted an entry, although evidence for that has not been found.

During spring 1941, the girls in Peggy's class were excited by news of the wedding of the film star Deanna Durbin, formerly of Winnipeg.

Durbin's photo, showing her smiling radiantly and wearing a full-length wedding gown, appeared on the front page of the *Winnipeg Free Press*, directly under a banner headline that announced twenty-eight Nazis had escaped from an Ontario prison.[177] By now, Grade Nine students were accustomed to having events of varying significance commingled in the newspaper and in their lives.

In May, as Europe confronted Fascist ideology, students who had assembled for the school's Empire Day observance heard the guest speaker address the topic: "Democracy Whither Bound?" That was followed by the reading of a letter that an airman had written to his mother — a letter that was to be delivered only after his death.

At the end of the school term, each Grade Nine student was mentioned in the school paper. It noted that Peggy Wemyss is cheerful "except when she loses her temper"; she enjoys arguing with Mona Spratt; and her characteristic saying is: "If at first you don't succeed, try, try, try again."[178] It is interesting that, even at this point, classmates took note of Peggy's determination. The *Neepawa Press*, the town paper, published the students' grades. That year Peggy's marks were among the highest in the class. Her best subjects were Literature, Grammar, and Music.

On the evening of June 8, students gathered in Knox Presbyterian Church for the annual Baccalaureate service and Achievement awards, the most coveted being the Governor General's Medal. This annual presentation went to a Grade Eleven student who best combined excellence in academic subjects with involvement in school activities. Before closing with the singing of "The Maple Leaf Forever" and "God Save the King," the Honour Roll for the armed forces was read.

As the weather turned warmer, many Neepawans enjoyed the Saturday-night custom of shopping or sitting in parked cars along Mountain Avenue, just watching folks coming and going. Stores remained open that night, so farmers and their families could come into town to shop and socialize. Mona Spratt's father would park his car where his daughter and her friends could take in the passing scene.

One night in June 1941, a terrific wind and electrical storm struck Neepawa. Trees were toppled, a stable was blown down, shingles were ripped from the south side of a home, and a caboose was turned over. The town held a "bee" to repair the house and replace the shingles. In many ways, Neepawa was like one big family. Such neighbourly concern was the positive side of living in a small prairie town. There citizens helped one another in the face of natural disasters, while Neepawa's fathers, sons, and brothers, who were abroad, faced disasters of an entirely different order as members of the armed services.

By August 1941, over one hundred thousand Canadians were serving overseas. Although many boys from Neepawa had enlisted and the town's youngsters were involved in salvage activities to aid the war effort, the war, of course, still seemed remote to Peggy and her friends. After all, the battlefields across the Atlantic were thousands of miles away.[179] In September 1941, however, when Peggy began Grade Ten, everyone was talking about the new airfield under construction a mile west of Neepawa. The town watched as work went forward on EFTS, No.35, one of a series of Elementary Flying Training Schools established in Western Canada by Great Britain for the training of RAF pilots.[180] These central-Canadian training bases were preferred over more vulnerable locations near the sea. On the Manitoba prairie, the pilots did not have to contend with coastal fog or worry about a naval attack. Soon a branch of the Air Cadets of Canada was formed at NCI. When the new cadets visited the EFTS base, they made a simulated flight in a Link trainer, and inspected small, single-engine training planes called Tiger Moths.

Since the town still suffered from the effects of the Great Depression, NCI students decided for financial reasons to adopt a school uniform, and, by mid-October, the girls had become accustomed to wearing the required blue tunic and white blouse.[181] The pranks of "freshman day" were over; student council elections finished, and convenors of the various subcommittees had been announced. The first class party, a "straw-stack burn" for Grade Twelve, was held two miles east of town. Full of hilarity and high spirits, students scrambled up one side of the stack and down the other before it was set on fire. Then, gathering around a smaller bonfire, they heated cans of pork and beans for supper. Singing songs as the smoke rose in the cool night air, whooping students followed their teachers, Connie Offen and Mildred Musgrove, as they led a war dance around the flames.[182]

That month a poem by Peggy was published in the high-school paper.[183] Entitled "Scholar's 'If,'" her poem is a humorous imitation of

Rudyard Kipling's well-known poem "If," which appeared in *Rewards and Fairies*.[184] Peggy had read that book as well as its sequel, *Puck of Pook's Hill*, and a good deal more of Kipling. "If" was also among the poems in *The Canada Book of Prose and Verse, Book Three*, which was used in Manitoba schools. One of Kipling's biographers remarked that even those who question Kipling's sentiments continue to acknowledge the "metrical and technical brilliance" displayed in "If."[185] For Peggy, imitating a work by Kipling was another step toward trying to develop her literary talent.

During the autumn term, students assembled for a special presentation by Watson Thomson, a faculty member of the Adult Education League at the University of Manitoba. He showed films of the war and the training of RAF pilots in Britain and spoke about the escalation of "the great battle in which we are now engaged." Peggy Wemyss could not have guessed at the time that Watson Thomson's presence in Winnipeg would later have an effect on the future direction of her life, but his presentation that day reinforced the impact of the war on their young lives. During the autumn, the Air Cadets were occupied with drills and training, while the girls at NCI worked on their war-readiness. After school hours, classes in physical training for girls had also begun.

As the war in Europe escalated, rationing of butter, sugar, and gasoline became a fact of life. At NCI the entire student body, as well as the faculty, were involved in assisting the war effort at home. NCI became the centre for the collection of salvage items such as metal toothpaste tubes, tin foil, bones, and rags to aid the British War Relief Fund. In addition, classes competed in purchasing War Savings Bonds, and the staff of the *Annals of the Black and Gold* decided "to save extra money for the war effort" by cancelling the customary colour printing of the Christmas issue.[186] The students' involvement with these activities, as well as the various debates and guest lectures about the world situation, brought the "Front" closer to Neepawa. Yet, the war in Europe continued to feel rather unreal.

That changed dramatically, however, after Japan's surprise attack on Pearl Harbor on December 7, 1941. No longer did the Manitoba prairie seem secure. Several months before that attack, reports of German U-boats off Canada's Atlantic coast had been announced in the newspapers and on radio. Now, worried citizens considered the possibility of a Japanese attack on the Pacific coast. A few days after Pearl Harbor, students gathered for an assembly listened to a broadcast by U.S. president Franklin D. Roosevelt, who informed listeners that the United States had declared war and would join its Canadian and European allies. At the conclusion of Roosevelt's address, the NCI students "voluntarily stood to attention when the American national anthem was played."[187]

Canadians soon learned another war tragedy had occurred on December 7, one that Margaret Laurence refers to several times in her memoirs. On that day, two thousand Canadian troops had been sent into battle to defend the ill-prepared British garrison and colony of Hong Kong. The effort to defend Hong Kong has been likened to Britain's infamous "Charge of the Light Brigade" during the Crimean War, and was described as "an act that sent inadequately trained and ill-equipped men to defend an island that was indefensible."[188] As a result, the Canadian troops suffered enormous losses.

While those battalions were engaged in combat in Hong Kong, construction work on the huge air base near Neepawa continued at a feverish pace. The base had twenty-five buildings, including a medical unit and a tremendous drill hall. By the time construction was completed "approximately 3,000,000 feet of timber, mainly spruce and fir," had been used.[189] By Christmas the age for joining the Neepawa Air Cadets had been lowered to fourteen in order to build up a larger flight. The cadets had been measured for uniforms and officially recognized. These lads, who were classmates, neighbours, and brothers of Peggy and her friends, were now studying navigation, gunnery, theory of combustion engines, signalling, and first aid. In June, they would be sent to camp for a week of further military training.[190] The growing impact of the war on the town's teenagers is evident in the Christmas 1941 issue of *Annals of the Black and Gold*, which described in detail NCI's war-relief efforts. In addition, it featured letters from former students who were presently serving in the armed services. A short story by Peggy, "Goodwill Towards Men," signed with her initials, appeared in that issue.[191]

Her story focuses on a wartime situation and is set in Scotland on Christmas Eve.[192] "Goodwill Towards Men" opens with a conversation between Black Tomas McDuff and his young son Robert. Black Tomas sends Robert on an errand. Although the boy is afraid to venture out alone at night, he summons his courage and goes forth. Along the way, he spots a German parachutist caught in a tree. The boy cleverly manages to disarm the young German and bring him home. Because the family's older son is serving overseas, Black Tomas and his wife decide to extend to the captured soldier the sort of kindness they hope their own son might receive in similar circumstances. The young German is given a bed for the night and spends Christmas day with the family before being turned over to the authorities.

While the story is clearly the work of an amateur, it shows a marked improvement over "The Case of the Golden Spaniel" and "The Case of the Blond Butcher." In "Goodwill Towards Men," Peggy creates suspense, uses dialogue effectively, and incorporates both internal and external conflict. She makes liberal use of Scots' dialect in phrases such as: "Dinna' boggle — ye arena' afeared o' the muir the nicht, are ye?" and "Come in and have a wee bit parritch." That Peggy, who was only beginning Grade Ten, could handle extensive dialect and not have her story become incomprehensible or downright silly indicates that she had been working on short fiction for some time.

"Goodwill Towards Men" is also interesting in terms of its themes and narrative style. The presence of dialect, danger, intrigue, and suspense may reflect Peggy's reading of adventure tales such as Stevenson's *Kidnapped*, but it may also reflect her mounting personal anxiety about the war and the safety of classmates and friends, many of whom were then serving overseas. The plot could have been influenced by articles in the *Winnipeg Free Press*, which described prisoner-of-war camps in Canada where captured Germans, lads of eighteen and nineteen, were being held. But whatever the source, this short story is an interesting apprentice effort.

After the celebration of Christmas and the New Year, classes resumed on January 5, 1942 with temperatures registering at -35°F. Three months later, in the midst of a howling March blizzard, the worst in many years, the RAF, under Wing Commander H.R. Black arrived in Neepawa. This first contingent of about four hundred airmen came not only from England, but from as far away as Australia, New Zealand, India, Ceylon, and the Bahamas.[193] While the men were kept very busy during their training sessions, from time to time there were station dances at the base, and the fine hardwood floor of the drill hall became an enormous dance floor.[194]

In spring, while, as the songwriter, Stan Rogers described it, farmers "put another season's promise in the ground," and "watched the field behind the plow turn to straight dark rows,"[195] the first RAF flight course (No.46) began training.[196] Soon the skies were filled with tiny Tiger Moths circling above the fields as the young pilots practised landing and taking off again. Inside Neepawa Collegiate Institute it was difficult to concentrate on lessons. Teenaged boys, remembering the bravery of Billy Bishop in the Great War, now imagined themselves in glory behind the controls of a Spitfire. One classmate, however, sombrely noted that "the drone of a training plane as it drifts lazily across the sky is a grim reminder that the world is not everywhere so fair."[197]

The idea of "Hitler in Manitoba" no longer seemed far-fetched. In fact, the city of Winnipeg launched a project — a "What If" Day. Citizens, dressed up as Nazi soldiers and officials, staged Fascist activities such as burning books, arresting "suspicious" people, and harassing clerics and ethnic minorities. This was filmed and turned into a thirty-minute documentary of the day's events.[198] In Neepawa, however, a film was not needed to bring home the fact of war. Now, when Peggy and her friends walked home from school, the afternoon air was filled with the sound of the planes and with nearby military commands. "Tennnnnnn-shun," barked the sergeant, as the girls passed uniformed classmates drilling smartly in the schoolyard or marching along the streets on their way to the base. Overseas in England, the Neepawa boys of the Queen's Own Cameron Highlanders were on manoeuvres in the spring countryside, languishing for lack of action.

Back on the Manitoba prairie, life also seemed predictable and uneventful. Peggy and her friends had plenty of time for lighthearted pranks and jokes. When Miss Osborn, who taught Home Economics, missed class because of illness, a mock apology was sent by Mona Spratt, Peggy, Jack Tyler, and others. They regretted "causing" their teacher's sudden illness. They wondered if it might have been the result of an "overdose of arsenic" in the tuna salad they had made, "the gopher poison" in the Bavarian cream, or "the sulphuric acid" in the coffee. Marjorie

Osborn, touched by their playful message, saved that note among other mementos of her teaching days.[199]

Another situation with Miss Osborn was later recalled by Margaret Laurence. In a letter to the writer Budge Wilson, Laurence noted that this teacher, who was not much older than the students, was made to teach another course to Grades Nine and Ten. "Of course, she [Miss Osborn] was terrified, and I think Mona and I even felt sorry for her, but in the presence of the great hulking boys we hoped to impress, we sure didn't stand up for her. . . . All these years later, I'd like to say sorry to her."[200] The theme of regret over words not spoken is repeated many times in Laurence's letters and in *Dance on the Earth*. It seems as if she was haunted by conversations interrupted by death or absence. Frequently it also indicates her capacity to empathize with others who were in pain or suffering in some way.

In Neepawa, once school exams were over, the longed-for days of summer unfurled, heralded by sweet strawberries and fresh rhubarb. All over town the baking of pies commenced and the aroma wafted along the streets and through the backyards. Although there were alarming newspaper headlines, they seemed only to startle for a moment like the sudden storms of summer. Life quickly returned to its usual routine for the town's teenagers. Whether splashing at the swimming hole in River Bend Park, racing down the streets on their bicycles, or laughing over a coke in Brooker's, Peggy and her friends felt all the exuberance and energy of youth.

Change, however, was around the corner. In July, when Peggy turned sixteen, she was required by Canadian law to register for military purposes at the post office. During that same month, a series of events that would affect Neepawa was unfolding in eastern Canada. A special train left Chatham, New Brunswick, and began its long westward journey from the Atlantic provinces across Quebec and Ontario to Manitoba, a distance of over two thousand miles. Fourteen Pullman cars were transporting the civilian personnel who had operated an Elementary Flying Training School (EFTS, No.21) near Chatham. A complete freight train was needed to carry all their personal effects, baggage, and equipment.[201] The group's task was to take over all the operations, except flight training, at the RAF Flying School in Neepawa.

As the August heat settled over the Manitoba prairie and "dust devils" rolled down the streets, news of war had become almost routine. Across the Atlantic, however, at British command headquarters, routine matters had given way to a hectic pace as generals and their staffs worked out the final details for a tremendous raid on the French coast, to be followed by a quick push into German-occupied France. The Canadian infantry, including the Queen's Own Cameron Highlanders, had been moved from their camps in the south of England and were now massed near the English Channel awaiting orders.

Back in Manitoba, curious townsfolk gathered to watch the plumes of steam which rose into the sky and floated over the prairie as the long train from New Brunswick slowly approached the Neepawa station. Soon 180 members of the Miramachi Flying Training School and their families stepped down onto the dusty station platform. The civilian personnel who were to staff EFTS No.35 had arrived.[202] They would need housing, and their children would have to be enrolled for the new school year. All sorts of adjustments would be required as the civilian operating company took over the management of the air base.

At about the same time, across the Atlantic, in the darkness before an August dawn, the Queen's Own Cameron Highlanders, with battalion piper Lance Corporal Alec Graham, waited in landing craft off the French coast at Dieppe for the signal to attack. The bloodiest nine hours in Canadian military history were about to commence. At the signal, five thousand Canadian troops from seven regiments charged the French beaches: three thousand one hundred were killed, wounded, or captured.

The first reports to reach Neepawa were guardedly optimistic, with rumours of victory. But the Winnipeg newspapers soon filled with news of Dieppe's casualties. Neepawans, anxious and sleepless, awaited further details of the assault on the French coast. Each day the front pages of the Winnipeg papers were filled with photos of the casualties from Manitoba and, as the days passed, the captions above those faces shifted from "missing" to "wounded" to "gravely wounded" to "dead." Peggy's hometown would never be the same.

The losses were overwhelming, due in part to the method of recruitment. Since Canada did not employ a lottery system, men from the same family often served together in the armed forces. Sometimes these relatives, hoping to stay beside one another on the battlefield, enlisted in the same branch of the service. The Winnipeg newspapers frequently had photos of family groups of servicemen — sometimes brothers; sometimes father, sons, and uncle. If Canadian forces were attacked and routed, however, the casualties could be from the same family or the same town. In places such as Neepawa, the town itself was like one large family, and the losses were deeply felt by all its citizens. A person did not require Peggy's active imagination to grasp the magnitude of Dieppe.

Now all those battles on the pages of fiction, the gallant skirmishes in *Kidnapped* and the medieval battles of *The White Company*, became dim and remote beside the reality of modern twentieth-century warfare, when a burning tank became a tomb for the boy next door, and the body flung forward on the stony beach at Pourville was that of a friend or relative.

In Grandfather Simpson's house, Peggy sat in a big oak armchair, staring at the photos on the front page of the *Winnipeg Free Press*, remembering the Cameron Highlanders who had bivouacked on the fairgrounds at Scotty Burnett's farm before going overseas. She recalled the smiling young faces of the Neepawa boys marching through town in kilted uniforms to the skirl of bagpipes, and she stared again in shock at the newspaper headlines and the columns of photographs: "I was sixteen that year [1942], and for the first time I knew, really knew, what war meant. It meant that young men from your own town, your friends or brothers of your friends, boys only a couple of years older than yourself had been mutilated and killed."[203]

The Second World War, particularly Dieppe, affected Peggy profoundly. Sensitive and thoughtful, she was overwhelmed by the magnitude of the losses. "They were boys I had known. They were a part of me." She had known death before, but this was different. This time death's losses came from her peer group. Thoughts of war — the nightmare of past wars, the horrors of the unfolding world war, and the possibility of future wars — permanently altered the way she would look at the world, and in the years ahead she would realign her priorities accordingly. As a well-known novelist, Margaret Laurence would work to ban the manufacture and testing of nuclear arms and to support a secure world peace. These efforts were undertaken as a consequence of her sense of a moral imperative, and not, as some have alleged, because she was not able to summon her powers as a writer. Margaret Laurence's convictions about war had been etched deeply into her character during her youth, a fact that she mentions frequently in interviews as well as in her memoirs:

> In one sense Dieppe perpetually has happened only yesterday. It runs as a leitmotif through all my so-called Manawaka fiction and, in a way, it runs through my whole life, in my hatred of war so profound I can't find words to express my outrage.[204]

Forty years after the casualties of Dieppe, Laurence explained in a letter to the writer Paul Hiebert, why, despite a certain natural shyness, she felt compelled to take a public stand against war and to participate in peace groups. "You are quite right — America and Russia are scared sick of one another. . . . I may be working for no possible effect, but Paul, if I don't do it I cannot face myself. . . . I also, of course, want to continue my own writing, my own work, but this seems related to the state of the world in general."[205] Margaret Laurence felt a great urgency to act on behalf of world peace because of the terrifying possibility of nuclear war. She would have agreed with Jonathan Schell's statement in *The Fate of the Earth*: "Because everything we do and everything we are is in jeopardy, and because the peril is immediate and unremitting, every person is the right person to act and every moment is the right moment to begin, starting with the present moment."

In September 1942, a few weeks after the battle of Dieppe, classes resumed at NCI, giving students a sense of normalcy, but the whole town was still deep in shock over the losses sustained by the Canadian troops. News of more deaths among those who had previously been reported as wounded continued to reach Neepawa throughout the weeks of autumn. However, young men did not stop enlisting, and during Grade Eleven only two boys remained in Peggy's class. By Grade Twelve there would be none. "They were all at war," she said.[206]

During her last two years in high school, Peggy, as the busy editor of the *Annals of the Black and Gold*, was "never known to slow down to a graceful walk." She dashed about determined to solicit a wide range of articles and art work for the newspaper.[207] The paper's adviser, Mildred Musgrove, remembers that Peggy rarely submitted her own writing to the paper, but instead put time and effort into getting other students to contribute.[208] The actual production of the paper presented a challenge. Peggy worked closely with Miss Musgrove and a few students to obtain the articles, type the master sheets, and arrange page layouts for a school paper that was now more than twenty pages long. Peggy was learning the practical side of "literary" production. Cranking out the newspaper on the shiny new Gestetner machine in the principal's office, she had to place blotting sheets between the pages to prevent the thick black ink from blurring the good copy. Fifty years later, she recalled the process as "messy and difficult," but "a labour of love."[209]

The first issue of the *Annals of the Black and Gold* with Peggy as editor appeared in the autumn that she was in Grade Eleven. Her earnest editorial stressed the importance of achieving readiness for the post-war era. "Remember, it is you and I," she wrote, "the students of today, whose task it will be to build up the world after the war. The fact that it will not, by any means, be an easy job, makes it that much more important that we learn all we can while we can."

On Remembrance Day in November, the assembled students listened as the names of eighty-four former students presently serving in His Majesty's Forces were read out. During the previous February, the British had surrendered Singapore to Japan, and by November the American and British forces had landed in French North Africa. Clearly the war was not going to end soon.

A grim editorial from the new principal, Herb Ray, in the December *Annals of the Black and Gold* underscored the effects of the war. Although the ravages of polio had left Mr. Ray physically unable to enlist, he was determined to contribute to the war effort at home. Principal Ray's graphic editorial is typical of his columns in subsequent issues of the high-school paper: "In Karkhov, desolation reigns. Hungry cats prowl warily through deserted streets and periodically death falls from the sky and walls crumble. Little starved children lie dead in the streets of Athens, and the grim specter of famine stalks through France. Smoke drifts lazily from the desolate ruin that was Cologne; and across the Channel, Canterbury is laid waste."[210]

At home in Grandpa Simpson's Big House, things remained unchanged. Peggy found it increasingly irksome to return from school to the place where her aged and autocratic grandfather continued to reign, exercising total control over the household. "He ruled it," she said, "like Agamemnon at Mycenae."[211] After the death of Peggy's father and her Uncle Stuart in 1935, there were no other significant males in the Simpson—Wemyss households. Her grandfather, who was known to many Neepawans for his miserly and rude behaviour, remained unchallenged within his domain on First Avenue. John Simpson's house was not a place where Peggy's school chums felt welcomed, and only a few of them ever passed beyond the foyer.[212]

Although Mum, Peggy, and Bobby continued to live with Grandfather Simpson, the Big House was by no means a "grand" place. In fact, a number of other homes in Neepawa would more aptly fit that designation. John Simpson's once-lucrative business ventures were no longer under his control. However, his daughter, Marg, somehow managed to run the household on a very small budget, although she never stopped worrying about finances. While the new air base was being built, Marg quietly made arrangements to take in a boarder, "the man from Miramachi."[213] He was assigned to Bobby's room, while Bobby was moved to the little alcove adjoining his sister's bedroom. Peggy, unhappy with the whole situation, stalked about the house. Mum realized that despite the additional income, these changes were upsetting to Peggy. After a few months, the boarder was told to leave and the indomitable Marg devised an alternate source of income. She took a part-time position doing bookkeeping and accounting at the Neepawa Hospital.[214]

After the boarder left, however, Peggy continued to chafe under her grandfather's reign. No longer a child, she resented his domineering manner. She observed her mother's and her aunts' acceptance of the "status quo." They seemed powerless to effect any significant change. Marg

Simpson Wemyss, intent on keeping peace in the house, silently yielded. Peggy realized that to be outwardly rebellious would only distress Mum, and that, in the end, Grandfather would surely prevail. Although for Peggy the difficult scene at home was relieved a bit by Mum's love and concern, Marg Wemyss was herself under enormous pressure throughout those years. At the time of Peggy's graduation from NCI in 1944, it was not clear whether there would be enough money for her university tuition. Mum also had nagging financial concerns about Bobby's future, as well as the complex problems of dealing with her elderly and increasingly irascible father. At times Marg Wemyss's anxiety was almost palpable.[215] Peggy, sensitive to the undercurrents in the household, looked forward with relief to classes and activities at NCI, where she was an involved, respected, and well-liked member of the student body.[216] In high school, Peggy was also encouraged by Miss Musgrove and Miss Offen in her dreams for the future.

"The chief joys of high school, and they remained so for four years," she recalled, "were being able to work on the school newspaper and studying English literature."[217] One day in Miss Musgrove's English class, the opening lines of a dramatic monologue by Robert Browning captured Peggy's imagination:

> That's my last Duchess painted on the wall,
> Looking as if she were alive. I call
> That piece a wonder . . . ("My Last Duchess")

Here was mystery, subtlety, obsession, verbal description, and an intriguing narrative, all delivered in the first person. As Peggy read more of Browning's monologues, she felt "as though a whole series of doors were opening."[218] During Grades Eleven and Twelve, her class studied poetry from *The Pocket Book of Verse*, which showcased the work of great English and American writers. It was an excellent volume for a budding writer.

First published in Canada in 1940, *The Pocket Book of Verse* was an anthology of 249 poems, chiefly lyrical, by "Great English and American" poets. It opened with Geoffrey Chaucer and concluded with Stephen Vincent Benét. Fifty years later Laurence remarked, "I have carted that book around the world with me ever since High School. . . . with the poems marked that we studied."[219] Noting that, while in high school, she had read a good deal of Wordsworth, Shakespeare, and the Bible, Laurence also mentioned seventeen poets and a number of titles that she liked. She may well have had *The Pocket Book of Verse* in hand when she composed this passage, since the sequence of authors cited there adheres exactly to the sequence in that little anthology.

While Peggy relished English literature, Maths was a different matter. The subject did not interest her. Nevertheless, in order to be certain of passing the Manitoba requirement for college, she and her friends Margie Crawford and Mona Spratt were tutored in Maths during the summer by her former neighbour Jack Coutts, then an undergraduate at the University of Manitoba. He recalls that the girls were "rewarding tutees," and mentions with some amusement Peggy's fascination with words: "A sheepish grin of discovery and gratitude came over Peggy's face when she learned that when 'arithmetic' was used as an adjective, the correct pronunciation was 'arith-MET-ic,' not 'a-RITH-metic.' Her teacher, apparently, had used the wrong pronunciation.[220]

Outside school hours there was plenty of time for fun or youthful escapades. Occasionally some boys and a few reckless girls, seeking a dangerous thrill, would venture out onto the railroad tracks that crossed the huge Trestle Bridge over Stoney Creek at the southwestern end of town. There they listened for approaching trains and then raced one another to safety on the other side.[221]

Once during Grade Eleven, Peggy, and several others, were caught smoking a cigarette in the library during an NCI dance, a daring act of a different sort, and a serious infraction of school rules. "For weeks afterwards, I trembled at the real possibility of public disgrace and expulsion."[222] A reprimand was considered sufficient, however, and the incident did not adversely affect her position at NCI.

Several nights a week during the winter, the teenagers went skating at a fine indoor rink near the King Edward Hotel. Peggy and her friends enjoyed skating to music there.[223] The teens could also skate on the outdoor rink near Neepawa Collegiate, and, if the snow was not too deep, they might skate on Park Lake, weaving in and out among the reeds along the frozen creek that led into the lake and gathering later for songs and snacks around a huge bonfire near the little dam at the eastern end.[224] "Evenings, coming back from skating," Laurence recalled, "the sky would be black but not dark, for you could see a cold glitter of stars from one side of the earth's rim to the other. And then the sometime astonishment when you saw the Northern Lights flaring across the sky, like the scrawled signature of God."[225]

In March 1943, a typical Manitoba blizzard struck Neepawa. Winds whipped across the prairie, temperatures hovered at -40°F, and piles of snow obliterated the runways at EFTS. All flights were cancelled and the young airmen were delighted to be guests for Sunday dinner in the homes of Neepawa citizens, a practice that continued while the base remained active. After it closed, the base manager J.W. Humphrey would speak gratefully of "prairie hospitality" and thank the town for the "many kindnesses" that had been extended to both civilian and military personnel during the war years.[226]

On the evening of June 11, the high school's graduation and awards ceremonies were held, and Peggy, who was completing Grade Eleven, received the "most coveted award" at NCI, the Governor General's Medal, which traditionally was granted to a student in that grade.[227] Despite the honour, Peggy did not want her award to be written up in the school paper. Nevertheless, the news did appear in "Here and There," a gossip column, signed "I.M. Nosey." It is important to note that the column, which praises Peggy, was not written by her, as one biographer asserts, but by a student in Grade Twelve. Only Miss Musgrove knew that I.M. Nosey was a sobriquet for Dorothy Coutts, who was the secret author of the column.[228] Peggy was editor of the school paper at that time and, Coutts states, refused to have an account of her award put into the NCI paper. The account did appear, however, and provides an interesting overview of Peggy's high-school years, indicating that Peggy was a participant in many NCI activities. Dorothy Coutts wrote:

> Jean Margaret Wemyss (more commonly known as Peggy) has an average of 81% in her studies for the past two years. Her most outstanding activity is editing the *Annals of the Black and Gold* which is well known to us all as a fine paper, credit for which is due largely to

Peggy for her untiring efforts. She has been faithful to
the Collegiate Orchestra for three years as an accomplished violinist. Dramatics and debating have also
played a part in Peggy's school life, as well as curling....
She possesses outstanding business ability, as was illustrated by her able handling of a refreshment booth at
the '42 track meet. Her initiative, fine leadership and
enthusiasm certainly prove Peggy Wemyss worthy of
claiming the honour of such an award, and to her, I
extend my heartiest congratulations on behalf of my
fellow students.[229]

With final examinations over and the summer months before her,
Peggy felt fortunate to have an interesting summer job at the *Neepawa
Press*, a local weekly, published by owner-editor, Blake Dunlop, a former
neighbour. Seated at a roll-top oak desk in the *Neepawa Press* office,
Peggy "worked as a reporter and as an editor for the district news."[230]
Her practical experience as editor of the *Annals of the Black and Gold*
now proved useful outside high school, and her summer apprenticeship
at the *Neepawa Press* fit in well with her plans to become a journalist.[231]

When Peggy returned to NCI for Grade Twelve in September 1943,
only a handful of girls remained in her class. There were no boys. What
would life be like after graduation next June? Would there still be war in
Europe and the Pacific? Could she afford to go to university? Questions
such as these formed the uncertain backdrop of Peggy's last year at
Neepawa Collegiate Institute. Her friendships, however, remained fixed.
Among her chums, Mona Spratt was now president of the Student
Council and Margie Crawford, the vice-president. Another friend, Louise
Alguire, was the diligent convenor of the War Services Committee, which
managed to collect a thousand pounds of rags for the war-relief drive.[232]
Peggy herself was convenor of NCI's small orchestra in Grade Twelve, and
she continued to play the violin with that group.[233]

When the fall issue of the *Annals of the Black and Gold* appeared,
Peggy again was editor. The cover now featured the NCI shield and a
motto: "To strive, to seek, to find, and not to yield."[234] Those noble sentiments from Tennyson's "Ulysses" were meant to challenge Peggy and

her classmates during that tumultuous period in history to hold fast to high ideals and dreams of a better world. Principal Herb Ray's editorial remarks once more emphasized the war's effect on NCI students. "Three years and nine months have now passed by since the German Panzer divisions rolled into Poland, and Britain, at long last rallied to the cause of freedom. *Your entire high school career has been spent in an atmosphere of wartime stress* [emphasis added]."[235]

As editor, Peggy would have been involved with comments relating to the national scene, such as the *Annals*'s announcement of the recent death of Sir Charles G.D. Roberts, the "Dean of Canadian poets," which was carried in the next issue of the paper.[236] Although few Canadian literary works were then studied at NCI (partially as a consequence of the Manitoba literature requirements for entry to college), Peggy had studied Canadian poetry in elementary school and knew Roberts's work. His place was secure in Rhodenizer's *A Handbook of Canadian Literature*, Dickie and Palk's *Pages from Canada's Story*, as well as A.M. Stephens's *The Golden Treasury of Canadian Verse*. In addition, Marg Wemyss and several teachers at NCI had strongly encouraged an interest in Canadian literature. While she was growing up, Peggy and her Mum used to quote poetry to each other when they doing the evening's dishes, taking turns line by line.[237]

For the traditional Drama Night in December, Peggy had a part in the class play. Behind such familiar events at NCI, however, her life had undergone a major change; this had begun earlier that year at a dance. Saturday-night dances were a regular feature of life in Neepawa — part of the ritual of growing up. Peggy, like her friends, had dated several boys during high school, but she lacked confidence in her ability to attract young men. She was 5 feet 6 inches and slender, but she felt insecure about her looks, believing that she was too tall and lacked good features. Another problem came from the fact that Peggy's interests were very different from those of the few boys her age who were still in town, and she felt her dating prospects were slim.[238] That situation changed dramatically, however, when the EFTS base opened nearby. Now numbers of young men were in the area. The Neepawa girls no longer had to dance with each other. Although there were frequent dances at the base, Mona Spratt recalls that the girls in Peggy's circle were expected to be chaperoned when they occasionally went to dances at the base. On Saturday nights, however, the airmen came to dances at the Arcade in town. "There were the usual brash girls, some from Neepawa in their Canadian Women's Army Corps uniforms loudly flirting with the RAF boys," Laurence wrote. "There was the usual complement of drunks and half-drunks, both men and women, uniformed or civilian. And a number of high-school girls, such as myself, in our party dresses, with our stiff imitation curls, wearing our blood-red lipstick and nail polish, smiling, smiling, dreading the ever-present danger of not being asked to dance."[239]

American jazz and boogie had come to Neepawa with the young airmen and over the radio. Jitterbugging was the rage. "The uncertainties of war meant we danced with a heightened tribal sense of being together. Dancing was a passionate affirmation of life and the desire to go on living."[240]

At one of those dances, between July and December 1943, Peggy met and fell in love with a British airman named Derek Armstrong. "He was not only handsome and ten years older, he was also well-read."[241] They shared an interest in music and books, and he introduced her to the work of important contemporary English poets, such as Stephen Spender and W.H. Auden.[242] This was Peggy's first serious romance. At twenty-seven, Derek had much more experience than the seventeen-year-old girl from Neepawa or the other lads in town. As the weeks passed, Mum began to worry that Peggy and Derek might elope. In her memoirs, Margaret Laurence recalls the situation. Although written more than forty years later, her description remains moving:

> None of the boys I had ever gone to school with would have given poetry the time of day, but here was an older man who not only could quote reams of the stuff, he also (could it really be?) wanted to spend time with awkward, shy, nervous, clever, often loud-mouthed me. I include clever because I knew I was smart, but I certainly didn't regard it as an asset. It was more of a millstone around my neck. I couldn't believe my good fortune. There was Derek, with all those remarkable qualities, interested in me.[243]

This is Laurence's retrospective view of herself at seventeen. She thought it was an unusual piece of good fortune that this good-looking airman, intelligent and mature, had become seriously interested in her. In addition to feeling insecure about her own looks, Peggy felt — and this was not uncommon at the time — that being a bright and clever young woman was a distinct disadvantage in dating situations. This negative sense of self was not confined to Peggy's adolescence. It prevailed during her college years and affected her subsequent romance with Jack Laurence and her marriage to him in 1947. It lasted, moreover, well into her mature years, when Margaret and Jack were living in Vancouver. She continued to worry about her appearance and put considerable effort into trying to look attractive and appealing for her handsome engineer husband, whom she felt fortunate to have married and whom she knew other women found to be good-looking.

Peggy's high-school romance with Derek coloured her entire year in Grade Twelve, but it ended when he completed the training course and left Neepawa. They exchanged letters for a while, but then, like a scene from one of Browning's poems, the letters stopped. Later Peggy learned that Derek had cruelly deceived her. He was already married, and he was not, as he had confided to her, the British composer Benjamin Britten. It seems hard to believe today that the airman identified himself as one of Britain's most outstanding contemporary composers, but at the time Peggy accepted his information. Although Derek may have amused himself with the subterfuge, his deception left Peggy feeling "hurt and betrayed."[244]

When classes at NCI resumed in January 1944, the usual hockey games got underway, and on Wednesday nights the Air Cadets went out to the base for instruction in engines, aircraft recognition, and armament.[245] Many women from town worked on the base as postal clerks, telephone operators, food-service workers, and propeller girls. The latter went onto the field to assist in starting the engines of the Tiger Moths. By then the town and the base were so intertwined that one could scarcely avoid thinking often about the war.

In February 1944, there was a welcome change of pace at NCI when René Dussault, from the University of Manitoba, came to deliver three lecture-demonstrations in drama. One day, students mimed scenes, which

Dussault then critiqued. Peggy and another student participated by miming a game of chess.[246] Peggy's interest in drama and her experience with high-school plays were strengthened by such activities. As an aspiring young writer, she was beginning to understand the importance of spoken dialogue and the creation of dramatic situations.

In March, a lighthearted performance of "Les Huîtres et Le Cheval" ("The Oysters and the Horse") was presented, first in French and then in English, by Miss Offen's students. It was followed by an award-winning drama, "Airman's Forty-Eight," a play that dealt with the current war. It had been written by a Grade Ten student in Alberta, who received a scholarship to the Banff School of Fine Arts as an award. Such recognition of another teenage girl's achievement further encouraged Peggy's own desire to become a writer.

The last issue of the school paper with Peggy as editor was produced at Easter 1944. It included her poem "Song for Spring, 1944 \ Canada," a sonnet that she signed with her initials.[247] This joyful poem celebrates the absence of fear in a world at peace. "Song for Spring" opens with a strong trochaic beat suitable to its affirmative stance. Decasyllabic lines are used throughout and, in the closing sestet, as will be seen, she brings the poem to its conclusion with interlocking rhymes. In the sonnet, Peggy uses alliteration well, but her ability to create sophisticated internal links within the poem is particularly noteworthy. The most successful of these occurs with the sound of "l" which is carried throughout the poem from the opening word "April" to the words: "unfold," "children," and "gladly," until the final line, where the "l" resounds in "glory." The sonnet's hyphenated adjectives and attention to specific details in nature underscore a prayer-like note of hope for a future of peace without fear.

Song for Spring, 1944 \ Canada

April has brought the youngest time of year,
With clinging cloaks of rain mist, silver-gray;
The velvet, star-wreathed night, and wind-clad day
And song of meadowlarks from uplands near.
The new-formed leaves unfold to greet the sun,
Whose light is warming fields still moist with rain,

While down each city street and grass-fringed land,
Children are shouting gladly as they run.
Free they are to hold with careful hand
A robin's egg; to welcome every morn;
To glance up, unafraid, at peaceful skies;
Joyfully free to plant a piece of land
With miracles of flowers yet unborn....
Nothing must blot that glory from their eyes.
                    J.M.W.

The poem's sentiments may express Peggy's romantic optimism during that April, as well as a wish for the future, but they are not a realistic depiction of the situation in spring 1944; as the poem "came off the press," the Second World War was still raging in Europe and the Pacific.

That issue of *Annals of the Black and Gold* also included several war-related items. There was notice of the wedding of a former NCI student to an airman from New Brunswick and a short story about a young serviceman who had returned to Manitoba after four years at the front. The most striking layout in the paper, however, was the following sad notice:

REGRETTING THE DEATH OF F/O MURRAY COUTTS,
KILLED IN ACTION MARCH 27, 1944
THE STUDENTS OF THE N.C.I.
EXTEND THEIR SINCEREST SYMPATHY
TO MR. AND MRS. W. COUTTS AND FAMILY.

The tragic death of Murray Coutts, who had been Peggy's neighbour on Vivian Street and was the older brother of her friends, Dorothy and Jack, put another familiar face to the statistics of the war dead. In addition, three cousins of her good friend Mona Spratt died during the war. By 1944 the Prairie provinces, which had already suffered from years of drought and financial depression, were reeling under the pain of war. The mood during that period is reflected in the *Alberta Poetry Year Book* 1943-1944, a chapbook filled with poems such as: "Missing in Action," "Malta:

War Wife," "To One Who Died in 1918," "Mother and Soldier," "To One Who Returns Not," "Vimy," and "Green Leaves Falling."[248] The latter poem was written by Elsie Fry Laurence, who later became Peggy's mother-in-law. Elsie then had two sons in active service and her own husband had served in the First World War.[249]

Peggy's four years of high school had been permeated by public and private events relating to the Second World War, and it comes as no surprise, therefore, that, a month after her graduation, she applied to join the newest women's unit of the navy, the Women's Royal Canadian Naval Service. A few months before Peggy made application, the *Winnipeg Free Press* had featured the work of several Manitoba WRCNS who were assigned to the HMS *Chippewa*. The women of this elite unit, wearing traditional navy-blue uniforms with brass buttons, not only performed important services, but were also given the promise of travel while in the navy.[250] When the Naval Service phoned Peggy about her application, however, she was not at home; a short time later they informed her that new recruits were no longer needed. Speculating in her memoirs as to why she had volunteered, Laurence states that the navy seemed "mysterious and glamorous."[251] But it is more likely that her desire to enlist also represented a way to "escape" from Neepawa — the farthest she could get from that small prairie town where the only waves were in the fields of grain.

With the option of serving in the navy closed, Peggy began to plan for college, applying for a Manitoba scholarship, which she was granted on the basis of her academic record and financial need. Mum did not have to sell the family china to augment Peggy's college fund.[252]

During August, she went with several friends to relax at Clear Lake in Riding Mountain National Park. The Wemyss's cottage there was not a secluded rustic retreat, although its decor was certainly basic. A short, half-mile walk brought the girls from the cottage to the centre of the town of Wasagaming, a popular summer resort, where there was a general store, a lodge operated by Louise Alguire's family, and a large dance hall. After their August holiday, the girls returned home to pack for college in Winnipeg. Mona and Louise were going to the University of Manitoba, while Peggy and Margie Crawford would be at United College, also in Winnipeg. Peggy looked forward to the excitement of living in the city and was curious about the University of Manitoba, where her neighbour Jack Coutts had distinguished himself. She wondered what her life at United College would be like. Years before, as Wesley College, it had been the alma mater of two of Peggy's cherished teachers, Mildred Musgrove and Connie Offen.

CHAPTER FIVE

The College Years

As summer 1944 gave way to autumn, Peggy set out for Winnipeg, leaving behind the confinement of Grandfather Simpson's place — a house that was his and had never truly felt like home to her. Now, she felt a terrific sense of excitement. She was eager for the freedom and new experiences that lay ahead. As the miles sped by, the prairie horizon, broken only by the familiar outline of the grain elevators, gave way to the taller buildings of Winnipeg, capital of the province of Manitoba and "Gateway to the West." Although Winnipeg, one of Canada's largest and most important cities, is only 125 miles from Neepawa, for young people from small prairie towns, the city then might well have been on another planet in terms of its tempo, size, and structures.

Winnipeg is situated at the confluence of the Red River and the Assiniboine River, where the Red River, flowing northward from the American prairie states, meets the Assiniboine that flows from west to east across the Canadian prairies. The city is a major centre of business, commerce, trade, and agriculture. When Peggy arrived there in September 1944, a vast network of railroad tracks carried passengers and freight into Winnipeg from all over Canada and from there to other regions of the country. Its historical significance and current importance were apparent in its diverse population, newspapers in eleven languages, and a host of varied activities. In addition to many businesses and a huge commodities exchange with fierce trading in grain, Winnipeg was also a cultural centre: home to the Manitoba Opera Company, the Royal Winnipeg Ballet, and a symphony orchestra.[253]

Peggy enrolled at United College alongside other undergraduates who had grown up during the "Dirty Thirties." Shaped by a decade of severe drought and economic depression, threatened by the cataclysmic events of the Second World War, the collegians' future seemed very uncertain. But despite that uncertainty, these determined young men and women, who had been forged by hardship and sacrifice, regarded the opportunity for a university education as a privilege and a trust. They longed for an end to war and felt ready for the challenge of imagining and building a better world.

United College (which today is the University of Winnipeg), was then one of several church-related colleges affiliated with the University of Manitoba. The university itself had been formed in 1877 by the federation of three existing colleges. "It sprang from the Presbyterian faith of the Selkirk Settlers," notes historian W.L. Morton.[254] By 1944, the main campus of the University of Manitoba had moved southwest from the city to Fort Garry. However, a few classes were still held in some buildings that had been retained in downtown Winnipeg, its "Broadway campus." United College, like the other affiliated colleges, had its own campus, faculty, and administration, but the students wrote common final examinations set by the University of Manitoba. United College, despite its small size, was known for its fine faculty and excellent liberal-arts curriculum.

Although the college was denominational, the student body represented "a wide range of ethnic and religious backgrounds" and had an enviable record for openness, tolerance, and academic excellence.[255] A number of Jewish students attended United College, because of its liberal faculty, the absence of fraternities and sororities, and its classes in Hebrew and Biblical studies.[256]

In the early 1940s, the state of the economy and the burden of the Second World War prevented many Canadian high-school students from attending college. Given the financial difficulties in Peggy's family, it is amazing that funds were found to send her to university. She later explained that this was due to her Mum who saved every penny possible to help her through, and diligently searched out information about scholarships and bursaries.

Students who had completed Grade Twelve in high school, which was then the equivalent of first-year college, were admitted to the second year at United and earned their degree three years later. However, students who had gone only to Grade Eleven were first required to complete Grade Twelve in United's Collegiate Division. Because many small towns did not offer Grade Twelve, over a third of United's entering class went directly into the Collegiate Division. This meant that there were many students on campus who were only sixteen years of age. Since Peggy, who was eighteen, had completed Grade Twelve at Neepawa Collegiate Institute, she was enrolled as a second-year student.

As she stood on Portage Avenue in central Winnipeg in September 1944, Peggy looked across a wide expanse of lawn to the buildings of United College. The campus occupied five and a half acres and had two main structures: Wesley Hall and Sparling Hall Residence. Wesley's cornerstone had been laid in 1894. An impressive grey-sandstone structure with twin towers that gave it a slightly medieval appearance, Wesley housed administrative offices; Convocation Hall (which was used for assemblies, some classes, and chapel services); the men's residence on the fourth floor; classrooms; and Tony's tuck shop in the basement. Near Wesley stood Sparling Hall, which contained the women's residence. On the first floor of Sparling, there was a music room, a common room, and a dining room, where men and women students took their meals together. At the rear of Sparling Hall, a rough storage building served in winter as a change-house for skating. The rink itself was simply a large open area in the field north of Wesley Hall.

Life in the women's residence was not unpleasant. In 1943, Dorothie Neil had been appointed Dean, replacing Eleanor "Pansy" Bowes, who had been at United for nineteen years. Dean Neil, still in her early twenties and a recent graduate of the University of Manitoba, held a dual appointment as Dean of Residence for Women and Dietitian. Although she could be strict, Dean Dorothie Neil found the women residents cooperative, and she was tolerant of their liveliness.[257]

Peggy Wemyss was assigned to share a room on the fourth floor of Sparling Hall with another "W," Helen Warkentin. Two years older than

Peggy, Helen had worked before entering college. She recalls that Peggy was mature in her concerns and focused in her studies. Although Helen's interests ran to music, curling, and French, rather than literature, she liked Peggy and remembers lots of laughter and good fun. The young women got along well and roomed together in Sparling Hall for two years.[258] A snapshot shows them seated side by side on one of the iron bedsteads in the dorm. A smiling Peggy has shoulder-length hair and is dressed in skirt and blazer. She is wearing nail polish. In another snapshot, Helen and Peggy are wearing slacks and men's plaid flannel shirts, which they considered de rigueur for studying. The girls look happy and confident as they pose for the camera. They are standing at a rakish angle, boldly brandishing cigarettes.

The student body at United College was small and closely knit. The entering class of 1947 had approximately forty students, although by graduation time it had increased to sixty-seven. All first- and second-year students attended lectures together. In a letter sent back to her high school, Peggy remarked that registration at the university had been a "horrible ordeal" that involved standing in line for hours. It was difficult for her to adjust to early classes, and she needed to work "much, much harder" than she had at NCI.[259]

On "Freshie Day" in September, classes were cancelled and the undergrads from the university and its affiliated colleges assembled in the Civic Auditorium for speeches, followed by a faculty-student track meet and picnic in Sargent Park. "By the end of the day everyone had a sore throat from shouting." Perhaps she fell asleep that night to echoes of United's cheer, which began:

> Katana! Katana! Kasula! Kasah!
> United!! Katara! Katah!
> Wesley! Toba! White and Red!
> Ever leading! Never led!

"Life in residence is a lot of fun," Peggy reported. She mentioned some practical jokes and described a night when the boys in residence caused a commotion by bringing a goat to the fourth floor of the women's residence. The boys were jubilant. However, Dean Dorothie

Neil was somewhat less enthusiastic. She remembers working hard with the caretaker, Carl Pye, and several students to get the goat safely down the stairs, which had metal treads, and out of the building.[260] All in all, however, those years were a time of innocence, when pranks by undergraduates involved no more than the occasional dropping of water balloons from the fourth floor of Wesley Hall or telephoning the dean to ask if the college was located on Portage Avenue, and then, in tones of muffled laughter, instructing her to "Move it!"[261] For all the students' highjinks, they were not unmindful that the Second World War was still raging. Peggy continued her involvement with the relief effort by working on Wednesday afternoons at the Central Volunteer Bureau, where she did typing and filing and phoned round for volunteers.[262]

Not long after arriving on campus, Peggy felt ready to plunge ahead with her writing. In a bold move, she submitted some pieces to *The Manitoban* (University of Manitoba) which was published more frequently and had a larger circulation than *Vox* (United College's literary journal). Although she mentions submitting work under the male pseudonym "Steven Lancaster," nothing under that name has been located. At that time, it was not uncommon for women writers in England and North America to use a man's name, but it is significant that Peggy chose the name "Lancaster," after the Lancaster Bomber, one of the most successful and powerful bombers of the Second World War era.[263] This plane, which typically carried fourteen thousand pounds of bombs, flew on virtually every major bombing raid in Europe and, despite its size, handled "as easily and dexterously as a Tiger Moth."[264] In choosing the strong pseudonym Steven Lancaster, Peggy was declaring her seriousness and determination as a writer. This is also reflected in the fact that she lost no time in submitting her literary work to various college publications.

From United's campus, it was only a short walk down Osborne Street to the Broadway office of *The Manitoban*. There, Peggy saw Jack Ludwig, its former editor, who had been dismissed from the University of Manitoba during the previous spring, prior to his scheduled graduation.[265] By the time Peggy arrived in Winnipeg that September, Jack Ludwig's situation had become a cause célèbre, for his "offence" had to do with freedom of speech. As editor of *The Manitoban*'s literary supplement, Ludwig had approved the publication of a war-protest poem

"Atrocities," written by Burt Hamilton, president of the student body.[266] The *Winnipeg Free Press* picked up the information and, describing the poem as treasonous, hinted that it was the result of Communist interference. An investigation was launched, and, despite the lack of evidence, both men were dismissed without their degrees. Young Hamilton's penalty was military duty; after serving in the navy, he was later reinstated at the university. However, military service for Ludwig was out of the question. He could not have passed the physical exam because of the effects of a serious childhood illness. The university was abuzz with talk about the injustice of the boys' dismissals. Although Ludwig was not the author of "Atrocities," his penalty was much more severe than Hamilton's. Many students believed that the administration's harshness against Jack Ludwig stemmed from the fact that he was Jewish.

The University of Manitoba, under President Sidney Smith, was then in the throes of a big upset, because the medical college had a quota system limiting the number of Jewish students accepted to its program.[267] A "numerus clausus," or "specific quota," had effectively blocked many Jewish students' admission to medical school, including, as Peggy would later learn, that of Miriam Wiseman (the older sister of her friend and fellow writer Adele Wiseman). In an effort to remedy the injustice, many undergraduates at United took action. A classmate of Peggy's recalls a writing campaign spearheaded by the campus Student Christian Movement (SCM), which successfully protested that quota system to members of the provincial parliament.[268]

During Peggy's first year at United, she followed a rigorous liberal-arts program, taking courses in English, history, ethics, psychology, French, and German. After the first class each morning, the bell for chapel rang. The simple service was held in Convocation Hall, the only room on United's campus that could accommodate several hundred students. The service, which was taken by members of the faculty and administration, was meant "to strengthen faith and practice fellowship." It included scripture passages, hymns, meditation, and a brief talk. Afterwards there would be announcements and a few minutes to greet friends. Attendance was optional, but Lois Freeman Wilson, who sang in the chapel choir, recalls that, during the war years, it was difficult to find a seat even in the galleries.[269] It is not clear whether Peggy attended chapel service regularly, but it seems likely that she went occasionally. One classmate, Charlie Forsyth, recalls that he and Peggy hotly debated the merits of the Scottish Psalter with Professor Doris Peterson, who had joined United's English department in 1946.[270]

At that time, strong friendships, fierce loyalties, and a deep concern for the less fortunate were among the hallmarks of United College students and faculty. The college was known for the earnestness of its faculty, who fostered the students' intellectual life. On the whole it was politically liberal, and the professors often took an unpopular stand. Lois Freeman Wilson recalls being "encouraged to think, question, critique, and debate, not only with other students, but also with my professors."[271]

In that setting during the mid 1940s, students suspended their complaints about the food, which was wartime fare, and the acrid fumes that filled the air when caretaker Carl Pye, mindful of the college budget, stoked the furnace with assorted pieces of lumber and rubber tires.[272] Although it was the era of wartime constraints, there was no rationing of intellectual fare, however, and Peggy's intellectual curiosity and eagerness to learn found generous support on campus. She wrote: "I had wonderful teachers of English at United College: as well as Arthur Phelps there were Meredith Thompson, Doris Peterson, and especially Robert Halstead. He and his wife Anne became valued friends. Malcolm Ross taught me a course on Milton and seventeenth-century thought at the University of Manitoba, a course that profoundly affected my life."[273]

During her first year, however, the teacher who clearly had the strongest influence on Peggy was Arthur L. Phelps, who had been at United College for over twenty years. By 1944, when Peggy took his literature class, Phelps's somewhat dramatic teaching methods and unorthodox style had made him a legend on campus. Peggy's classmates affectionately recall Phelps, who had bushy black eyebrows and dark hair that was balding on top, as a memorable teacher. "He had a golden-edged voice, read poetry beautifully, and was very interested in Canadian writers."[274] Peggy never forgot his lectures in Convocation Hall:

> I remember Phelps, twisted fantastically around the lectern, his face looking uncannily like that of an Irish leprechaun, and I remember the sad solemn portraits

of Very Important Persons, gazing down perhaps a little perplexedly, at this decidedly unsolemn man who
yet possessed something of almost Shakespearian dignity in his manner and in his expressive voice, and who
had somehow managed to put his finger on the very
pulse of literature.[275]

Phelps "was a fascinating man: enthusiastic, intellectually curious, and a great encourager." He had a "pixie-ish look" and several
mannerisms and eccentricities that delighted his students. One day
when workmen had left a stepladder in the room, Professor Phelps
climbed up it, talking all the while, and then, seated on the top step,
completed his lecture.[276] At other times, Phelps, clad in academic
gown, would look over his pince-nez and smile at the class. "We got a
sort of warm feeling," remembers Alan Hockin. "But he wouldn't
allow any nonsense, although he was part of the fun."[277] Seated in
Arthur Phelps's class during her first year at United, Peggy "sometimes became too interested in the lecture and forgot to take notes."[278]
She later summed up Phelps's impact: "The chief thing one remembers are, first, his awareness of Canada and its people, and secondly,
the way in which he linked literature of the past with the present. . . .
Literature to Phelps was not something famous, calm and dead. It was
vitally connected with life, always a living commentary that passed
from age to age."[279]

Arthur Phelps was also moderator of the prestigious English Club,
which met monthly at his home. Peggy, unaware that upperclassmen
became members through invitation, asked Phelps how she might go
about joining the club. He simply invited her to come. At the next meeting, however, he informed the members that Peggy Wemyss would be
joining their group that evening, and asked them to accept her graciously, although this was only her first semester at United. Then, taking
aside the club president, Alan Hockin, Phelps confided: "She is very
remarkable and you will hear of her in the future."[280]

The Phelps family lived in a large, comfortable older home on
Assiniboine Avenue near the big bend in the river at Armstrong's Point.
The living room had high ceilings and an impressive rough-hewn stone

fireplace, which Phelps himself had built and into which he fed well-seasoned wood brought down from his cottage in the country.

Mrs. Phelps usually greeted club members at the front door. As Peggy walked in, the welcoming fragrance of logs burning in the large stone fireplace filled the living room, summoning memories of her own family's cottage at Clear Lake. In the Phelps's living room, students gathered and chatted before the meeting began. Usually one member gave a paper on a topic not covered in the curriculum; then there would be questions, discussion, and argument. Sometimes Phelps invited a visiting writer to speak to the group; once it was Morley Callaghan.[281] At the evening's close, members adjourned to the dining room and, near a large samovar of coffee, enjoyed sandwiches and Mrs. Phelps's famous sesame buns. She was a very motherly person, concerned about the students, and occasionally offered worried collegians "a shoulder to cry on."[282]

Belonging to the English Club under Professor Phelps was indeed a special opportunity for Peggy, bringing her for the first time into contact with a group of peers who cared deeply about literature. "It was one of my happiest and most rewarding college experiences."[283] The rigorous intellectual discussion and the deep appreciation of literature fostered in Phelps's class and in the club meetings made a lasting impression on Peggy.

When Arthur Phelps left United College the following year to join the newly established International Service of the Canadian Broadcasting Corporation (CBC), the English Club would continue under the auspices of Professor Doris Peterson ("Petie"), who had come to United from Connecticut College for Women.[284] She had been told by the department's chairman that she would enjoy Winnipeg's "salubrious cold."[285] Professor Peterson would soon earn a reputation as a fine teacher, and her review lectures before final exams were so effective that crowds of students from the Broadway campus of the university also attended them. An active scholar, Doris Peterson also taught a memorable course in "Poetry from the Metaphysicals to the Moderns," which included T.S. Eliot's *Four Quartets*.[286] During those years, T.S. Eliot was all the rage on campus. His quest for meaning against the backdrop of the twentieth century's sense of malaise, and his explorations of time and memory appealed strongly to Peggy and her fellow collegians.

In those days, the pulse of United's students could be felt throbbing in an unlikely place, "Tony's tuck shop" under the southwest tower of Wesley Hall. It was presided over by an extraordinary man, Tony Kozyra, who was more like an uncle than a proprietor. Being neither a member of the faculty nor of the student body, he was in a unique position vis à vis the young people. The shop was not just a convenient place for coffee and snacks. Tony Kozyra cheered up students who were discouraged, listened to their problems, and from time to time lent money to those who were broke. At the tables in "Tony's," the walls "ringed with graduates' pictures, and carved with students' names," students as well as faculty gathered to talk and argue ideas.

Peggy's roommate, Helen, remembers sitting in Tony's in the late afternoon, arguing politics for hours with a group that usually included herself and Peggy as well as Madge Hetherington, Charlie Forsyth, Stirling ("Red") Lyon, Rayburn McCall, Heath MacQuarrie, Jack Borland, and Lyall Powers. At least three of the men were veterans of the Second World War, and in the years following graduation, many from that group in Tony's went on to important careers in public office or university teaching.[287] Lyon and MacQuarrie were Conservatives, while the others were Liberal. Several classmates describe Peggy as "keenly intelligent, thought-provoking, an exciting person to be with." Both MacQuarrie and Forsyth recall that "Peggy was always one of the gang. Very definitely. She was always in the thick of any discussion."[288] In that group, however, the discussions were not about social life, but about social movements.[289]

Madge Hetherington was another aspiring writer, with whom Peggy had made friends in her first year and who also lived in the women's residence. Bright and attractive, with dark hair and blue eyes, Madge was the daughter of a minister from Carman, Manitoba. She too had found her hometown stifling and was excited by the intellectual ferment at United. She describes herself as rebellious and somewhat unconventional, though she achieved high marks.[290]

Another close friend of Peggy's was Patricia Jenkins, an intellectually gifted young woman, who also had a strong determination to become a writer. Pat Jenkins, a striking blonde with classical good looks, was voted Freshie Queen. Peggy worried a good deal about her own looks and was convinced that she was unattractive. As she noticed the boys gathered around Pat and Madge, she probably felt twinges of jealousy, although she later remarked that it was a drawback to be valued more for one's looks than for one's mind. On the whole, Peggy felt it was wonderful to have friends and classmates such as Pat and Madge, with whom she could have long talks about writing and literature and their shared desire to become writers. Recalling those days, Madge now remarks that, "if you didn't know Peggy well, you would think she was an extrovert, but inside she was just as scared as the rest of us."[291]

Patricia Jenkins had been born in Souris, a small prairie town that she later fictionalized as Mouse Bluffs in her novel *A Candle to Light the Sun*, published posthumously in 1960.[292] When Pat was in elementary school, her family had moved to Winnipeg. She lived with them on Qu'Appelle, near United's campus. "I used to go over to her place fairly often," remarked Laurence, "and we would also talk in Tony's. We showed each other our writing a good deal. . . . I don't think either of us had the slightest doubt that we would be writers — it was the only work either of us wanted to do."[293]

A few months after starting college, Peggy attended her first Canadian play, "Dark Harvest" by Gwen Pharis Ringwood, which was produced by the University of Manitoba Dramatic Society in January 1945. *The Manitoban* noted that Ringwood was present and "won the hearts of the audience, with her pleasant, excited manner, her natural unaffectedness." Recalling that play years later in her preface to *The Collected Plays of Gwen Pharis Ringwood*, Laurence noted: "It made a deep and lasting impression on me. . . . It was set in the prairies during the drought and depression, my own land and the time of my own growing up."[294] These remarks are similar to those that Laurence made about the impact of reading Sinclair Ross's novel *As for Me and My House* with its depiction of life on the prairies.[295]

During her first year at college, Peggy remained troubled by the awful consequences of the war. Her concerns were echoed in *Vox*, which had many features dealing with war; one issue carried a particularly moving story "Phineas Student Goes to War" as well as an angry anti-war poem "The Children of Europe: A Pastoral." In addition, there were many veterans on campus, and Peggy's friendships at United made her painfully aware of the human tragedy of war as it affected the families of those friends and their classmates.

As Peggy's first year drew to a close, the news of Germany's surrender on May 8, 1945, brought great excitement to the campus and the city. Nearby a large banner "THANK GOD FOR VICTORY" hung from the façade of the Hudson's Bay building, and the Union Jack proudly waved from double flagpoles above Portage Avenue. The euphoria was tangible, as crowds poured into Winnipeg's streets, laughing and celebrating. In the days following the surrender, collegians eagerly discussed plans for a world without war, where countries might exist side by side in peace.

That euphoria was rudely shattered three months later by the alarming news that American planes had dropped atomic bombs on the Japanese cities of Hiroshima and Nagasaki. People flocked to the cinema, spellbound by newsreels showing the billowing cloud from the atomic explosion as it rose high into the atmosphere. That image of the atomic blast was to haunt Peggy and many of her classmates. Though deeply grateful that the war had ended, they were profoundly troubled by the magnitude of the atomic destruction and its ominous portents.

The collegians' concerns are evident in the pages of several undergraduate publications. A long satirical poem, "Democritus Walks at Hiroshima" by Jack Borland, a good friend of Peggy's and himself a veteran, appeared in the autumn 1945 issue of *Vox*. The intertextuality of his poem significantly enhances its effectiveness. In addition to incorporating fragments of contemporary conversation, Borland makes arresting use of lines from Tennyson's "The Charge of the Light Brigade" (a nineteenth-century pro-war poem); T.S. Eliot's "The Hollow Men" (conveying the mood after the First World War); and Abraham Lincoln's "Gettysburg Address" (delivered at the site of one of the most devastating battles of the American Civil War). Jack Borland's poem reads in part:

> Just press the button on the left there, lady,
> And we all go up with a bang.
> . . . .
> Button, button, who's got the button?
> Into the valley of death
> Rode the millennium.

. . . .
You were wrong, Mr. Eliot,
Dead wrong.
We are to be spared the whimper,
Rather it's for us the living,
To die as we lived,
Fast.[296]

Campus authors were writing about the war in prose, poetry, and essays. Margaret Laurence later commented on that period in her life:

> My generation was the first in human history to come into young adulthood with the knowledge that mankind now had the terrifying power to destroy all life on earth. . . . I still remember — and I was a young woman at college at the time — when the bomb fell on Hiroshima and Nagasaki. I remember discussing this with all my friends. We realized that the world would never be the same again and I have been concerned about the whole issue of peace since that time.[297]

When classes resumed in September 1945, Peggy was in her third year academically, although it was only her second year at United College. The campus scene had drastically changed. The University of Manitoba and its affiliated colleges had run out of space. An influx of returning veterans caused a swift, sharp rise in enrollment, and additional faculty were needed immediately. United College's student body had almost doubled, while the number of its accommodations had remained the same. The bustling, crowded, seemingly chaotic campus was very different from the tranquil scene that had greeted Peggy the previous September. Now classes had to be temporarily scheduled in the basements of nearby churches, in old army barracks, in the Legion Hall, and in United's "skating shack," which had been quickly winterized and refurbished as a "classroom." Hundreds of experienced veterans now sat side by side in class with seventeen-year-olds who had just completed high school, some of whom had never before travelled on a streetcar or been to a city.

One of the most formative influences during Peggy's college years was the Social Gospel. The term refers not to something that she studied in class, but rather to a group of ideals shared by many of United's faculty and "felt" in the atmosphere at the college. Although the term sounds religious, it does not apply to a particular denomination.[298] During the years following the First World War and the Great Depression, various leftist political movements allied to Fabianism or Communism or Socialism sought to change the political agenda in Canada, especially in the Prairie provinces. In addition, there was a strong movement for change endorsed in a particular way by many nonconforming Protestant churches. Referred to as the Social Gospel, this movement was very strong on the Prairies. Its tenets were espoused, wrote Laurence, by "the founders of the Social Democratic party, the CCF [Co-operative Commonwealth Federation], people such as J.S.Woodsworth, Stanley Knowles, Tommy Douglas."[299] At United College, many of the faculty endorsed the Social Gospel and sought concrete ways to bring about change in the social order. One classmate recalls: "While we didn't talk a whole lot about it, the Social Gospel was in the very air we breathed. We absorbed it like osmosis. At United, the ideals of the Social Gospel were all around us."[300]

The enduring significance of the Social Gospel in Margaret Laurence's life is reflected decades later in her 1982 Convocation Address, given at Emmanuel College, Victoria University:

> Ours is a terrifying world. Injustice, suffering and fear are everywhere to be found. It is difficult to maintain hope in such a world, and yet I believe there is hope. I want to proclaim and affirm my personal belief in the Social Gospel. I speak as a Christian, a woman, a writer, a parent, a member of humanity and a sharer in life itself, a life I believe to be informed and infused with the holy spirit. I do not think it is enough to hope and pray that our own lives and souls will know grace, even though my entire life as a writer has been concerned with my belief that all human individuals matter, that no one is ordinary.[301]

A year after she delivered that address, Margaret Laurence wrote in 1983 to another Manitoban, Professor Paul Hiebert, whom she had known as an undergraduate. She confided to him the following thoughts about her own work:

> [I want] of course to continue my own writing, my own work, but this seems related to the state of the world in general. I keep coming back, again and again, all the time, to the Social Gospel. Our Lord's new commandment, 'Thou shalt love thy neighbor as thyself: ... 7 words. Seven words only. And yet — how incredibly complex, how incredibly <u>difficult</u>, how incredibly <u>necessary</u>, at least in our very imperfect ways to <u>attempt</u>. There are things I want to say in fiction, not in didactic ways but through human individual characters, and have not as yet found the way to do so.
>
> I keep on trying, and pray that it <u>will</u> be given to me. We will see.[302]

Over the years, Laurence consistently described her political position as that of a committed Social Democrat, a position which, she explained, was close to the tenets of the Social Gospel. Her enduring concern with the Social Gospel is apparent even in the last months of her life. After learning that she was terminally ill, Margaret Laurence began to plan her funeral service. Among the hymns to be sung, she chose "Guide Me, O Thou Great Jehovah," partly because "it expresses to me some of my life's struggles for peace and justice and partly because it reminds me of the Social Gospel."[303]

From September 1939, when Canada had joined England in taking up arms against the Axis powers, until the surrender of Japan in 1946, Peggy and most of her classmates had lived under the cloud of war. It made a profound impression on her during the formative years of adolescence and early adulthood. The uncertainty that hovered over that period in her life repeated the pattern of uncertainty that had formed the background of Peggy's childhood. Nevertheless, as a young adult she did not feel as powerless as she had in childhood, and while at college her days were also permeated with the optimism and energy of youth. Peggy and her friends took time to relax after classes were over. They went off campus to grab a hamburger at the nearby Salisbury Steak House, a snack at Kelekis Chip Wagon, or an ice-cream soda at Blue Boy. They walked downtown to the cinema, and sometimes, as Joyce Friesen recalls, they even trudged seven miles to see a film at the Bijou in the North End.[304] They also enjoyed United College's annual social events, such as Stunt Night, various tea dances, the "beard and mustache contest" for resident men, and "the Grads' Farewell."

By September of Peggy's senior year (1946-1947), the University of Manitoba had a record enrollment of over sixty-five hundred students, and the affiliated colleges were also bursting at the seams.[305] Peggy was busy as an associate editor of *Vox*, United's literary journal, then edited by her friend Jack Borland. Borland, an RCAF veteran with lively dark eyes, dark hair, and a slim build, was serious about his writing. Within the group he was known as Ariel, probably after the character in *The Tempest*. Jack Borland and Peggy dated frequently, and many of their friends thought they would marry. Years later, Laurence opened her apocalyptic novel, *The Fire-Dwellers* (1969), with these four lines from a children's rhyme: "Ladybird, ladybird / Fly away home; / Your house is on fire, / Your children are gone;" lines that apply very appropriately to a major theme of that novel. The same rhyme, however, had been used quite prominently by Jack Borland in a powerful short story published in *Vox* when he and Peggy were undergraduates. Borland's story focuses on a young soldier, the death of the soldier's mother, and her "haunting of him." In that same issue of *Vox*, an essay by Peggy and several of her poems appeared. She would have been moved both by Borland's style and by his story about war and the death of the mother. Laurence's later use of those lines in *The Fire-Dwellers* may have been a coincidence or it might have been her private homage to Jack Borland and to that important period in her life.

Although Laurence's memoirs only briefly mention her connection to *Vox*, that engagement was very important to her. *Vox* served as a forum for literary talent and provided an opportunity to enhance skills needed to work with others in putting together a good college publication. As an assistant editor, Peggy was able to build upon the skills she had developed while working on her high-school paper and at the office of the *Neepawa Press*.

During her last year at United College, Peggy enrolled in Malcolm Ross's honours course "Seventeenth-Century Non-dramatic Literature," which was also open to graduate students. Ross was on the faculty at the University of Manitoba, and his class met at the Fort Garry campus. The ride out there was "terrible," recalls one student; "The bus was always full and we had to stand."[306] But once they arrived in Professor Ross's seminar, those discomforts faded.

A dozen students met informally around a large table and engaged in heated discussion about topics such as the poetry of John Donne and the influence of the cosmology of Copernicus and Galileo on Donne's writing. Laurence described that class in a later tribute to Professor Ross:

> We talked about these matters as though they had happened only the day before yesterday. Our sense of the *immediacy* of great literature we owed in no small measure to Malcolm Ross. He encouraged — indeed, insisted upon — our thinking for ourselves. He made accessible to us many aspects of the literature we were examining, but he also helped us to trust our own responses to it. . . . I still recall with great clarity the excitement and enthusiasm of those classes.[307]

Malcolm Ross, who was then in his mid-thirties, had earned his doctorate at Cornell University and, prior to his appointment to the University of Manitoba, had worked with the National Film Board of Canada. A dedicated scholar, Ross had genuine concern for his students. It seemed to the collegians as if Professor Ross himself was always learning. He was an exciting and creative lecturer. One former seminar member described Ross as a man who dealt in ideas as "if they were pulsating, live things. Where other people might pull off the petals of a daisy in order to show it, Ross put the daisy together."[308] He thought dialectically, and that was one of his strengths. He could always find opposites and the resolution of tensions.[309] Although Ross had been attracted to left-wing causes while at Cornell University, he became an Anglo-Catholic during his Manitoba years. His book *Milton and Royalism* had been published in 1943, and his University of Manitoba lectures were later published as *Poetry and Dogma*.[310]

Margaret Laurence's life-long passion for the great English poet, John Milton, and her respect for his achievement certainly owed much to Malcolm Ross's class. In that seminar, despite the professor's erudition, she felt free to express her own opinions about Milton and to raise questions about his ideas. Many years later, she showed an interviewer her old and battered leather-bound copy of *Paradise Lost*. He then remarked on the numerous annotations Peggy had made in the book and noted that, in one margin, she had written, "What would Mrs. Milton have said!!!"[311]

Peggy could be witty and firm in her opinions. Once Professor Ross took an entire lecture to set forth the anatomy of Aristotelian philosophy and demonstrate how Thomas Aquinas had built a theology on it. After Ross left the room, Peggy turned to fellow student John Speers and, commenting on the length of the lecture, said with a smile, "And Kant only needed two pages to tear all that to pieces!"[312]

John Speers, who had studied with Northrop Frye at the University of Toronto, was then pursuing a Master's degree at the University of Manitoba. He recalls Malcolm Ross as "a great teacher." Although he found Ross and Frye to be very different, Speers felt "both men had a spirituality. They had a sense of seeing wholeness, of seeing forms and putting things together. Both men were highly original and you felt they were discovering as they were lecturing and you were making the discovery with them."[313]

Adele Wiseman, two years younger than Peggy, was then enrolled at the University of Manitoba, where she also studied with Malcolm Ross.[314] Wiseman was to become an accomplished writer and lifelong friend of Margaret Laurence. Adele Wiseman concisely described the situation in Professor Ross's class during the years that followed the influx of returning veterans:

> The encounter with a teacher of the calibre of
> Malcolm Ross, who had the rare ability to communi-

cate intellectual passion, had the effect of awakening
the faculties to something far more exciting and more
importantly binding than the divisive worries about
differences in age and experience. We shared the
excitement of learning a way of learning, an attitude
to experience, to standards, to larger goals. We became
comrades, grew in self-confidence and determination
to enter and help create and extend the cultural life of
this country. Malcolm Ross taught us to look to literature not simply as a by-product but as a prime value,
as the expression of the quality of a society, as witness
to the soul of a culture.[315]

In addition to that memorable seminar with Malcolm Ross, Peggy
also studied with another stimulating teacher during her senior year,
Robert N. Halstead, who with his wife had come to Winnipeg from the
United States.[316] Peggy became friends with the Halsteads and occasionally baby-sat for their son.[317] Professor Halstead was a vibrant and creative
teacher with an enthusiasm for modern literature. His talent for encouraging creative writing had a positive influence on Peggy, and Bob Halstead
became one of the very few persons with whom she corresponded frankly
about her fiction after she had married and moved abroad.[318]

The exciting atmosphere on campus and in the city of Winnipeg
made an ideal setting for an aspiring writer. In addition to being in
Malcolm Ross's class, Peggy also knew about several faculty members at
the Fort Garry campus of the University of Manitoba, among them Roy
Daniells, chair of the English department. However, Daniells left
Winnipeg in 1946 for the University of British Columbia. He subsequently sent back letters and poems that were published in *The
Manitoban*. He wrote with enthusiasm about the West Coast poet and
teacher Earle Birney, mentioning in particular his long poem, "Daniel."
That same issue of *The Manitoban* carried a modernist poem by Malcolm
Ross called "New Day."[319] Chemist Paul Hiebert was another remarkable
and colourful literary figure at the University of Manitoba, who seemed
to prefer literature to the Bunsen burner. Although Peggy was not in his
class, she attended several of Hiebert's readings, where he regaled the

undergraduates with chapters from his humorous tour-de-force *Sarah Binks*. Using style with great adroitness, he recounted the fictional literary career of Sarah, "sweet songstress of Saskatchewan." Hiebert subsequently received the Leacock Medal for Humour for *Sarah Binks*. In later years, Margaret Laurence and Hiebert exchanged letters in which they discussed philosophical and religious matters, particularly as these were expressed in his books: *Tower in Siloam* (1966) and *Doubting Castle* (1976), which explore the place of humans in the universe.

Beyond Tony's tuck shop in Wesley Hall and not far from the campus of United College, a number of interesting developments aimed at creating a more secure future for Canada and the world were under way in Winnipeg. One effort involved the establishment of co-operative residences within the city. On Balmoral Street, several student co-operative houses sponsored by the Student Christian Movement were set up during the mid 1940s. Some Japanese-Canadian students were welcomed there as residents after their release from Canadian internment camps.[320] During that same period, Watson Thomson, a dynamic Scot and "controversial activist educator," launched an ambitious plan to change the world order. Thomson, with a group of like-minded persons, established a group residence that was designed to effect transformative-communitarian living. It was referred to in Winnipeg as the Roslyn Road Community. After its beginnings in the province of Alberta, a core group under Watson's leadership had moved to Winnipeg and set up an "intentional community" at Roslyn Road.[321] Some of the members collaborated in preparing a study of Manitoba's pressing economic and social problems, *Pioneers in Poverty*; others were involved with the Prairie School for Social Advance.[322]

Members of Thomson's group believed that study-groups within a communal setting would become "spearheads of social change," and that "guided by the vision of a fully co-operative society, similar groups would gradually initiate a social and intellectual revolution."[323] Because Watson Thomson had inaugurated the Adult Education Division at the University of Manitoba (1941) and frequently broadcast on the radio, he was widely known in Winnipeg and had friends in the academic community. A number of collegians, aware of the Roslyn Road community, met at the house from time to time with visitors from all over Canada for discussion and an occasional meal with the group. The Roslyn Road house, a magnificent old building with floors of quarter-cut oak, had a wide entrance hall and a panelled library, where discussions were held. Other attractive features of the house included a huge fireplace in the living room, a dining room large enough to hold the whole group, and a carved oak stairway that led to the second and third floors.[324] As an undergraduate, Peggy knew about the group's utopian ideals. She may have recalled Watson Thomson's visit to NCI when she in high school, and she probably attended a few meetings of the community at Roslyn Road.

By the autumn of 1946, however, Watson Thomson and his wife had left Manitoba for Saskatchewan, and the group was in a period of transition. As members moved, and apartments became available in the former co-op house on Roslyn Road, Peggy and some friends took an apartment there. She had decided to move off campus for her final year at college. As things turned out, Mary Turnbull, a shy poet and an aspiring journalist, agreed to share a place there with Peggy. The yearbook describes Mary Turnbull as a "blue-eyed idealist . . . a frequent contributor to *Vox* and *The Manitoban* . . . interested in all literature with a preference for Canadian poetry and [William] Saroyan." Mary and Peggy lived in several places during the next year. Once they sublet a faculty member's apartment, where they cheerfully painted a marble fireplace and its mahogany mantel a shade of purple.[325] For at least part of the winter they moved into a boarding house in the North End of Winnipeg, about a mile past the terminus of the Selkirk Avenue streetcar line.[326] The streetcar ride gave Peggy the background for one of her most experimental poems: "North Main Car," which will be discussed subsequently.[327] Winnipeg's North End was the site of several richly diverse ethnic communities. Although Peggy lived in the area briefly as an undergraduate, she returned to live there the following year. The unique features of that place and period have since been captured in memoirs, artwork, and literature.[328] Margaret Laurence on a number of occasions also spoke movingly of the impact that living in the North End had on her life.[329]

From there Peggy and Mary Turnbull moved to a small flat at 356 Broadway, not far from United College. As roommates they talked earnestly about literature and about becoming journalists. Mary recalls Peggy wearing "À Bientôt" perfume, and sitting at her desk consulting a thesaurus, a book that Mary had never seen before.[330] In July, brimming with good cheer, they sent out invitations to a soirée, at which they planned to serve "beer, salami, Roquefort cheese, dill pickles, and pink ice-cream."[331]

They subsequently moved back into the former co-op house on Roslyn Road, along with Madge Hetherington and her roommate Joyce Friesen. The girls could easily walk from United's campus, past the impressive Manitoba legislative buildings, and across the Osborne Street bridge to 139 Roslyn Road (no longer standing). The house was set on a large, deep property that stretched down to the Assiniboine River. According to her memoirs, Peggy first noticed her future husband, Jack Laurence, an RCAF veteran, on the staircase of that Roslyn Road house: "I thought his face not only was handsome, but also had qualities of understanding. I said to myself, 'That's the man I'd like to marry.'"[332] And so she did, four months after her graduation from college.

The description of seeing Jack Laurence on the staircase is reminiscent of an earlier life-altering decision that she recalled making at the age of fourteen on the staircase of the Big House in Neepawa — her decision to become a writer.[333] Margaret's account of noticing Jack conveys the impression that she had not seen him before; that is doubtful, however. Jack Laurence had been in Winnipeg for some time.

Prior his discharge from the RCAF, Jack had been stationed at an airbase about one hundred miles from Winnipeg, and had joined the Roslyn Road group "every other weekend for about a year."[334] One of the original members of the co-op, Kay Bolton, recalls that, after Jack was discharged, he resided full-time at Roslyn Road and "used to bring Peggy to the house quite a lot."[335] Margaret Laurence's description of seeing Jack on the staircase probably reflects the moment when she realized she had fallen in love with him, rather than the first time she actually saw him. Jack's bearing and good looks made people take notice. No doubt, Peggy also had seen him on campus at United College, where Jack took an accelerated program in the Collegiate Division in order to gain admission to the University of Manitoba. He finished the required classes while living at Roslyn Road, and then entered the engineering program at the University of Manitoba.

John Fergus (Jack) Laurence had been raised in Alberta and had met Watson Thomson as a result of his mother, Elsie's Laurence's, prompting. In the summer of 1939, Elsie Laurence, along with the playwright Gwen Pharis Ringwood and her husband, had attended a weeklong session under Watson Thomson's direction at the Alberta School of Community Life.[336] Elsie Fry Laurence had respect for the ideals of Thomson and his group and was familiar with his experiment in communitarian living.[337]

It was natural, therefore, for Jack and another comrade, Frank Collier, to come frequently from the airbase at Carberry to visit the community at Roslyn Road, and eventually the two men moved in there. They enjoyed the challenging intellectual discussions and contagious optimism of the group. Jack, however, was not drawn to Roslyn Road solely because of Thomson's ideals for a new world. He had become fond of a vivacious and attractive young woman who was a member of the group. She and Jack dated quite seriously for some time, and members of the Roslyn Road community expected a wedding. But the young woman had a little son, and Jack made it clear to her that he did not want to be burdened by that. However, his attachment to her is reflected in the fact that he wrote to her from time to time over the next twenty years.[338]

Peggy's friends were taken by surprise when she became engaged to Jack Laurence in 1947, because she had been dating another undergraduate, Jack Borland, a veteran and fellow writer. Friends thought their romance was serious, and it is not clear why the couple did not marry. In any event, when Jack Laurence and Peggy Wemyss began dating, the timing seemed right for both of them. Although Peggy's oldest and dearest friend, Mona, liked Jack Laurence, she could not imagine Peggy as his wife. It all seemed rather hasty. Mona didn't think their personalities were suited to one another, but when she mentioned her reservations to Peggy, she was strongly rebuked. Other friends also thought that Peggy was making a mistake in marrying Jack, but Peggy was "very much in love."[339] It is easy to see why.

Jack Laurence was strong, intelligent, and sympathetic. The eldest of six children, he was born in 1916, while his father was serving overseas in the Great War. As a young adult, Jack left home and Canada just before the outbreak of the Second World War. He had travelled a good deal while in the armed services, and had an air of confidence and calm. He also appreciated literature. Jack's good looks reminded some people of the film actor Clark Gable. Margaret Laurence's comments about Derek, her "first love," shed light on why she was later attracted to Jack Laurence. As a young woman of twenty, Peggy would have been surprised and grateful to receive the attention of this handsome veteran.[340] The fact that Jack's mother was also a writer led Peggy to assume he would be open to having a wife who was a writer. She was not aware then that Jack's father had neither valued nor encouraged his wife's literary efforts.[341] Peggy had no intention of returning to her hometown after graduation. She was hungry for broader horizons and intellectual challenge. In Neepawa, there would be no real future for her. To be in Neepawa would have meant stultifying town life and proximity to her elderly grandfather, "old man Simpson." It would have meant forfeiting her freedom and her life's goals. On the other hand, as Jack's wife, Peggy could look forward to mutual love, children, companionship, travel, and the chance to pursue her writing.

It is significant that Peggy's two serious romantic interests in her youth were with men ten years older than she, both of whom had served in the RCAF. If one examines the photographs in *Dance on the Earth*, there also appears to be a strong likeness between Peggy's father, who died when she was eight, and Jack Laurence. The resemblance may have contributed at some unconscious level to the attraction. In any case, everyone agrees that Peggy was in love with Jack.

Although their romance flourished during Peggy's last months at college, she sustained her dedication to her writing. Her literature classes had given her an important background for her own work. Under the aegis of excellent teachers, she had studied the finest writing in English literature from the Anglo-Saxon period to the twentieth century. At the same time, her interest in, and appreciation of, Canadian literature had grown. Although Peggy's introduction to Canadian literature had begun at home and been encouraged in Wes McAmmond's Grade Seven classroom, it was at United College that Arthur Phelps's knowledge of — and undiminished enthusiasm for — Canadian literature deeply affected her. In her memoirs Laurence refers to Phelps as "one of the greatest teachers of literature in our country."[342] A sense of his abiding interest in Canadian literature may be gleaned from his monograph *Canadian Writers* (1951), which was an outgrowth of his class lectures at United College and his radio broadcasts on the subject.[343]

While an undergraduate, Peggy had enjoyed the fellowship of other collegians who were interested in ideas and in literature. One of them recalls that "Peggy, unlike some of her classmates, did not seem to be interested in romantic attachments, but was absorbed in the world of writing and the world of ideas. She had an inquiring mind and a rebellious spirit."[344] At that time the intellectual ferment at United was especially stimulating. Peggy and Cliff Grant, another Honours student, were keenly interested in theological inquiry and would discuss religious matters for hours. Cliff and Peggy also enjoyed music, and he often took her to the Winnipeg Symphony.[345] One friend summed up the stimulating and lively atmosphere of that period in Wordsworth's lines: "Bliss was it in that dawn to be alive, / But to be young was very heaven!"[346] More than fifty years later, many alumni from that era recall their days at United College with affection, respect, and gratitude for attitudes toward learning that were fostered there, for friendships that were formed, and for a dedicated faculty who challenged and encouraged them.

During her college years, Peggy resolutely pursued the craft of writing. An overview of her apprentice work during that period will show her determination and ambition, even as an undergraduate, to develop her literary gifts.[347]

UNDERGRADUATE PUBLICATIONS

In her last year at college, Peggy wrote publicity notices for campus events when she served as publicity president of the Students' Council. This was literary training of a different sort. It is important to note that she seized the opportunity to write for publication almost as soon as she arrived on campus in 1944, and that she managed within a few weeks to have poems published in the literary pages of *The Manitoban*.[348] This was a major accomplishment for her. As an undergraduate she succeeded in publishing at least eighteen poems, three short stories, and a critical essay in *Vox* (United College) or *The Manitoban* (University of Manitoba). With one exception, those pieces are signed not as "Peggy," but with her full name, Jean Margaret Wemyss, or a variant.[349]

One poem, "Pagan Point — Wasagaming — Approaching Night," actually had been written while she was in high school, and may have been published in the *Annals of the Black and Gold*. The typed text of the poem was saved by Peggy's high-school English teacher, Mildred Musgrove.[350] The word "Wasagaming" appears in the typescript, but was dropped from the published version in *The Manitoban*. That decision could have been made by an editor who found the word distracting or pretentious, whereas people in Neepawa would have recognized Wasagaming as the Cree name for the largest lake in nearby Riding Mountain National Park (later known as Clear Lake).[351]

The poem's opening line is self-consciously dramatic, but Peggy's choice of particular details is effective, and the varied metrical pattern provides interest.

> The blood-tipped rushes thrust their clutching roots
> into firm sand. Cool water, darkly blue,
> Laps on the beach, leaving a clinging ridge
> Of moisture with each small, retreating wave.
> And in the background, dark and splendid spruce
> Uplift their arms to an untroubled sky.

The poem concludes serenely at dusk:

> The lake is stilled, the marsh birds cry no more
> This is a dim cathedral — full of rest
> Remote from pain, where Man may find his God.
> This is the oldest chapel in the world.

This romantic description of the woods, the lake, and the cry of a loon suggests the peace and serenity that were tangible at Clear Lake, where Peggy spent many happy childhood holidays. Although in the poem she uses the words *pagan* and *heathen*, those terms are intended to mark periods of time stretching back though millennia, rather than to distinguish between a "pagan" and "Christian" era. The longing for serenity and a place free from anguish was deeply felt.

During all of 1944, the progress of the Second World War involved wrenching personal losses for Peggy and her friends. That year her Neepawa neighbour, Murray Coutts, a pilot, died overseas, and her cousin Bob Pennie perished at the age of nineteen in a burning tank during the last Allied offensive in Europe. Her roommate's brother, also a pilot, had died in a massive bombing raid over Berlin the year before, and Patricia Jenkins's brother, Walter, a Winnipeg Grenadier, had been captured in Hong Kong "handy to Christmas day" 1941, and was still being held prisoner by the Japanese. Such grim personal tragedies had a strong impact on the sensitive young writer, who had already experienced so many deaths in her own family. It is not surprising, therefore, that war and death, as well as isolation and fear, are themes that occur frequently in Peggy's published work in 1944-1945, her first year at college.

"Thought," written in blank verse, appeared prominently in the top-right column of the "Features Page" of *The Manitoban*. It opens with the words of a person who is seeking refuge from fear and war. The language, which might appear melodramatic in another context, here seems apt:

> I have need of wind and hilltops,
> Far away from the terror and brutality,
> Away from the strangled cries of women,
> The great dry sobs of men whose sons are dead
> And the sickening torrents of bright blood
> Of young men who wished desperately to live.

These detailed descriptions of wartime recall the grim editorials by Principal Ray in NCI's *Annals of the Black and Gold*. The poem's closing lines suggest that healing will take place in a setting reminiscent of the British Romantics: in solitude amid nature, where the music of the pines and sweeping gusts of wind will lessen "the aching fear in me." Although the poem refers to healing, it closes with the poignant line: "my heart is sick with the heartsick world." In a poem about her father, which may not have been published, she wrote these bitter lines: "Under the stone lies my father, ten years dead, who would never know as his this bastard world he sired."[352]

"The Imperishable," an ambitious poem of fifty-four lines arranged in four sections, develops against a background of crumbling cities and wasteful wars, where "on the battlefield are left the twisted, dead bodies of young men." The last two parts move away from the horrors of war to ponder the beauty of the earth, which is "untouched by stupidity and insincerity." The poem affirms that the earth will not only survive but will remain untainted. The notion that nature will endure despite the ravages inflicted by humankind appears frequently in works by Robinson Jeffers, a poet whom Peggy greatly admired.[353]

In "Bus-Ride at Night," she tries to combine external description with metaphysical insights. Amid the timeless fields of night, the shrouded domains of the unknown, where there is "no safe light holding back the darkness," a wanderer finds himself alone and lost, "with only his brave heart's shining to show the way / Over rough furrows to the friendly fireside." Isolation is underscored here, and although the opening lines mention the consolingly solid shape of the bus, its headlights "steadily devouring the darkness," and the comfortable sound of its engine purring through the night, there is no communication among the bus's passengers, who remain apart and alone, "afraid to look beyond the headlights' narrow glow."

During her second year at United, eight poems by Peggy appeared in college publications, an impressive number in that competitive literary milieu. "Quest: Clay-Fettered Doors," written in five free-verse stanzas of unequal length, is quite different from her earlier undergraduate poems.[354] The tone and form are new for her, but carry echoes of T.S. Eliot. The poem's abrupt opening lines "I know you. I've seen you before" are addressed by an interlocutor to a person wandering in a large, impersonal city, seeking some sort of answer to a religious crisis. However, no answers are forthcoming from officially sanctioned places: Parliament, the CCF, or established religion. The interlocutor then remarks: "All right, where did you expect to find it?" The poem moves into its final stanza as the seeker shuffles along bleak, dusty pavements, "glancing around for someone who answers to the name of God." The final lines suggest a resolution, as the seeker ponders to himself:

Wait a minute, maybe you've forgotten one place.
But perhaps it wouldn't work after all
. . . .
Because it's hard to look people straight in the eye,
And tear away gently the carefully woven mask.

In another vein are three poems for children that were also published in *Vox*. For the first time in Peggy's undergraduate work, joyful lines leap from the page. An element of the magical is also present as she gives free rein to her imagination. "Cabbages," written in rhyming couplets, offers children a charming depiction of a butterfly:

I once knew a butterfly, silver and green
Whose wings had a flimmery, shimmery sheen.
. . . .
She lived in a cabbage all crinkly and cool
And had three large rooms and a small swimming pool.

That mood and metre are sustained for the remaining eleven short stanzas, and the poem's formal structure actually allows Peggy great freedom.

A pair of lyric poems that appeared in the same issue are in a different mode.[355] They present a strong, confident speaker who has found a way to deal with some undefined, enigmatic pain and loss. In both poems, "alone" is used to describe a speaker who finds solace in nature and apart from others "listening not to their bitter talk." Solace resides in making a song — a suggestion that could apply as well to making a poem: "Someday I shall make me a song for singing, / Shaped of laughter and woven of pain."

During Peggy's last year at college, her poems show a decided shift toward classical subject matter: "Thetis' Song about Her Son," "Classical Framework," "Song of the Race of Ulysses," and "Bread Hath He" (the title is taken from a line in *Electra* by Euripides).[356] In each poem, she tries to use the timeless aspects of the classics in a more personal way.

It is significant that "fear" is almost tangible in "Bread Hath He," her last published undergraduate poem. Here the poet attempts to explore and explain alienation in modern society, an appropriate theme for that post-war era. The sentiments in "Bread Hath He" are akin to those in "Thought," her first published college poem. Both mention a solitariness that cannot be shattered, and an "aching fear" so palpable that, as the speaker notes, "fear is the texture of the penetrating ache within my bones." Feelings of isolation and anxiety about an uncertain future, whether personal or world-wide, remained concerns of Peggy and many of her fellow collegians. In referring to their class in his valedictory address (1947), Heath MacQuarrie noted that, whether the collegians were veterans or not, "the magnitude and significance of world-shaking events was ever pressing upon every day and every activity."[357] Indeed, the impact of the Second World War remained with those graduates. "Bread Hath He" comes to a sombre conclusion as the speaker urges: "because there is no breaking through / — Let us sing songs against the impending shadows." For Peggy herself the cessation of pain and aching fear would be found near at hand within her own writing and in "reaching for the right sound of her own voice."[358]

Although she was awarded the prestigious Aikens Poetry Prize at graduation for "Bread Hath He," many of the poem's lines seem seriously flawed by her choice of words. Distracting phrases such as "electric vitality," "synaptic space," and "the plastic years have hardened immaculately over our faces" diminish the poem's impact.

The shift to classical subject matter in Peggy's poetry during 1946-1947 seems unfortunate. Her poems feel forced and contrived, despite their origins in rich classical texts such as those by Euripides and Sappho. The lyricism and appropriate rhythms of some of her best undergraduate poems are now forfeited, and these poems based on classical material are the least successful of her college period. It is clear that Peggy was struggling to find the right poetic vehicle for her ideas, but the tone is more confident and natural in a number of her earlier poems.

As an undergraduate, the challenge that Peggy set for herself as a poet is obvious in her exploration of a variety of forms: from the traditional sonnet in its several variations to blank verse and free verse. She used varying line lengths, inserted speakers, and experimented with rhyme schemes. Her classmates and others from that era expected Peggy to become a writer, but they thought of her chiefly as a poet.[359]

It is clear, however, that she was drawn to write fiction as well as poetry. Although only two significant short stories seem to have been published while she was in college, "Calliope" and "Tal des Walde," looking more closely at them provides an opportunity to see what the apprentice writer was trying to accomplish.[360]

"Calliope," published in the fall of her second year, drew upon an experience Peggy had had while on a summer visit to Carman, Manitoba. There she and her friend Madge Hetherington had picked cherries and helped run a hot-dog stand at the Carman Fair. "This story," Laurence noted, "came out of my observations of the carnival people, the 'carnies.'"[361]

The events in "Calliope" take place on a rainy day at a country fair. The tawdriness of the place is deftly sketched. The plot centres on several men and a five-year-old boy who has "run away." Two of the men look after the little boy and show him around the fair. When the carnival boss comes looking for a "lost child," the lad goes with him to be reunited with his mother and family. The characters include German Joe; Carl, a Swede; Steve, a gambler; Charlie, who operates a fast-food stand; and Spike, a performer with snakes. Spike's face is scarred, an "ugly gouged pit where his nose had been." His scars are the result of war injuries received when Spike's ship hit a mine and he was badly burned.

In this short story Peggy also handles various dialects with assurance: from German Joe's brand of English to Steve's rough talk. The carnival men have been touched by their brief association with the lad. The last sentence of the story suggests that, as the little boy leaves the place, these men, who have neither children nor families of their own, will find solace in telling tales. "'C'mon Joe,' it concludes, 'tell me the story about yer castle on the Rhine.'"

In commenting on this story, Margaret Laurence later said: "If it were shown to me by a young writer today, I would tell her (as tactfully as possible) that it showed promise, had some good moments and turns of phrase, showed some subtlety in the ending, and was overwhelmingly sentimental."[362] The very fact that Laurence was willing to comment rather favourably on her early effort is untypical of her and probably relates to her personal attachment to the theme of this story — a lost child is cared for and happily reunited with his family.

"Tal des Walde," which has a self-consciously obscure title, was published in *Vox* (1947). Told from the point of view of a young man who has been travelling, it unfolds as a story within a story and is very different in style and plot from "Calliope." The male narrator stops at a watchmaker's shop and chats with the old proprietor. As they talk, the watchmaker mentions the town's earlier days, remarking: "There are a great many tales which I remember. It seems a pity that so few people know them." He then relates a suspenseful story set in the early twentieth century about an Austrian count, who after mismanaging his estate and amassing gambling debts, seeks a new opportunity in Canada. The consequences of his emigration to Manitoba, where he establishes a feudal-like estate, involve an underlying ethnic conflict and relate to labour, management, and exploitation.

Peggy's use of formal diction for the Austrian count is very appropriate, and somewhat reminiscent of the Latinate diction in tales by Edgar Allan Poe. Her attention to detail is noteworthy; for example, the nobleman has an Austrian name, but the peasants who work for him have Ukrainian names, because the story takes place when the Ukraine was part of the Austro-Hungarian empire. These distinctions are those that she deliberately put in place.[363]

Thirty-one years later "Tal des Walde" was reprinted in the *Journal of Canadian Fiction*, along with Laurence's comments about it. She did not disparage her youthful effort and noted that the most interesting thing about the story is the fact it connects to all her subsequent writing in this way: namely, a basic life-view that could say, even then, a man is never God, even in his own domain, and "one should not mould the lives of others." Laurence explained: "My views have, I hope, deepened throughout the years, but they have obviously grown from a basic view that was there early on. Parts of the story are, of course, wildly melodramatic, notably the birth scene. But youthful and naive as much of the story is, I would not reject it even now, for it expresses some of my tenets of belief that are as true to me now as they were then."[364]

A minor but significant point in both "Tal des Walde" and "Calliope" resides in the fact that the telling of tales provides the means by which these people find the courage to go on with their lives. In one sense, Peggy herself also was doing that.

In addition to her undergraduate fiction and poetry, Peggy wrote an important essay which appeared in *Vox* a few months before her graduation: "The Earlier Fountain: a Study of Robinson Jeffers, in his Early Poems and Philosophy."[365] She writes with assurance and demonstrates a wide-ranging knowledge of Robinson Jeffers's work. It may be that her familiarity with his lengthy poem "The Stone Axe" lingered in her memory to provide some background for her later short story, "A Queen in Thebes." This little-known grim, apocalyptic story was published in *Tamarack Review* (1964) and deals with the ominous consequences of nuclear war.[366] It may be found here in Appendix C.

Being a student at United College during the mid-1940s had a positive effect on Peggy Wemyss's development as a writer and on her maturing as a young adult. The college was not large and she was fortunate in having excellent, concerned faculty. She found friends such as Madge Hetherington, Mary Turnbull, and Pat Jenkins, who also appreciated and enjoyed literature. She worked steadily at her writing, relished the comradeship of the staff of *Vox*, and discovered a cadre of like-minded students, who appreciated thoughtful conversation, questioned the relevance of religious belief, supported schemes for improving the world, and thoroughly relished good fun.

As college graduation approached, Peggy was planning to get a newspaper job in Winnipeg. Journalism was a natural route for an aspiring novelist and it was also considered an acceptable career for women. In Peggy's last year at United, the campus was abuzz with talk of the *Winnipeg Citizen*, a new morning newspaper that Professor Harry Ferns was planning to launch. Peggy's roommate Mary Turnbull, and Jeannette Grosney, a friend of Mary's, were eager to become involved in this unique enterprise. Ferns, an idealist, had recruited students to canvass the city, selling subscriptions to the *Winnipeg Citizen*, which was to be owned co-operatively by citizens. The concept of a genuinely independent paper was very exciting in that postwar era when the young graduates wanted so very much to build a better future for Canada and the world.[367]

After her graduation, Peggy did work at the *Winnipeg Citizen*, but prior to that she held at least two jobs, one seems to have been in the book department at Eaton's, the other was at *The Westerner*, a weekly newspaper. As summer drew to a close, she was busy with plans for her wedding, and on September 13, 1947, Peggy and Jack Laurence were married in the United Church in Neepawa. She wore a gown of ivory satin brocade and a full-length veil of silk embroidered net. The best man was John Marshall, a friend of Jack's from the Roslyn Road community, who had been instrumental in founding the Prairie School for Social Advance.[368] Peggy's college friends, Jack Borland and Lyall Powers, were ushers. Two of her friends since childhood, Louise and Mona, were unable to attend because they and their families had moved to another province.[369] A modest wedding reception was held afterwards in Grandfather Simpson's Big House on First Avenue. Peggy and Jack then spent their honeymoon at her family's cottage at Clear Lake, beside Peggy's beloved Lake Wasagaming in the majestic autumn setting of Riding Mountain National Park, splendid in September's green and gold.

After returning to Winnipeg, Jack Laurence continued his engineering studies at the University of Manitoba, and the couple managed to make ends meet during the next two years on his small DVA allowance and Peggy's salary from her work at the newspaper.

CHAPTER SIX
Journalism

Between 1947 and 1949, Peggy worked for two newspapers successively. She was hired not long after her graduation as a staff correspondent for *The Westerner*, a weekly paper that was affiliated with the *Canadian Tribune*.[370] According to her memoirs, she did not realize *The Westerner* was a Communist paper, although she was vaguely aware that it was left-wing.[371] The staff was small and she did the typical work of a young reporter, covering the Winnipeg scene and writing an occasional book review. Several months later, when financial problems arose with the paper, Peggy was let go, but she was subsequently hired by another newspaper, the *Winnipeg Citizen*.

Her articles in *The Westerner* and the *Winnipeg Citizen* offer an interesting window into a formative period in Margaret Laurence's literary apprenticeship.[372] Because she rarely spoke about that period, it might be assumed that her experiences as a young journalist were not significant.[373] The very opposite is true, however. The multi-faceted influences of this newspaper work on Margaret Laurence's literary development may be gathered from more than one hundred and twenty columns that carried her byline in *The Westerner* and the *Winnipeg Citizen*.

While covering assignments for those papers, Peggy was in the midst of an exciting and controversial scene. The papers carried articles about social, political, and economic issues in Winnipeg, one of Canada's most important postwar centres; and also carried lengthy reports on developments in Europe after the armistice. As a young reporter, Peggy Wemyss was thus brought into contact with a fast-paced and varied national and international scene.

From July through December 1947, she contributed about fifteen signed articles to *The Westerner*. Its banner proclaimed "Truth and Justice for the West," and the editor stated that the paper would convey honest news of the events and life around us — with the moral courage and the strength to tell it. "We will have none of the traditional press: cheap sensationalism and shoddy scandal."[374] Those idealistic goals appealed to Peggy, and she was excited by the prospect of working for the newspaper.

As a cub reporter, Peggy attended public hearings and wrote about housing, welfare, health, and labour issues. Having grown up during the Depression, she would have been aware of some of these matters, but as a young Winnipeg reporter with an urban beat, she must have discovered a dimension and an immediacy to them that had been lacking in her own experiences within the protected environs of Neepawa.

Peggy's first signed article for *The Westerner* was a lengthy report dealing with the severe postwar housing crisis in Winnipeg. Approximately fifteen hundred people were then in emergency shelters, and the city was in desperate straits trying to meet their needs as well as the housing needs of returning veterans and their families. Peggy provided details about a situation in which fifty-seven families were scheduled to be evicted from Immigration Hall by order of city authorities. A fellow reporter, Ann Henry, in her autobiography, *Laugh, Baby, Laugh*, has given a detailed description of the dreadful conditions that then existed in Immigration Hall.

In August 1947, Peggy wrote about the recent distribution of anti-Semitic leaflets in Winnipeg, quoting a barrister who had called for a police investigation of the incidents.[375] She also contributed a lengthy article about the province's polio epidemic, noting that the opinions of doctors in Toronto differed from those of the medical authorities in Winnipeg, and referring to the United States's newly established Infantile Paralysis Foundation.[376] Perhaps her coverage was so thorough because she had witnessed the ravages of polio during her youth. In fact, she did bring the memory of those experiences into her final novel *The Diviners*, in which the parents of Morag Gunn, the main character, die as a result of polio.

During the summer of 1947, Adele Wiseman, who was still an undergraduate at the University of Manitoba, became "guest" columnist at *The Westerner*. Substituting for her friend Roland Penner, she wrote the entertainment column. It is not clear whether she and Peggy knew each other then, since Wiseman's column did not require her to spend time in the newspaper's office. As Wiseman recalls it, their friendship stemmed from a meeting at the Labour Temple, where they had both gone seeking employment as writers.[377]

One of the most frightening and disturbing news events that Peggy Wemyss covered as a reporter for *The Westerner* took place on September 1, 1947, when a disastrous train wreck occurred fourteen miles east of Winnipeg, causing at least thirty-one deaths. It virtually wiped out six area families who were returning on the Minaki holiday train when it crashed into the No. 4 Transcontinental, standing at Dugald. Because Victorian-era gas lamps had been used to light the thirteen flimsy wooden coaches, fire engulfed the train and compounded the tragedy. Large headlines and photos accompanied Peggy's front-page article. Here is an excerpt:

> Tanks at the Imperial Oil depot went up in flames, and the Dugald grain elevator was demolished by fire. . . . The coaches were burned until nothing but their twisted skeletons of steel were left. Decapitated bodies and corpses, charred until unidentifiable, were part of the nightmare, as dazed survivors wandered around looking for friends and relatives and hysterical mothers screamed for their children lost in the blaze.[378]

Eight days after that terrible accident, the city's flags flew at half-mast, while thousands of Winnipeggers lined the funeral route and twenty-two hearses passed the legislative buildings en route to the grave site. The experience of covering the fire and the subsequent municipal hearings into the crash probably contributed to the background, whether consciously or not, for the devastating fire that the fictional Morag has to deal with as a reporter for the "*Manawaka Banner*" in *The Diviners*.[379]

During September 1947, only two signed articles by Peggy Wemyss appeared in *The Westerner*. She was on her honeymoon, having married Jack Laurence on September 13, in Neepawa. On the marriage certificate she gave her occupation as "journalist." The byline "Peggy Laurence," her married name, appears for the first time in *The Westerner* on October 4, 1947, when she contributed a lengthy account of the public hearings that she attended following the Dugald train wreck. Her analysis raised a series of important questions about the circumstances of the tragedy.

Later that autumn, Peggy had a very different event to report. Approximately three thousand workers had gone on strike in six Manitoba packing plants. She interviewed men who were picketing at Swifts, Burns, and Canada Packers. Her article is particularly interesting, because here, for the first time as a journalist, Laurence slipped away from the journalistic mode and into a style more typical of fiction. Her description of the two strikers, Alf and Bill, was followed by eight paragraphs of alternating dialogue between the two men: "Alf was cleancut, fairhaired, probably in his early twenties. His alert eyes looked as if they knew how to laugh. Now he was in dead earnest, though . . . ." "That's right." Bill said, shifting his massive frame on the bench beside the gateway. "And they say our demands aren't fair."[380]

The style here differs significantly from her previous articles for the paper. As a result, one may speculate about Peggy's own literary efforts at the time. Had she continued to write short stories after college? Was she struggling with a novel? The answers to such questions, however, remain elusive.

In December 1947, her employment at *The Westerner* ended. A few months later, she secured a position at the *Winnipeg Citizen*.[381] Her byline appears in its premier issue on March 1, 1948. Years later when interviewed, Margaret Laurence said that she "loved working on the paper; the staff was small; everybody did three jobs."[382] Her college friends, Mary Turnbull and Patricia Jenkins Blondal, also wrote for the *Winnipeg Citizen*. When the Canadian Authors' Association prizes were announced in May of that year, Peggy's ambition to become a writer was reinforced by the news that Manitoba had received more honours than any of the other provinces: Gabrielle Roy, Paul Hiebert, and Dorothy Livesay were among the award recipients. If people from St. Boniface, Pilot Mound, and Winnipeg could reach their literary goals, perhaps, in time, she could too.

The *Winnipeg Citizen* was an exciting and singular experiment in newspaper publishing. Before its first issue appeared, there had been hours of theoretical and practical discussions, months of fund-raising, and door-to-door soliciting of subscriptions. Many students at United College were involved in these efforts because Professor Harry Ferns, a faculty member, was a key figure in founding the *Winnipeg Citizen*.

The concept of such an innovative morning paper also attracted a number of excellent and experienced newspaper personnel from other parts of Canada who joined the staff of the *Winnipeg Citizen*.[383] Laurence said later that her own work for the paper involved writing a radio column, doing book reviews, and covering the labour beat.[384] Her signed articles, however, do not include labour news. In the opinion of several of her contemporaries, Peggy had no understanding of the complexities of the labour scene in Winnipeg.[385] If she did cover the labour scene, it may have been in a secondary role to more seasoned reporters. In any event, both J.C. Woodbury, who was then working as a copy boy at the paper, and Shirley Lev Sharzer, who covered City Hall, remember Peggy as animated and self-confident when she returned to the office from assignments. People there knew that she intended to become a writer.[386]

During Peggy's first few months at the *Winnipeg Citizen*, she interviewed the lieutenant governor when he visited Winnipeg to view the destruction resulting from the spring flood damage in 1948. Her chief responsibility at the *Winnipeg Citizen*, however, involved writing a daily radio column, "In the Air."[387] In it she informed readers about upcoming programs and discussed recent radio offerings. This experience of listening to hours of varied radio broadcasts provided a rich apprenticeship for her. Radio in Canada was then a very significant medium of expression and communication, especially in the Prairie provinces, and her column had many readers. The routine of daily deadlines for a morning paper also afforded her an important discipline and many opportunities to reflect on the elements of effective writing.

While she was reviewing radio programs for the *Winnipeg Citizen*, the CBC series "The World's Great Novels" was broadcast. In her column, Peggy commented on Henry James's *Washington Square*, Robert Louis Stevenson's *Kidnapped*, and Flaubert's *Madame Bovary*, among others. Radio also presented adaptations of Shakespeare's plays and classics such as *Antigone*, *The Arabian Nights*, and *Murder in the Cathedral*. In addition, it featured contemporary dramas, for example, *Queer Heart* by Manitoba writer Laura Goodman Salverson, which told of the province's Icelandic community in pioneer days. In her column, Peggy also referred to other Canadian writers such as Lister Sinclair, Len Peterson, and Joseph Schull — each of whom wrote adaptations for radio as well as original scripts.

Although at least eight radio stations could be heard in Winnipeg, Peggy rarely mentioned the American stations (NBC and CBS). She preferred to review programs from Canadian stations, including CKSB, St. Boniface, Manitoba, which sponsored French broadcasts, and the provincial station CKY which also carried programs from the Canadian Broadcasting Corporation .

Her column included remarks about widely diverse radio programs such as: "The Farm Roundup," "Sports Digest," "Movie News," "20 Questions," "Music of Ukraine," "Cuckoo Clock House" (a children's program), and "Saturday Night Party." She also wrote at length about specific broadcasts that she had heard, for example, "The Dybbuk," a Jewish folktale; Bach's *St. Matthew Passion*; and Shakespeare's *Richard II*. Radio gave her the opportunity to listen to broadcasts and to discussions of literary works by authors such as Dorothy Sayers, Jane Austen, Alexander Dumas, John Donne, and T.S. Eliot. Listening to and writing about some these works was an excellent way for Peggy, an aspiring author herself, to ponder important elements of good literature.

While working for *The Westerner* and later the *Winnipeg Citizen*, Peggy also contributed at least a dozen book reviews. Her tone in these reviews is confident, emphatic, and more assertive than in reviews done in her later years when she was more sympathetic and less caustic toward authors. Although as a young journalist Peggy applauded good Canadian writing, she did not hesitate to criticize work that she felt was stylistically ineffective or superficially Canadian. She even found fault with writers such as W.O. Mitchell and Martha Ostenso.

Peggy's review of Mitchell's novel *Who Has Seen the Wind* appeared in *The Westerner*. Although his novel was to become a Canadian classic, Peggy found much to critique in it: "After the round of applause being given to *Who Has Seen the Wind* has died down, it may possibly be found that the book does not, after all, entirely capture the spirit of the west."[388] She notes, "Those of us who have lived all our lives on the prairies and among its people, may perhaps doubt the validity of presenting so many characters as merely 'quaint.' Western Canada has its oddities, but they are not specifically those of Dogpatch."[389]

Although she praised the characters of Ben, the district ne'er-do-well, and his young son, she believed that "philosophically the novel is slim":

> The total effect is one of vagueness of thought plus an attempt to portray the prairies and their people as charming and odd. The beauty of the prairie is here, but not its awe, its bleakness, its vast, terrifying presence. The amusing qualities of people, and some of their pettiness, is here, but not the depths of their feeling. Gabrielle Roy, in *The Tin Flute*, and, in novels of the west, Sinclair Ross in *As For Me and My House*, have both done more to write Canadian novels that intensely portray people and their environment.[390]

Despite the fact that she had praised an earlier novel by Martha Ostenso, Peggy here declared sharply that the tone of Ostenso's recent book, *Milk Route*, was "just about as vigorous as the uninspired clip-clop of the milk-wagon horse on the route which she describes." Her review concluded: "The tales of *Milk Route* are obviously calculated to inspire a little smile, a little tear. In this reviewer they inspired more than a little annoyance."[391] At times, Peggy may have intended to be ironic, but her comments seem harsh and flippant. In reviewing *Everybody Slept Here*, for example, she stated, "Rarely can one get such a complete résumé of the plot from the book's cover."[392] And referring to a book about the Canadian Pacific Railway, she declared that the most dramatic element was its title: *When the Steel Went Through: A C.P.R. Saga by an Engineer*. Peggy's penchant for the caustic remark or witty phrase was tempered somewhat after she was contacted by an author whose book she had found unsatisfactory. Laurence later recalled that, following their conversation, she felt bad and was more inclined to look on book reviewing as "a great responsibility."[393]

Radio also provided an opportunity for her to celebrate many aspects of Canadian life and culture, including drama, art, music, and literature. She was particularly impressed with two movements from Alexander Brott's suite "From Sea to Sea," a musical portrait of British Columbia and the Prairie provinces.[394] Because she believed that Canadian music had been "badly neglected" by the public, largely because it had not been accessible to them, she suggested that the CBC continue symphonic broadcasts which featured the work of young musicians. She also empha-sized the fact that contemporary symphonic music would reach a wider audience only through radio.[395] In other articles she recommended "Music of the Ukraine," and referred to the "richly varied" composite of Canadian culture.[396] She also praised Winnipeg's CKSB, a French-lan-guage station, for its classical musical offerings and commended its direc-tor on several occasions. In April, she remarked that she had enjoyed a recent tour of their St. Boniface broadcasting station.[397] She applauded CKSB's program, "Let's Learn French," which then had two thousand active English participants who received scripts for every broadcast.[398] And she lamented a network's decision to discontinue Lister Sinclair's Friday-night radio talks. Her comments about that situation reveal a good deal about her own literary standards at that time.

> We shall miss Sinclair's biting, pithy wit in "Mainly About Music." Perhaps we liked Sinclair because he agreed with our own ideas about *Canadian art*, (e.g., that a novel doesn't have to be crammed full of beavers and maple leaves to be Canadian). Although one might accuse Sinclair of a degree of intellectual snobbery, he never failed to criticize the cheap and tawdry and never used his wit to harm the genuine. For our money he is a good critic, and we'd like to see him back on the air, surveying Canadian books.[399]

In longer reviews Peggy addressed issues that would later become central to her Manawaka novels, namely, the realistic evocation of small prairie towns and the creation of authentic characters.

She liked the gentle humour in *The Happy Time* by French-Canadian writer, Robert Fontaine, and called the radio series based on his book "the very best of Canadian humour."[400] She praised Stephen Leacock's *Sunshine Sketches of a Little Town* and enjoyed Wayne and Shuster's comedy routines, which she recommended because the writers were less self-conscious than American comedians and were "our boys." The things they talk about are known to Canadians, "not gags which center around happenings in Ohio."[401]

Preparing a radio column six days a week over a period of several months had a significant impact on Laurence's development as a writer. It helped sensitize her already keen ear to the nuances of speech, and her mind to the importance of character and plot. The single most important aspect of her work at the *Winnipeg Citizen* stemmed from the fact that she was expected to listen attentively to many hours of radio drama. As a result, Laurence came to admire the way in which radio appealed to a listener's imagination, and to believe, for example, that the staging of *Peer Gynt* could not possibly satisfy in the same way as "radio drama can do by relying on the listener's own mind."[402]

Her enthusiasm for radio drama, however, did not cloud her critical judgement or blind her to some of radio's limitations. As early as her second column for the *Winnipeg Citizen*, she found fault with a drama by John Drainie, which "fell far beneath the average" and was too much a "patchwork of events."[403] She also criticized several scripts that were broadcast on "Prairie Showcase" and "Winnipeg Drama." Laurence felt that some writers had been attracted to "the myth of the prairies and not its real self."[404] Plays from the Prairie region, she maintained, did not have to be "crammed with Manitoba maples, wheat fields and people who called each other 'pardner.'" She then raised the following questions: "What of the prairie's harshness and bleakness? What of the long snows and the unbearable winds? It seems to me that writers could do worse than admit this is a godforsaken, hard country, and take it from there. Why, despite its harshness, do people find beauty on the prairies? Why do farmers hate it, yet refuse to leave it? If these things were explored, we might have a 'Prairie Showcase' that would really justify its name."[405]

Laurence issued a rallying cry: "It's about time we aimed ourselves up and got rid of the national inferiority complex." She declared that Canada was tops in radio drama and the CBC's "Stage 48" was "head and shoulders above most American productions."[406] She was convinced of the superiority of Canadian radio over American programs, particularly those of the "superficial Hollywood variety," and believed that advertising sponsorship had had a deleterious effect on the style, type, and content of U.S. programs.

She also maintained that Canadian radio drama was far better than most offerings of the British Broadcasting Corporation, including "London Playhouse."[407] At least one of their dramas became a target for her quick pen. She wrote: "Moving with the sprightly pace of a lame elephant, *The Pile of Wood* was a mystery drama which concerned a young man who was killed and another young man who killed him. Beyond that I failed to penetrate. . . . *The Pile of Wood* sounded as if it had been written and produced by people whose mental equipment unhappily resembled its title."[408]

In her columns Laurence consistently applauded contemporary radio writers who were dealing with modern issues. She praised Max Shoub for his series "My City," and Len Peterson, who had done "the best job" of handling problems of the contemporary world.[409] She had frequent and unqualified praise for Joseph Schull's "Shadow of the Tree," which addressed the problems of living in the atomic age. Laurence, then twenty-one, predicted that Schull would become Canada's leading radio dramatist because his technical accomplishment had "matured amazingly."

Although in Neepawa, the well-established Wemyss and Simpson families were certainly middle-class, Peggy's comments about radio reflect a distinct preference for the working class. She had praise for "The Trouble with Yesterday," written by a London cab driver, because the tone was down-to-earth and the harshness of the main character's early life as a Russian Jew in the factories and slums of the cities had been accurately depicted; "the language was simple and direct, the words of a working man who knows whereof he speaks."[410]

In addition to being keenly interested in language appropriate to the character and subject, Peggy was intrigued by the way in which voice in radio drama can denote, through slight changes of tone, the development of personality as well as mood shifts. In the broadcast of *Madame Bovary*, for example, she thought that listeners could practically see Emma Bovary changing "from a slightly ethereal girl to a self-centered, brittle woman, as the note of greed for excitement became more pronounced."[411] She praised the actress who played Gertrude in a broadcast of *Hamlet*, remarking that through her voice she had been able to depict "the touch of decadence that surrounded Hamlet's mother, her full-blown and fast-disappearing beauty, and her essential weakness."[412] In another program, she criticized the speech of an Indian woman. "One minute she would say in excellent English 'Are you badly hurt' and the next, 'Me, Indian.'"[413]

When "Fire in the Snow," a drama that dealt with Captain Robert Scott's ill-fated expedition to the South Pole was broadcast, Peggy called attention to the female narrator. Because the woman's voice was so far removed from the icy wasteland of the barren Antarctic, Peggy felt it provided a fine contrast for the harsh suffering voices of the explorers and gave an ominous tone to the whole. She then suggested that producers seriously consider the idea of having a woman narrator: "Until fairly recently, women had no great part in radio. Men were always used as announcers, and still are, to a great extent. However the actresses on Stage 48 and some CBC produced talks have shown that women can speak over the radio without sounding as though they were in a receiving line at a tea."[414]

As a result of listening to so many varied radio broadcasts, Peggy confidently put forth a number of suggestions.[415] She proposed that the ten best contemporary plays be published in an annual anthology and recommended that sets of records be placed in libraries at CBC branches in Canada's chief cities.[416] In addition, she suggested that good radio programs be made available for school children, since radio brought a drama to life in a way that no amount of text reading could do. Her praise for CKRC's free radio school and its drama lab under the direction of Mauri Desourdy and Kay Parking, as well as her comments about their productions, underscore this point.

Laurence's appreciation of excellence in Canadian arts is apparent in her columns. She was impressed by a radio adaptation of E.J. Pratt's national epic, *Brébeuf and his Brethren*, an evocative narrative poem that deals with the seventeenth-century Jesuit mission to Canada. She noted that Pratt's sharp, realistic descriptions give the poem the sweep of the Canadian wilds. "It is," she declared, "one of the most moving of all Canadian poems."[417]

Laurence thought that the adventures of La Vérendrye or the explorers Radisson and Groseilliers would make good radio drama. After listening to a program about U.S. President Abraham Lincoln, she pointed out that the radio broadcast managed to convey the main features of the Lincoln legend, with his funeral train as focus, and using flash-back as method. Then, referring to Canadian history, she asked, "Why not write a play based on the life of Louis Riel?"

In fact, as a young journalist she made several references to Riel, the controversial Métis leader:

> There are few Canadian historical characters with enough color and significance to work into a similar drama. There are few Canadians who gather into themselves the salient features of their times and represent not only their individual story but part of the story of a growing country.
>
> Louis Riel is one of these. Whether you think of him as a madman, a misguided reformer or a sincere man, . . . the drama of his life is indisputable.[418]

In this 1948 column, her remarks are significant, because Margaret Laurence was to use Riel, as well as other Métis characters and their stories, in her Manawaka novels, most notably in *The Diviners* (1974). Laurence's understanding of the complexities of Canadian history and her desire to have stories that dealt with that history set down and produced are evident here at the outset of her professional career. This was to remain a major concern, rather than, as some have alleged, an interest that emerged only after her African sojourn in the 1950s.

While Peggy was working as a journalist, she and Jack lived in an upstairs apartment on Burrows Avenue in the home of Anne and Bill Ross in Winnipeg's North End. This was a vibrant and exciting part of the city, with a strong Jewish population as well as many diverse ethnic groups. Laurence says in her memoirs, "North Winnipeg in the 1940s decided a lot of my life."[419] Anne Ross remembers Peggy's excitement over her newspaper work and her joy in her marriage to Jack. Peggy was comfortable talking with Anne Ross, and often stopped by to see Anne's infant son or to chat after work at the *Winnipeg Citizen.*

The Wiseman family lived nearby. One of their daughters, Adele, was to become a lifelong friend of Margaret Laurence, and was then completing her senior year at the University of Manitoba. Peggy had previously lived in the North End for several months with fellow collegian, Mary Turnbull, and out of her experiences there wrote a very lengthy and ambitious poem, "North Main Car" (1948), which captures the variety and vibrancy of this working-class area of the city. It also offers evidence of themes and concerns that were to emerge in her later work, though not in the same garb. The poem's narrator, who is on a streetcar travelling from the North End to downtown Winnipeg, gives memorable descriptions of a variety of passengers, among them a young man who works in a slaughter house, a middle-aged Irish mother, and a Jewish shopkeeper who is going to visit his daughter.

While living on Burrows Avenue, Laurence herself travelled by streetcar from the North End to the *Winnipeg Citizen*'s office on Selkirk Avenue and to assignments in various parts of the city. Living on Burrows Avenue, she also had the good fortune to be brought into the Wiseman family by Adele, whose mother, Chaika, treated Peggy with affection. She felt "bathed in her kindness and concern."[420] Chaika Wiseman and Anne Ross were fond of Peggy, and she appreciated being welcomed into their homes and families. Margaret Laurence was to remain in contact with these older women throughout her life, whether in person, by mail, or by telephone. Although her connection to each was quite distinctive, they were very important to her and she cherished each of them. Anne Ross remembers Peggy's "easy laughter. She was buoyant, full of vigor, and interested in people." Peggy had an inquiring mind and plied Anne and her husband with lots of questions. She wanted to understand everything, and was eager for new experiences.[421] Anne Ross, who was about fifteen years older than Peggy and a nurse, became something of an elder sister to her.[422] Although her husband, Bill, was an active Communist, Anne was not a member of the party.[423]

Across the street, Chaika Wiseman always had a warm, smiling welcome for Peggy. Although Chaika had little formal education, she was fluent in several languages, and worked beside her husband in the small tailor shop in their home. The Wisemans' income was modest, but the family was rich in love, warmth, and open-handed hospitality. For Peggy this was a wonderful shift from the household of Grandfather Simpson, where spontaneity was frowned upon and every member seemed to be "walking on eggshells."

Laurence left the *Winnipeg Citizen* in the summer of 1948, and then worked for a while as registrar at Winnipeg's YWCA.[424] In her memoirs, she states that she left the paper in protest over the editor's accusation that she was a Communist.[425] She did return to its office, however, on the morning of April 13, 1949, when staff members gathered after the last issue of the paper appeared on the streets of Winnipeg.[426] Serious financial difficulties had plagued the paper for several months, and, as Harry Ferns himself once noted, "falling in love with an idea is one thing, attempting to translate an idea into an instrument of social action is quite another matter."[427] Although Peggy and Jack's political sympathies were to the Left, Peggy was never a member of the Communist Party and always identified herself as a Christian Social Democrat.[428]

In her last signed article for the *Winnipeg Citizen*, she focused on freedom of speech and celebrated the unique freedom of radio programs such as "Points of View," which aired opposing views on difficult questions. In an earlier column, she had praised the freedom, diversity, and initiative traditionally displayed by speakers in England's Hyde Park and in that last piece for the *Winnipeg Citizen* (September 1948), she wholeheartedly endorsed responsible freedom of expression:

> Our radio writers must be allowed to keep every iota
> of writing freedom and even to extend and broaden it.
> I believe that it is the business of all of us to insist
> upon this. For perhaps, after all, the most important

job the CBC has to fulfill is that of holding up a mirror to our difficult times.

Public school history texts relate that Good Queen Bess destroyed all the mirrors in her house when she felt that she was losing her beauty. If the CBC ever reaches the point, as various information sources have been known to do, of allowing only one side of any picture to be shown, we shall have smashed our mirrors, and for reasons similar to those of the queen.

Although the mirror has flaws, the fact that it exists at all is a thing vigorously to be maintained through every apparent crisis.[429]

Laurence elaborated here on a theme that she was to return to throughout her career: the significance of freedom and responsibility, both for individuals and for nations. Not only does she refer to it in these newspaper articles, but also in her book reviews. Thirty-six years later, this theme appeared again in one of Margaret Laurence's last essays "The Greater Evil" (1984). There she quoted F.R. Scott's words, "Freedom is a habit that must be kept alive by use." She then added a characteristic note of her own: "Freedom, however, means responsibility and concern toward others."[430]

Reading Laurence's early newspaper columns helps to illumine a significant period in her literary development. The young Peggy Wemyss, who had moved from a small prairie town to the bustling capital of Manitoba during the tumultuous closing years of the Second World War certainly had her horizons expanded and her literary ambitions fostered while writing for *The Westerner* and the *Winnipeg Citizen*. The cultural diversity mirrored in the sights, sounds, and pace of life in North Winnipeg, as well as the competing agricultural and labour interests of the city and its outlying areas, all combined to claim her attention as a young journalist. In 1949, following Jack's graduation from the University of Manitoba, they left Winnipeg and set off by ship for England, where they remained for several months before Jack found a position as an engineer with a British government project in distant East Africa, in the British Somaliland Protectorate.

Although Peggy Wemyss/Laurence's involvement in the world of journalism lasted less than two years, it was, nevertheless, of great importance in her personal and professional development. In Peggy's newspaper columns, this young woman, who had the drive to become a professional writer, used the opportunities of journalism to hone her skills. Of course, she had to meet newspaper deadlines, carry out her responsibilities, and fit her remarks to the allotted space, but undoubtedly one of the most important contributions to her development as a writer came as the result of writing a daily radio column. Hours of listening to excellent radio drama constituted an important part of Margaret Laurence's literary apprenticeship. Listening helped to train her ear to the nuances of language, the effectiveness of dialogue, and the subtle rhythms of the spoken word.

CHAPTER SEVEN
New Territory

In her mature years, Margaret Laurence was well aware of the advantages and disadvantages of her place of birth. The limitations of her hometown and a host of sad memories made it impossible for her to consider living in Neepawa as an adult. The sudden deaths of her mother and father, her uncle, and her favourite grandmother had created in her deep feelings of insecurity. It was clear to her that, at any moment, the established order of things could change forever, whether from a virulent flu, kidney infection, polio, or pneumonia. For Peggy Wemyss Laurence, a future away from Manitoba and Neepawa would be no more uncertain than the sudden tragic losses that she had already experienced there.

After Margaret Laurence's husband received his engineering degree in 1949, the world seemed to beckon. Peggy shared Jack's idealistic career goals and was grateful that he, too, valued literature. She was eager to set out with him for adventures overseas. In the summer of 1949, although they were "almost penniless," they sailed for England, hoping that from there Jack would find significant work in a developing country.[431] He wanted "a job that plainly needed doing ... [and] whose value could not be questioned, a job in which the results of an individual's work could be clearly perceived, as they rarely could in Europe or America."[432]

This would be Peggy's first trip abroad, but for Jack, who had served overseas during the Second World War, England was familiar territory. Peggy was tremendously excited at the prospect of spending time in the land of Chaucer, Milton, and Shakespeare, and the many other English poets whose works she had memorized in high school and college. Now, that "sceptred isle" was to be her home, at least for several months.

The couple found lodgings at Fairfax Mansions on Finchley Road in northwest London. It sounded rather grand in her letters home, but, in fact, their accommodations were rather shabby. No doubt the inconveniences seemed slight to Peggy when measured against the amazing fact that she was actually living in England. Twenty years later, however, she reported that their London "apartment" had been "a bed-sitting room," with a shared bath in the corridor and a nightly bath schedule that resembled a railway timetable.[433] She and Jack wrote a lively letter to family and friends in late November. High spirits are evident in that account of their months in England. On the first page, they pasted humorous cartoons, for which they supplied their own captions. Several pages were written by Jack, who commented at length about the postwar situation in Socialist Britain.[434]

Peggy secured a clerical job at an employment agency nearby, and later wrote reassuringly to Adele Wiseman, who had expressed interest in finding work in England, noting that jobs were available and the cost of living not too high. Jack also urged Adele: "Do, come over. England is a dynamic country . . . a vital provocative land and as such worth experiencing." Then, using a line from T.S. Eliot, Jack assured her that she would no longer be "measuring out her life with coffee spoons."[435]

Peggy, with a touch of bravado, reported that they had been managing quite well on their combined wages of nine pounds per week. She did not mention the bleaker aspects of life in postwar Britain. Although they had to monitor their budget carefully, she bragged that they were able to cook nourishing meals on a single gas ring, and often had salads and fresh fruit:

> We buy three daily papers and one weekly magazine. . . .
> We entertain a bit, not lavishly, but we frequently have
> people in for meals. We do not drink, but we sometimes

buy bottles of ale or cider, altho' we can't afford hard liquor. We smoke about 10 cigarettes a day. We are, in fact, living in relative luxury and comfort.[436]

Although their income was limited, Peggy and Jack decided to put a shilling a week into the English football pools. Once they won sixty-four pounds, which was a small fortune to them: "We were absurdly happy about this 'found' money, and have decided to spend it recklessly. Half of it will go towards our holidays, which we fervently hope to spend in France and Italy. The rest is being spent on concerts, theatres, ballet, clothes and books."[437]

With their winnings they were able to see *The Bicycle Thief*, attend performances of *The Heiress* and *Black Chiffon*, and several concerts at the Albert Hall; at one of which Sir Malcolm Sargent conducted the London Philharmonic Orchestra in Beethoven's Ninth Symphony. Peggy remarked on the chorus celebrating the brotherhood of man (based on Schiller's "Ode to Joy") and told Adele, "Beethoven was really a revolutionary, respectable as his music may be today."[438] Peggy's letters are filled with comments about sights, activities, and customs that she found interesting in England. They also reflect her ongoing concern for ordinary workers during Britain's difficult postwar years.

During their first months in London, Peggy and Jack also attended a play about a Jewish working-class family, *The Golden Door*, and toured the plant of the *Daily Worker*, a Communist paper. Recalling her summer job at the Neepawa Press, Peggy noticed that the plant had about thirty linotype machines and "a beautiful Goss rotary press." She and Jack were "particularly impressed with the printers themselves, who, altho' they were busy were extremely courteous, and even anxious to explain how the various machines worked."[439] The couple also went to Highgate Cemetery to see the grave of Karl Marx. "Bizarre though that tomb was, covered with red roses placed there by a delegation of Yugoslavians who were just leaving as we approached, we found another part of the cemetery which was yet more bizarre." That was the tomb of the writer Radclyffe Hall. In an area of locked crypts filled with weeds, her coffin lay on a marble slab behind an iron grille. There were fresh flowers and a card from her companion, Una.[440]

Peggy, like many of her generation, had become interested in Marxism during her college years. Later, while working for two Winnipeg newspapers between 1947 and 1949, she had become keenly aware of class and race issues amidst the struggle for jobs and decent housing in the city. The ideals set forth by Marx appealed to Jack and Peggy, as they did to many others who had struggled through the years of the Great Depression. Communism, as it was then understood in North America, seemed to offer hope for a more equitable future and a more just distribution of goods. Although Peggy always considered herself a Christian Socialist and was never a member of the Party, she did have friends who were Communists.[441] At United College, she and other collegians could be found from time to time singing "The Internationale," the international song of both Marxist and non-Marxist socialist parties. According to Helen Warkentin, it is not quite clear whether they did so in jest or in earnest.[442] The same group of undergraduates had been roundly upbraided at United College for attending a lecture by Tim Buck, General Secretary of the Communist Party of Canada.[443]

Peggy's concern for greater social justice and respect for non-Christians was keenly personal. It had been fostered by the atmosphere at United College and augmented by her close friendship with Adele Wiseman's family and others such as Anne and Bill Ross in the Jewish community of Winnipeg's North End. Her abhorrence of anti-Semitism and concern for workers and matters of social justice were to remain strong throughout her life.

Within a few months of arriving in England, Peggy sent off at least two poems to the *Canadian Tribune*, a Communist paper. One of them, "Let My Voice Live," was published there on January 9, 1950. She remembered that the layout was attractive and had two photographs appropriate to the poem's subject. Peggy signed herself simply as "Meg — A Canadian in England." Narrated by an old woman who is making a plea for peace and the cessation of war, "Let My Voice Live" is a moving poem about old age and war. It opens as follows:

> I am a childless woman, old,
> And like my frail world, bled to grey.
> A dry husk, my seasons' fruitfulness

Dead as those lads whose bones now melt
Like lifeless leaves into that hillside
Hideously mellow with their fallen flesh.

It is not surprising that Peggy was writing poetry at this time. She had studied a great deal of poetry in college and written many poems then, but her choice of an aging narrator is unusual for a twenty-three-year-old, and seems to point forward to the elderly Hagar, the unforgettable central character in *The Stone Angel* (1964), the first of her Manawaka novels. Although parts of the poem are self-consciously dramatic and over-wrought, the theme is a significant expression of Peggy's abiding concern about the ravages of war.[444] She also submitted to the *Canadian Tribune* a poem that dealt with the revolt of the Italian peasants in the autumn of 1949. She felt it was better than "Let My Voice Live"; however, the poem has not been located and may never have been published.[445]

While Jack and Peggy were living in England, they managed a trip to Paris, where they stayed in the Latin Quarter and visited many famous art museums and historic buildings. In August 1950, Adele Wiseman arrived from Canada and was warmly welcomed by them. Peggy had been able to secure a job for her at the Stepney Jewish Girls' Club in London's East End. Adele and Margaret were delighted to see one another and eager to hear about the progress of their respective manuscripts. Adele was absorbed with the manuscript that was to become her award-winning novel *The Sacrifice*, but it is not clear what Peggy was then working on. Impressed by Adele's book, which was nearing completion, Peggy sent off this enthusiastic account to the Wiseman family: "We read each other's scripts and told each other that we were going to write the two great novels of the century! In actual fact, however, if she [Adele] gets this novel of hers finished the way she wants it to be, it will be infinitely better than anything I shall ever write. She has got a tremendous amount of talent."[446]

The friendship between these two young women was to endure, becoming a lifelong source of strength and joy as they continued to develop their respective literary talents against the backdrop of their uncertain futures.

Within a few months of the Laurences' arrival in England, Jack had been offered a position with the British Colonial Service as an irrigation engineer in East Africa; it was the sort of work he had been hoping for and, by mid-November, they were busy packing crates and shopping for the voyage to the Horn of Africa. "What do you take to such an out-of-the-way place," Peggy later wrote, "when you have no idea of what life will be like there? Tents or topees, evening dress or bush boots, quinine or codeine, candles or sandals?"[447] Jack purchased an evening suit for the first time in his life, and Peg "got a lovely formal dress, fully washable as there is no dry cleaning in Somaliland." They finally embarked, like Melville's Ishmael, during a "sleet-sodden English December," and went to Rotterdam, where they planned to board the *Tigre*, a vessel bound for the British Somaliland Protectorate. However, their departure was delayed, because the ship had not yet arrived in port.

Despite their keen disappointment at the delay, Peggy and Jack decided to make the most of their time in Rotterdam. They strolled the cobblestone streets, looked at the old buildings, and examined Delft pottery, which Peggy found "awfully traditional." She much preferred the modern ceramics displayed in the Handicrafts Centre. Writing to Adele in the tone of a sophisticated traveller, Peggy noted that the town's fourteenth-century cathedral was "hideous" and, referring to Ruskin's essays on architecture, remarked that the cathedral had "none of the mounting lines or impression of having grown out of the earth and striving towards heaven" that one finds in French and English Gothic.[448] In Rotterdam the couple was impressed with the ultra-modern buildings that had been erected after the war, and spent hours at the new Museum Boymans [Boijmans], admiring its modern construction of grey marble and white stone. There they studied paintings by Rembrandt, Rubens, and Van Gogh, and admired bronzes by Epstein, Henry Moore, and Zadkine. Peggy was struck by Ossip Zadkine's bronze "Orpheus," which she noted was "very angular and tree-like, with his lyre growing out of his ribs like a branch."[449]

When the *Tigre* finally docked in Rotterdam, Jack and Peggy discovered they were to be the only passengers on board and would occupy the owner's suite: "an unbelievably spacious three rooms, full of polished brass, green plush and shiny mahogany."[450] It was a marvellous change from their lodgings in Rotterdam and their cramped, cold bed-sit in London. The Norwegian ship's accommodations were like a fantasy come true. The journey was to take over a month, and en route to Africa, Peggy and Jack had a memorable Christmas celebration, thanks to a thoughtful crew. One chap, after discovering that Jack's people were from the Shetland Islands, originally settled by Norsemen, leapt to his feet and proposed a Christmas toast: "To our ancestors and yours — the Vikings!"

By December 27, 1949, the *Tigre* was off the coast of Portugal and approaching Gibraltar. They had time to observe the sights, talk with the sailors, and read. Jack was finishing *War and Peace*, while Peggy was engrossed in *The Brothers Karamazov*, "a joy to read." She told Adele: "I've never read a book that impressed me so much with its sharpness of perception, vividness of dialogue, and way of catching the full complexity of its characters. It really is tremendous."[451]

Peggy and Jack savoured their journey by ship. After rounding Gibraltar and passing into the Mediterranean Sea, the *Tigre* remained in Genoa for several days. There they climbed the nearby hills and visited the Staglieno cemetery, where Peggy noted the marble angels among the dark cypress trees. Her memory of that sight was to give her, fourteen years later, the paradoxical image that provided the title for her first major success as a novelist, *The Stone Angel*.[452]

Peggy found the Mediterranean at that time of year awe-inspiring. It was "truly the wine-dark sea of Homer." One passage in *The Prophet's Camel Bell* captures some of her excitement: "High up on the *Tigre*, whipped by the icy winds, we watched the wild hills of Sicily pass by. At night we saw a far-off red glow in the black sky, Mount Etna in eruption. And sometimes in the darkness we saw a phosphorescence, plankton perhaps, frothing up suddenly in the waves and seeming to run along the surface of the water like sheet lightning."[453]

During the voyage, Peggy worked steadily on a novel and managed to complete three chapters, although she only briefly alludes to that in her extant letters.

As the ship made its way towards Port Said, their anticipation grew. Soon they would be in the Horn of Africa. A more exotic destination could hardly be imagined. Sailing on the Mediterranean in February, far from Neepawa's snow-covered streets, with responsibilities only for herself and her husband, Peggy's sense of excitement was tangible. She was twenty-three; there would be plenty of time for adventure.

EAST AFRICA: 1950-1952

At last the *Tigre* was past the Suez Canal, through the Red Sea, and into the Gulf of Aden, where, in addition to freighters, hundreds of fishing dhows with "their curved prows and triangular sails" dotted the sea.[454] Peg and Jack disembarked at Aden, where their baggage was put on board a "little tramp steamer." Jack, who had spent a number of years in transit during the war, slept well on the straw mattress, while Peggy, who had "an unpleasant suspicion that they were not the only living creatures in the cabin," slept fitfully. Later, on deck, holding onto her broad-brimmed straw hat and with warm salt spray on her arms, she caught sight of "a Somali coolie," perched on the ship's prow. "As the boat rode high, caught in a sudden swell of waves, I saw his face against the sky . . . a face I could not read at all, a well-shaped brown face that seemed expressionless, as though whatever lay behind his eyes would be kept carefully concealed. I wondered if his was the face of Africa."[455]

The Horn of Africa was still under the colonial rule of three European powers: France, England, and Italy. While France had the smallest section, England and Italy had carved out significant portions of Somaliland, attracted not by Somalia's negligible natural resources, but by its strategic location along the Gulf of Aden, the water route to the East.

At last Jack and Peggy reached the British Somaliland Protectorate and disembarked at Berbera. Arrangements had been made for their arrival, and Jack returned with a Somali lad of eighteen, Mohamed, who was to be their houseboy. The couple's difference of opinion about that situation quickly surfaced. Peg thought it "absurd" to have a servant so soon, and she was distressed by the prospect of being called "memsahib," a word that was familiar to her from the fiction of Rudyard Kipling and Somerset Maugham. To Peggy, memsahib had connotations of the "white man's burden" and paternalism — colonial attitudes she deplored. Jack, with dwindling patience, tried to explain: "This isn't Winnipeg or London. You don't tote your own luggage here. It just isn't done. Maybe we don't agree with the system, but there it is."[456] His practical approach, born of experience in those parts of the world, could be summed up: "You have to learn that if you can't change something, you might as well not worry about it."[457]

From Berbera the couple continued their journey by truck toward the city of Hargeisa, the government centre of the Protectorate. Situated on an ancient caravan route that went from the interior to the port cities, Hargeisa had a population of about forty thousand people.

As the truck lurched over some of "the worst roads in the world," Peggy's brown eyes scanned miles and miles of yellow sand stretching away in the distance. Glistening with mica, the sand slid down into long, ribbed dunes. Occasionally the scene changed near a water-hole or a *tug* (dry river bed) that was still a bit moist. Then Peggy saw "bright green grass, bulrushes, a tangle of palms and pepper trees, marvelously green and alive."[458] Such places were rare, however, and they drove for hours across a barren, seemingly empty landscape. It was the *Jilal* season: the hot, arid period of the northeast monsoon.[459] There in the Horn of Africa, the pages of the *National Geographic* magazines that Peggy had pored over as a child came to life for her. As a youngster she had written simple stories about travel to exotic places and drawn intricate maps of imaginary lands. Now that world of her youthful creation encountered the more complex and subtle realities of her new life in an ancient land.

As the journey continued, they passed nomads' encampments with their *akhals*, portable dwellings made of woven grass and twigs. Peggy noticed Somali women in long robes helping with the burden-camels. Once in a while, a turbaned man holding a spear could be seen with a small herd of black-headed sheep gathered around him. During most of the long, bumpy truck ride, however, the dusty land seemed devoid of life.

After finally reaching Hargeisa, they moved into temporary quarters, while Jack became acquainted with details at the government office and made plans to assemble men and begin work. His assignment was to construct thirty *ballehs* (shallow earthen reservoirs) at ten-mile intervals in the southwestern part of the Protectorate. These *ballehs*, each holding about three million gallons, were intended to hold water from the seasonal rains and thereby ease the drought that afflicted the Somalis' herds of grazing camels, upon which their lives and livelihoods depended. The *ballehs* were to be situated in the Haud, a high plateau that covered about twenty-five thousand square miles, and lay partly in the Somaliland Protectorate and partly in Ethiopia. During the grazing season that followed the rains, approximately three hundred thousand

Somalis moved into the Haud for several months in order to graze their camels and livestock.

Before Jack went off to begin construction of the *ballehs*, he and Peggy were able to move out of the busy city of Hargeisa and into Sheikh, a small station high in the mountains. They were glad to do so because, as Canadians on contract, they did not feel very comfortable among the set of British colonial officers and their wives. Peggy especially felt out of place in the midst of what to her seemed to be an extension of the British empire. Furthermore, her frank style of stating her opinions was not well received by them.

Although Sheikh was small, it was the educational centre of the Northern region, where the chief government school had been established.[460] It was also one of the few places in the Protectorate that remained reasonably green all year round. There was always "a merciful breeze," and the climate was "absolutely perfect."[461] Peggy described Sheikh as "the best place in Somaliland." Indeed, it seemed quite marvellous after the previous year in their cold London quarters.

Peggy's excitement and curiosity were boundless as she and Jack settled into their timbered bungalow. They were delighted with such comfortable quarters. After three years of living in various apartments, this was their first home! The Sheikh bungalow had a wonderful view of the hills and a good-sized living room, with a big stone fireplace that they used when the evenings were cool.

Peggy quickly set about making curtains of unbleached cotton for the living room and bedroom. She designed block prints of autumn leaves, and embroidered a large green-and-yellow snail ("one of the few things I can draw") on cushions for their wicker chairs. She felt she had become "surprisingly housewifely."[462] Peggy's description of the view from their new home makes clear why she found Sheikh so special, almost enchanted:

> Our front door is like a picture frame, and the picture contains the soft line of hills; the red sand of the valley and the blue-green rocks; the green flat-topped trees; a flock of tiny white sheep, grazing a few feet from the house, and tended by a brown-robed Somali woman

with a scarlet headscarf. The *yerki* (little boy) is there too, with his little switch of dried grass, rounding up the stragglers in the flock. I think it is the quiet one notices most about Sheikh. During the whole sunny day, only the odd scrap of birdsong; the strange minor-key chanting of the boys as they work; the early morning clank of water-tins as the Somali woman brings up our three donkey-loads of water each morning; the frantic chirp of the *yerki*, a little boy so tiny that one can hardly see how he copes with the relatively large cows he drives through the valley; and the occasionally tic-tic-tic of a lizard in the walls of the house. There is a strange air of peace here, almost a Shangri-la atmosphere.[463]

In this letter to Adele Wiseman, Peggy undoubtedly drew upon the diary that she was keeping in Somaliland, but her carefully structured descriptions are different from her rather casual remarks in other letters. The colours of the place and people are precisely presented before the focus shifts and the description of the little *yerki* leads directly to the sounds she noticed. The passage is evidence of the sort of challenge Peggy had set herself as a writer — to capture in words Somaliland and its people.

In Sheikh, their neighbours were several British and a few Somali teachers who were connected with the government school. Peg remarked that the director of education, Chris Bell, and his wife, Jane, were extremely nice people, "very interested in literature." The others were "passable."[464] Jane Bell, from whom Peggy learned a great deal, taught a class of local Somali girls and instructed them in the care of their homes, children, and health. She was also careful to use materials that would be locally available to the girls after they married.[465] Jane Bell realized that some of these girls might leave their nomadic way of life and became settled in towns or cities. Then, such instruction would be quite important to them.

While Jack Laurence was away in the Haud, Peggy was able to spend much of her time writing and, by the end of the first month in Sheikh, she had completed chapter four of the novel she had been writing on board the *Tigre*. She now had the opportunity for uninterrupted time to write in pleasant surroundings where housekeeping tasks were done by local servants. It was, she realized, a rare privilege; one not shared by her female counterparts back home. With servants and with quiet, Peggy was able to pursue her writing with a single-minded diligence.

The profound peace of Sheikh was almost tangible. One night while Jack was away, Peggy set out at dusk under a dark-blue sky to fetch a dog they had been minding. The dog would not remain with the Laurences, however, preferring his master's place about a mile away. Whenever an opportunity arose, he headed back home. As Peg was returning to the bungalow with the dog, she began to feel anxious:

> I won't say I wasn't a bit scared. I kept thinking of wild boars (plentiful here) and camels. Especially the latter, which are ugly tempered and very nasty. But I saw nothing unusual, and suddenly I felt much better — the sky was pitch dark, but the earth was lit by a huge bright moon and thousands of the clearest stars I've ever seen. Everything was silent — only the faint dry rustling of the brown trees, and the sound of my sandals on stone. It was lovely and peaceful and a little sad because it was such a short way away from perfection. The hills could be seen in the starlight, looming blacker than the sky. Then suddenly I heard a tiny voice. The voice, which appeared to be coming out of a bush, chirped brightly, "Good Morning!" It was a pint-sized Somali herd-boy, proudly using his one English phrase.[466]

The vast starlit sky seemed familiar to her prairie eyes. Indeed, there were certain features of this unfamiliar land that did remind Peggy of home: the limitless horizon, the stalwart natives enduring extremes of weather, the ability to "make do" in the face of adversity.

The next month she sent Adele an enthusiastic letter summarizing the highlights of her first trip to several sites where the *ballehs* were to be constructed: "We camped in our big tent. . . . It was great fun. We went out shooting, and got several deer for meat, and visited *ballehs* in the surrounding area, and talked to the local inhabitants."[467] As the days passed, Peg reflected: "It's a wonderful life out here in camp, though, despite any difficulties, and we both enjoy it tremendously. We were so glad to get away from Hargeisa, with all its constant and unvarying drink-parties, its bed-hoppers, and its gossip."[468]

One day, however, Jack returned from surveying in the Haud covered with red dust. He looked weary and grim. Peggy assumed there had been problems with the engineering scheme, but that was not the case. Jack had been overwhelmed by what he had witnessed in the Haud: Somalis were dying of thirst, and all along the road he had passed bodies of burden-camels that had died before they could reach the wells.

His dismal report caused Peggy concern, but in their bungalow, amid the tranquil and beautiful Sheikh hills, it was difficult for her to fully comprehend the significance of Jack's report and the extent of the suffering. In *The Prophet's Camel Bell* she frankly remarks, "I had not seen them die, and so I did not really know at all."[469] As time passed, however, she was to share his experience of both human and animal suffering during the *Jilal* season.

Jack was able to obtain permission for Peggy to accompany him regularly on treks into the Haud. There the Somalis, the animals, and the land were reeling under the impact of a terrible drought, which had gone on for the better part of a year. Peggy described the scene: "For miles across the flat plains we could see only the long expanse of dark red sand and a few grey thorn trees, dry to the core, looking frail and brittle in the glare of the sunlight. From time to time in the distance there were great structures that looked like towers."[470] Those structures were termite mounds, which sometimes reached twenty to thirty feet in height. The landscape on all sides was exotic and unfamiliar.

Peggy lived in the work camp in the Haud for weeks at a time and had unique experiences that were not encountered by British wives, who generally remained in the government stations. With Jack, she saw the impact of the *Jilal* on humans as well as animals. As their Land Rover crossed the desert terrain, they observed small bands of Somali nomads leading their lean, thirst-weakened camels across the waterless plains in a desperate effort to reach the already-overcrowded wells. One day on the Awareh—Hargeisa road, Jack and Peggy noticed an exhausted young woman squatting in the sand, a baby carried across one hip. Nearby were two forlorn burden-camels, laden with "crescent-shaped hut-frames and the bundled mats."[471] Seeing the woman alone in the desert, Peggy wondered: Had her tribe had gone ahead or was this poor woman the last survivor? They stopped the Land Rover and offered water. The woman silently filled a little tin and carefully held it for the child to drink first. Then she drank, rose, and walked on slowly, leading the parched camels. The incident was one that Peggy never forgot.[472] She returned to it again in *A Tree for Poverty*, in *The Prophet's Camel Bell*, and in *Dance on the Earth*.

While Peggy was on trek with Jack, she developed a deep respect for their servants, as well as for his work crew. She also became intrigued by Somali oral literature and developed a keen interest in Somali culture. C.J. Martin, an Englishman then working in the Protectorate, shared his memory of her uniqueness: "Peggy is outstanding in my recollection because of the intensity of her interest in everything around her and her transparent fascination with the Somali scene. Unlike most of her housewifely contemporaries there, she made conscious, deliberate efforts to identify with the Somalis and to discover and learn all she could about them."[473]

Peggy was often intolerant of the British in the colonial service and her impatience with them seems a natural outcome of the situations in which she found herself. Her scathing descriptions of the worst of the sahib and memsahib types may be found in "The Imperialists" chapter of *The Prophet's Camel Bell*, written ten years after leaving Somaliland. By that time, however, she had tempered some of her initial responses, achieving enough distance to analyze the situation. She was able to report, "Yet, I do not feel the same anger now."[474]

During one of their trips, the drought ended abruptly with the arrival of the rains. Jack and Peggy had set out in the Land Rover with their driver to make a quick check on one of the sites. The man lost his way, however, and decided to take a shortcut across the plateau towards their destination. Suddenly the rains began. Within an hour the vehicle was mired in sticky red mud right up to the front axles: "The spring rains came with violence, the sky opening, a black flood of water cloaking the land, the storm winds screaming through the nights, for no rain is as sudden and attacking as the desert rains."[475] During a break in the rain, the driver spoke with passing camel herders, who agreed to send help. After several hours, men arrived and managed to pull the Land

Rover out of the mud. No sooner had that been accomplished, however, when the rains began again.

This time the three of them were in imminent danger, as the water roared violently down the dry river beds that served as roads. In the Land Rover they could do nothing against the powerful force of the water. While forked lightning, "a bright, terrifying pink," crashed to earth all around them in the middle of that vast, treeless plain, they said, "We are in the hands of Allah."[476] Fortunately they remained unharmed and were able to continue the journey the next day. Peggy felt safe with Jack at her side even in those alarming conditions. She had complete confidence that his military experiences, maturity, and general expertise would be adequate to any situation.

As the journey continued, they came to a Somali teashop along the caravan route. There, the impoverished owner spread his best embroidered quilt for Peggy to rest on and, in the spirit of hospitality which is a characteristic of many nomadic cultures, he offered them dried dates, bowls of steamed rice, and hot tea. He would not accept any payment.[477]

After the rains fell, the Haud was transformed:

> Now the grass grew several feet tall, ruffled by the wind and swaying greenly. . . . The whole land was laced with flowers. White blossoms like clover were sprinkled through the short grass under the acacias. There were pale yellow flowers the colour of rich cream, and small mauve "wahharowallis," and the scarlet flowers of the aloes spreading out on slender branches like some mythical tree. The air was full of the songs of birds.[478]

Peggy noticed small, light green butterflies gathered around pools of water along the road. Clustered together they looked like a gigantic flower with innumerable fluttering petals.[479]

The Somali nomads, relieved to have survived months of the *Jilal*, were threatened after the rains by another danger — malaria, the largest child-killer in all Africa. Across the region, hundreds of children as well as adults, struck by malaria, were now suffering and dying. It was difficult for Peggy to see those young children: "Their small limbs burned to the touch, and they shuddered spasmodically with the fever's compulsive chills. Their eyes occasionally flickered open in a kind of bewilderment. And I turned away, unable to meet those eyes."[480]

Out in the Haud, Peggy usually remained in camp with their servant, Mohamed, and a few labourers, while Jack and the crew went off to survey or drill test holes. Jack and his native advisers soon began to realize that the *balleh* scheme was not well understood by the wandering tribesmen, who deeply resented the European presence in their land. A rumour began that the English had poisoned the water in the *ballehs*. Jack was worried that the tribesmen's fear and resentment might cause a situation in which the whole camp would be in danger, so he suggested that Peggy learn how to use a rifle. She agreed and they walked to the edge of camp. There he loaded the powerful .303 and advised her, "Hold it tight against your shoulder."[481] Trembling, Peggy aimed it off into the empty distance and fired. "Whoom! Stunningly, I found myself sprawled on the ground, the rifle beside me."[482] That brought the effort at armed defence to an end. They decided, instead, to exercise more caution when delegations of tribesmen arrived in camp to inquire about the *ballehs*.

Another day, after watching the *Illaloes* (the native police) practice spear-throwing, Peg decided to give it a try. She threw a few spears, without much success, but she had learned something: "The chief skill to be mastered was balance."[483] Peggy appears undaunted by going on trek, sleeping in the back of the Bedford truck, facing the barren Haud or the Somali tribesmen. While she may have been shy socially, she was not timid or fearful. One contemporary said that what she most remembered from knowing Peggy then "was her enthusiasm and curiosity about everything. She just seemed to fall into Somali life quite naturally, and was without naiveté or preconceived ideas that might have interfered with her happy acceptance of this quite different life."[484]

From her letters and from comments by others who were in Somalia at the same time, it is clear that Peggy embraced the many new experiences and was remarkably open to the intricacies of a completely new culture. She even took driving lessons from Jack, but the prospects were not good:

I lose all semblance of poise and become like Stephen
Leacock in a bank. I have a terrible desire to drop the
wheel and take my eyes from the road while I am
changing gears, and apply both hands to the gear lever.
The day when I can successfully put the car into reverse
and drive it out in the required manner without back-
ing into the fence, shines like a beacon in my mind —
a far off goal to be aimed at but not really expected. Jack
is very patient.[485]

In the evening when she and Jack were on trek, they gathered with
his crew under the desert sky, which was open from one side of the horizon to the other, reminding Peggy of the great prairie sky in Manitoba.
During that respite from their labours in the harsh desert, the group's
tribal differences seemed less pronounced and there was a sense of community and peace as the men chanted age-old poems, accompanied by
gestures. Then Peggy may have felt she was at the "still point of the turning world."[486] One night after a fierce storm had passed through, they all
remained around the campfire until nearly morning. "Hersi led the
singing, chanting the verse of a long narrative poem, while the others
joined in the chorus."[487] In the background they heard the rustle of water
as the streams poured across the desert, and from time to time the
"mournful cry of the night-flying *ghelow*." Peggy remarked, "All this was
good, in ways we could not explain, better than anything we had ever
known before." A sentence reminiscent of Hemingway.[488]

Although Jack and Peggy wanted to learn Somali, they found the
language "awfully difficult as it contains many sounds not made in
English at all."[489] At mid-twentieth century, the Somalis, speaking an
ancient Cushitic language, still had not adopted an alphabet. In part this
was due to a disagreement within the country over whether a Roman or
Arabic script should be chosen. The language was indeed tantalizing
and, even after years in the Protectorate, only a few Englishmen in the
colonial service had achieved fluency.[490] Nevertheless, Peggy was impatient and frustrated by her inability to comprehend Somali. Within a
few months, however, a fortunate coincidence made possible a partial
resolution to her frustration.

Bogumil Witalis Andrzejewski, born in Poland, and his English wife, Sheila, took up residence in Sheikh. Andrzejewski, who was known as Goosh, had made a hazardous escape from Warsaw during the Second World War and had joined the Allies.[491] After the war, he remained in England. Goosh Andrzejewski was an accomplished poet in his native tongue and a linguist educated at Oxford University.[492] He subsequently taught at the University of London, became a world authority on the Somali language, and was widely respected both for his erudition and for his unassuming demeanour.[493] A friend remarked, "One always came away the richer in mind and spirit from having been in his company."[494] Andrzejewski had come to the Protectorate at the British government's behest to further his study of the Somali language and to develop a grammar and an acceptable plan for implementing orthography — all very challenging tasks.[495]

Living in Sheikh, the two couples visited frequently. Goosh recalled that Peggy "was very anxious to become a writer and was always keen on describing her experiences."[496] He also remembered that she enjoyed listening to Somali songs and had a nostalgic love for the hymns of her childhood.[497] His wife, Sheila, was open-minded, well-read, fun-loving, and an excellent cook. The couples enjoyed many meals together. Sometimes Sheila used an inverted saucepan as an oven and made delicious biscuits. Goosh had a warm sense of humour and both he and his wife were very engaging conversationalists. It was a great relief for Peg and Jack to feel so much at ease with the Andrzejewskis, "with whom we could discuss anything, freely, not worrying what we said." Jack was more adept at simulating the English reserve, which was usually manifest in an extreme caution in speech, but that reserve did not come easily to either of them; now with Goosh and Sheila they could "occasionally shed it."[498]

As Peg continued to accompany Jack on treks, she had many opportunities to observe animated renditions of Somali oral literature. However, aside from comments by her household staff about their traditional poems and tales, Peg had no inkling of how ancient and sophisticated Somali oral literature was until she came in contact with Goosh Andrzejewski. "Even the Director of Education, Chris Bell, was amazed when Goosh told him that the songs he heard the Somalis singing were proper poetry."[499]

As a result of Peggy's conversations with Goosh and her own experiences in the Haud, she began to realize she was living in a veritable "nation of poets," and she subsequently became interested in the challenge of translating some Somali poems and tales into English. As a scholar and linguist, Goosh himself did not wish to rush precipitously into making translations at that point in his career, but he generously assisted Peggy in her efforts.[500] Goosh's presence in the Protectorate made possible developments that Peggy could never have imagined when she first arrived in the country. Now, she badgered him with endless questions about the meanings of words, their cultural contexts, and the intricate features of Somali poetry. He responded with kindness to her interest and shared his notes with her. She wrote enthusiastically to Adele:

> What I really want to do is to be able to understand the Somali stories and poems, of which there are a huge number, all unwritten of course, but a vast body of folk literature passed on from generation to generation. Some of these poems are highly complex, and also very symbolic . . . the Sheikhs, and other "wadaads" (holy men) and notables, are always arguing about the interpretation of a poem — it's just like a college at home in that way! I don't know any of the poems yet, but have had a few odd lines translated for me — one is "in the green Haud there is a tree for poverty to sit under." It sounds just like Eliot, doesn't it?[501]

That casual reference to her college days and the poetry of T.S. Eliot, whose work had often been discussed while she was an undergraduate, may partially explain Peggy's enthusiasm for the Somali world. It was, after all, a unique place, where poetry was essential to life and had a central place in Somali culture. In the barren Haud, where time had a different dimension, lines from *The Wasteland* may well have echoed in her mind.

> Here is no water but only rock
> Rock and no water and the sandy road.[502]

As Peggy increased her efforts to learn Somali, Hersi Jama, who was their interpreter on trek, became her language instructor. Despite his diligent efforts, however, Peggy found it was a "hideous task" and concluded that Somali must be "the hardest language in existence."[503] At college, she had studied some French and German, probably without much enthusiasm, but this complex, ancient language was indeed another matter. As one of her contemporaries explained, "Somali is a difficult language for Europeans to tackle and it was especially so in those days when there was no official version of its orthography and even educated Somalis when writing to one another were accustomed to using English, Arabic, Italian, or French."[504] In the absence of orthography there was nothing Hersi Jama could do by way of written instruction. After a few months, Peggy realized she was able to say only "silly things," such as "the country is looking well this morning." The puzzled Somalis, hearing her efforts, concluded that she was still speaking in English! It was very discouraging. Although she did not learn to speak Somali, Peggy did manage to make herself understood in basic situations of daily life and she persisted in trying to understand the language, regardless of whether or not she was able to converse in it.

At first, her approach to translating Somali poetry was a collaborative effort. She worked with Goosh Andrzejewski and Musa Haji Ismail Galaal, his Somali associate, who was a very fine poet. It was a three-way process. Goosh and Musa Galaal provided Peggy with literal translations of Somali poems. Musa knew a great many poems and had an extensive knowledge of the background and styles of Somali poetry.[505] He later studied at the University of London. Although he was fluent in English, Musa needed to discuss the subtler connotations of words with Goosh in both Somali and English.[506] Then Peggy and Goosh would discuss the lines in English, as she explained: "I took notes on the literal meanings, the implications of words, the references to Somali traditions or customs. I would then be able to work on this material later, and attempt to put it into some form approximating a poem, while preserving as much as possible of the meaning and spirit of the original."[507]

Peggy was aware that at this point Goosh and his wife would be able to stay in the Protectorate for only a few months, so she tried to gather the necessary linguistic information in order to continue with her translations after the Andrzejewskis returned to England. Goosh now explains, however, that the number of hours that he and Peggy were able to spend in the process was very limited because he was busy with additional linguistic research. He remarks that Musa made rapid progress in English, and Peggy "learnt more and more about Somali culture and acquired the skill of collaborating with Musa Galaal."[508] More than a decade later, Margaret Laurence and Musa Haji Ismail Galaal would again collaborate, this time in London (1967), where they produced a program, "Somali Poetry," for Professor Dennis Duerden's Transcription Centre there.[509] Musa Galaal chanted the poems in Somali, and Laurence's English translations were read by Robert Serumaga; the narrator was Andrew Salkey. The program closed with the famous *gabay* by Mohammed Abdulla Hassan, "Blessing to a Friend." Here is Peggy's translation of the opening lines:

> Now you depart, and though your way may lead
> Through airless forests thick with "hhagar" trees,
> Places steeped in heat, stifling and dry,
> Where breath comes hard, and no fresh breeze can reach —
> Yet may God place a shield of coolest air
> Between your body and the assailant sun.[510]

In order to broaden her understanding of Somali culture and history, Peggy embarked on a study of the available literature in English. She also realized that, even if a person did learn the Somali language, a further challenge remained, namely, "discovering how the tribesmen actually looked at things." Without that knowledge of basic concepts, communication would be "impossibly confused."[511] She wanted to understand, for example, the context in which the Somalis made so many references to camels in their poems, and she was intrigued by the ancient tribal system and its significance in Somali life. She had come to realize, too, that the Koran held a central place in their lives, and she embarked on a study of that sacred text in order to better appreciate Somali religious and cultural beliefs and practices. While this was interesting, it was also daunting. For Peggy to undertake translations of Somali literature in the face of so many complex features of the language and culture is evidence of her determination and dedication, as well as her increasing respect for the Somali people. As Marguerite Yourcenar once pointed out, you can't translate poems, you have to create them.

Since many Somali poems, especially the *gabay,* use a highly specialized, literary vocabulary, Peggy needed assistance. Her efforts alone could never have produced the desired result.[512] In the following passage she provides additional information about her approach to making translations into English: "I have tried all along to be as true as possible to the original, and yet not to be too hidebound and thereby lose the implied meaning in the original. In some of the poems I've added a line, in order to explain something that was implied in the Somali, or perhaps phrased something in six words instead of one, because often a Somali word is very compressed and there is no single counterpart for it in English."[513]

In one poem, for example, the Somalis use a special word which, in addition to meaning place, also means "the grace of God," thereby implying that the place referred to is particularly fortunate or blessed in some way. In Laurence's introduction to *A Tree for Poverty*, she states, "I have in no sense embroidered the original text or developed the thought of any poem."[514] However, to bring out the second meaning of the word "place," for which there is no English equivalent, she translated the single Somali word into English with six words: "a place of Allah's kindly grace."

In *A Tree for Poverty*, Laurence reports that her own translations would have been impossible if she had not been given a literal translation of the poems by Goosh Andrzejewski and Musa Galaal.[515] This acknowledgement is appropriate, but it is also a bit misleading, because it does not sufficiently describe the process that she engaged in while trying to shape a translation. Only when her English renditions of these poems are compared with the literal translations that she worked from, can one appreciate the diligence and skill which Laurence brought to the challenge of shaping an English translation that would convey the spirit, beauty, and sophistication of the originals.[516] It was not an easy task.

The following excerpt will serve to illustrate some of the hurdles that she had to overcome. Archived documents show that she was given the following rough translation of lines from a Somali poem: "No one can do anything alone, without help and I am now without anyone by my side, though you, my cousin, should have come to my aid. Sailing ships do not sail in the windless season, just before the 'karan' rains."

Here is Laurence's English rendering in poetic form:

> Before the "karan" rains, when the wind is still,
> The wide-sailed dhows do not put out to sea
> A heavy log cannot be set ablaze
> Without the assisting fire of tinder straw:
> And no man lives who will not one day need
> His brother's help to lighten his distress.[517]

The complex and challenging process of shaping satisfactory translations sharpened Peggy's literary skills. Translation, even for an accomplished writer, can be very difficult. For Peggy, who was still in her apprentice period, the process of translation proved to be a stimulating literary exercise, one that she later referred to as "a labour of love."[518]

In addition to these translated tales and poems, which will be discussed subsequently, Peggy was working on a novel and some short stories. She also kept a diary, which has not been preserved. In it she made extensive notes about her experiences in the Somaliland Protectorate and confided to Adele: "I write about 40 notebook pages every couple of days, and how I'll ever weed it all out when the time comes, I just don't know. There are so many things to describe, especially the Somalis, who are a fascinating people, tremendously complex. From time to time I try to describe one of our chaps in words, and I wonder what makes me think I could ever write a novel."[519]

Later, after she returned to Canada, Laurence worked with that diary and with letters she had sent home to Mum, in order to garner material for *The Prophet's Camel Bell*, which one critic summed up as "a metaphysical travel memoir." The fine photographs in *The Prophet's Camel Bell* were taken by C.J. ("Bob") Martin, who recalls that "Peggy was intensely interested in everything around her. It was clearly a great novelty and adventure for her to come to a little-known African country populated by a remarkable race of people with a highly developed culture based on their limited natural resources, and a remarkable oral literature!"[520] *The Prophet's Camel Bell* offers a thoughtful and absorbing account of Jack and Peggy's experiences in the British Somaliland Protectorate and gives fuller details about how *A Tree for Poverty* came to be published.[521]

During April and May 1951, there was no lack of excitement in Jack and Peggy's lives. First, a huge poisonous snake and then a hyena were killed near their camp. One night Peggy awoke in the truck where they were sleeping and thought she saw a figure trying to creep in underneath the mosquito netting. When she shone her torch on it, nothing was there. The next morning, however, they realized that thieves had stolen valuable engineering equipment as well as the typewriter, radio, and Jack's briefcase, which held important papers. Everything was soon recovered, however.

Back in Sheikh a short time later, a more dangerous situation developed. During the night "a man was taken by a lion in the nearby Sheikh Pass." The following night "a boy was taken by a lion in the same hills."[522] At that time of year, Peggy explained, people in the Guban were moving up through the mountains, en route to their traditional inland grazing grounds in the Haud. They took their flocks and camels through the Sheikh Pass at night when it was cooler. Because a lion had killed a man and a boy, rather than animals from the nearby flocks, people believed it was a man-eater. Everyone in the station was nervous. Jack cleaned his rifle and went out to check for tracks, but found none. Then he had to return to his headquarters in Hargeisa. Peggy no longer went out at night to bring back the dog or to gaze at the stars.

During one encampment a nasty accident occurred. Hersi Jama's hand was badly mangled by a machine. There, in the midst of a vast barren plateau, the distressed Somali workers stood talking excitedly, but seemed unable to come to Hersi's aid. Peg managed to remain calm and, with the help of Arabetto, one of their drivers, Hersi's hand was bathed and bandaged. Perhaps Peggy's childhood interest in nursing stood her in good stead. She described the situation to Goosh and Sheila: "I've never seen a bad accident before, and this was really awful — the bones were sticking out the ends of the three middle fingers of the left hand, and the fingers themselves were completely flattened, like a rag doll's. Hersi, of course, had nearly passed out from shock."[523]

Arabetto and Peggy then managed to get Hersi into the Land Rover, and the driver took them into Hargeisa, "Arabetto holding Hersi as gently as a child. I was convinced that the fingers would have to be amputated, but thank heaven, they didn't have to be."[524] Everyone felt very upset about the accident, which was their first, and as a gesture of appreciation to Hersi, Jack Laurence decided to name the new *balleh* "Balleh Hersi Jama."

During late June and July, a challenging and exhausting aspect of Jack's job commenced. Essential equipment that was needed to continue the *balleh* construction was due to arrive by ship in Djibouti, a small port city that was the capital of French Somaliland. Jack, Peggy, and several workers set out for Djibouti to oversee the unloading of the equipment. They were accompanied as far as Borama by Goosh, Sheila, and Musa Galaal. After leaving Borama, the Land Rover bumped over the rough desert towards Djibouti and they were shaken "like seeds in a gourd rattle." The heat was so intense that Peggy breathed "raspingly, gulping at the air." Whenever they stopped and got out "the sun was like a hammer blow" upon her head and neck.[525]

They waited in the frightfully hot town of Zeilah, which was virtually deserted, until the freighter finally docked in Djibouti. Peggy wrote to Goosh that Zeilah was "as close to being a genuine hell-hole as one is likely to experience."[526] The whole trip, both going to and returning from Djibouti, was full of hardship and backbreaking labour. A substantially different account, however, has been put forward by one biographer, who described the Laurences in Djibouti as frequenting nightclubs and enjoying a rather jolly time, "no one went to bed before two or three in the morning."[527] In fact, the heat and almost ceaseless labour in Djibouti made their trip exhausting and frustrating. Jack, working with his men to get the shipment unloaded, suffered sunstroke and Peggy became very alarmed. He nearly collapsed "since he had to work all day, every day, on the docks, in the burning sun, trying to get the Cats unloaded and onto the diesel truck that was to take them [to Hargeisa]."[528] To her dismay, the dreadful return journey seemed almost bewitched. First the diesel truck got stuck in the sand, then the steering apparatus broke, and while Jack and his mechanic tried to patch it, a fierce sandstorm blew up. "The wind was howling like a demon, and the sand whipped against us with all the fury of flames."[529] The men had to cast planks in front of the wheels so the truck could move slowly forward on a makeshift road. After they finally reached Hargeisa, a few days later, Jack had to begin at once training his men to operate the equipment. The whole business had taken a month, and Jack, who had all the responsibility as well as the problem of communicating in several languages, was thoroughly exhausted.

At that time of year, the *Kharif*, the summer monsoon, came up from the southwest and blew until autumn, "filling the days with dust devils and the nights with moaning."[530] Jack and Peggy were looking forward to returning to the peace and quiet of their bungalow in the hills, but Peggy realized that a regular two-day journey to Sheikh would now add more stress to Jack's life. She suggested they apply for a house in Hargeisa, where Jack's office and the transport maintenance yards were located.[531] This they did, thereby ending their days in their "House in the Clouds" in the Sheikh mountains.

Peggy, however, continued to accompany Jack into the Haud, even after they had moved back to Hargeisa, and she described their situation to Goosh and Sheila:

> We are getting the reputation of being anti-social, as there are very few people we bother to see when we're in town. No longer do the morning tea-party girls try to rope yours truly into their charmed circle. No longer do the eligible married women make sheep's eyes at Jack. No longer do the cocktail invitations pour in. And just as well, too, in our opinion. We have grown a bit sour on life in Hargeisa. . . . We're glad to be away from it, and out in the Haud, where we can breathe. We work like the dickens out here, and we often don't even talk very much, but somehow, we're perfectly happy here. I suppose it's because one doesn't have to put on an act.[532]

A British couple who lived in Hargeisa recalled, "Peggy was not one of us";[533] and another colonial officer stated, "Peggy seemed to think that she could empathize with Somalis in a way that the British Colonial Officer could not. This caused some resentment and increased the self-imposed isolation in which she seemed to glory."[534] This impression of Peggy was probably the result of comments by the officers' wives. Jack, however, seemed to get along well with the colonial staff and enjoyed hunting with some of the men.[535]

Peggy, on the other hand, never really felt comfortable in the social circle of colonial wives in Hargeisa, but she and Jack did come to know and admire several British persons who were in the colonial service there, among whom were Michael Wilson and Bob Martin.[536] Martin was an excellent photographer and head of the Government Information Department, which included radio as well as print. Michael Wilson, was editor of the *Somali News* Sheet, and the acting public-relations officer for the British government in Hargeisa. His principal job, however, was that of a district commissioner. He had administrative responsibility for the tribal people in the region where Jack was constructing the *ballehs*.[537] Michael Wilson was to remain friends with the Laurences for many years, corresponding with each and later visiting Peggy in England.[538]

When Peggy and Jack went out to the Haud in mid-October 1951, they were accompanied by a large number of workers and a good deal of heavy equipment. Around the camp the men built a large *zareba*, a thornbush structure that typically enclosed nomads' encampments. Inside the *zareba* was the Bedford three-ton truck in which Jack and Peggy lived; a big caravan belonging to their Italian mechanic, Gino; a mobile workshop, complete with an electric generator; and many tents for the caterpillar drivers, the native police, the labourers, the cooks, and several important members of the crew.

The workers then constructed a *wob*, a little brushwood structure, where Peg and Jack took their meals. During the day, while the men laboured on the *ballehs*, Peg continued writing at an improvised desk inside the *wob*, which almost seemed magical. "It is always beautifully cool inside the *wob*, and it is a very attractive little shelter, too. It is made by weaving branches together, and filling in the spaces with clumps of a silver-grey weed, rather like dried herbs. With the sun shining through the clumps of weed that hang down from the roof, it looks just like the silver tinsel one used to put on Christmas trees."[539]

Somaliland and Laurence's Development as a Writer

Peggy continued to work at her writing: in the *wob* or the back of the Bedford truck, at the mountain bungalow at Sheikh, or in the city of

Hargeisa. At the age of twenty-four, writing had clearly become her calling and she was very disciplined in addressing that work. By November 1951, she was pleased with the results: four completed stories set in "an East African colony." She was especially pleased because Jack liked these stories and told Adele: "It really is the first time I've ever written anything that he thought was good, as a whole.... There have been odd bits in the novel that he liked, and his criticism was always very helpful, but this time was a bit different."[540] Thinking things over, she had come to the conclusion that the improvement was the result of two factors: "(a) for the first time in my life I really tried to write as I thought my character would think, and not as I thought myself, i.e., both stories are without propaganda entirely; (b) they are both written mainly in conversation. I am beginning to feel that this may be the start of a new way of doing things. I'm unsure of the method, of course, but I do feel it's the most hopeful thing that's happened."[541]

When Peggy reread her stories later, however, she was less content. She felt that her descriptions of people's reactions were not as convincing as the dialogue: "It seems that when I go much beyond conversation, I get pompous and rather unsubtle. I seem to do better sticking to what people actually say, and letting the reactions and feelings and any deeper significance show up between the lines, rather than actually stating it. I don't know if this will lead to anything, but I feel quite hopeful at the moment."[542]

Peggy's ability to reflect on the strengths and weaknesses of her writing and analyze the problem areas were essential stages in her development as a writer. Because she thought that, on the whole, those four stories were "the best things" she had ever written, she sent them off to various publishers.[543] Two months later, however, she dejectedly reported to Adele, "All my stories so far have come back like homing pigeons, blast them" (a reference to the editors).[544] She was further aggravated because the manuscripts were frequently returned with coffee stains, making it necessary to retype the offending pages or, in some instances, the whole story. Regardless of her annoyance, Peggy was determined to circulate her short stories, even though she knew of only a half-dozen places in England and America where they could be submitted. She sent them out again, despite the fact that publishers' replies often took months to reach her in Africa.[545]

On November 5, 1951, Peggy mailed "The Uncertain Flowering" to Whit Burnett, editor of *Story: The Magazine of the Short Story in Book Form*. In her accompanying letter she enclosed an international stamp coupon for "the return of the manuscript, should it be rejected."[546] Her decision to submit her story there was not a random choice. She must have known something of *Story's* reputation. By sending her work to *Story*, Peggy was, in fact, tossing her literary hat into the ring with the finest of the century's short-fiction writers. She was able to do that because, as Whit Burnett once remarked, *Story* never closed its doors to new authors or was unwilling to deal with unsolicited manuscripts.[547]

Peggy's ambitious move in contacting *Story*, one of the premier places to publish short fiction, highlights again her desire to produce fiction that could be judged alongside the best being written at that time in English. *Story* had been launched in Vienna in 1931 by Whit Burnett and his wife, Hallie. It later moved to New York and, for over twenty-five years, *Story* "introduced more young writers who eventually became famous than any other magazine."[548] It had, for example, published works by Graham Greene, Thomas Mann, Kay Boyle, Luigi Pirandello, William Faulkner, Tennessee Williams, Carson McCullers, and Ignazio Silone. Laurence's choice of *Story* was to prove ultimately rewarding, but before she learned that "The Uncertain Flowering" had been accepted, a series of postal misadventures occurred. These will be described in a later chapter.

An interesting account of this period in Laurence's life may be found in a five-page typed letter to Goosh and Sheila, who were still in Sheikh. Written while Peggy was out on trek with Jack, single-spaced and on legal-sized paper, it is one of only a few extant letters to them written while she lived in the Somaliland Protectorate. These letters to friends who knew the same places and people are filled with details about Peggy's work on the translations, as well as lively bits of Somaliland chit-chat that never appear in her other letters. It is unfortunate that more letters like those written to the Andrzejewskis do not survive, since the tone and content are quite different from letters to the family in Canada or to Adele in England.

The existence of these letters, replete with spontaneous comments and descriptions, makes one regret the loss of several hundred letters that she wrote to Michael Wilson. It is also unfortunate that the weekly letters from Africa that Peggy sent to her Mum over a period of more than six years were either destroyed or lost.

There does remain, on the other hand, her extensive correspondence with Adele Wiseman, her letters to the Andrzejewskis, and a few extant letters to Jack's parents — correspondence that contains a vivid picture of the couple's adventures in the Horn of Africa. These letters have an immediacy which is different from, yet complementary to, the account of that period related a decade later in *The Prophet's Camel Bell*, one of her finest books. In addition to memorable descriptions of Somaliland, the book recounts, with the advantage of hindsight, Peggy's growth in self-awareness and her developing appreciation of a culture that was markedly different from her own.

After Peggy and Jack moved back into the city of Hargeisa, she accepted "a terribly interesting job" in the Secretariat, which was located nearby. There she worked for Philip Shirley, the Chief Secretary to the government of the Protectorate. He was the top administrative officer in the country.[549] Several months later, however, Peggy reluctantly had to give that up that work, as well as her trips into the Haud with Jack; she was pregnant and under doctor's orders to rest, since she "had a tendency to miscarry."[550]

Although they had moved into Hargeisa, Jack had to continue his work with the *ballehs* in the Haud. Peggy noted, "He is able to get back every weekend but it's rather lonely for both of us, though especially for him."[551] She used the time to get her Somali translations into final shape and, by April 1952, she had completed the manuscript. Her pregnancy, now at five months, was no longer a cause for concern. Peggy was feeling quite well and the doctor permitted her to resume work at the Secretariat, which she enjoyed: "I'm glad to be working again, as it was pretty lonely before, with Jack away all the time. The time goes much more quickly when I'm working."[552] Through conversations with Philip Shirley about Somaliland, Peggy began to realize how little she actually knew of the country, and to consider "how impossible it was to blow in from the sea and size up a land's centuries in a few months."[553] Nevertheless, she showed some of her Somali translations to Philip Shirley, who had been serving in the Protectorate since 1923 and was "deeply attached to the Somalis, spoke their language, and had amassed an extensive knowledge of their culture, traditions and clan politics."[554] He was very favourably impressed and decided that the government should undertake to publish her translations.

Shirley's wife, Mary, was one of the exceptional people living in the Protectorate. During the *Jilal*, she had been working at a *miskin* camp (a camp for the destitute) set up by the government in an effort to save people who were dying from thirst and starvation.[555] Peggy understood that desperate situation after her first-hand experiences in the Haud, and she had great respect for Mary Shirley, "who had worked day after day among the nomads dying of thirst and starvation to portion out the careful rations to their clamouring desperation — this took courage. Such courage I knew I did not possess."[556] Later Laurence commented on Mary Shirley's dedication in *The Prophet's Camel Bell*. When Philip Shirley read that book, he wrote as follows to Margaret: "Your tribute to Mary was most warming to me as I know she deserved praise for her act and it needed some determination to live cut off by rains entirely on her own in a camp of desperate people who both needed help but also had to be disciplined to ensure fair shares for the weakest. This I think, with your deep understanding you have appreciated."[557]

Although Peggy had not done such courageous work, her determination to shape the first English translations of Somali literature did require strong resolve of a different order. In addition, her responses to various situations in the Protectorate underscore qualities of her character: her adaptability to a country and climate that most Westerners found uninteresting and difficult; her growing appreciation of the Muslim religion and its role in Somali life; her eagerness to look more deeply into Somali culture and customs. Peggy's experiences in the British Somaliland Protectorate were entirely different from what she had known growing up in Neepawa. Undoubtedly her attitude of openness and acceptance had been fostered during her years at United College, where the ideals of the Social Gospel were, as another collegian remarked, "the very air we breathed," and by her life in Winnipeg's North End.[558] Peggy Laurence's approach to the land and people of Somalia was in sharp contrast to the dismissive attitudes and strong sense of superiority that prevailed among many of the British living in the Protectorate, and which is also reflected in writers such as Elspeth Huxley and Isak Dinesen.[559]

Michael Wilson, recalls the lasting impression that Margaret Laurence made on him. Forty years later, he remarked: "I have yet to have met anyone who was so impartial, and without prejudice and able to analyze situations and people so 'caringly' and with such deep sympathy and understanding."[560] Margaret Laurence's translations of Somali poems and tales in *A Tree for Poverty* are evidence of her appreciation of their oral culture. Her respect is mirrored in her endeavour to present a sampling of Somali literature in an English translation, so that it would not be "lost," and so that others, hopefully the Somalis themselves, would thereby be encouraged to set down and preserve that unique heritage.

Out of her experiences in the British Somaliland Protectorate during 1950-1952, Margaret Laurence wrote two books: *The Prophet's Camel Bell* (1964), a travel memoir, and *A Tree for Poverty* (1954), her translations of Somali poems and tales. When a second edition of *A Tree for Poverty* was issued in 1970 for the use of Peace Corps volunteers, Laurence acknowledged in the preface that, although translations more scholarly than hers had since been published, she stood by her early endeavour.[561] In 1989, Professor Andrzejewski summed up Peggy's unique contribution: "Her book publicized Somali poetry and showed through the excellence of her translations that it was not just anonymous folklore poetry but was a form of high art."[562]

While Jack and Peggy Laurence were living in the British Somaliland Protectorate, Peggy persevered in developing her writing skills. She produced at least four radio scripts and worked diligently in several literary genres: the novel, short fiction, and translation. Each had its own challenges and rewards. After spending a great deal of time on a novel, she finally abandoned various versions of it. She was disappointed that only one of her stories, "Uncertain Flowering," had been published. Nevertheless, her translations of Somali oral tales and poems met with acclaim in Africa and remain among her enduring works.

TRANSLATIONS

When Peggy undertook her translations, she faced overwhelming difficulties. She put a substantial amount of time and energy into trying to understand the context of the Somali poems and stories in order to render them into literary and reasonably accurate English. When the translations were completed, Laurence chose as her title a phrase from a Somali *gabay*, "a tree for poverty." Although that phrase is baffling to Westerners, Peggy found it appropriate to the subject. In Somalia, poetry and folk-tales are always available; they cost "nothing" and are "as free to the impoverished nomad as to the Sultan." The title of her book suggests that the whole of Somali literature is meant to function as "a tree for poverty to shelter under."

The book is divided into three sections: Laurence's lengthy critical introduction, her translations of poems and tales, and extensive notes about Somali vocabulary and customs.[563] Although *A Tree for Poverty* is not long, it constitutes a considerable body of work. It includes ten Somali tales in translation, as well as paraphrases of another twenty-six tales that are either Somali or Arabic in origin. In addition, she offers her translations of thirty Somali poems and provides information about approximately ten different types of Somali poetry.

Somali Poetry

Although there are many types of Somali poetry, Peggy focuses on the *belwo* and the *gabay*. The *belwo*, generally two to four lines in length, is a genre of love poetry. It became popular in the mid-twentieth century and was frequently sung to the accompaniment of tambourine and flute.[564] The following examples from two different poems on the same page indicate the success with which Peggy accomplished two of the essential requirements of the *belwo*: the single image and a strong alliterative pattern.

> Woman lovely as lightening at dawn
> Speak to me even once. (*Tree*, 48)

> I long for you, as one
> Whose dhow in summer winds
> Is blown adrift and lost,
> Longs for land, and finds —
> Again the compass tells —
> A grey and empty sea. (*Tree*, 48)

Among Somalis, the *belwo* is considered acceptable for younger poets, but the most highly regarded and the most difficult to compose is the *gabay*, a long, intricate narrative poem, which follows complex rules of composition. The style is formal and strict rules govern its composition. In addition, a special literary language must be mastered by a poet before he can even consider composing a *gabay*; and since there is no formal instruction, the process of "learning by doing" usually takes years, even when a poet has considerable natural talent.[565]

The *gabay* is highly alliterative and contains many allusions to Islamic theology, Somali genealogy, history, and legend.[566] It may serve, Laurence explained, as a vehicle of political persuasion, personal invective, admonition, or philosophical speculation. "Through the *gabay* a man can express what is closest to his heart and mind — his grief, his rage, his faith, his love, his resolution."[567]

In *A Tree for Poverty* Laurence did not include an entire *gabay*. Westerners would have found the form and content unfamiliar and lacking in interest. Although Peggy sent Malcolm Ross an excerpt for *Queen's Quarterly*, he did not publish it. However, her translation of an entire *gabay*, "To a Faithless Friend" by Salaan Arrabey, did appear in the *Somaliland Journal*.[568] In shaping that translation, Peggy once again set herself a significant challenge. The poem, which is very long by North American standards, fills six pages with single-spaced verse and is divided into four parts. By placing her translation of this famous *gabay* in the *Somaliland Journal*, Peggy was setting it before an audience that could be most severe, for it would be scrutinized by persons who knew both the Somali language and the country. Her translations were well-received by them, however, and the reviews were complimentary, as will be shown.

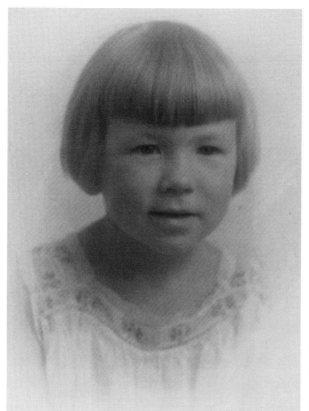

LEFT: Peggy Wemyss

BELOW: Former CNR railway station, Neepawa. Now the Beautiful Plains Museum.

Bronze War Memorial and County Courthouse, Neepawa

Winter Fun
BACK ROW, left to right: Alice Dahlquist, Louise Alguire,
Margie Crawford
FRONT ROW, left to right: Peggy Wemyss, Shirley Dunn,
Mona Spratt

Friends, Neepawa Collegiate Institute
BACK ROW, left to right: Jim Simmons, Earl Whiteman,
Jack Tyler, Charlie Joyce
FRONT ROW, left to right: Peggy Wemyss, Bob Ferris,
Mildred Ishenberg

Wesley Hall,
United College.
Stone building
to the left is
Sparling Hall
Residence.

Sparling Hall Residence, United College
Left to right: Peggy Wemyss and roommate Helen Warkentin

United College, Winnipeg
Left to right: Helen Warkentin and Peggy Wemyss

ABOVE: Jack
Laurence, c.1945

LEFT: Signing the
wedding register,
Jack Laurence and
Peggy Wemyss,
13 September 1947

B.W. (Goosh) Andrzejewski and boy on the beach at
Mogadishu, British Somaliland Protectorate, c. 1952

Professor L.H. Ofosu-Appiah and his wife, Victoria, with their
daughters, 1960

Peggy and Jack, the Gold Coast, c. 1954

Margaret, David,
and Jack, Vancouver,
c. 1960

Adele Wiseman on board the
Demostenes D, 1961

Cemetery, Neepawa

Tales

After Goosh and Sheila Andrzejewski returned to England in August 1951, Peggy was able to collect more tales with the assistance of Hersi Jama, their interpreter; Ahmed Nasir, a Somali teacher; and Arabetto, a driver. In the men's spare time, they conveyed the stories to her, partly in Somali, but mainly in English. Their renditions were accompanied by lively gestures and facial expressions. These performances gave Peggy a sense of the manner in which, for centuries, the Somali people had orally passed on their literature, but she did not have any rough translations, such as she had used with the poems.[569] Consequently Laurence's English versions of the tales are more properly called "paraphrases of the stories" she heard, or, as Professor Andrzejewski remarked, they are "tales retold." Nevertheless, because of her diligence in working on the tales, Peggy felt that her translations did remain true to the "tone and spirit of the original."[570]

One of the very interesting Arabic tales that she paraphrased was the story of Ahmed Hatab ("Ahmed the Woodseller").[571] Describing Ahmed as a Charlie Chaplin figure, Peggy told Goosh: "He is both funny and sad. Laughing at him, we laugh at ourselves, and weeping for him, we weep for all the tragedy we know exists."[572] Ahmed Hatab had a misshapen body and a nagging wife. Each morning he set out to gather and sell firewood. Although his life took many unfortunate turns, somehow Ahmed Hatab also experienced strange and wondrous things and in the end he married the Sultan's daughter. "You laugh at him," said Peggy, "but tenderly, as someone who is one of yourselves."[573] Her translation not only appeared in *A Tree for Poverty*, but it was one of only two tales that she decided to include in *The Prophet's Camel Bell*.

Ahmed had a special appeal for her because the portrayal of his character was "realized on a very high level."[574] Her translation later brought added pleasure to her when a musical version of "Ahmed the Woodseller" was commissioned by the British Broadcasting Corporation as a cantata for school children in England, with music composed by Gordon Crosse and a libretto by Ian Serraillier. It was shown on BBC-TV twice weekly during the summer term 1965, and the BBC published a booklet illustrated by John Griffiths to accompany that school series.[575]

Critical Reception

Soon after *A Tree for Poverty* was published in 1954, the book received generous acclaim from several persons who were knowledgeable in the field of Somali studies. It was favourably reviewed in the first issue of the *Somaliland Journal* by V.H.W. Dowson, an Englishman with an excellent command of the Somali language.[576] Dowson wrote: "[Mrs. Laurence] is to be heartily congratulated not only for being the first to undertake the publication of so large a collection of translations from the Somali, but also for the felicity of her verse. . . . [She] has caught well the spirit of the original songs."[577]

Another reviewer in *War Somali Sidihi* noted: "[Margaret Laurence] has written an introduction full of understanding and sympathy, and in her translation of the poems has shown 'a vision beyond her fellows' in capturing the imagery and imagination of the originals."[578]

The Somalis, too, were impressed by her accomplishment, as Professor Andrzejewski noted, "Somalis speak of her with admiration and affection and regard her as one of their great friends."[579]

Although Peggy realized *A Tree for Poverty* would not have a wide circulation, she was proud of her achievement and confident that she had done a good job. And she remained deeply committed to that book and to the work of translating Somali tales and poems.[580] Several years later, when she learned that some of her translations had been appropriated by a Danish writer, John Bucholzer, and published as if they were his own, she was enraged at his unauthorized use of her work. Further details about his plagiarism will be discussed in the following chapter.[581]

THE NOVEL

Peggy's letters indicate that she was struggling to complete a novel during her first six or seven months in Somaliland. This was the same novel she had been labouring over on board the *Tigre*. By June 1950, eight of eleven projected chapters were completed, but she had become uneasy with its length: "I don't know if I can cut it down properly. It's kind of top-heavy, particularly since half-way through I introduced an entirely new theme (it really did seem to arise quite naturally, so I let it take its course, so to speak)."[582] She had further difficulties with the plot's complexities and told Adele, "The thing doesn't hold together properly."[583] Her summary of the problems with this novel shows there was simply too much to handle:

> The girl falls in love with a young Ukrainian boy she's known at college, and fluctuates between (a) unconscious prejudice against his background, expressed at first in a sort of fear of his making love to her, even while she's very attracted to him, and later in a desire for him to leave the small town (and his family) forever, so that he can be dis-associated from them in her own mind; (b) a later realization of the prejudice of those who think they have no prejudices, and the consequent violent reaction — against her family, to whom Ukrainians are beyond the pale — and a desire to marry him at once, just because he is Ukrainian. Does that sound crazy? I don't think it is, really, but it's so hard to explain in a few words.[584]

After wrestling with the plot, however, Peggy concluded optimistically, "Maybe I've learned something from it."[585] Although she abandoned that particular novel, her summary provides an interesting window into elements that were to reappear fifteen years later in *A Jest of God*. The book's central character, Rachel, lives in a small prairie town, and has an affair with Nick Kazlik, a Ukrainian. *A Jest of God* received a Governor General's Award in 1966 and later was adapted as a successful film, *Rachel, Rachel*.[586]

Short Fiction

During January 1952, while Peggy was still waiting for news about "Uncertain Flowering," she was struggling with the plot of a short story "about an eastern Jew in Africa." She knew what she wanted to accomplish, but admitted that, when she tried to plan the story out, it got absurdly tangled up. She felt the plot was good and noted that it was based "to some extent on fact, i.e., the character of the man, not the plot itself."[587] That remark points to how she worked to develop a fictional character. Aspects of that person might be drawn from an actual individual, then modified or merged with features of another person, and, as imaginative ingredients were added by Laurence, the person became a new and entirely unique individual, one of her fictional creations.

Peggy had been pleased with a half-dozen stories that she had written while in Somaliland, despite the fact that only one was published. The steady work of trying to "get it right" was to be ultimately rewarded, however, and the time spent labouring over those short stories proved to be a good learning experience for her.

Summary

Peggy had lived in the British Somaliland Protectorate for a little less than two years, but the land and its people had a radical and lasting impact on her. Working on Somali literature while in her late twenties marked an important phase in Peggy's literary apprenticeship. It enabled her to concentrate on features of good writing that might not have come to the fore if her work had been strongly autobiographical, as is often the case with a young writer. Trying to translate Somali poems sharpened her attention to wording and rhythm; working on the tales immersed her in the essential elements of good fiction — many of the tales move swiftly with dialogue advancing the action. They often have surprising conclusions in which there are role reversals, the clever outwit the bold, impossible challenges are overcome, and shrewd plans resolve insoluble dilemmas.[588] Some of the longer tales have subplots, high suspense, and a good deal of character development.

After working steadily for months on her translations of Somali oral literature, she finally completed that manuscript. She also had finished a number of chapters of a novel, but subsequently decided to abandon it, having learned a great deal from trial and error with such a lengthy manuscript. In the area of short fiction, she had received a number of rejections, but "Uncertain Flowering" had been accepted and published in *Story*. Referring to "Uncertain Flowering," the scholar William J. Keith has stated that, although it is an apprentice work, for serious students of Canadian literature it marks an important first step in Margaret Laurence's development as a writer of fiction. He also praised her ear for dialogue, calling it "remarkably effective."[589]

In the light of Margaret Laurence's subsequent accomplishments as a writer, the account of her engagement with *Story* may seem rather inconsequential at first, but knowledge of the background of her first professionally published short story adds to an understanding of her goals as an apprentice writer. It also highlights her determination to persevere with her writing in the face of rejections and the absence of a timely response from *Story*. Her correspondence with friends and publishers makes clear that Peggy felt committed to writing as a vocation. Although she had the necessary solitude and had worked diligently as well as steadily, from a professional point of view, there was very little to show in terms of tangible results. From a personal perspective, however, that sojourn in Somaliland had been in many ways like an extended honeymoon, as she and Jack met the challenges and relished the pleasures of living and working in such a remarkable country during the 1950s.

CHAPTER EIGHT

Heart of a Stranger

The Gold Coast, 1952-1956

When Jack's engineering work was completed in the British Somaliland Protectorate, they planned to take a holiday in England. As events turned out, however, Peggy scarcely had time to reflect on the fact they were leaving Somalia. She was expecting a baby in August and, naturally, was focusing on that and on plans for the immediate future. She and Jack had decided it would be best to be in England for the birth, and Peggy was both excited and apprehensive. Although England was familiar to them, neither she nor Jack had any relatives there. They would have to manage on their own, although her Mum intended to come from Canada and stay with them for a few weeks in London.

As they boarded the plane that would take them from Somaliland to England, Peg could not have dreamt that, more than a decade later she would be flying back, one of a small, exclusive group of Westerners who were invited to return to the country as guests of the government to attend the sixth anniversary celebrations of Somalia's independence.[590] Peggy would never have guessed that her diary entries from Somaliland and her letters home would, in the future, form the basis for her memorable travel memoir *The Prophet's Camel Bell* (1963), which earned praise from Canadian, British, and American publishers and readers.[591] That was hidden in a future yet to unfold. For the present she and her husband were eager for the birth of their first child and for time to relax and enjoy England again after Jack's demanding work in the Horn of Africa.

Shortly after arriving in London, they settled into a flat and, at the end of August 1952, Peg went into labour. She wanted to have natural childbirth, but when the baby's shoulders became stuck, she agreed to an anesthetic. The infant's collarbone was broken during the forceps delivery, and Peggy wasn't allowed to hold her child for two days. The difficult delivery was not the only problem, however. Peg had not been told promptly about the baby's collarbone, and before she ever held or nursed Jocelyn, the infant had been taken out of the hospital twice (unbeknownst to Peg) to have her collarbone X-rayed.

When Jocelyn was finally brought to her, "[It] was a moment of revelation. I had always wanted to bear a child with the man I loved. . . . Holding this miracle in my arms, seeing her quiet contented breathing, her latching onto my breast for nourishment, taught me something I had never begun to guess."[592] Two months later, as Peggy and Jack were preparing to depart from London for his new engineering post in West Africa, Jocelyn went into convulsions. They rushed her to the hospital, but no diagnosis was forthcoming and they had to leave her there. Peggy, who was twenty-six, was determined to continue breast-feeding, even while little Jocelyn was in the hospital. "I walked nearly two miles, four times a day, to feed our daughter. Jack was heroic. When I got back to our flat I cried until I had to go to the hospital again. It was dreadful for him. I cried constantly."[593]

In this passage, she stresses that Jack was heroic; things were dreadful for him. But it is not clear whether Jack was upset more by Peggy's constant weeping or by worry over their infant. Clearly, Peggy was distraught over the baby and exhausted from trekking to the hospital four times each day.

The medical staff offered scant information about Jocelyn's condition, however, and when the doctor finally met with Peggy, his comments only fuelled her anxiety. He thought Jocelyn might have contracted spinal meningitis. Years later Laurence told Gabrielle Roy, "They neglected to tell me the disease was not always fatal. In my terrible pain, believing she would die, I remembered Rose-Anna's experience [in *The Tin Flute*]."[594]

Jocelyn remained in the Lawn Road Fever Hospital for more than a week. At last, her convulsions ceased and she came out of hospital quite healthy, having gained several pounds. When their son, David, was born in 1955, Peggy finally learned the cause of Jocelyn's illness. She was told that Jocelyn's convulsions occurred because she had received the yellow fever and smallpox inoculations too close together and in the wrong sequence.

During Peg and Jack's last weeks in England before departing for the Gold Coast, they had to deal with exhausting details in the midst of bitterly cold weather. Finally, the little family was ready for the flight to West Africa, where Jack was to be involved with a massive engineering project: the construction of a deep-water harbour that would give the Gold Coast's capital, Accra, a much needed major seaport.

After they arrived in Accra, they were guests for several weeks of Jack's supervisor and his wife, an older couple who had never had children. Jocelyn's vaccinations had made her uncomfortable; she was cranky and cried a lot. Peggy walked the floor with the baby, "hoping she wouldn't disturb the boss and his wife too much, while Jack tried to accustom himself to the new job."[595] At last, they were able to move into their own place five miles outside Accra "on the crest of a hill where you could get a bit of sea breeze."[596] A row of modern bungalows had recently been built there by Jack's firm, Sir William Halcrow and Partners.

Although their new lodgings were modern, spacious, and attractive, with shining hardwood floors, Peggy had to find curtains, china, and "all the accoutrements of a household."[597] She was in a dilemma, because she did not want to leave the baby for a second, but she lacked the "self-confidence to say, 'Somebody else has got to go.' I did what was expected of me, and Jocelyn was cared for by several African servants" while Peggy shopped for furnishings for the bungalow.[598] "I began to realize," she said, "[that] I was going to have to be a memsahib, a concept I hated and despised."[599] Other adjustments also had to be made in their new quarters.

> [The bungalow] had no screens in a land replete with bugs. The living room and dining room had louvers, as did the bedrooms. . . . Either you opened the windows and took the chance of thieves, or you closed the windows and opened the lower-level louvers, inviting in scor-

> pions and snakes. Occasionally we'd leave the dining-
> room doors open and bats would flit in. I was petrified of
> bats, and would stand turned to stone, as Jack, under-
> standably annoyed, yelled, "How the hell do you expect
> me to get this damn bat out unless you help me?"[600]

Despite the adjustments required by such situations, Jack and Peg realized they liked the Gold Coast (which became Ghana in 1957). The hot climate seemed to suit them and they bought a secondhand car so they could get about more easily. Peggy was ready to try driving once again. She sat behind the wheel and tried to accustom herself to handling the car. She was not very adept, however, and reported to Adele, "Every time I back the car out of the garage, I seem to knock over our lovely tall bougainvillea bush — I've never broken it yet, but it's taken an awful beating."[601]

At the end of November, their baggage (including Peg's typewriter), which was coming by sea, finally arrived. She was relieved to have it with her once again, and hoped get back to writing as quickly as possible. Soon after furnishing their bungalow, however, Peggy learned that they might have to move again — this time to Tema, a small fishing village near the construction site. Peg told Adele she'd be sorry to leave the house in Accra, but she expected to enjoy Tema, a lovely spot, right on the sea with many palm trees surrounding it.[602] She realized, however, that she would miss the "nice young neighbors on either side," with one of whom she shared babysitting arrangements.[603] Whatever a future move might require, Peggy and Jack intended to become acquainted with and enjoy the capital, a large, bustling city, where thirteen daily newspapers were published in English, in addition to several vernacular papers.

Accra had a "fascinating" marketplace. "The streets buzzed and clanged with voices and bicycles, and the air was heavy with the rich cloying smell of plantains being fried in palm oil, as the trader women beside their roadside stalls blew and stirred at the red coals of their charcoal pots."[604] On the streets of the capital, Peggy heard not one language as in Somaliland, but all of the Gold Coast's five main languages. It was a city where the drive and pace of change and growth were insistently present, and many new buildings were under construction.

The Gold Coast was in a great state of excitement under the leadership of Prime Minister Kwame Nkrumah, and everyone was talking about the prospect of independence and self-government. Many people believed the transition would be peaceful, gradual, and effective. But competing political parties flourished and there was a great deal of political unrest.

After the difficult months in their chilly London flat and the anxiety about their baby daughter, it was a delight for Jack and Peggy to be settled in the Gold Coast. She described the lovely view from their porch at Accra:

> I can look out across the valley. Just beyond our compound the bush begins . . . a thick tangle of vines and bushes and where spitting cobras have their dens in the underbrush. The sunlight is piercingly bright, and it makes the green of the bushes and trees so vivid that they hurt the eyes. Across the valley are the hills — long ridges of dark blue with the clouds hanging low over them. Some of the grass in our compound is as tall as a man, and around these giant stalks the white butterflies hover, absurdly pale and fragile. There is an electric power pole standing in the bush outside the compound, and the wild morning glories have twined to the very top of it, their pink blossoms looking out of place against the rough wood of the pole.[605]

Peg, ever observant, noticed that their cook's wife had a little garden covered with a lattice of sticks and leaves to protect it from the sun. "Every morning at dawn she goes from one end of the lattice frame to the other, kneeling and touching her forehead and murmuring something that sounds like an incantation. We do not know why she does this, but we suppose it is an appeal to her gods, whatever they may be, to make the garden fruitful. We do not ask her, because she would not tell us anyway, and would be offended if we forced her to speak of it."[606] The situation that Peg describes here later became the background for her short story, "A Fetish for Love," published in *The Tomorrow-Tamer and Other Stories.* The details in the story are changed and the European woman, Constance, while she may be partially based on Margaret, is clearly an amalgam of several persons.

In the Gold Coast, much more than in Somaliland, Peggy became aware of the juxtaposition of the "new" Africa, emerging from colonial rule, and the "old" Africa, the traditional Africa. She hoped to meet some educated Africans in the Gold Coast, perhaps faculty connected to the nearby University of Ghana. Through letters from their friends Goosh and Sheila Andrzejewski, now in England, Peggy and Jack were introduced to Professor Lawrence Henry Ofosu-Appiah. He was a distinguished Classics scholar who had completed secondary school at Achimota College in Achimista. He then majored in Classics and Philosophy at Hertford College, Oxford, and did postgraduate studies in Anthropology at Jesus College, Cambridge. Ofosu and Goosh Andrzejewski had been friends since their student days at Oxford.[607]

At first, Peggy found it difficult to appreciate Professor Ofosu-Appiah's comments about the Gold Coast or grasp his complex concerns for the future of his country. In talking with him she often felt uncomfortable as the result of her naïveté and his disillusionment with the political situation in West Africa. As time passed, however, they did became friends; and after he married, the couples visited one another in Tema and in Legon, where Ofosu lived with his wife, Victoria. Their bungalow was covered with purple bougainvillea and surrounded by paw-paw trees and giant clusters of canna lilies, a low wall around the garden gave a feeling of privacy.[608]

Peggy and Ofosu-Appiah remained in contact over the years, and later he and his wife visited her at Elm Cottage in England.[609] On several occasions Margaret Laurence wrote about him, underscoring the important role Professor Ofosu-Appiah had played in her developing sense of the complex situation in the Gold Coast. He is the subject of her article "The Very Best Intentions," which appeared in *Holiday* (November 1964). There, however, Laurence changed his name, occupation, and other details in order to protect his identity during a time of great political strife in the Gold Coast. She reprinted "The Very Best Intentions" and provided some background information in her collected essays *Heart of a Stranger* (1976). Thirteen years later in *Dance on the*

Earth, she again mentioned Ofosu-Appiah and the ways in which their friendship helped to provide her with a more nuanced understanding of the situation in West Africa.[610]

While living in the Gold Coast, Peg worked steadily at her writing. It was a bit easier to do since Jocelyn was still an infant. She managed to complete five short stories during the first four months in the Gold Coast, and she worked again on her Somaliland novel. She was satisfied with only twenty-six pages of it, however, and told Adele she was relying very much on Jack's comments for her revisions.[611] His response to her work was valued by Peggy since Jack had an appreciation of literature, and at that time and in that place there was no one else to whom she might turn for comment and advice. In addition to working on the novel, Peggy had also completed several radio scripts about Somaliland and sent them to the Canadian Broadcasting Corporation (CBC), but she was worried that their reply would be delayed in reaching her "I suppose," she wrote to Adele, "we'll have left this country before I hear . . . that's the worst of moving around."[612]

Margaret Laurence's first short story to be accepted by a professional journal was "Uncertain Flowering," set in contemporary British Somaliland. Although she had completed the story while living there and sent it to *Story* in November 1951, the reply from Whit Burnett, the editor, had been much delayed in transit. Burnett's congratulatory letter of acceptance was sent to Somaliland, but arrived there after Jack's work had ended and the Laurences were back in England. Burnett's letter then went from Somaliland to England and from there it was forwarded to the Gold Coast of Africa. Peggy finally received it on January 20, 1953, a year and a half after Burnett had written it and two years after she had mailed him the manuscript with a note saying "an early reply would be very greatly appreciated."[613]

Although the postal delays meant that Laurence's manuscript had arrived too late for *Story 2*, Whit Burnett assured her it would appear in *Story 3*. As she read his letter, Peggy became alternately angry and pleased. She was distressed over the months of waiting for a reply from *Story*, when all that time Burnett's letter was actually in transit to her. What other correspondence, she wondered, might have been delayed or lost in the international mail services? On the other hand, Whit Burnett's letter was a welcome breeze blowing upon the coals of her creative talent. It was full of praise and went far beyond any reply that Peggy might have anticipated. He wrote encouragingly:

> We were delighted with the writing quality and the story, "The Uncertain Flowering." You have a fine fictional and character sense, and we wonder if you have a novel we could consider for book publication.[614]

Publication in *Story* was indeed cause for celebration. "In those days for a young writer to be published in *Story*," remarked Norman Mailer, "was enough to give you the beginnings of a real inner certainty that perhaps you were meant to be a writer."[615] Peggy had already abandoned her first novel, but now, in the light of Burnett's interest, she decided to give it another try. She confided frankly to Adele, "It is hard not to seem too eager, isn't it, when in fact one is?"[616]

The subsequent correspondence between Burnett and Laurence contains interesting information about her development as a writer. Laurence told him rather disingenuously that she "had not thought of writing a novel," but had a number of short stories set in Somaliland, and asked if he would be interested in seeing them when they were completed in about a year's time. Whit Burnett informed her that collections of short stories were often hard to place, and told Peggy that she might be well advised to attempt a novel with an East African setting rather than working entirely on short stories.[617] In April 1953, she sent word to Burnett that she had begun writing a novel set in Somaliland. Seven months later, however, she informed him that, although the novel had not worked out as she had hoped, she still intended to send him the first half when it was ready. That seems not to have happened.

At last, "Uncertain Flowering" was published in *Story 4* (1953).[618] The volume, which ran to more than 240 pages, contained eighteen short stories. "Uncertain Flowering" appeared prominently as the first story in the book.[619] This was indeed an accomplishment for Peggy, her first professional publication. She was further encouraged when *Story 4* was favourably reviewed in the *New York Times*. Peggy's excitement could be likened to that of Edmund Hillary and Tensing Norgay, who in that same year became the first persons to reach the summit of Mount Everest. Peggy had attained her own summit, one that to her had seemed virtually impossible after all the letters of rejection that she had received.

After a spate of seven letters between Laurence and Burnett, there is only one further letter from Burnett. It was written seven years later. In it he refers to an hiatus in *Story*'s publication and notes that the magazine is now resuming publication. He also asks for news of her novel. It is doubtful, however, that she received Burnett's letter, which is in the *Story* archives at Princeton. It was dated November 1960 and had been sent to Accra. Peggy had left Accra three years earlier (January 1957) for Canada where she remained for the next six years. Moreover, at the same time Burnett was writing to her for an update, Margaret Laurence's first novel, *This Side Jordan,* had already been accepted for publication and was being released in Canada, England, and the United States. Her earlier appearance in *Story* was mentioned on the dust jacket.

In 1959, *Prism*, a new Canadian journal, published another story by Laurence. The contributor's note, which she had composed, also made reference to the fact that her work had previously appeared in *Story*.[620] However, she later dropped all mention of *Story* and cited the *Queen's Quarterly* as the place of her first publication. This is not only incorrect but, given the stature of *Story*, it is also puzzling. It is impossible to believe that Margaret Laurence had forgotten about her earlier achievement and recognition.

There may be more than one reason why Laurence thought it best to drop any reference to *Story* after *The Prophet's Camel Bell* (1963), despite the fact that "Uncertain Flowering" was indeed her first professional publication.[621] The following explanations seem plausible. As her stories improved, Margaret Laurence, like many other writers, may have eschewed her earlier efforts and decided "Uncertain Flowering" was not worth mentioning, since it was not equal to her best fiction. But a more compelling reason for her later omission of this publication may be due to the fact that several paragraphs from "Uncertain Flowering" were also used in her later travel memoir, *The Prophet's Camel Bell*.

In that book, Laurence describes a morning when she and Jack began to climb Malol, the highest mountain near Sheikh. After clambering through a rocky pass in the afternoon, they came suddenly to a hidden valley: "a green place where the grass was thick and soft, hair-like, and where mauve flowers grew." Before returning to Sheikh, they rested for more than an hour in that seemingly enchanted valley, which she then describes in further detail. Those descriptions had appeared in "Uncertain Flowering" ten years before, although the place is given a fictional name in the short story. It is possible, of course, that in both instances Laurence relied on the contemporary diary that she had kept in Somaliland. Whatever her reasons may have been for neglecting further mention of "Uncertain Flowering," she did retain her copy of *Story 4* as well a laudatory clipping from the *New York Times*, in which she is mentioned by name as a writer whose work is "first-rate."[622]

As a Canadian living in the Gold Coast, not only was Peggy isolated from contact with other writers, but she was also far from friends who might have shown interest in her writing and provided occasional encouragement. As a result, her correspondence with Adele Wiseman became a life-line amidst the waves of self-doubt and anxiety that often beset her. One letter to Adele provides a window into Peg's typical situation during the years that she and Jack lived in the Gold Coast: "Tonight you are the only person I feel like writing to, since Jack is at the moment going through Episode #4 of my story, & I am sitting here trying not to chew my nails. Jack is a very good critic, you know. . . . The first two times he read this episode he tore it to bits (it had then been rewritten about five times already), so I hope he thinks it stands up better this time. I am fed up with it."[623]

Peggy's reliance on Jack's judgement of her work had already been questioned by Adele, who wisely realized that Peg's dependence on Jack's approval could put a strain on their marriage and undermine Peg's assessment of her own writing.

At this juncture, Peggy was having trouble with the novel, because in it she was trying to handle two different narrative points of view:

> I am doing the story mainly from the European woman's point of view. In the (necessary) places where the Somali world is the setting, it is mainly seen though the Somali girl's eyes — This combination is risky, obviously, but better I think than my original idea of

writing it from the man's [the district commissioner's] point of view. I have not got the necessary scope of talent to write from a man's point of view. Sorry to pour out all this, Adele — it is only because I know how well you know the anxiety that the whole thing may not turn out right.[624]

Peggy was also discouraged because, in the Gold Coast, unlike Somaliland, she could manage only two or three hours a day for writing. At night she was too fatigued to write, and she and Jack retired early. In any case, she felt that working at night was out of the question, since the noise of her typing might awaken Jocelyn or the children in nearby bungalows.[625] By July, however, driven by her need to find time, Peggy was writing by hand at night. She tried to put her situation in an optimistic light, reporting that she hoped writing by hand might force her "to write more slowly and weigh words more carefully."[626]

On the domestic side, she was busy overseeing the regular cleaning of the house and its environs, since she believed that, in the Gold Coast, this was "the only way of avoiding disease." Jocelyn, now six months old, naturally took up a good deal of Peggy's time and her letters are full of comments about her infant daughter. She was delighted with the baby's development and amused by her use of language. At one point Peggy noted, "[Jocelyn] is getting very entertaining now, and Jack is very fond of her, thank goodness."[627] The remark "thank goodness" seems to imply that Peg had been uncertain about how Jack would respond to having a child. Their friend Kay Bolton, who had known Jack during his years at the Roslyn Road community in Winnipeg, remembers that Jack was not eager to have children, perhaps because, as the eldest in his family, he had had responsibilities for his younger siblings. Kay recalls, however, that after her own son was born, Jack, who was completing course work at the University of Manitoba, took an interest in their little boy and seemed to change his mind about having children of his own.[628]

By early June 1953, Peggy's conflicted feelings about the time that was available for writing and the time she wanted to spend with the baby and with her husband began to surface. She had new ideas for a radio series and wanted to incorporate some contemporary African music into the broadcasts, but she realized that might not happen since "there seems to be so much to do, and . . . so darned little time."[629]

Although her translation of the Somali poems and tales had been completed and was now scheduled for publication under the auspices of the government of the British Somaliland Protectorate, Peggy continued to work on additional translations. Goosh Andrzejewski, who had returned to England, was sending her literal translations of several *gabay*. She remarked that the form was longer, more complex, and very effective in the Somali language, but "terrible to translate with anything [like] the same effect."[630] Goosh's assistance was essential, of course, and Peg also asked his permission to submit her translations of a *gabay* for possible publication in *Queen's Quarterly*. Although she was now living in West Africa, Peggy continued to work on those challenging Somali translations, both for their own sake and because she realized it would help to keep the Somali mode of thought and expression fresh in her mind while she endeavoured to complete a novel set in Somaliland.[631]

Despite diligent efforts, Peggy felt her writing was going too slowly. After completing a hundred pages of the novel, she had become discouraged by thoughts of Graham Greene's accomplishment in *The Power and the Glory*, "a terrific novel and only about 250 pages." She told Adele, "I don't know how people manage to compress like that . . . perhaps it comes only with years of experience. I try very hard to be brief, but find I am always spreading myself to dozens of pages where a couple should suffice."[632]

In the course of the next few weeks, however, Peggy did complete five chapters of the Somaliland novel and tried to improve its organization. "I keep telling myself that one learns with experience, but sometimes I wonder," she reflected.[633]

During July, the rains finally ended and the days became hotter. To relax one evening, Jack and Peg went to a dance at the European Club, but they decided afterwards that they would "never go again." It was only the second time they had been to the club, and they found it dull. The African band played waltzes and fox trots, not jazz and high-life. Peg, who was twenty-seven, remarked, "everyone dances around sedately, looking bored stiff. It must seem odd to the African band."[634] Although the European Club had actually changed its name to the "Accra Club," it remained colonialist.[635] Peggy and Jack preferred the African clubs, where they enjoyed the music and the relaxed ambience much more. Years later Laurence recalled how, as a young woman, she had loved to go dancing: "One of my greatest pleasures when my husband and I lived in Ghana was to dance in one of the African nightclubs in Accra, to West African high-life music with its counterpoint rhythms of the drums. I was pretty good at it, too. When young African men asked me to dance, I was honoured — they didn't ask just anyone."[636]

In September 1953, the CBC finally offered $50 for Peggy's radio scripts. Their offer, however, generated some anxiety, because she had been led to believe that the CBC intended to rewrite her scripts. "Since I would have no knowledge of what they did with it, and no control over it, I have refused," she told Adele. "I hated to refuse the money, quite honestly, but you know what re-written things are like . . . generally they bear no resemblance to the original."[637] She was further aggravated by the CBC's error in linking the African Sahara with Somaliland in East Africa. The distinction between those two separate and very different geographical regions of the African continent was important to Laurence because she did not want the radio program to give the "wrong impression" of Somaliland. In an animated reply to the CBC, she informed them of Somaliland's location and rejected their offer for the scripts.[638] Peggy later received a letter from the CBC's Elizabeth Long, in which she explained things to Peggy's satisfaction. As a result, she felt sheepish and remorseful about her peremptory response and the "harsh" letter she had sent them. She decided to accept the CBC's offer.[639]

During October 1953, encouraged by Whit Burnett's comments about her writing, Peg worked diligently on her Somaliland novel, then scrapped it, started to write it all over again, and finally put the new effort aside. The novel simply was not working out. It was difficult for her to do any concentrated writing because Jocelyn was now walking and "constantly getting herself into trouble of one kind or another."[640] In addition, the hot season had begun and Peg felt tired "all the time."[641] She was worried about Jack, who was "working far too hard, as usual," and becoming exhausted. "He will really need his leave," she told Adele.[642] It was uncertain at that point whether they would return to the Gold Coast. Their decision would depend on whether Jack could get the appropriate salary for the work he was doing. Peg was concerned about his situation. "I shall feel terrible if anything goes wrong at this point with the prospective job, as Jack has worked so hard this tour and done so well, and he really deserves the new post. It would be third in command on the Tema Harbour Project, a big job, and a big step up in his profession."[643]

As she reflected on the situation, Peggy realized she had "become unexpectedly fond" of the country, and she hoped they would be able to return.[644]

In December 1953, Peggy resumed work on her Somaliland novel. It was being written in two parts, instead of chapters, and within those parts she put related, but separate, episodes. That structure, she felt, was determined internally by the material. The novel took place in two worlds: the Somali and the European. However, she was satisfied with only twenty-five pages, a "very small bit after all the time I've spent on it. A year now."[645] That same month, a letter from Peg's former professor, Malcolm Ross (then at Queen's University in Canada and editor of *Queen's Quarterly*) brought a welcome invitation. Professor Ross suggested that Peggy forward translations of some of her Somali poems and tales for possible publication in the journal. Ross's initial interest was chiefly due to Adele Wiseman's enthusiasm for *A Tree for Poverty*, which she had reviewed in *Queen's Quarterly*. It is doubtful, however, that anyone in North America paid much attention, since Laurence was unknown at the time and her book, on such an obscure topic, was difficult to obtain. Reviews in African journals, however, were consistently favourable.[646]

Adele Wiseman had remained in contact with Professor Ross after her graduation and recently had given him Peggy's address. Peggy, in addition to sending Ross an excerpt from a new *gabay*, also forwarded a short story, "Amiina," about a Somali girl. It was, she told him, the first of the Somali stories that she had written in 1952. Although that story has not been traced, its title comes from a *belwo,* a Somali love poem that Peggy had translated and sent to Adele two years before.[647] Professor Ross rejected both the *gabay* and the short story. Peggy thought his decision was based on a misunderstanding and replied with a long, feisty letter defending "Amiina." Although she conceded that the story should have had more background, she assured Malcolm Ross that "the Englishman wasn't pathetic," and "the native girl was certainly not vicious."[648] The paradox in that story, she explained to Adele, is that the European accepts the African girl as "good" by his British standards, but later in disillusionment he turns from love to hatred. "I suppose it was silly to explain it [to Ross] . . . but I did so because I hated to think he had the idea that I'd got to the point where I'd write simple little tales about pathetic Englishmen and vicious native girls."[649] Undaunted by Professor Ross's unwillingness to publish that story, Peggy remained eager to have her fiction appear in print and quickly sent off another story for his consideration.

Although in her memoirs, Peggy described her life at this point as "rather uneventful," her contemporary letters convey a very different impression. It is possible, of course, that after living for a year in the Gold Coast, she had become accustomed to life there, and by using the word "uneventful," she may simply have meant "routine." Things were far from routine, however, on the political front. During 1953 there was turmoil in the Gold Coast and considerable unrest in anticipation of the elections that were to be held in 1954. On the domestic scene, too, there had been a good deal of excitement and several crises to worry about. Two spitting cobras had been sighted in the yard in June and Peggy was terrified.

Adding to her other worries was the fact that thieves entered the bungalow one evening through a window in the baby's room. Ordinarily theft of that sort did not involve any personal harm to the occupants. Fortunately Jack and Peggy awakened and the thieves fled. But Peg noticed that an enormous crowbar had been dropped outside and wondered, "What would have happened, if the baby had awakened?"[650]

In October, a servant killed a large scorpion in their living room and a few weeks later, the three-year-old boy next door died in a matter of hours from cerebral malaria.[651] His funeral was "somehow even more sad here than it would have been at home. The hearse was a government Land-Rover, and the tiny coffin jolted around in it. The flowers picked that morning, were all dead."[652] Peg then became even more vigilant with Jocelyn, especially when the child played with toys in the baby tub. If Jocelyn somehow had managed to drink water from the little plastic scoop, there would have been real danger of typhoid.[653]

Tropical diseases posed a terrifying threat. Cholera, typhoid, tuberculosis, anthrax, yellow fever, trachoma, polio, guinea worm, and schistosomiasis were common diseases in that part of Africa. Peggy herself came down with her first bout of malaria just before Christmas; fortunately it was a mild case, and she recovered quickly.[654]

When Peggy wrote to Adele soon after New Year's Day 1954, there was much to relate. She described their Christmas celebrations, Jocelyn's growth, and her own delight in Jocelyn's use of language and her funny sayings. She summed up her young daughter's personality as "very outgoing & gay . . . yet sometimes she can be very serious and thoughtful."[655] One evening Jocelyn fell and cut her head; it bled so much that Peg and Jack were "nearly frantic." The doctor discovered, however, that the cut was actually quite small, and they then felt "silly about the fuss they had caused."[656] A few weeks earlier, Jocelyn had broken her thumb, and Peg, as a result, spent some days in a rather distracted state.[657] Domestic concerns about her daughter's "adventures," her eating preferences, and use of new words continue to pop up regularly in Peggy's letters home. Adele, meanwhile, had made good progress on her novel, and Peg rejoiced in that news. Although Peggy thought that the progress of her own novel had been "slow and uncertain," she also felt encouraged that the current version seemed "closer to the mark."[658] She was looking forward to reading Adele's manuscript when she and Jack were in London on leave later that year.

For several weeks in 1954, Peggy had been doing secretarial work for the well-known British economist Barbara Ward, who, with her husband, Commander Robert G.A. Jackson (later Sir Robert Jackson), was also living in Accra. Commander Jackson was head of the Volta River Preparatory Commission, which had been set up to make a detailed study into building a massive dam and hydro-electric power station on the river.[659] His wife had been trying for a number of months to complete the book that subsequently became *Faith and Freedom*. However, she found the climate of the Gold Coast very difficult to deal with and had fallen behind in completing the manuscript. Faced with engagements for lectures overseas and a publisher's deadline, Barbara Ward was distressed, and sought the assistance of a good typist. She turned to Peggy who agreed to work for her. In looking back on that, Jack Laurence remarked: "We weren't short of money; perhaps Peggy just wanted something to do. Or else she wanted to practise typing. I honestly cannot think why she did it."[660] Peggy, on the other hand, may have welcomed the opportunity to engage in stimulating conversation with a woman writer who had been educated at the Sorbonne and Oxford and who had joined the staff of the British *Economist* while still in her twenties. Peggy also may have been pleased with the opportunity to earn some extra money rather than request it from Jack.

In the process of typing the draft, Peg realized that she respected many of Barbara Ward's analyses.[661] The opening sentence of *Faith and Freedom* would have resonated with her: "Surely no previous age has known the sense of foreboding that hangs over the modern world." Barbara Ward then proposed an analysis of freedom, and made the point: "We cannot learn from history unless we are free to learn. We cannot profit by the lesson unless we are free to act."[662] In many ways Margaret Laurence's own writing may also be construed as an examination of the question of freedom through the prism of fiction. But freedom was not only on the page. At that time it was also in the air. In the Gold Coast the rallying cry of the Convention People's Party (CPP) was heard over and over again in the streets and on the radio: "Free-dom, free-dom." The sound of people chanting that slogan echoes later in Laurence's "A Gourdful of Glory," one of her most successful and moving short stories.

Although the Laurences were not in the same social circle as Commander Jackson and his wife, they did have dinner in their home on at least one occasion, according to Jack.[663] On another evening in February, after Jack and Peggy returned from a cocktail party, Jack took his bicarbonate of soda and retired for the night, while Peggy took a cup of coffee and a biscuit into the bathroom, because it was fully screened and neither bats nor mosquitoes could disturb her while she wrote to Adele. Peg described their boring evening and reported: "[Jack] never gets drunk in the slightest, so he has all the ill effects of alcohol with none of the good ones. Neither of us can drink much in this climate — I have virtually given up altogether — I'm not made sick, just dopey the next day."[664]

Peg informed Adele that the novel was moving along steadily, although progress was "painfully slow."[665] Peg thought she was losing sight of the book as a whole because she was focused on small sections, but she described the problem to Adele in humorous rather than frantic tones: "Who dares to disparage the tortoise in my presence? I do feel I am writing much too slowly & tend to become very despondent when

I realize how much more there is to work out & set down. I hit the all-time low recently when I spent 2 weeks on 1 paragraph — that is just neurotic, say what you like!"[666]

Since Adele was nearing completion of *The Sacrifice*, Peg passed along a few suggestions from Jack's mother, who was also finishing a novel. Elsie Laurence had cautioned Peg that the sense of discouragement as one nears the end is often due to fatigue and impatience. "Don't rush to finish the work," Elsie had advised.

By March, Adele's novel was almost completed and she was feeling rather empty. Although Peggy had yet to experience that feeling, which frequently accompanies the completion of a novel, she tried to cheer Adele with these comments: "I suppose having a novel is similar to having a baby — when you're carrying it you think everything is going to be wonderful as soon as it's born, only to find that you enter then a new phase of existence that carries with it its own special problems. I do feel, however, that you should talk yourself into a certain feeling of achievement — after all, you *have* achieved a great deal."[667]

The two women would continue to encourage and support one another both personally and professionally through their ongoing correspondence, especially while living abroad.

The March weather in the Gold Coast became "horribly hot," and Peg and Jack were looking forward to going on leave to Canada with a stopover in London.[668] Although Peggy's scripts had been accepted for broadcast by the CBC, she was now assailed with doubts about their quality. In one letter to Adele she apologized for lengthy remarks about her own writing and explained: "Now I've done nothing except talk about writing. You know, except for Jack—who is always a very helpful critic — I never talk to anyone about writing — in fact, most people here don't know how I spend all my time, and probably think I'm lazy as hell. It's such a relief to be able to write you about it — I expect you sometimes feel, too, that it's odd that such an important area of one's life is shared with so few people, in fact, hardly any."[669]

From the time that Peggy had ceased working as a journalist in Winnipeg and moved overseas with Jack, only a few people seem to have been aware of her intention to become a writer. It is not clear why that was so. For a woman to keep silent about her writing, especially while unpublished, was not unusual then, but one wonders. Had Peggy not yet met her goals? Did she feel that identifying herself as a writer would evoke too many unwanted comments and questions? Did she feel a bit guilty about being a writer and wish to be seen only as the wife of Jack Laurence and, later, as the mother of Jocelyn and David? Perhaps the answer is a combination of these factors.

Although Peggy's desire to be a writer was not common knowledge, even among some of their close friends, she continued to apply herself to learning the craft. That ambition came to dominate her life. Without writing, life for her simply would not be possible. Trying to write well took on an urgency and became a necessary way of "being in the world." However, it was only many years later, after the publication of her first novel, that Margaret Laurence publicly embraced for herself the word "writer" — with all that it implied.

In May 1954, Jack and Peggy decided to spend their leave in Canada. Bringing Jocelyn, then a year and a half old, with them, they went by train from Montreal to Vancouver and then by ferry to Victoria, where Peg's Mum had moved to join Aunt Ruby after Grandfather Simpson's death.[670] Jack's parents also lived in Victoria and they were able to spend time with them as well. Jack and Peg remained in Canada for over a month and she remembered it as "a wonderful leave. Jocelyn was talking non-stop, totally captivating her two grandmothers." They had waited to have her christened in Victoria for the sake of the grandparents, and Peggy's brother Bob, who was working nearby, and was to be Jocelyn's godfather.[671]

One of the highlights of that trip was a stopover in Winnipeg, where they were warmly welcomed by the Wiseman family. Over the years Peggy had grown to love the Wisemans, especially Adele's mother, Chaika, whose affectionate greeting always made Peggy feel comfortable. In the Wiseman's home, unlike Grandfather Simpson's house, Peggy felt relaxed, accepted, and loved. Among Adele's friends, the Wiseman family's hospitality was legendary. When Jack and Peggy arrived in Winnipeg, the Wisemans naturally hosted a small reunion for the couple's friends. Peggy later instructed Adele to convey to Chaika "how very much we appreciated all her kindness to us. She is pure gold and we really love her."[672] For Margaret Laurence, the encouragement and support of older women, whether her Mum, Anne Ross, or, later, Ethel Wilson, always meant a great deal.

By September 1954, they were back in the Gold Coast, where a letter from Malcolm Ross was waiting for Peggy. It had been posted four months earlier! He informed Peggy that her Somaliland short story would be published in the *Queen's Quarterly*. Peggy, aggravated by the four-month delay in receiving his letter of acceptance, told Adele, "I always have that kind of rotten luck [with delays in receiving mail from publishers]."[673] She replied at once to Professor Ross, asking him not to publish that story, but to consider as a replacement a "much better" and more recent story, "Drummer of All the World." She confided optimistically to Adele, "I think it is the best story I've ever written, and so does Jack."[674]

Malcolm Ross received Peggy's letter in time to make the substitution and sent her a check for fifty-four dollars. "Drummer of All the World" appeared in the *Queen's Quarterly*, Winter 1956. Several years later she gave it prominence as the opening story in her collection *The Tomorrow-Tamer and Other Stories* (1963).

The Laurences had left their residence in Accra and were now settled and comfortable in a "really nice bungalow" in Tema, closer to Jack's work. Peggy, wanting to make the bungalow look like home, once again had embarked on ambitious decorating projects. "I've made curtains, shower curtains, made shelves for Jocelyn's room out of concrete blocks and planks, painted Jocelyn's furniture green and decorated it with red and yellow peasant-like designs."[675] She was also busy decorating inexpensive earthenware jars and bowls from the African market with oil paints, and "turning them into very posh . . . ashtrays and plant pots."[676] She had put up pictures, attempted to turn a mahogany plank into a low table, and learned to put in Rawlplugs (which were used to hold screws or nails in masonry) by herself. "I have enjoyed it all very much," she wrote, "but will be quite glad when everything is in shape and I can settle down to some serious work."[677] Peggy's delight in decorating and making things for their home is reminiscent of her father's pleasure in building cabinets and painting their Neepawa home on Vivian Street. Creating a warm, welcoming space, even with the most ordinary of objects, was very important to her.

At the end of September the rains that had been expected since June finally arrived. One night there was a tremendous storm, with sheets of lightning accompanied by eight hours of rain. Peggy was feeling homesick for family and friends in Canada; she yearned for the opportunity to talk with Adele, Chaika, her own Mum, and Elsie Laurence.

Later that month her spirits lifted with the arrival by mail of her first book, the Somali translations, *A Tree for Poverty*. Although for many years that small book was little-known outside Africa, "it was the first collection of Somali poems and folk-tales to appear in English," Laurence later noted. "The doing of it was a labour of love, and I could not help feeling that for the Administrator [Philip Shirley] to take the time and trouble to get it published, it had been much the same sort of thing."[678]

In November, Peggy was suffering from some sort of foot problems. Not long after, a mass of long burn-like blisters appeared on her arm. It was the result of "tumblo fly," she explained, a tropical insect that "lays eggs under the skin and the larva burrow merrily along."[679] Fortunately the problem did not last very long, and there remained only a lot of temporary scars. Her health troubles were not over, however. After getting a bad case of food poisoning, Peggy felt terrible, "[I] couldn't have cared less whether I lived or died." By mid-month she had recovered, although she was still "full of sulpha and a bit weak at the knees."[680]

At last she felt well enough to settle again into work on her novel and she pushed hard to complete the first draft. As 1955 dawned, Peg sent New Year's greetings to Adele. Their Christmas had been fine and little Jocelyn had played for hours with her new kiddy-car. The youngster had been upset, however, at the beginning of her parents' Christmas-morning party: "We had about 40 people and they all arrived at once. We couldn't pay any attention to Jocelyn for a while, and when I finally found her she had apparently been saying 'It's my house, and I can't find my mummy!' However, I took her with me after that and she perked up considerably."[681] This letter also announced "the big news . . . we're expecting another baby."[682] Although she was three months pregnant, Peg reported feeling well, except that, instead of morning sickness, she seemed to have "[early] evening sickness, a rather inconvenient time to feel ill."[683] She was frustrated about her lack of energy and had felt an overwhelming sleepiness for about a month and a half.

I could hardly keep my eyes open, and was sleeping for about 2 hours every afternoon. This was really depressing, as I haven't done any work on the book for about a month. . . . Never mind, it's wearing off now, and I'm beginning to feel like normal again, so hope to get cracking on the book again. I must try to get it finished, at least the first draft, before the baby is born, or it will be delayed for another 6 months. . . . I'm delighted about the baby, though, and hope everything will be o.k. I try not to count on it too much just yet — one doesn't feel quite safe until the first 4 months are over.[684]

Peg remarked that Jack was not as thrilled as she and Jocelyn were about a new baby, but he was "at least philosophical about the whole thing and admits he will probably be crazy about this one, too, when it is actually here — it is difficult for a man to feel very enthusiastic before the event . . . especially as 9 months is a long time. Anyway, the baby will be born here, and we will be going on leave in December."[685] Writing to Adele a few months later, Peggy reported that her novel was half-finished: "I want to get it done before the baby is born, but don't know if I will manage it. Still, even if it is nearly done, it won't be impossible to complete it afterwards. But I must get a lot more done before July. I'm doing my own housework now, which means I have much less time than I had before. However, the story is moving on at its usual snail's pace, so one of these years it ought to be completed."[686]

She cheered Adele's writing efforts and asked about the progress of her novel and whether she yet had a publisher. The following year Adele Wiseman's first novel, *The Sacrifice*, was published in Canada, the United States, and Great Britain. Wiseman received the Governor General's Award for Fiction, and the Beta Sigma Phi Award. One of the struggling pair of young writers had made it to the top.

In March 1955, Peggy was five months pregnant and relieved that this pregnancy was "less eventful than the last."[687] She was feeling quite well and was busy preparing for the new baby and still fixing up their bungalow. She was now doing the housework and ironing, partially to save money and partially because she claimed that women in the tropics needed "to keep physically active."[688] On the other hand, this change may have come from a desire to lessen expenses. Given the semi-tropical climate, however, and the fact she was pregnant, managing those tasks would have been a challenge. It is not surprising, therefore, that at this juncture Peggy's issues about having time to write reappear in a letter to Adele:

> I've painted both the cot and Jocelyn's bed and made bedspreads for each, which I've printed with enormous fish designs. . . . That sort of thing takes up a lot of time, and I know I don't have to do it, but when it is for one's kid, the temptation to fix things up nicely is overwhelming. I won't get the novel finished before the baby is born — but I still hope to get much of it done by then. I waste a lot of time resting in the afternoon — it is so hot these days, and now I find I just have to sleep for 2 hours every afternoon, which is a bore and a waste of time but I can't stay awake. I feel very fit if I get that sleep but hellish if I don't. The heat at this season saps one's brain — I feel wonderful physically, but mentally every thought is like lifting a ton weight. I hope the rains come soon.[689]

Peggy's comments about the weather and her need to sleep in the afternoon are typical of Westerners' response to the hot season in the Gold Coast. The heat and humidity were so enervating that people generally began their shopping at 8 a.m., because two hours later it was too hot to go out. The economist Barbara Ward found the weather in the Gold Coast very taxing. In her letters to England she frequently mentions the terrific heat and complains that it not only affects her ability to concentrate, but also diminishes her productivity as a writer.[690]

Local people were also affected by the climate and the sudden severe changes in the weather. One afternoon in June 1955, after ten days of unremitting rain, there was a tremendous storm: "It was as though the clouds had formed a solid bowl across the sky, and the bowl had now tipped, spilling its entire contents in a sudden deluge. The water drove into the ground, hammered and thudded at trees and bungalows. A ravenous wind tore at the bougainvillea and casuarina branches."[691] In the marketplace people drowned "by falling into large, deep drains hidden under the flood waters."[692]

During that same month, Peggy was engrossed in working out her Somaliland novel. Through careful scheduling and diligent effort, she had managed to finish nineteen chapters of the book. However, the realization that she would only be able to complete one or two more chapters before the baby was born, made her focus even more rigorously on bringing the Somaliland novel to its conclusion. Accomplishing that was a new experience for the apprentice novelist, since she had abandoned at least two other novels before their completion. Writing the conclusion to this one, however, was proving to be very difficult. Peggy was also dogged by insecurities. She told Adele about "terrible spells of feeling the characters are weak and unconvincing" and the recurring anxiety, "is the thing going to be interesting? It's interesting to me, but will it be to anyone else?"[693] Moreover there was the question of a publisher. Recently many novels had been set in Africa, and Peg thought publishers might reject her book, even though it had a different focus: her book was not political nor was it axe-grinding against the "white man's burden." It was not primarily concerned with the type of European who hates Africa, but with the type who is completely bound up with it. "And not, I hope, in the manner of so many Africa-lovers in novels — 'God! The Masai are wonderful people! Nature's gentlemen!' — that sort of thing makes me sick."[694]

Her letters make clear that Peg's attention was centred on her writing and her family. Her delight in Jocelyn's development is apparent in the many descriptions and anecdotes that she includes in letters to Adele. She mentioned, for example, that one day, when Jocelyn was in the car with Jack, she said, "'Well, mummy's not here, so I guess we can go really fast now, eh?'"[695] Jocelyn had been well, except for the typical bruises of a three-year-old. "Whatever is wrong, she has to have a bandage on it. She has taken once more to saying her prayers at night, and she intones them in a voice that could be heard miles away. The religious effect is slightly offset by the fact that she insists on following [her prayers] with a loud rendition of the children's song, 'I'm a Little Teapot.'"[696]

Peg and Jack had decided that their second child would be born at Ridge Hospital, Accra. Remaining close to their home in the Gold Coast appealed to Peggy after the dreadful days in London following Jocelyn's birth in 1952. However, it turned out that things were not to be simple. In July, she had bouts of false labour on and off for three weeks, and went into the hospital twice only to go home again. The second time was frightening and hectic. She went into labour one evening while Jack and several Africans were trying to deal with a spitting cobra in the garage. In the midst of having contractions, Peggy paced the floor and worried herself sick at the thought of Jack blinded for life. "Spitting cobras," she explained to Adele, "aim for the eyes and have dead accuracy up to seven feet."[697] Fortunately, the men were able to take care of the snake. At last on August 9, Peg gave birth to a healthy baby boy, who weighed eight pounds, twelve ounces.

In her memoirs, Margaret Laurence devotes two and a half pages to a description of the situation before and after the birth of her son, David. It was "an easy labour of 8 hours" and an "easy birth."[698] A "wonderful" African midwife, Salome, was with her and put the infant on Peg's abdomen even before the cord was severed. "I felt as though I were looking over God's shoulder at the moment of the creation of life. I was witnessing a miracle."[699] Jack, however, did not arrive at the hospital right away, and Peggy was very concerned. "He turned up at four o'clock, the beginning of visiting hours," looking terribly upset.[700] Jack had been phoning the hospital trying to get information and did not realize their son had been born.[701] They decided to name him Robert David Wemyss Laurence.[702] Peggy soon felt fit enough to go home, but she acquiesced to the doctor's orders and remained in hospital for a week. When David was "just over a month old," she was able to resume work on her novel.[703]

In letters to Adele, she describes this period, and thirty years later returned to it in her memoirs. Laurence's letters make resoundingly clear that writing was essential to her life. That view, however, was not shared by Jack. Her description of their differences on this matter is significantly understated in her memoirs, however, where Jack's opinion is presented in a matter-of-fact manner, without qualification: "The kids had to be in bed and asleep before I could begin [writing]. This was my own rule; no one imposed it on me, least of all Jack, who was always patient and understanding about what he conceived of not as his wife's vocation but as a kind of work she was interested in doing."[704]

In fact, writing, for Peggy, was never merely "something she was interested in doing." She was distressed that Jack viewed her work this way, as if it were a hobby analogous to other wives' interest in tennis or knitting. Jack did not fully understand that Peggy considered writing "a gift," something unexpected, but given to her from God. It was her vocation, and she felt a responsibility, very much in the biblical sense, to both respect and nurture that gift.

It is surprising, therefore, that as this passage in *Dance on the Earth* continues, Peggy actually defends Jack's view of things. One may wonder why she defended her husband, since this major difference between them was the cause of some serious problems: "If you haven't published a thing except one story in *Queen's Quarterly* and a small book of translations from Somali poetry, you can't really claim to be a professional writer, or so I felt."[705]

Peggy's remarks throw a smoke screen over the reality of her situation. She minimizes her literary efforts by referring only to tangible results. She cites one published short story and omits any mention of the prestigious appearance of "Uncertain Flowering" in *Story*. She also downplays her impressive and hard-won achievement in *A Tree for Poverty*.

Even though Peggy had not published much at that point, it certainly was not due to a lack of effort. Given the layout of their bungalow, Jack must have been aware of how diligently his wife worked at her writing, regardless of whether she used the typewriter or wrote by hand. Obviously it was not a hobby. Furthermore, her daily routine of writing made clear that she was determined to overcome whatever shortcomings she felt her work might have. Peggy continued to wrestle with the written word, regardless of the lack of tangible success in terms of publication. She had the sort of determination that an apprentice writer must possess in order to achieve. Despite setbacks and obstacles, Peggy persisted in her efforts. She tried to create authentic characters, laboured with the shape of the novel, and experimented with point of view.

In mid-October 1955, Peg and Jack went on leave to London. They looked forward to a reunion with Peg's Mum and Aunt Ruby, who were to arrive a bit ahead of them. Although Peg and Jack had visited with them in Vancouver the year before, David had been born since then. The anticipated reunion and time together turned out to be very stressful for

Peg, who later simply said, "[It was] not one of the easiest times of my life."[706] Unfortunately Aunt Ruby had slipped and broken her wrist shortly after arriving in London. As a result, it was impossible for Peg and Jack and their young children (Jocelyn was three and David only three months old) to stay with the older women. They had to find a place of their own, regardless of their limited finances.

"Affordable flats were hard to come by and we needed one quickly. Jack spent several days of weary and solitary looking, while I stayed with the children and Mum and Aunt Ruby in their expensive flat, trying to keep Jocelyn entertained and David from yelling, simultaneously talking to Mum and my aunt."[707]

Finally Jack found a third-floor flat in Knightsbridge and they moved: "The flat was dark, dusty, gloomy, and when we first arrived, filthy. I scoured, scrubbed, and almost literally threw Dettol around the place. David never adjusted to the time difference between West Africa and England, with the result that he awakened for his morning feeding at about 4 a.m. . . . The flat was supposed to have central heating but it didn't work."[708]

Living on the third floor necessitated dragging the baby's carriage up and down two flights of stairs every day. Despite such difficulties, Peggy felt the visit in London had been worthwhile. Mum had been able to see her grandson for the first time and to be with them for his private christening in a nearby Anglican church. She also enjoyed seeing how much little Jocelyn had changed in a year and a half. When it was time for Mum and Aunt Ruby to return to Canada, Peg gave Mum a long letter that she had written and asked her not to open it until they were aboard the ship. "I simply wanted to tell her (and for me, this was more possible on the page than in speech) how much I loved her, how much she meant to me, and how much her encouragement of my writing had strengthened me, even though I had had nothing published professionally. I also wanted to tell her that she could not have been more my mother if she had actually borne me."[709]

Conveying her feelings in a letter may seem to be an impersonal gesture, especially since Peggy had the opportunity to do so in person. Although she was a good conversationalist, in matters of the heart Peggy found it easier to write than speak. After many years of writing letters, that form of communication seemed more natural and enduring. A letter could be reread when the voice could no longer be heard, just as viewing the old photos in Peggy's family albums brought the deceased back to life, at least for the moment.[710]

The return journey from England to the Gold Coast was dreadful for Jack and Peggy. Although they had left their London flat early in the morning, the flight to Africa was much delayed due to heavy fog. They spent a "miserable" day getting "on and off many different buses with a good deal of hand luggage and the two children."[711] Finding a place to heat David's bottle was a further difficulty. In addition, they had no idea when they would eventually reach the airport or what the situation there would be. At last, twelve hours later than their scheduled departure, they were on board the plane. En route to the Gold Coast, they landed at Tripoli where they were delayed for another two hours while the plane was reloaded properly. Then there were more problems. At the Idris airport, baby David needed to be changed and little Jocelyn became sick all the way to the restroom. This return trip to the Gold Coast had none of the delights of their leisurely sea voyage to Somaliland six years earlier.[712]

Once back in the Gold Coast, however, they settled into a routine and Peggy was able to work again on her manuscript. Regardless of her objections to being a "memsahib," she now had an advantage which many women writers of the time lacked: a good deal of domestic help. Because of Jack's position as engineer, it was taken for granted that they would have servants. This meant at least a cook and housekeeper. While Jack was away at work, Peggy did not have to attend alone to shopping, house cleaning, and caring for the children. For most of those tasks she had some help.

By April 1956, her writing was at an important juncture. Peg had decided to take a break from her Somaliland novel, and she began working on a short story that had been on her mind for over a year. It quickly grew to eighty pages and Peggy could not "seem to get it down fast enough." She found herself working on it regularly four nights a week until one or two o'clock in the morning. The short story was becoming a novel. Set in the Gold Coast, the plot was "mainly about an African schoolteacher who's lost the old life and not yet firmly grasped the new." In sharing this news with Adele, Peggy made a positive comment, something she rarely did, "Parts of it are good."[713]

Although corresponding with Adele was important to Peggy, sometimes it made her very frustrated. Even when the women wrote frequently, the time lag between letters was significant, and Peggy longed for a real conversation face to face with Adele:

> Sometimes in this intellectual desert I wish I could drop into your flat for a talk. I hardly ever talk about anything that interests me here, as I'm sure people would be bored. Jack and I are going to as few parties as possible this tour, as we are thoroughly sick of the incessant small-talk. Not that I am being condescending about people here — no doubt everyone feels sick of small talk, but no one dares to break the pattern.[714]

By the next month, Peg had completed the first part of the novel which eventually became *This Side Jordan*. Nevertheless, she continued to struggle with its structure because the novel did not adhere to strict chronological sequence. "The various parts," she said, "will have to be inter-leaved in some miraculous fashion."[715] Moreover, she wanted to write the second part from the point of view of a European woman, and that was proving to be more difficult than the first part, which had been done from a man's perspective: "Mainly, I suppose, because I tend to be rather fed up at this point with the European community here and that is not an attitude to have for writing. I don't want to condemn even them — I only want to understand them. . . . You know, I don't think I am capable of writing anything unless I like my characters."[716]

After detailing the progress of her novel, Peggy describes for Adele the children's development: David was healthy, weighed about twenty pounds, and was very strong. "Fortunately he's happy most of the time," she said, "but I can see he's going to be a little demon when he's a bit older."[717] By May, he was crawling and "rapidly developing into a menace." But he was "so good-natured that one cannot get annoyed with him."[718] Jocelyn was now paying attention to clothes and dresses. She also had a three-wheeler bike that she parked beside her bed at night. During the day, she zoomed around on it and was "into everything."[719] Perhaps seeing her daughter's delight brought back memories to Peggy of her own birthday present at age four, "a splendid green-and-silver" tricycle, which she had lugged up the back stairs of the Simpson house to show to her ailing mother.

After congratulating Adele on *The Sacrifice*, Peg mentioned that she had recently read Mordecai Richler's *Son of a Lesser Hero*. She then praised Adele's novel: "You have something [quite different from Richler] . . . without which no writer can ever be great and maybe not even good, and that quality is love and compassion."[720] Peggy then recounted some difficulties she had grappled with as she tried to complete her own novel:

> It is now approaching 6 months since I began working until 2 or 3 a.m. four nights a week, and I think the strain is beginning to show! I feel at the moment rather discouraged, as I'm afraid I'm just about at the end of my tether, and I haven't finished the story yet. Can't get rid of headaches, and feel generally beat-up. However, I have a very strong constitution, thank God, and so if I can only make a last burst and finish the damn thing off (rough draft, you understand) I shall then take about three weeks off and do nothing but sleep. I hope the effort proves worth it. Did you feel discouraged when you were nearing the end? I feel awful. I think the story is terrible. It is probably the worst piece of prose in history. Also, who am I to write about Africa? I don't know a damn thing about it, relatively speaking. I've had the nerve to write half the thing from an African's point of view. Also, it's too long (344 pages now and with an estimated 50 to go). (Time out while I remove David from under the table where I am working!) The Europeans will hate the European parts and the Africans will hate the African parts. Never mind — it has a good title, *This Side Jordan*.[721]

Peg had put aside her earlier Somaliland novel, even though it was nearly completed, in order to work on this new novel, which was set in the Gold Coast. On the whole, she was pleased with the way it was developing and told Adele, "I feel strangely fanatical about it. (Excuse me a moment — David is standing on his head and appears about ready to collapse)."[722]

Peggy's comments about young David, interjected at several points in this letter, indicate how difficult it was for her to find time to write during the day when the children were active and needed attention. "David goes like a bomb all day long. He crawls very fast, too fast, and is on the verge of walking. He is a terror, and has a terrible temper and an equally large amount of charm."[723] Her letters from West Africa, such as this one, rarely have the kind of detailed descriptions of people or events that appear in Laurence's letters from Somaliland. Now, with two active youngsters and several literary projects under way, she simply did not have the time to include those sorts of descriptions in her letters. However, her observant eye and attentive ear absorbed all that for future writing. Before concluding the letter, Peg apologized for mentioning such "boring details" about her struggles, but she emphasized again that Adele was the only person she knew who would understand her dilemmas.

Laurence's delight in her children and concern about them while struggling to develop her talents as a writer are in stark contrast to the choices made by another contemporary, Doris Lessing, who let nothing stand in the way of her writing and her political activities. Lessing walked away from her first husband and her children, when they were three and five years of age, and for many years had almost no contact with them.[724]

Writing again to Adele, Peggy apologized for sending her the previous "stupid letter," full of her own doubts and depressions. Now she reported things were going "quite well":[725]

> I've got one more episode to do in the first draft, then a heck of a lot of fixing up . . . to do before I start turning my attention to re-writing proper. In other words, the story has to be hammered into shape before I start worrying overmuch about the style. Maybe that's wrong — I don't know. I think perhaps in the past I may have fussed over writing too much, bleeding it to death in the process. . . . I feel my great flaw in the past

has been mulling over something much too long, and kind of losing the thread in the process. This, I may say, will be the third novel I have written (the other 2 never got quite finished as they were no good, especially the first — the second, the one set in Somaliland, I still have some feeble hopes for). I am thirty years old. This is not good enough.[726]

Remarks such as these made to Adele over several months in 1956 make clear that *This Side Jordan* developed in the midst of a great deal of worry and effort on Peggy's part. Thirty years later, however, she remembered it very differently. In her memoirs, Laurence relates that the process was easy: "Those late-night hours when I wrote the first draft of *This Side Jordan* were exhilarating. I scribbled on and on, as though a voice were telling me what to write down. It was the easiest novel I ever wrote because I knew absolutely nothing about writing a novel. The pages poured out."[727] Perhaps that statement reflects her initial engagement with the manuscript, but it is certainly misleading as a description of the composition of *This Side Jordan*. Moreover, contrary to her assertion, Laurence did know a great deal about writing a novel, having struggled with at least two previous novels which were never completed. However when she penned her memoirs in her late fifties, with many literary accomplishments behind her, the memory of her first published novel may have taken on a glow that is not reflected at all in her contemporary letters.

In the process of writing *This Side Jordan*, moreover, she had done a considerable amount of research and reading.[728] Laurence familiarized herself with Asante proverbs, religious beliefs, and customs. She also spent time with the principal of an African school, visiting the classrooms and meeting with the teachers to determine if her impressions as reflected in the novel had been correct; "they were. . . . I was delighted to find that I hadn't been wrong."[729] Peggy was preoccupied with her manuscript and expressed her concerns over and over in letters to Adele:

I'm sorry I keep chattering on about all this to you. The thing is, I can't talk about it to anyone except Jack, and altho' he is wonderful about it, and has an excellent critical mind, he hasn't actually done this kind of work himself. I often feel I am leading a double life — do you? It seems a kind of irony to me that the thing in life which is most important to me, next to my husband and kids, is something I can never talk about, never let anyone know about, even.[730]

It may seem strange today that Laurence felt unable to mention her work, but in the early 1950s, concealing the fact she was a writer was not untypical for women writers. It was as much a sign of those times as it was the result of Peggy's shyness. Her younger contemporary, the writer Alice Munro, recounts similar behaviour at the beginning of her own literary career in the 1950s.[731]

Peggy's efforts to shape the novel were further complicated because of her efforts to lose weight. She related to Adele an anecdote about Jocelyn, who had cut out a magazine picture and said to Peggy: "Wouldn't you like to be SLIM like this girl? You'd better keep it as your diet picture!"[732] As the wife of a handsome and important engineer, Peggy was determined to look slender in order to be attractive to her husband and his associates. She was afraid that extra weight would make her less desirable in her husband's eyes. The rigour of trying to diet while she was struggling with a manuscript took a toll, but in photographs from that period she does look quite trim. Margaret Laurence's appearance during those years is remarkably different from the worn, rather heavy features in photographs of her that were taken in the late 1970s and 1980s.

In July, Peggy sent Adele a long letter that filled two airmail letterettes. She congratulated Adele over the news that the prestigious firm of Victor Gollancz had plans to publish *The Sacrifice* in Great Britain and told her she intended to purchase a copy because "it is a mistake for an author to give away free copies — let your friends help sales!"[733] She reported that she had been laid low with a terrible cold and fever, which made it hard for her to get up and look after the children. The letter also summarized themes in *This Side Jordan*. Peggy explained that the novel unfolds partly from the point of view of Nathaniel, an African schoolteacher, and partly from the point of view of Miranda, the young wife of a European accountant in Africa. "It is really the story of her attempt to make friends with a few sample Africans . . . her serious but blundering attempts to understand them; and her final realization that intellectual 'racial tolerance' is not enough — it is, in fact, only the beginning. She fails, of course, as we all do who try the same thing and with the same naiveté, but she begins to realize why she has failed."[734] Nathaniel dreams of the "past glories of Ghana, and the glory that will be in the future, but he doesn't know how to achieve it." She told Adele that Nathaniel's story is told "in very emotional terms, and Miranda's is on a much more subdued level, as I think would be the case."[735]

Some of Peggy's nagging uncertainties about her work also surface in this letter. She refers to it as "a very plain story in the sense that nothing much happens, I suppose. No one is raped or seduced, there are no riots or anything like that. Maybe not enough happens. I don't know."[736] She told Adele that she was sick of books about Africa that were "full of wildly dancing tribesmen, human sacrifices, and Europeans who are always drunk and always leaping in and out of bed with each other. That isn't the Africa I know. Maybe the Africa I know doesn't have enough sensation to make it book material. We shall see. I can see there is a lot of work still to do."[737]

Although she described many uncertainties about her novel, Laurence's contemporary letters also convey a real sense of excitement about that book.

In early November 1956, however, things became more complicated. Peggy's Aunt Ruby wired Jack from Canada to say that Peg's Mum was seriously ill with cancer, and surgery would be necessary. Aunt Ruby wanted Jack to break the news to Peggy, thus continuing a Simpson family pattern of meeting adversity with indirection.

Greatly concerned about Mum's health, Peg and Jack decided that she and the children would leave Africa after the New Year and return to Canada before Jack's contract ended in the spring. Doing that would ensure Peg some quality time to visit with Mum and provide an opportunity to assess the state of her health. Once she and Jack had reached that decision, she pushed forward with changes to the novel, knowing it would be "virtually impossible to work at it for some time" once she was back in Canada.

By the end of November, "after working terrifically hard" on the book, Peg felt that the manuscript was completed.[738] Although she knew that some chapters would need to be polished when it was retyped, on the whole, she considered it "finished." Moreover, Jack had "read the first few chapters and liked them."[739] At this point she felt "absolutely beat" and wanted Adele to riffle through the pages, even though "the script is in a shocking state, all scribbled over." She also realized that "the pleasure is in the doing of the story — irrespective of what happens to it now, I am beginning to feel a bit empty, and to wonder what I shall do without it to work on. I shall have to type it all out neatly to send it somewhere, I suppose — I hate the thought of that job. So boring."[740] She believed that the manuscript was completed; she had no inkling that work on *This Side Jordan* would actually drag on over the next two years.

In trying to get the novel into shape before she and the children returned to Canada, Peggy had overextended herself. Then, as she set about preparing to leave the Gold Coast, there were disturbing events to deal with. First, David, fifteen months old, had a "bad bout of malaria." The impact of coping with malaria, whether in their family or among others, was to leave a deep impression on Laurence. She mentions it more than once, most notably in a moving convocation address at Emmanuel College in May 1983.[741] Now, she described her anxious state in a letter to Adele:

> I have been worried sick about him [David]. However, he is o.k. now and eating once more. For days he was absolutely listless and it nearly broke my heart to see him that way. He goes for his second blood test tomorrow, to see if the parasites are gone. The day before he got malaria, he fell and gashed open his head, and had a very nasty wound. Troubles certainly don't come singly. If anything else happens I shall be a candidate for a mental hospital. However, now that the story is finished, I aim to try to get some sleep for a change![742]

A few weeks later, both David and Jocelyn became sick "either with food poisoning or worms."[743] Not long afterwards a thief broke into the house. Then, in the midst of great concern about Mum's cancer and her own children's health, Peggy herself again came down with malaria. She wrote Adele: "Thank God my story is finished for the moment — I simply couldn't concentrate on it now."[744]

CHAPTER NINE

Stolen Time

In early January 1957, Jack Laurence stood at the Accra airport and watched his wife cross the tarmac toward BOAC flight #272, carrying David in her arms and holding young Jocelyn by the hand. This would be their longest separation since their marriage ten years earlier. On the morning of January 9, the plane finally landed in London, where Peggy and the children visited for several days with Adele Wiseman.[745] The two women spent hours catching up on news of family and friends and talking about their writing. Then, within a few days Peggy and the children were on their way to Canada. Fortunately, little Jocelyn and David slept during most of that long transatlantic flight.

The years in Africa had followed upon Peggy's work for *The Westerner* and the *Winnipeg Citizen*. Without her weekly or daily newspaper deadlines, Peggy had time to experiment with her literary gifts. Living in the Horn of Africa and the Gold Coast had a significant intellectual as well as literary impact on her development as a writer. When Peggy left Africa in 1957, it was only a physical departure. The continent and its people were to remain with her. Her homes in Vancouver would have African items as part of the décor, and friends who came to dinner recall that Peggy would serve traditional African foods from time to time. She would also review books about Africa for the *Vancouver Sun* and *Canadian Literature*, and later, when living in England, she continued to read literature in English by authors from the newly independent African countries. She attended London performances of new plays by African writers, such as Wole Soyinka and went to the Commonwealth Literary Festival with Marjory Whitelaw of the CBC. Margaret would also spent a good deal of time researching her seventh book, which is her only work of extended literary criticism: *Long Drums and Cannons: Nigerian Dramatists and Novelists 1952-1966*, published in 1968. When it was reissued in 2001, the noted scholar, Douglas Killam, remarked that "it has lost none of its validity as a way into understanding the literature that was produced between 1952 . . . and 1966."[746] Considering the number of times that Margaret Laurence moved after she left Africa, it is worth noting that, at the time of her death twenty years later she still had almost a hundred books by or about Africa and Africans in her library.[747]

While living in Africa, Laurence's short fiction had not met with the success she had hoped for in terms of publication. Nevertheless, out of her experiences in the Gold Coast and her omnivorous reading about the customs and beliefs of West Africans, Laurence was later to produce a very fine first novel, *This Side Jordan,* and a remarkable collection of short stories, *The Tomorrow-Tamer and other Stories*, which captures the former British colony on the threshold of independence and sheds light on that situation from various perspectives. But these achievements were not on her horizon in January 1957; they lay in the future.

Arriving in Montreal following their long flight, Peggy and the children were welcomed by Elliot and Kay Bolton, old friends from Winnipeg, and she was happy to relax for a few days at their home. But after living in the semi-tropical Gold Coast, Peg and the children found it challenging to adjust to Montreal's January temperature: -40°F! The children, who had never seen snow before, played in a dishpan full of snow, brought in by the Bolton's son.[748] Kay Bolton recalled that David Laurence, who was still in diapers and unaccustomed to stairs or shoes, kept walking right off the top step at their home and into the air.

After relaxing with the Boltons, Margaret and the children boarded the plane for another long flight, to the West Coast, where Peggy's close friend and former school chum, Mona, was to meet them. The plane's arrival in Vancouver was delayed for hours, however, and when it finally landed before dawn, Mona greeted a weary and very bedraggled trio.[749] As they sped from the airport, Mona's car was stopped by the police, but after listening to her explanation, the police, with sirens blaring, escorted her car through Stanley Park to North Vancouver.

A few days later, Peg made the short flight to Victoria where Mum now lived. Aunt Ruby met her and exclaimed with relief: "'Here you are. You're young and strong. You'll take over. You'll manage things.'" Peggy's body tensed as she realized her life was about to undergo a radical change. She had two young children to care for, her Mum was dying, and her husband was not due to arrive from Africa until late April, four long months away. "I was suddenly petrified," she recalled. "I felt like my life had changed irrevocably. The fun was over. I was thirty-one."[750]

Not only was Peggy filled with dread as she faced the reality of Mum's condition, but many routine tasks also became difficult as they settled in. That month temperatures in British Columbia plunged to record lows and snowstorms enveloped the area. Greater Victoria was hit with its heaviest snow in forty years, and within the week southern Vancouver Island was digging out of a nine-inch snowfall. From the time of Peggy's return to Canada in that cold and snowy January, which was so reminiscent of Neepawa's weather at the time of her father's death, through the months that followed, she felt that her life on all sides was enveloped in gloom.

The international situation also was fraught with dangerous uncertainties. Overseas, Great Britain endeavoured to secure its hold on the Aden protectorate in Yemen. The Gold Coast prepared to celebrate its new, but fragile, political independence as Ghana. On the domestic front, there was an outbreak of red measles in Vancouver during February. Then city officials, overruling citizens' protests, mandated fluoridation of the city's water. A twenty-six-year-old woman plunged from the Granville Bridge and a boy was trapped in the ice on Burnaby Lake. The murderer of a nine-year-old child was hanged in British Columbia, and two elderly women sitting on a bench were struck and killed by a car that careened out of control.

Events such as these fuelled Peggy's anxieties about the precarious nature of seemingly ordinary situations, especially in Jack's absence. These grim domestic disasters were eclipsed, however, by the international arms race. This characterized the Cold War period when Russia and the United States, the two military superpowers, were rushing to test and stockpile atomic weapons. Russia exploded its fifth atomic bomb a month after Peggy's return to Canada, and Vancouver launched a civil-defence plan for the evacuation of the city "in case of atomic attack." The newspapers tried to assure worried citizens that Vancouver could be evacuated in less than twelve hours, provided all available sea and land transport were deployed![751]

These powerful reminders of man's hubris, folly, and vulnerability were not lost on Peggy, and the young mother-writer would later call upon memories of that period to provide the anxiety-ridden backdrop for her novel *The Fire-Dwellers* (1969). The tense situation in Vancouver also inspired a bleak, futuristic science-fiction story, unusual for Laurence, that dealt with the possibility and consequences of an atomic disaster, "A Queen in Thebes" (*Tamarack Review*, 1964), which is included here in Appendix C. Laurence later said, "It seems a strange story for me to have written, and indeed it is the only science fiction story I've ever done."[752]

When Margaret Laurence returned to Canada from the Gold Coast, she brought with her the manuscript of *This Side Jordan*, which she hoped to discuss with Mum. After getting settled in Victoria, Laurence described her situation to Adele and apologized again for not writing sooner. Getting settled, writing to Jack, and typing her manuscript had kept her fully occupied.[753] The letter also related the difficulties and tension she had experienced trying to adjust to life in that very small house, with two children under the age of five and two elderly relatives, one terminally ill with cancer.

Although Mum was home from hospital, she was weak and needed large doses of painkillers. Peg did not want to alarm David and Jocelyn, who were two and a half and four and a half years old, respectively. The children missed Jack and the familiar routine of their life in the Gold Coast. For Peggy, keeping them busy, happy, and quiet was a major challenge. She later described those months in Victoria as "among the most difficult and anguished of my life."[754] The little one-storey house on

Windsor Road was too small for three adults and two young children, but Aunt Ruby put a folding cot for Peggy in her own bedroom and placed the children in a finished basement room, adding a crib for David. Peggy found those arrangements completely unacceptable. She lacked privacy, the children were far from her, and there was no place to work on her manuscript or write letters to Jack. She became increasingly irritable: "Without privacy, I knew I would break down entirely."

One day when the two older women were out, Peggy took action. Her description of what followed is significant. In *Dance on the Earth* the tone at this point shifts markedly from the previous section and the passage becomes very animated. In recounting what took place, Laurence uses several sentences commencing with the pronoun "I" and followed immediately by a series of strong verbs ("wrestled," "dragged," "rigged," "strung," "slung"), which convey how she dealt with the unacceptable arrangements in Aunt Ruby's house:

> Regarded with glee and astonishment by my prancing and excited young, I constructed a bedroom for myself in the basement, right beside theirs. Their bedroom had walls and a door and was furnished with a rug, a single bed, my brother's bookshelves, the old Wemyss desk that belonged to Bob, and a crib Aunt Ruby had borrowed for David. My room was somewhat different. The basement was a jumble of old trunks, cast-off furniture, clotheslines, and assorted junk. I wrestled the fold-up bed and mattress out of Aunt Ruby's room and down to the basement. I dragged two trunks and spaced them at the end of the bed. I found an old door and placed it with one end on each trunk; I had a desk. I rigged a discarded lamp from the ceiling light with an extra socket. I strung up clotheslines across the open sides of my room and slung blankets from them to act as walls. I had my own space. (*Dance*, 114)

When the women returned, Aunt Ruby became furious. She could not understand Peggy's need for privacy or her desire to sleep near the children. Under great strain, Ruby lashed out at Peggy, and Peggy replied angrily: "You don't understand, you just don't! You've never had children. I'm not going to have them sleeping away down there if I'm not near them. And I'm not a child! I can't sleep in your bedroom!"[755]

After Laurence recounts that situation, she quickly rationalizes Aunt Ruby's behaviour and relates how, once again, indirection in the face of disaster became Ruby Simpson's modus operandi: "Aunt Ruby was, as she always had been, efficient and capable. . . . When personal emotions threatened, she became all practicality, concentrating on the details of everyday life: meals, medication, the evening glass of sherry, news of neighbours and friends. She was magnificent. As for me, I tried my best. What held me together was that I had to follow Aunt Ruby's lead for Mum's sake and for the sake of my children."[756]

On days when Mum was feeling a bit better, she read the manuscript of *This Side Jordan*, offering comments and suggestions to Peggy. Her feedback was genuinely helpful and very reassuring. "It was," said Laurence, "her final gift to me."[757]

Fortunately Peg had additional support from Jack's parents, Elsie and John Laurence, who also lived in Victoria. They had raised a large family and now had many grandchildren. John and Elsie were accustomed to youngsters. Peg and the children visited them weekly and frequently stayed overnight. They felt welcomed and more relaxed there. Elsie was also a published writer, who understood the tension that Peggy felt as she tried to make time to write and to be an attentive mother while having the many responsibilities, even temporarily, of being a single parent.[758] Peggy told Adele that Elsie had been "wonderful" and "an enormous help." In her memoirs, Laurence states that she could hardly believe the strength Jack's mother had given to her.[759]

Not only did Elsie Laurence give Peggy emotional support, but she also gave her practical encouragement, urging her to enter *This Side Jordan* in the annual fiction contest sponsored by the *Atlantic Monthly*. In addition, Elsie Laurence typed a third of the manuscript for her. Although the deadline was June 30, Peggy was fearful that Mum's condition might worsen at any moment, and she raced to complete the book. By March 17, the typing was done, three months ahead of the contest's deadline. She did not expect to win, but she was canny enough to realize that the *Atlantic Monthly* returned manuscripts quickly and often took other scripts in addition to the winning one. Peggy intended to await comments from the *Atlantic Monthly*, then revise her novel and submit it to Macmillan, Canada, the firm which had recently published Adele's first novel, *The Sacrifice*. Peg, however, was uncertain of how to proceed with Macmillan and turned to Adele for practical advice about submitting the manuscript.[760]

The completion of a novel, especially a first novel, is a major event in a writer's life. Once Peggy had sent off the manuscript, she was prey to conflicted feelings:

> Well, now that it is done I don't know what to do with myself, and feel very lost without it, as though a lot of people I knew suddenly went away. Also, I wonder how long I will go before I start anything else. Quite awhile, I hope, as I feel I must get settled down somewhere first, and I have an overpowering urge to make up to my family (i.e., husband and kids) for all the neglect they have endured over the past year. Not really neglect, you know, but half my mind was elsewhere. I wonder what I shall want to write about next?[761]

In the months that followed, she continued to work on several literary projects. She told Adele she was struggling with the "previous half-finished novel on Somaliland," as well as editing her diaries from Somalia, and thinking about a novel that focused on an old woman at the end of her life (this became *The Stone Angel*). Peggy had already put months of effort into that novel set in Somaliland, but she still was not satisfied with it:

> Its trouble, I can see now, was a basic lack of simplicity — a theme should be as simple as birth or death — something that can be summed up in a single sentence and yet whose ramifications are so wide that it can never be entirely said at all. The theme of that one wasn't simple — it was superficially very complicated

because I didn't really know what I was trying to say and therefore camouflaged it with intricacies of plot. I think I loved Somaliland too much to write about it so soon after being there.[762]

This letter, written two months after Peggy's return to Canada, also contains significant information about Laurence's approach to fiction and provides a fascinating glimpse into some of the ideas that she later developed in *The Stone Angel*:

Old age is something which interests me more and more — the myriad ways people meet it, some pretending it doesn't exist, some terrified by every physical deterioration because that final appointment is something they cannot face, some trying to balance the demands and routine of this life with an increasing need to gather together the threads of the spirit so that when the thing comes they will be ready — whether it turns out to be death or only another birth. I think birth is the greatest experience of life, right until the end, and then death is the greatest experience. There are times when I can believe that the revelation of death will be something so vast we are incapable of imagining it.[763]

Peggy's interest in writing about old age pre-dates her return to Canada. She had written a moving poem about old age, "Let My Voice Live," which was published in the *Canadian Tribune* when she was only twenty-four and living in England.[764] Peggy had continued to think about old age as a subject for fiction during the following years, and this letter to Adele indicates that, by 1957, she had already begun to imagine in specific detail the inner world of an elderly woman who would later become Hagar, the central character in *The Stone Angel* (1964). The gestation of that novel was a gradual and lengthy process.

I picture a very old woman who knows she is dying, and who despises her family's sympathy and solicitude and also pities it, because she knows they think her mind is partly gone — and they will never realize that she is moving with tremendous excitement — part fear and part eagerness — towards a great and inevitable happening, just as years before she experienced birth. I probably sound off my rocker. *It is only because you are the only person, apart from Jack, to whom I can spout these vague and half-formed ideas.* [emphasis added].[765]

This letter to Adele included the news that Peggy was on a strict diet: "I have lost 10 lbs. Am living on celery & cottage cheese!" She was "gleefully ticking off the days" until Jack arrived in Canada.[766] Peggy wanted to look attractive when her husband reached Vancouver, but the worries of the past months had taken an enormous toll on her. The stresses of living with Mum, who was very ill, and with Aunt Ruby; the adjustments to life in Canada, and the climate of British Columbia after four years in the Gold Coast; the sole responsibility for two small children; and the difficulty of finding the necessary time and place to edit and type her manuscript — all these issues had turned the months in Victoria into something of a nightmare for her.

By early June, Jack had arrived and the family was together again. Jack had secured a position with an engineering firm, and soon was busy with a project involving the highway to Squamish, north of Vancouver. Peggy noted: "[He] is outdoors most the time and loves it." A harbour and town development had also been proposed there and Jack expected to be involved with that project. They both wanted to move up to Squamish within the next six months. "We like the idea of living in a small town," she wrote to a friend, "and I have highly coloured daydreams about a picturesque old fishing lodge at Squamish with all our friends coming for weekends."[767]

In the meantime, they had found other lodgings in North Vancouver below the brooding ridges of Grouse Mountain, and had become "reasonably well settled" in the ground-floor flat of a large house at 1540 St. George's Avenue (no longer standing). Peggy and Jack decided to make some of their living-room furniture and began with a black-walnut coffee table. In describing their new "home," Peggy was pleased and in high spirits:

> It is really perfect for us right now — there is a large yard where the kids can play; large kitchen, small living room; two bedrooms. The house is owned by an elderly Italian woman and the garden reminds me of your two old ladies' garden in Rome. There are grape vines all over the place; a profusion of somewhat untidy classical circular flower beds, a cement chair made to resemble one made out of tree branches; a weird concrete tree with concrete snake eternally coiling round it; tiny birdbath-cum-fish pool with concrete cat forever chasing concrete fish and remaining for all time unsuccessful — the whole thing is rather like a burlesqued version of Keats' "Ode on a Grecian Urn." All our bathroom plumbing is a rich burgundy color! When I have a bath, I get into a positively Homeric mood and keep muttering "wine-dark sea. . ."[768]

This lively description conveys Peggy's pleasure in her new surroundings, but the letter also contains worried comments about her writing. She had not heard from the *Atlantic Monthly*. Although she didn't believe her novel really stood a chance of winning the contest, she hoped they would return the manuscript soon. In the meantime, she wanted to complete another novel, her Somaliland book, "but it won't be a matter of rewriting — it is very poor stuff." After looking over that manuscript, she concluded that it would "have to be redone completely. Perhaps even entirely chucked out and something else tried."[769]

Peggy's conflicted feelings about juggling her roles as mother, wife, and writer are obvious in her postscript to Adele Wiseman, who had received a Guggenheim Fellowship and was then living in New York City: "Sometimes I envy you the freedom of mind — I've got too damn much on mine, in the way of practical concerns, like what's for dinner and when am I going to get this week's ironing done."[770]

Although Adele replied in late July, she had no further news from Peggy for several months. The reason for the delay lay in the fact that all summer long Peggy had been preoccupied with Mum's condition and assailed with worries that were reminiscent of her early years in Neepawa: there was widespread concern that a polio epidemic raging in Japan would reach British Columbia. In addition, an outbreak of the flu was expected that fall, and thirty thousand doses of the vaccine had been prepared for distribution. When Peg finally wrote to Adele on December 1, she summarized the anxious and anguished months. They had been worried about Jack's job, because there was a possibility that his company might have to declare bankruptcy. In the meantime, Mum had grown weaker and been admitted to hospital, where she needed large doses of painkillers. Then, on September 25, Mum had died. During the three preceding weeks, Peggy had been at her side in Victoria. She admitted to Adele that she had been "pretty close to the breaking-point after her Mum's death." It was, Laurence said, "the most ghastly period I've ever lived through."[771]

The relentless course of Mum's painful illness had worn down both Peggy and her brother, Bob. Although he was working in Nanaimo, he frequently made the trip back to Victoria. There he and Peg would go to the hospital and spend time together afterwards. Her brother was, she said, "a great help and support to me."[772] Thinking about Mum, Peg confided to Adele that "it didn't seem fair that a person who had had such a hard life should have such a hard death." Peggy's early years had been filled with death's losses, and now the dearest and closest member of her family had died after months of suffering. All the joy and exhilaration of the African years were eclipsed by that irrevocable loss and the painful return of memories of the deaths of her own parents and beloved grandmother. Although Peg was a wife and mother, now once again she was an orphan.

A short time after Mum's death, the family's troubles multiplied when Jack had to be hospitalized for kidney stones. Aunt Ruby came from Victoria to help out with the children so that Peg would have time to visit Jack. His illness and hospitalization awakened in her further anxiety. Then, Aunt Ruby came down with the Asian flu. Soon both children had caught the flu. Meanwhile, Jack had to remain in hospital longer than expected because he had developed two sets of complications following surgery. As these misfortunes multiplied, Peggy admitted to Adele, "Honestly . . . for a few weeks I thought I would go out of my mind. I guess I hit the bottle pretty hard."[773]

Fortunately, everyone made a good recovery from the Asian flu, and Peg was offered a job that winter as a marker for Professor Gordon Elliott, who was teaching English to Engineering students at the University of British Columbia in a program under the auspices of Watson Thomson. She wanted that job in order "to make money as we have been hit hard by Jack's illness."[774] Finally he was released from hospital and their life became a bit less chaotic. Within a short time Jack and Peggy were talking about resuming the search for a home of their own.[775]

After such a turbulent year, it is not surprising that Peggy felt glum when she wrote to Adele in February 1958, "So much of one's thought, time and emotions are drained away from work, with a family." As the children grew older, Peggy found that her

> greatest "inner demon" — one which no amount of wrestling with seems to quell — is that I constantly lose my temper with the children, mainly out of a frantic desire to get all the housework done so I can get to work & a sort of impotent fury when they create more & yet more domestic work to be done before I can do any writing! It isn't right, & they will probably be very maladjusted — whatever that means.[776]

By the spring, Peggy and Jack had moved again. This time from North Vancouver to a small house in the Dunbar area, not far from the University of British Columbia and Jack's old associates from Roslyn Road, Watson and Mary Thomson.[777] There were a few stores nearby and the local school was within walking distance. The school, named Lord Kitchener, was an ironic reminder of some of the worst phases of the British colonial era.

In early May, Jack's job again took him away from home. This time he went farther up north, near Fort St. John, where he remained for at least four months as resident engineer involved with the massive project of dismantling the old Peace River Bridge. During that long separation, there was little relief for Peggy in terms of household management and child care. Jack's absence also necessitated more complex domestic arrangements since Peggy no longer drove.

During most of July and August, however, Peggy and the children were able to join Jack in Fort St. John. Fortunately, they were together there when the Second Narrows Bridge in Vancouver collapsed while under construction in July, killing nineteen men. It was the city's worst disaster in many years. If Peggy had been in Vancouver, she would have been worried sick about the safety of Jack and his men who were trying to dismantle the Peace River Bridge.

The family's summer together was "idyllic." The countryside with its mountains and northern rivers was beautiful, and the children enjoyed picnics, swimming, and berry-picking, as well as the Stampede and full "Wild West atmosphere." Peg reported that she and Jack "would like to settle down somewhere like this — in the Cariboo country." Although she realized earning a living in that remote area would be difficult, she told Adele, "Maybe someday we'll have a brilliant idea on the subject. At the moment it's impossible. But both of us are country people at heart, you know. . . . We have some wild and wonderful schemes for 'our own business' but no capital!"[778]

Despite Peggy's cheerful description of the summer months, she also made oblique references to marital problems between herself and Jack. She told Adele they had had "a long depressing time," although things now seemed to be all right. Peggy thought that working outdoors had done Jack "a lot of good," and explained that she had been depressed for a long time because it seemed as if she would never be able to finish the "damn novel."[779]

She was struggling once again with revisions of *This Side Jordan*, and had decided to throw out twenty-five of the fifty chapters and start all over. "I cannot understand how I could have written it the way I did the first time. I only had half a novel. But the other half was there waiting to be picked up, as it were, only I hadn't seen it before." This time she did the European chapters from the man's point of view, which she "ought to have done the first time."[780] The following comments, which were omitted in the published version of the novel, refer to material about Johnnie's religion and indicate the complexity of Laurence's revisions. "The European character, Johnnie, goes back to the R.C. [Roman Catholic] Church at the end of the book. I didn't know whether he was going to or not, but he did. For him, it was necessary. But there is a subtle point which I don't really emphasize — the European is the one who returns to the past, in this fashion. The African for all his weakness, does not."[781]

Despite pages and pages of changes, Peggy remained uncertain about whether the novel was good enough. However, since she now found that she enjoyed reading it aloud to herself after everyone else was in bed at night, she took that as a sign that her extensive changes really had improved the novel. Reflecting later on her struggles with *This Side Jordan*, Laurence stated, "There is no job in the world in which one puts greater effort with less assurance of success and less knowledge of the true quality of one's work."[782]

In September 1958, Jocelyn, who had turned six, began Grade One and Peggy returned to marking essays for Professor Gordon Elliott. Although she could have found that work boring and very time-consuming, she actually found it interesting and was pleased to be "quite well-paid." She described Professor Elliott as "a real prince," noting, "we work very well together, and see many things the same way."[783] He was also a regional "scout" for the publisher McClelland & Stewart. In that capacity, Gordon contacted Jack McClelland about *This Side Jordan* and thus initiated a publishing connection that was to prove critical to Margaret Laurence's future success.

During the following year, 1959, Peggy was on a veritable roller coaster in terms of her work. She had "a great many ideas" for more short stories, and decided to work at them while editing *This Side Jordan*, since "new work is always so much more interesting."[784] However, she was quite discouraged by the fact that the *Atlantic Monthly* wanted further changes in the manuscript of *This Side Jordan*.

In addition to trying to satisfy them, Peggy was exploring other channels in an effort to published. She had contacted Macmillan, England, where one of the editors had admired her Somali translations and expressed an interest in her novel.[785] Peggy also wrote to a New York agent, Ruth May, who represented her new friend, the Vancouver writer Margaret Hutchison.[786] Laurence planned to send Ruth May the revised version of *This Side Jordan*, but she was in an ethical quandary about multiple submissions and queried Adele:

> Do you by any chance know what the legal position is regarding publication in England and America? That is, could I send my script to this bloke in England, and at the same time send it to Miss May for possible place-ment with an American publisher? Or would this not be cricket? . . . I am beginning to see that I am a verita-ble babe in the woods, and am beginning to feel that this whole process is fantastically complicated.[787]

For Peggy, such dilemmas were further compounded by a practical problem — she had only one fair copy of the manuscript! Determined to wrestle *This Side Jordan* into shape, she decided to sharpen her red pencils and edit ruthlessly. "I only hope I won't have to completely re-type the blessed thing," she told Adele; "It took me 3 months to type it the last time."[788] Subsequent readers' reports from the *Atlantic Monthly* added to her uncertainty; for while they complimented her on the revi-sions, they found *This Side Jordan* was still too long and declined to publish it.

Adele decided that Peggy needed a break from her labours and invited her to come to New York City for a visit. Although Peg very much wanted to see Adele, she realized the trip would be impossible: she had two young children, her husband's engineering work often took him away from home, and their limited financial resources would pro-hibit such a long journey. "How I envy you," she wrote, "with all that stimulating company! I don't think a writer should be too group-mind-ed, but it must be wonderful to know people who like to talk about such things from time to time. I miss that communication very much."[789]

Three months later, Peggy sent a poignant letter to Adele in which she confided her frustrations, her unsuccessful efforts to get her work published, and her recurring uncertainty about the quality of her fic-tion. Earlier in the day, Peggy had received a rejection letter for a story and she wrote to Adele that, when rejections arrived, doubts about the quality of her work again assailed her:

> How can one tell? Without periodic encouragement, how can one possibly know if one's own standards are any good or not? . . . The main point is — if one is writing, & more or less gambling one's whole existence on it, & cheating family & etc. of one's time and care, & putting into it very nearly the whole of one's identity, & it turns out to be no good — what will you say to them? "God, I bought the wrong stock? I invested in a mine that wasn't capable of production?[790]

Peggy continued to feel guilty about the time required for her writing, although she cared deeply about her work, and wanted to see it published, for she believed her ability to write was a "gift," a talent given to her, not earned. It is clear that writing was not an option; it was as necessary to her well-being as food and love and family. She dismissed the suggestion that she might write solely for the work itself, and not necessarily for publication. She explained, "What I try to write about is rooted in this world. It is not a purely private vision." She then elaborated further: "One does it presumably, to create a private world in which somehow one can breathe better than in this one."[791] However, Laurence also believed strongly that the private world has to become public:

> If it remains private, it is shrivelled as a stillborn child. One wants to get rid of it, finally, to bear it, to cease to be obsessed with it — & this can only be done if it is published & hence forgotten. So there we are. What all this waffling amounts to is that I am bloody discouraged with myself & my own ability to create living creatures on the printed page. I read Joyce Cary's *Mr. Johnson* not long ago, & I could have wept in rage and frustration — and admiration — because he had done it. How?[792]

Earlier that spring, Peggy had reworked *This Side Jordan* and managed to complete three short stories, one of which, "The Merchant of Heaven," she submitted to a new Canadian literary magazine, *Prism*, housed at the University of British Columbia.[793] Peg told Adele that she also had ideas for at least a dozen more stories to be set in West Africa. In that letter, her determination to write is manifest, as is her anger and frustration about her current situation: "I'll do the bloody things even if no one will publish them, because it is the only pleasure in life, apart from sex and one's children. I wish to heaven I could drop the whole sorry business & become a *Good Housekeeping* mom, complete with home-baked bread & glamour, but I can't, so why talk."[794]

While Jack and Peggy had lived in West Africa, they usually had the customary household staff. After her return to Canada, however, the rhythm of life in West Africa was gone, and life in Vancouver was complicated by the fact that Jocelyn and David were older and needed more varied types of attention. Living in British Columbia, moreover, was proving to be expensive, and they could not afford household help. After the emotionally exhausting year of transition in 1957 with Mum's slow and painful death from cancer, Peggy felt as if everything was spinning out of control. Her ideas for stories, her revisions of *This Side Jordan*, and her struggles with a new novel were not exhilarating but rather tormenting.

In fact, Peggy was attempting an impossible task. Like most women of her generation, she lived in a world that had very specific and widely accepted expectations for wives and mothers. Such expectations were also given prominence in magazines, films, and television. It is not surprising, therefore, that at the same time Peggy was struggling to become a fine writer, she was also making diligent efforts to be the "perfect wife and mom." She dieted rigorously to look attractive for her husband and spent time in the kitchen making home-baked bread and cookies for the children. But the days were not long enough for her to do everything. When she tried, ineffectually, to be supermom, she was anxious about the lack of time for writing. When she immersed herself in a manuscript, she felt guilty about taking time away from the children. Few, if any, male writers of that era suffered from a similar conflict, but it was not at all unusual for women writers, particularly when the budget was not adequate to hire either secretarial assistance or household help. In this regard, Peggy's brief description of herself for the contributors' page of *Prism* is significant: "Profession: housewifery and motherhood in Vancouver; devotes much time to writing."[795] Such a simple description belies the fact that she was deeply torn between trying to live up to her husband's (and contemporary society's) expectations of a wife and mother, and her profound belief in her vocation as a writer. That struggle between her family life and her commitment to writing remained an undercurrent throughout her years in Vancouver. Later she could look back on that struggle with perceptive self-awareness. Writing later to the poet Al Purdy, Laurence described the enormous conflict she had experienced until she finally was able to accept the fact that the "professional writer" was "the Real Me."[796]

During the summer of 1959, however, Peggy had to face some depressing facts: the *Atlantic Monthly* had finally turned down *This Side Jordan* and some of her stories had been rejected by *Queen's Quarterly*, *Atlantic Monthly*, and *Tamarack Review*. Although that was chiefly due to their length, she felt as if she were trapped in "a vicious circle." In addition, she was very concerned about Jack, who was not content with his job and wanted more interesting work. It was a difficult time, and Peggy wrote a long letter to Adele that was so negative and gloomy that she decided not to send it. She burned the letter instead.[797]

The situation seems to have improved, however, because later that year "The Merchant of Heaven" was scheduled to be published in the first issue of *Prism*. While that was good news, Peggy did not consider it especially significant. *Prism* was new; it had a small list of subscribers and an uncertain future. She and Jack made plans to take Spanish courses during the winter at the University of British Columbia in the event that he might have job prospects in South America.[798] The house was now quieter and she could concentrate more easily since Jocelyn was in Grade Two and David was attending a co-operative playschool at the Unitarian Church. Peggy admitted that she had been tired and impatient at her young son's incessant chatter, but now that he was in playschool, she missed him.[799] Her description of David's "world" indicates an attentive mother with insight into her young son's developing personality. She notes that David wanted only two things for his fourth birthday: "a real hand-drill and a real pipe-wrench."[800] She commented further: "The back yard is full of his bridges, dams, irrigation systems, parking lots, etc. . . . He uses all the basic carpenter's tools, including saw, vice, hammer, wrench, screwdriver, drill, spanner etc. And his understanding of the ways machinery works is astounding to me. He is very aggressive and at the same time very shy, a not uncommon combination."[801]

Peggy's letters express concern, delight, and a keen interest in her children's remarks and accomplishments, but her letters also underscore a deep anxiety. Without the household help that she had had in West Africa, and with Jack out of town on engineering projects, sometimes for weeks at a time, Peggy felt overwhelmed as she struggled with her desire to spend time with the children, the pressure of keeping up with laundry, groceries and household tasks, and the lack of time to write. This dilemma, felt by other writers and creative women in the 1950s and 1960s has been movingly described by Adrienne Rich in an essay "Anger and Tenderness."[802]

Laurence hoped that, if some of her stories appeared in magazines or anthologies, it might pave the way for publication of a collection of her African short stories.[803] She was eager, therefore, to have at least one short story published in Macmillan, London's, annual short-story anthology, *Winter's Tales*, edited by Alan Maclean, but was again in a dilemma about multiple submissions and asked Adele, "Do you know for sure what the ethical and legal position is regarding sending scripts to more than one place at a time?"[804] The stories that she wanted to submit to *Winter's Tales* were still in the hands of editors who, she assumed, would reject them. Another difficulty that she faced was trying to retain the integrity of her work while attempting to incorporate the editors' suggestions. As letters flew between Peggy and various editors, she must have felt like Tantalus: the goal was within sight, but inevitably out of reach.

At last, in September 1959, the Canadian firm of McClelland & Stewart agreed to publish *This Side Jordan*. Their acceptance, however, was contingent upon finding an American or British firm which would co-publish.[805] As if that were not enough to worry about, McClelland & Stewart also requested two additional copies of her manuscript. In that era before photocopy machines and computers, their request sent Peggy into a frenzy of typing: "I nearly blinded myself in the process, as I did the whole thing in 2 weeks, 300 pages. . . . If M & S don't find an American or British publisher, I am right back where I started."[806]

As the year drew to a close, Peggy again faced the fact that, although she had diligently pursued her writing, often at great personal cost, the measurable results were negligible. During the past ten years only three stories and her small book of Somali translations had been published.[807] More recently a fourth short story, "The Merchant of Heaven," for which she received twenty-five dollars, had appeared in the slender first issue of *Prism*.[808] Other contributors were Dorothy Livesay McNair, Earle Birney, Alden Nowlan, Raymond Souster, and Henry Kreisel. However, wonderful consequences were to follow publication of "The Merchant of Heaven," consequences that Peggy could never have foreseen. It would soon bring her satisfying recognition from fellow Canadian writers and an important lifetime friendship with an older, respected Vancouver author, Ethel Wilson.

By December 1, 1959, her prospects for publication had improved a bit, and the prestigious firm of Macmillan, London, had offered to co-publish *This Side Jordan*. Horatio Lovat Dickson, the firm's editorial director, had spent many years in Canada and, while an undergraduate at the University of Alberta, had studied under E.K. Broadus. Dickson, familiar with Canada, was enthusiastic about Laurence's writing. She could scarcely have had a better editor. Dickson was also editor for the popular Canadian author Mazo de la Roche. Known to his friends as Rache (short for Horatio), Lovat Dickson has been described by the distinguished biographer Michael Holroyd as: "a level-headed, humourous, trustworthy man, loyal and kindly, with a genuine interest in twentieth century writing."[809] Peggy's pleasure in the good news about Macmillan's offer was offset, however, by their stipulation that the novel be shortened. Determined to have her novel published, Peggy replied on the same day to Dickson, stating she was willing to cut ten thousand words! That grim prospect was to prove unnecessary, however. A short time later, Peggy announced that such an extensive revision would not be required. She planned instead to blue pencil the manuscript and return it to Dickson by January 7.[810] Thus relieved from hours of manual typing, which were mentally boring and physically exhausting, Peggy may have felt delighted by Macmillan's offer to co-publish, but as she recalled all the work that she had put into innumerable revisions of *This Side Jordan*, she probably felt weary and cautious rather than elated.

In the Laurences' social circle almost no one realized that Peggy was seriously committed to being a writer. She was known simply as the wife of a successful engineer and the mother of two attractive little children. Adele Wiseman remained the only person with whom Peggy felt free to confide her personal struggles about writing or issues around being a wife and mother. Although the two continued to correspond, Peggy did not have much time to write and her letters to Adele were often composed when she was at a particularly low point. While those letters constitute a singular record of Margaret Laurence's Vancouver period, they are by no means a complete record.

After Peggy and Jack moved from North Vancouver to the Dunbar area, they made some new friends and participated in a number of social events at their home and the homes of friends. In addition, there were meetings to attend in conjunction with the children's schooling. There are very few allusions to these friends or activities in Peggy's letters to Adele. But people who knew the Laurences at that time in Vancouver have clear recollections which help to fill out some details of Margaret Laurence's years there. This is fortunate, because those five years in Vancouver constitute a significant period in her personal life and in her development from apprentice to accomplished writer.

An early and very important literary association began there with Vancouver writer Margaret Hutchison, called "Hutch" by her friends. They were introduced in 1958 by mutual friends, Watson and Mary Thomson, who had been initiators of the Roslyn Road experiment in communal living. The year before, Hutch's first novel, *Tamarac*, which is set in a small lumbering town in British Columbia, had been published by St. Martin's Press, New York. At the time Hutch and Peggy met, *Tamarac* was about to be published in Canada, and Hutch was working on a second novel.[811] She taught at Lord Kitchener School near the Laurence's home and she and Peggy discovered they had a mutual friend, Muriel Neilson (née James). Muriel, who also had been part of the Roslyn Road community in Winnipeg, had attended Peggy's wedding in Neepawa, and had corresponded with Peggy when she and Jack were in Africa. A contemporary recalls, "Muriel James Neilson was a

teacher and a brilliant musician. She did all the early CBC music programs for school children and she conducted school choirs for most of
her life."[812] After moving from Winnipeg to British Columbia, Muriel
had married Einar Neilson, and together they had established an
extraordinary retreat, called "Leiben," on Bowen Island.

There Einar, who was skilled in woodworking, had single-handedly constructed a peeled-log chalet. He also had constructed many of its
beautiful furnishings from driftwood. The Neilsons welcomed people
in the arts and offered Leiben as a place where they might rest or work
at their discipline. Among their many guests over the years were
Malcolm and Margerie Lowry, Lister Sinclair, and Earle Birney, who
wrote most of *Turvey* there. Leiben had a stunning location overlooking the sea, and the property was covered with first-growth evergreens
and giant arbutus trees.[813]

Although Peggy did not frequent Leiben, she went there at least
once with Hutch, who was also Jocelyn's, and later David's, Grade One
teacher. In addition to being a writer, Margaret Hutchison was also very
talented musically, and she enjoyed the arts community at Leiben.

Living in the Dunbar area, Hutch and Peggy saw each other often,
since Hutch frequently stopped by to chat on her way home from
school. When Jack was out of town on business, Hutch sometimes
drove Peggy to a cultural evening at the Vancouver Arts Club, which
had space in a former art gallery on West Pender Street. Members
would go there for a lecture, an art exhibit, or simply a cup of coffee
after the theatre or a movie.

Hutch describes Peggy as "very alive, vibrant, with a lot of anxiety,"
and she remembers dinners at the Laurences' home when Peggy often
served African dishes.[814] While Hutch and Peggy were devoted to their
husbands, they were also ambitious and energetic about their writing.
Both women were interested in capturing the subtleties of "family relationships, speech patterns, and idiom." Margaret Hutchison was one of
the very few Canadians to whom Peggy gave a copy of her first book, *A
Tree for Poverty*, and with whom she discussed the challenges and satis-
factions of translating Somali literature.[815]

At the time the women met, Peggy was still struggling with the
manuscript of *This Side Jordan*, and it was at Hutch's suggestion that she

contacted the New York agent Ruth May.[816] Hutch remembers Peggy as "very disciplined" about her writing, "a conscientious mother and a dedicated writer."[817]

Over the years, Peggy and Hutch would remain in touch, and she and Muriel Neilson visited Margaret when she and the children lived in Elm Cottage in Buckinghamshire. When Laurence in later years returned occasionally to Vancouver, she usually visited Margaret Hutchison. And as adults, Jocelyn and David Laurence, Hutch's former pupils, retained fond memories of their primary-school teacher, and also visited with her when they were in Vancouver.

By coincidence, Peggy met another aspiring writer, Nadine Jones, at a Vancouver book signing in 1960 for *This Side Jordan*. Nadine was about to marry a Ghanian, Kwadwo Asante, and sought advice from Peggy. The two became friends and after Laurence moved to England in 1962, they, too, corresponded. By then, Nadine, like Peggy was struggling with the conflicting roles of wife, mother, and writer. Later Nadine and Kwadwo would move to Edinburgh, where he went to study medicine; and the women, now living in Scotland and England respectively, met from time to time and continued to talk on the telephone. Nadine occasionally stayed with the children when Margaret had to go to London or Canada. When Laurence's collection of West African short stories, *The Tomorrow-Tamer*, was published in 1963, she dedicated the book to Nadine and Kwadwo.[818]

Another good friend and neighbour during those years in Vancouver was June Schulhof. Born in Ireland, June was married to an Austrian, Fred Schulhof. They had emigrated with their children to Canada in 1958, the year after the Laurences' return from Africa. June and Fred first met Peggy at a "Living Room Learning" group (under the auspices of the University of British Columbia) in the autumn of 1958. About eighteen people belonged to the group, which met for discussion in members' homes. Peggy and the Schulhofs were members for at least two courses: one covered "Great Religions of the World"; the other was "An Introduction to the Arts." June notes that Peggy "was mentally alive and never asked stupid questions; her comments were always pertinent," and Fred Schulhof recalls that "at times Peg had very definite opinions and made no bones about that."[819]

Although Jack Laurence did not participate in the "Living Room Learning" group, the couples did become friends; both men were engineers and frequently played tennis together. At that time, Jack and Peggy, along with Gordon Elliott and his former student, Lino Magagna, were involved in wine-making. June recalls lots of laughs over the labels they created for their home-brewed vintages. June was delighted that Peg was a woman with whom she could discuss ideas, and fondly remembers conversations about everything "except trivia and recipes."[820]

While living in Vancouver, Peggy and Jack also enjoyed the company of Eva and René Temple, who had arrived from Europe in the late 1950s after the Hungarian Revolution. Both couples had young children and, despite the fact that Jack and René had good jobs, there was very little money to spare since living in Vancouver was expensive. However, the couples enjoyed an occasional meal together, a movie, or, for the men, a game of tennis. Eva had found it difficult to find other Canadian women with whom she could speak openly and frankly, but she found Peggy to be an exception. "When Peg talked it was with honesty and you trusted her." Eva said that Peggy was "appealing, animated and different from other women her age. She asked questions which was very unusual at the time. . . . I think she was the first person who asked me pertinent questions about what went on in Europe during World War II."[821]

Eva Temple also found that Peggy had an ability to share "interesting vignettes about her trips, about places she had been." Eva recalls that it was a pleasure to talk to Peggy "because she had seen things in minute detail and she remembered." According to Eva, Peggy was interested in everything. She wanted to understand "what made people tick." Eva was delighted to find a woman who was "interested in architecture, in wooden buildings, in movies and books, in anything beautiful." They talked a good deal about art and painting and about life in Europe. Eva realized that Peggy was politically aware and very concerned about "moral duties." Eva and René remarked that "it was the children who were most important to Peggy. She was totally devoted to them."[822]

The Temples were also members of the Arts Club. On one occasion the club's yearly costume party centred on a Roman theme. According to the rules for that night, a person could use only one sheet and two safety pins for the costume. Jack and Peg came to the Temples' house and there tried to pin on their "Roman" robes. The Temples remember that the party and its preliminaries made for "a fun evening with plenty of laughter."[823]

In addition to these friendships and activities with other young couples, Peggy felt fortunate to hear about the Unitarian Church in the Dunbar area of Vancouver. It was then flourishing under the dynamic leadership of Phillip Hewett, who had become pastor in the fall of 1956.[824] Hewett recalls that, shortly after his arrival, the church was inundated by a "tidal wave of young families with children."[825] The small wooden structure on West 10th Avenue could not handle the growing congregation, so other nearby buildings were used. Peggy and Jack and their children attended Sunday services at that church. Peggy had a wide embrace for the various ways in which people express their spirituality. After the couple's experiences in Africa, the Unitarian Church in Vancouver would have been a natural choice for them. On December 12, 1959, both Peggy and Jack formally joined the church and signed the membership register.[826]

Pastor Hewett recalls that new members frequently came through word of mouth, attracted by the church's unique education program for children, which was "entirely different then from that of the other churches."[827] Many academics from the University of British Columbia sent their children to the Unitarian Church school. Under Hewett's leadership the church had developed an experiential approach to religious education, which helped to augment the children's independence and enhance their respect and appreciation of world religions. The program aimed to help the children develop "a feeling of wonder and awe for all that was around them." These goals are reflected in the book used in their curriculum, *From Long Ago and Many Lands*, which contained stories and parables from various parts of the world and from major religions, including Buddhism and the African religions.

If parents wanted to enroll their children in the religious-education program, they were required to participate in the Unitarian parents' group. One might also volunteer as a teacher, which Peggy did. Philosophical and religious discussions were part of the parents' group. Noreen Foster, who was director of religious education for many years, says that the congregation's approach was more humanist than strictly Christian. The members, for example, "struggled over how they were going to deal with Christmas in a Unitarian setting." Pastor Hewett notes that the Christian story of the birth of Jesus was put alongside miraculous birth stories of Buddha and Zoroaster.

Noreen Foster has vivid memories of Mrs. Laurence introducing matters from the King James version of the Bible in the parents' discussion group.[828] She also recalls Peggy as a kind, quiet person who was very spiritual, a woman who listened intently, "a kind of listening with the whole body." However, she also found her to be very nervous. Sometimes when Peggy came to church-school meetings, Noreen would have to phone Jack Laurence to come and drive his wife home "because she had blinding headaches."[829] These headaches worried Peggy, and it is difficult to know whether they were due to dieting, stress, or marital problems.

During one of the parents' meetings, Laurence notes that she was "horrified" when it was suggested that the children should not be told the Nativity story "because we knew that angels weren't actually flitting around the sky."[830] Laurence felt that the story held "very basic truths, whatever the interpretation," and "rashly offered to try to write a version of the Nativity that would be acceptable." Since young Jocelyn and David were attending the Unitarian Sunday school, Peggy "wrote the story with both of them in mind."[831]

A few weeks before Christmas 1959, Peggy sent Mrs. Foster a small manuscript. It was an adaptation of the traditional Christmas nativity story. Her intention in writing that story for the children was "to emphasize the aspects of the family, joy in the birth of the child, and connection with all creatures."[832] Noreen Foster, pleased with the story, responded by writing to Peggy asking her to drop by so they might discuss it. Noreen thought that Peggy was shy and felt that contacting her by letter would be preferable to a phone call. She and Peggy approached one another quite formally because Peggy seemed somewhat nervous. Noreen Foster had no inkling that Peggy was a writer and she, therefore, offered some suggestions about the manuscript, which Peggy received favourably.

Mrs. Foster asked Peggy to tell the story to the children as part of their Christmas party that year. Peggy insisted that no adults be present other than Noreen. The children, seated on the floor, listened with "rapt attention" as she told The Christmas Story. "The rich timbre of her voice and the way she told the story really gripped the children," recalls Mrs. Foster.[833]

Peg lost the manuscript of the story, however, after she left Vancouver in 1962. Almost twenty years later, when she was living in Lakefield, Ontario, a copy would come back to her. One evening at the home of friends, Laurence met Nonie Lyon, who had also belonged to the Unitarian Church on West 10th Street in Vancouver. Nonie told Margaret that for many years she had read the story to her children at Christmas time. Margaret, pleased to have the story returned to her, made a few changes and decided to publish it.[834] *The Christmas Story* then appeared in the *Weekend* magazine section of the newspaper. Later she enlisted the talented artist Helen Lucas to illustrate the hardcover edition, published by Knopf, New York, with a slightly altered title, *The Christmas Birthday Story*. Margaret described Lucas's illustrations as "joyous, beautiful, and wise." She felt that, through the illustrations, Helen Lucas had really become "co-author" of the book.[835] Obviously pleased with the results, Margaret sent copies of *The Christmas Birthday Story* to Pastor Phillip Hewett and to Lovat Dickson at Macmillan. In her letter to Pastor Hewett, Laurence recalled that she wanted "to emphasize the birth of the beloved child into a loving family." "I said that Mary and Joseph didn't mind whether their baby turned out to be a boy or a girl. They just hoped their baby would be strong and healthy. After all, I myself had one of each kind, and I knew perfectly well that any mother who really wants her baby *never* asks first 'Is it a boy or a girl?' The first question is always 'Is my baby all right?'"[836]

Her lengthy letter to Pastor Hewett concluded: "It is with great joy and gratitude that I send you this book now. In this truly terrifying world of ours, some joyous things still do happen."[837] Thus, by a curious coincidence, this little story written in Vancouver in 1959 became Margaret Laurence's last published work when it appeared in 1980 with its illustrations by Helen Lucas.[838]

As 1959 drew to a close, Peggy must have been doubly grateful to work on that Christmas story for children since the year had brought her so little in terms of professional advancement or publication.

During 1960, however, the situation regarding publication of Peggy's fiction finally began to improve. In her professional correspondence she was now consistently using the signature Margaret Laurence or Mrs.

Margaret Laurence, and at this point in the story of her early career, it seems appropriate to refer to her as Margaret rather than Peggy.[839] In January, she mailed Macmillan, London, new photos of herself, done this time by a professional photographer, and substantive revisions of *This Side Jordan*, eliminating some passages which seemed to be melodramatic.[840] She received her first check from Macmillan for "The Perfume Sea," which they planned to publish in *Winter's Tales 6*, the short-story annual that Alan Maclean edited for them.

The important history of this anthology is summarized in Maclean's introduction: "The main purpose in starting *Winter's Tales* six years ago was to provide an additional outlet for the long story, whose only home for many years had been the literary magazine."[841] He noted further that each volume of *Winter's Tales* had been well-received and found it comforting to know "there is still a small but faithful market" for the short story in book form. Although Alan Maclean acknowledged that collections of stories were often commercially unprofitable, nevertheless he reminded readers that, in 1959, approximately *fifty short story collections had been produced by British publishers*. Maclean's comments fuelled Margaret's hope that a collection of her West African short stories would be possible.

A few months later, she was approached by Donald Stainsby, book-review editor of the *Vancouver Sun*. He had admired her work in *Prism* and now invited her to contribute book reviews to the paper.[842] The salary would be ten to fifteen dollars per review. Margaret agreed. She welcomed the opportunity to read some of the latest books, looked forward to the extra income, and told Adele she intended to do a conscientious job.[843]

By the end of April 1960, she had finished the demanding task of marking 250 end-of-term essays at UBC for Professor Elliott, and had received a cheque for another African story, "Godman's Master," which had been published in the third number of *Prism*.[844] At this point Margaret significantly altered the description of herself in the "Contributors' Notes." Gone is any mention of "housewifery and motherhood in Vancouver." Now she describes herself as a writer. Readers are informed that Mrs. Laurence's short stories have previously appeared in *Story*, *Queen's Quarterly*, and *Prism*. The journal also announced that Mrs. Laurence's novel, *This Side Jordan*, was scheduled for publication in Canada, England, and the United States.

Margaret's literary momentum was threatened, however, when Sherman Baker of St. Martin's Press, New York, sent her comments from three different readers; one of whom said he had been "reasonably nauseated" by a melodramatic passage in *This Side Jordan*.[845] Baker himself insisted on further changes in the novel. Margaret naturally was upset. Would such requests never end? How could she possibly satisfy readers at three different publishing houses? She had already spent many weeks revising *This Side Jordan* for Macmillan and now, just when publication seemed imminent, a list of requested changes from St. Martin's sat facing her on the table.

With characteristic determination, Laurence threw herself once again into the task of revising the novel, somehow managing within a few days to make changes in at least nine chapters of *This Side Jordan*: reworking some parts, dropping others, and tightening the sections dealing with ancient Ghana. However, she refused to alter the scene with Nathaniel's son at the end of the novel and later explained to Jack McClelland that she did not believe the ending was pat, "for Nathaniel's naïve hope that Joshua will somehow, in miraculous fashion, know how to cope with the problems of a new Africa, does not seem to me to be an easy solution, or indeed a solution at all, but I think that this is how *he* [Joshua's father] would feel at the time."[846]

Margaret also told McClelland she was worried that revisions at such a late date might result in publication of two different versions of *This Side Jordan*.[847] Although Sherman Baker at St. Martin's had told her, "we intend to get behind this book," his promise had little impact on Margaret, who commented wearily to McClelland, "I don't know what he means, . . . I need a long holiday." McClelland, however, was reassuring and noted that two different versions were not unprecedented.[848]

By the end of May, Margaret was relieved that both publishing houses had accepted her revisions. Perhaps the long labour had been worthwhile, for Sherman Baker now sent word that St. Martin's is "proud to publish *This Side Jordan*. . . . I can only assure you that in my opinion a good book has been made into a very outstanding one."[849]

Good news continued to arrive during the next month. *Tamarack Review* accepted her African story, "A Gourdful of Glory."[850] This would be her first publication in that important Canadian journal. A chapter from *This Side Jordan* was also published in *Prism*, which now carried an impressive half-page ad for her novel, due for release that autumn.[851] In addition, Laurence received advance royalties from both St. Martin's and Macmillan. With the royalty cheques in hand, she began to think her career as a writer might be truly launched. Within a few weeks she had finished correcting page proofs for the novel and sent them back to Macmillan. Publication was almost reality!

Two months later *This Side Jordan* was published by Macmillan, England. Margaret had been struggling with that novel for several years. Although she had arrived in Canada with a completed second draft, it required another three years and innumerable revisions before her first novel was published. Now a copy of the book was on the way to her from England. The dedication of her first novel was revealing: "To my mother Margaret Campbell Wemyss," not "Margaret Simpson Wemyss." By leaving out "Simpson," Mum's maiden name, Margaret eliminated reference to her mother's family, and hence to Grandfather Simpson.

Copies of the dust jacket reached Canada before the book itself arrived from England, increasing Margaret's eager anticipation of the moment when she might actually hold the novel in her hands. In the meantime, British reviews of *This Side Jordan* had been forwarded to her and she wrote to thank Lovat Dickson, commenting with pleasure on the book's jacket.[852] Dickson forwarded her letter to his colleague Alan Maclean, who was the fiction editor, along with a note asking why *This Side Jordan* was not being sufficiently reviewed. Maclean replied that the market was then saturated with African novels. Margaret knew nothing of their comments, however, and was, in fact, about to embark on another novel set in West Africa![853]

Although she had worked on a "Somaliland novel" during the previous year, mentioning it in several letters to Adele Wiseman, she must have put that work aside because now she specifically mentions West Africa. It would have been impossible for Laurence to use material intended for a book set in Somaliland in another novel which would be set in semi-tropical West Africa, where the people, languages, religion, and customs were totally different. No trace remains, however, of either the Somaliland or the second West African novel.

During the autumn of 1960, Margaret roughed out ideas for that West African novel and took steps to place one of her stories in the *Paris Review*. This was not mere wishful thinking. The fiction editor of that prestigious literary journal had read one of Laurence's West African stories and expressed interest in seeing another.[854] She then sent an important and confident letter to Jack McClelland, informing him that she had completed nine short stories set in West Africa and asking his advice about several publishing matters: how to sell her stories, the feasibility of securing an agent, reprint rights, and the publishing situation in England, the United States, and Canada.[855] The inexperienced, discouraged apprentice of 1959 was on her way to becoming a more confident and experienced author.

Jack McClelland replied promptly to her queries and suggested a New York agent, Willis Kingsley Wing. Margaret agreed and Jack McClelland wrote Willis Wing on her behalf. This is how he described her to the literary agent: "She has a somewhat unique style, powerful, virile and vigorous — when I read it [*This Side Jordan*] I found it hard to believe that the novel had been written by a woman. I'm not suggesting that she is the greatest literary discovery of the last ten years, but she is a serious writer, a writer of quality, and she tells a very good story."[856]

McClelland also told Willis Wing, with a touch of irony, that, after McClelland and Stewart had finally worked out complex arrangements with Macmillan, England, to co-publish, they had been "inundated with translation option requests" for *This Side Jordan*. In addition, they had received letters of interest from about a dozen American publishers — all as a result of British enthusiasm! He also told Willis Wing that a shipping strike would delay release of *This Side Jordan* in Canada since they had to wait for Macmillan's sheets to arrive from England.[857]

In securing Willis Kingsley Wing as an agent, Laurence was joining an accomplished group of writers. Although she could not have known it at the time, her New York agent numbered among his clients bestselling authors such as Allen Drury, James Michener, Nicholas Monsarrat, and fellow Canadians, Pierre Berton, Ralph Allen, and Brian Moore.

Margaret Laurence's many achievements during 1960, however, did not lessen her anxiety about the novel she was now attempting. In letters to three different correspondents, she relates that she is trying to summon enough courage to begin work on another novel set in Africa. Here, she elaborates on her problems with it:[858]

> I know so much more clearly this time what I want to say, but of course I don't want to say it. It has to be there. But it won't be there all tidy and neatly labelled, because if it were, the people wouldn't be real. The people are very odd, in some ways. I am not quite sure what some of them will ultimately do. I think that is the hardest act of faith — to free one's characters, to allow them to act, to be, to speak and move, without manipulating them to make them fit a thesis. At the moment I am still afraid to start, in case they don't come into being as themselves and not merely projections of me. In the last analysis, whatever conscious skills one develops, it is still a process of uncertain alchemy — it either happens or it doesn't.[859]

A few days later, Margaret was surprised by a phone call from New York. St. Martin's Press wanted her photograph "as soon as possible," because the *Saturday Review* planned to run a favourable review of *This Side Jordan* and her photo might be used on the cover.[860] After receiving that call, she wrote to thank Jack McClelland for approaching Willis Wing on her behalf. Her letter is focused, specific, and confident:

> I am writing to Mr. Wing today to tell him I would be glad if he would act as my agent, and I am sending him a number of short stories. I think it would be as well if he would take on the foreign rights representation of *This Side Jordan*. . . . I would be grateful, therefore, if you would turn over the relevant correspondence to him and also send him photo copies of my three contracts.[861]

Her letter continues on a more personal note. Aware that Jack McClelland had planned a promotional tour to Western Canada, Margaret tried to initiate a meeting with him: "I look forward to meeting you when you are in Vancouver. I don't suppose I could prevail upon you to have dinner quietly at our house one evening? I am sure you will be very busy and would probably not have the time to spare, but if you felt you could make it, we would be very pleased. I should add that we have a number of excellent homemade wines of which we are extremely proud."[862]

McClelland replied that dinner might not be possible, but concluded on a very cordial note: "May I thank you then for your kind invitation and say that if it is possible to leave it open until after I arrive, and if it can then be managed at a time that would suit you, I can't think of anything that would please me more."[863]

The dinner did not take place, but within a fortnight the young author and the dynamic Canadian publisher had met at a party in Vancouver. Margaret referred to that evening in her next letter, where for the first time she addressed McClelland as "Dear Jack": "I was very glad indeed to meet you at last, although a cocktail party is not the ideal place to talk with anyone. However, from a publicity point of view the whole thing seemed to go quite well, and that is the main thing."[864]

Margaret looked forward to having an opportunity to talk with McClelland under calmer circumstances and promised that in the future she would refrain from explaining "the more obscure points of the psychology of colonization."[865] She also congratulated him on his "tremendous job of promotion" in Vancouver, noting that "we watched you on Channel 8 TV last night, and greatly admired" the way in which he managed to mention many of his books.[866] Margaret also told Jack McClelland that, after his visit to the city and the accompanying publicity, her phone rang steadily for several days.

When Jack McClelland replied, he apologized for not writing sooner and told Margaret he had enjoyed meeting her, adding, "You were a tremendous success at the party." He was sure that *This Side Jordan* would get off to "a rousing start" because of the excellent impression she had made on everyone present. McClelland's enthusiasm was not singular. Although a rather negative review of *This Side Jordan* appeared in *Canadian Literature*, one that Margaret characterized as "vitriolic,"[867] reviews of her first novel were generally very favourable. Mary Renault, whose own novels had received much acclaim, noted in *Saturday Review* that *This Side Jordan* was a "first novel of rare excellence," and declared that Margaret Laurence's ear "is so good that one cannot wish it less than perfect."[868]

Jack McClelland mentioned to Margaret that he had only recently examined finished copies of the two editions of the book and told her: "I am not well pleased with either, but what is done is done. I think the book looks fairly adequate for our market and I can certainly promise you that on subsequent books, whether we manufacture here, in the U.K., or in the U.S.A., we shall certainly insist on designing our own jacket."[869]

When Margaret replied the next week, she asked whether McClelland had seen the reviews from England, and specifically mentioned the *New Statesman*'s review, which praised the book, and "for which one can be profoundly grateful."[870] She may have been aware that a good review from that distinguished journal had helped to launch the literary career of her new friend, Ethel Wilson. The *New Statesman* certainly had accolades for Laurence's novel, comparing it to the work of the prominent British novelist E.M. Forster:

> [*This Side Jordan* is] a really excellent novel set in the Gold Coast just before it became Ghana. Its chief character, a most haunting, interesting un-hero, is Nathaniel Amegbe, schoolteacher; shabby, unimpressive, conscience-ridden; a divided man, torn between the pull of the old tribal ways he has managed to half-educate himself out of, and the Christian-commercial life of the city. Accra, incidentally, and its inhabitants could hardly I imagine be better drawn. Miss Laurence has a natural instinct for proportion; her detail is exactly enough to bring place and people most vividly to all one's senses. . . . Were it not for a suspiciously sunny conclusion I would have said this book had an almost Forsterian quality of understanding.[871]

In the middle of November, six copies of *This Side Jordan* finally arrived from Macmillan. Excitement turned to dismay, however, as Margaret unwrapped the water-damaged parcel. She sent the damaged copies of *This Side Jordan* back to Macmillan and wrote to Alan

Maclean: "I do hope you will not be irate at my returning these books, but I am sure that you will understand that I am reluctant to give to friends and devoted aunts a number of copies which look as though they have been kept in a damp basement for half a century."[872] Returning the books was obviously the appropriate response. Why then did she use the word "irate"? The term is hardly an apt description of Alan Maclean's dealings with her to this point. In this context, "irate" seems rather to be a description of how Margaret felt. She was also very upset that Macmillan had not used the photo that she had chosen for the jacket. Although she did not mention that to Alan Maclean, she did inform Adele of her distress over the photo that they used.

Laurence's keen disappointment over the ruined copies was somewhat offset by the arrival of *Winter's Tales 6* later that month. Aware of Alan Maclean's high standards for that annual, she was excited to see "The Perfume Sea" in company there "with the work of writers whom I admire very much." The volume's ten selections included stories by Gabriel Fielding, Liam O'Flaherty, Jean Rhys, and Muriel Spark. Laurence told Alan Maclean "there is a quality of sorcery in Muriel Spark's writing that I find irresistible; in comparison, many writers of soberly realistic prose seem very heavy footed indeed."[873] Laurence's name appeared prominently on the cover as well as on the spine of the book; however, Jack Laurence was not at home to share his wife's good news. He had been up north, working in the Yukon for several weeks.[874]

During that autumn, Margaret had received further promising news. The Book Society in England had selected *This Side Jordan* for one of its October recommendations, and Macmillan wanted to include "The Perfume Sea" in a Braille edition of *Winter's Tales*. That story was also sold to the *Saturday Evening Post*, resulting in a much wider audience for Laurence's work, as well as a handsome cheque. "The Perfume Sea," renamed by editors as "The Exiles," appeared three months later in the *Saturday Evening Post*.[875] Despite the fact that they had also cut parts of the story, publication in the *Saturday Evening Post* was a new and exciting opportunity for Margaret since the magazine regularly featured fiction by many first-rate writers.

At last, copies of the Canadian edition of *This Side Jordan* arrived for distribution in Vancouver. On December 3, Margaret went to Franklin's bookshop for an autographing party and was assured that the attendance was good.[876] Since she had not yet received her own copy of the Canadian edition, she was very relieved to see the book on display with the "right" photograph of her, rather than "the bespectacled ape-woman one," that Macmillan had used.[877] She made plans to be at another bookshop for a signing on December 5.

Laurence's first novel was a handsome production. The attractive jacket, the heft of the novel, and the effortless turn of the pages put it worlds above *A Tree for Poverty* (1954), a slender book with a tan cardboard cover, printed in Nairobi.

Between May and December 1960, Margaret Laurence had also been busy writing book reviews for the *Vancouver Sun*, averaging two reviews a month. She continued to review books through March 1961, when the section was discontinued for financial reasons. Her reviews are well-written, confident in tone, thoughtful, and occasionally acerbic. They demonstrate Laurence's familiarity with a wide range of authors and works. Her concern with style is apparent. In those book reviews, Laurence uses periodic sentences, parallelism in phrasing, and witty images. The reviews are good-humoured, lively, and interesting; even today, they would be worthy of publication. Ethel Wilson, herself a consummate stylist, admired Laurence's book reviews and in a Christmas letter to her friends, Alan and Jean Crawley, she devoted an entire paragraph to praising Laurence's accomplishments:[878] "I admire Margaret Laurence's *This Side Jordan* enormously. . . . Simply, she *is* a writer. Whether she will find her material here difficult and arid, I don't know. I hope she will not be chiefly *an excellent reviewer* [emphasis added]. I think she's far beyond our average novelists.[879]

During that December, Laurence had been working ambitiously on her next novel, which would become *The Stone Angel*. She told Jack McClelland quite frankly that she thought it "a very good story," adding, "but I have no way of knowing at this point whether I will be able to tell it properly or not. This time I am determined to know a little more clearly where I'm going before I start," she said, referring to the false starts and many revisions of *This Side Jordan*.

Margaret's tumultuous inner state during the Vancouver period may have formed the basis for one of her finest stories, "Godman's Master," published in spring 1960.[880] That story frequently has been interpreted as a parable about the nations of Africa emerging from colonial control.[881] But "Godman's Master" may appropriately be viewed as an expression of Laurence's own personal concerns. Godman Pira is a dwarf, one of the *pirafo*, who formerly had been court jesters to the kings of the Ashanti. In Laurence's story, Godman has been kept in a box by his master, Faru. One day he is able to make his escape through the kindness of Moses, a young African who has returned from studying in England.

Although Godman had yearned for his freedom, he believes he is incapable of living on his own in the world and insists on living with Moses as a sort of houseboy. He is sure that he needs Moses's protection in order to survive. But as the story draws to its conclusion, Godman Pira has become more independent. He no longer needs the protection of Moses, and he leaves him to join a circus, where he will make a life for himself among the other performers and musicians. Godman's last words in the story might fittingly have been uttered by Margaret herself at that point in her life. They are also echoed by Stacey, the central character in Laurence's Vancouver novel, *The Fire-Dwellers* (1969): "I have known the worst and the worst and the worst, and yet I live. I fear and fear, and yet I live." With Moses looking on, the circus musicians take up their instruments and begin to play. As their notes sound, Godman Pira waves goodbye to Moses, hops onto the stage, and takes his place beside the other performers.

This moving story about freedom and friendship is set in Africa, but it probably serves as the externalized expression of Margaret's own feelings about her life at that period, her feelings of being trapped in Vancouver as both wife and mother at a time when Jack's expectations for her as the wife of a civil engineer clashed with her own deep need to give expression to her considerable talents as writer. On the other hand, it would not be unfair to say "Poor Jack." How could he have suspected that the young, inexperienced collegian from Neepawa whom he had married in 1947 would develop into a serious writer with great gifts and a passion for writing?

Jack had seen his mother, who was also a writer, produce short stories, a novel, and poems. Although her first novel was published before her marriage, she had since published a collection of her poems, *The*

Band Plays a March (1936), illustrated with fine linoleum cuts by her sister, Bessie A. Fry, who was an artist. In addition, two chapbooks of Elsie's poems were published by Ryerson Press, and several of her short stories had appeared in various magazines, including *Chatelaine*.[882] Nevertheless, Elsie Laurence had remained a traditional and dutiful wife, raising six children and putting aside her literary gift or hiding it when it displeased her husband. Moreover Jack Laurence knew that his father had been jealous of Elsie's writing. It seems there had even been a day when his father had insisted Elsie destroy some of her work.[883] In the light of his mother's acquiescence, how could Jack have suspected that the young woman who became his wife would have such a strong belief in her vocation and a need to write so great that quite literally Margaret could not survive without writing.

In 1957, when Peggy arrived in Vancouver from Africa, there were a number of writers living there; among them the attorney William C. McConnell, and his wife, Alice, who together had launched a very fine small publishing house, Klanak Press (1958-1979). Other writers in the area included: Bob Harlow, then with the CBC, Ethel Wilson, Earle Birney, Roderick Haig-Brown, Gordon Woodward (Margaret Hutchison's husband), and poets such as Anne Wilkinson, Anne Marriott, and P.K.Page. It was not precisely what one might call a literary community, but there were opportunities to meet other writers in the late 1950s. Gradually, Peggy became acquainted with some of them.

One New Year's eve, Margaret Hutchison ("Hutch") invited Peggy and Jack to a party at her home. That evening she introduced Peggy to Alice Munro, then living with her husband, Jim, and two little children in West Vancouver. Alice Munro remembers that Laurence was wearing an attractive dress at the party and had a very good figure. "She looked like a successful engineer's good-looking wife," Munro recalls. "She was terribly nice to me. And fun. We talked and laughed and had a good time. I can remember just having a wonderful time with her the first time I met her."[884]

Both women were shy and dedicated to the craft of fiction and to developing their literary gifts. They were also struggling with concurrent responsibilities as housewives and mothers of young children. Neither woman had household help and neither was really connected to the academic community at the University of British Columbia, where Earle Birney had begun to influence a new generation of writers. Although circumstances were such that Laurence and Munro were not able to meet often, Peg did invite Alice to her home at least once, where they talked about housework, the children, writing, and how each was trying to manage.[885]

The two women also met on several other occasions, once by coincidence at a Tattoo in Stanley Park. Although Munro had actually published more fiction than Laurence, she considered Margaret to be a more accomplished writer and a more experienced person. Recalling that time, Alice Munro remembers Laurence as vivacious and a good listener. "She was lively and funny. Her wit was the wit that was familiar to me: the wit between women who had been friends at college." Margaret Laurence often called her women friends "kid" or "kiddo," which harked back to college slang. There was a way that women talked to each other, explains Munro, which was not the way they talked in front of men. There was "a kind of jokey irreverence that went side by side with this trying very hard to do the right thing, but at the same time not let it absorb your soul."[886]

Munro notes that "Margaret was like a friend I would have met and really liked at college, with that subversive kind of intelligence that is, nevertheless, operating within the framework of what's acceptable, which was the smart thing to do." If Margaret had been more Bohemian, Alice would have been "frightened" and uncomfortable. She found Margaret Laurence to be an interesting conversationalist and "a nice comfortable person to be with." Munro clarifies further, "Not that Margaret was a conventional person, but she was sort of conventionally attractive and charming. She was intelligent and lively, and dressed very well. Most people would have been comfortable with her. She was not a person who demanded that people adjust to her."[887]

In late 1959, after publication of "The Merchant of Heaven," other doors in the literary community opened to Margaret. When the second volume of *Prism* appeared early in 1960, it included nine letters from readers to the editors of the new journal. In those letters, Margaret Laurence is mentioned more frequently than any other contributor. Comments from the distinguished Vancouver writer Ethel Wilson were prized by Margaret, but she was also especially heartened by accolades from two other established and respected writers: Roderick Haig-Brown and William C. McConnell.

In her letter to *Prism*, Ethel Wilson singled out stories by Henry Kreisel and Margaret Laurence, calling them "excellent" and "a milestone in the crucible of Canadian short stories." Wilson said, "The Merchant of Heaven" was a good story, well-told and "developed in depth with natural unobtrusive skill." Roderick Haig-Brown called it "a particularly fine piece of work. Finished, sensitive, vivid, and full of meaning. Every point is made with a subtlety and naturalness that make the whole a very powerful and moving piece." And, referring to "The Merchant of Heaven," McConnell wrote: "I particularly liked Margaret Laurence's story. If she can maintain a style like this in other stories, she's going to go far."[888] How refreshing such praise must have been to Laurence, who had been grappling with readers' comments and the demands of various editors throughout 1958 and 1959.

She was invited to join a creative-writing group that met at various members' homes in the city. Among the members were Bill and Alice McConnell. Not only were they the busy owners of Klanak Press, but they also had an important role in that group of writers. According to Bill McConnell, membership was fluid and required no formality beyond the writing of prose or poetry and the sponsorship of a de facto member (which was not lightly offered): "Margaret fitted in beautifully. She was not too vocal, though she did read some drafts of her stories." He remembers two or three meetings at the Laurences' home, where he met Jack Laurence, whom he liked. McConnell enjoyed Jack's outgoing personality and recalls, "He was interested in people and places. More places than people."[889]

According to McConnell, Margaret gave the impression of being a strong-willed person. She was not a writer, he said, who lived in a bygone era, but rather was very aware of current social and political matters. He found Margaret eager for conversation and for opportunities to expand her intellectual horizons. She had "a very strong face. A lovely face. And a marvellous, resonant laugh. Her laughter was wonderful." One night at a lecture given by Marshall McLuhan, Margaret laughed uproariously when Leonard Marsh, finding the discourse incomprehensible at the end of an hour, got up muttering under his breath and walked out. Bill McConnell also remembers this about Laurence:

> Marg (some called her Peggy) was an avid listener. She was eager to hear technical discussion of both prose and poetry read aloud by the group. Highly intense, somewhat camouflaged by a seeming outer self-control but betrayed by her chain smoking. A keen observer, she had a prismatic memory which made her depiction of both character and place sharp and exact. Though not reluctant to comment on the work of others, it was devoid of any trace of malice yet sharp and precise as to what she considered weaknesses."[890]

McConnell describes Margaret as "sandy," by which he means there was no slippage between her honest self-evaluation and the person she really was. After Bill and Alice McConnell first met Margaret Laurence, Alice remarked: "You can expect good things from her without the worry of what it will cost others." In their opinion,

> Margaret had no pretensions, realized she had to learn her craft thoroughly, that there were no shortcuts and then one could tiptoe into the kingdom of the imagination. . . . Her subsequent work did not disabuse our appraisal, though we were often wrong about some other developing writers. And unlike a few of her contemporaries, Margaret never pretended to be an expert at anything except what she believed to be an honest piece of writing.[891]

McConnell introduced Margaret Laurence to Earle Birney, who had been a member of the group, but was now starting his own creative-writing group in conjunction with his position on the faculty at the University of British Columbia. Not only was Bill McConnell busy with his own law practice, the older writing group, and Klanak Press, he was also one of the founders of *Prism*.

Meeting the McConnells and other members of that writers' group was important to Margaret Laurence, but there is no doubt that the most powerful literary and personal association during her Vancouver years was with the distinguished novelist and short-story writer, Ethel Wilson, then in her early seventies. As the wife of Wallace Wilson, a prominent and well-liked physician, Ethel had had many social responsibilities over the years. She had given priority to Wallace's career and to entertaining graciously his colleagues and their wives. Mrs. Wilson was fortunate, however, because Wallace had the financial means to employ household help. Her husband, while tolerant and generally supportive of Ethel's writing, was said to be "essentially clueless" about that aspect of his wife's life.[892] The Wilsons had no children and occasionally travelled together in Europe as well as Canada. When Margaret Laurence met Ethel Wilson, the latter had been writing for years, her literary talent developed, as the scholar and biographer David Stouck notes, by diligent practice and a long apprenticeship.[893] Although the Wilsons had enjoyed their summer cottage on Bowen Island for many years and had frequently gone trout fishing together in British Columbia, that early physical energy was gone by the time Margaret met Mrs. Wilson.

Ethel Wilson's demeanour reminded one of a proper English matron — a woman who was comfortable in the world of culture and manners, a woman who knew how high tea should be served. Yet Ethel Wilson also had real intellectual vigour as well as a roguish side. These qualities, combined with an honesty and directness in conversation, indicated there was more depth to the aging matron than might appear at first glance.[894]

Alice Munro, who then lived in Vancouver, recalls Ethel Wilson as "an eminence." Another person states, "Although she was very dignified — I always think of Ethel as pouring tea with the finest of china and the finest of silver — she could surprise you with her wonderful sense of humour."[895]

While Margaret was undoubtedly in awe of Ethel Wilson's literary accomplishments, they quickly became friends. Both of them had lived in Africa and Margaret noticed the camel-bell in the Wilson's home; she also had one in her own home. Despite the difference in age, the two women had much in common. Each was tall, with a clear gaze and a good sense of humour. They shared other traits: a passion for writing;

an appreciation of the finest in literature; an absorbing intellectual curiosity; a fascination with language; a natural shyness; an abiding love for Canada; quick wit; and an enjoyment of cigarettes and a cocktail before dinner. By a curious coincidence, both women were orphans, having lost their mothers at an early age and their fathers by the age of nine. Both had been raised by strict relatives. And both women had known fear and loneliness.

Ethel Wilson's fiction was first published in the *New Statesman* before the outbreak of the Second World War. At its best, the tone of her fiction is brilliant and defies imitation. Under the apparently simple surface of her short stories and novels lies a remarkable understanding of the human condition, which would have appealed to Laurence. The writer and translator Joyce Marshall notes that Ethel Wilson "wrote of the human heart and human entanglements," and praises her as "a fine writer of great individuality, the first Canadian writer of my acquaintance who did something quite idiosyncratic and even unique with the English sentence."[896]

After Margaret left Vancouver in 1962, she and Ethel Wilson corresponded for a number of years. At least fifty of Wilson's letters to Margaret Laurence are in the archives at York University, although Margaret's letters to her seem to have been lost or destroyed.[897] When Ethel Wilson died in 1980, a tribute broadcast on the CBC included remarks by Margaret Laurence. In addition, Margaret wrote a tribute that was published in the *Vancouver Sun*. Laurence recounted their friendship, which had its beginnings after Ethel Wilson wrote to *Prism* praising "The Merchant of Heaven." As a result, Laurence wrote to thank Wilson, who then invited Margaret to tea at her apartment on Kensington Place overlooking English Bay. "Thus began a friendship," said Margaret, "that I valued more than I can say. I was starved for the company of other writers, and here was an older fiction writer whose work I admired so much, taking the time to talk with and encourage a young and unknown writer."[898]

Although Margaret was neither living nor writing in great isolation, her remarks make clear that Ethel Wilson's interest and concern had made a deep impression on her, giving Margaret a sense that someone did understand. "There's no question," says Laurence, "that I would have gone on writing, but she provided me with an enormous amount of encouragement. I owe her a great, great deal. There is no way that I can ever repay her personally. The only thing I can do is pass it on."[899]

After her first visit with Mrs. Wilson (for Margaret did not address her as Ethel for many years), Laurence visited her from time to time:

> and grew to love and admire her just as I had long loved and admired her writing. She once said to me shortly before I left Vancouver and embarked on a new kind of life (and I can see the room now, the Wilsons' dining room and myself and Mrs. Wilson sitting down to lunch in a rather formal way, and yet her warmth taking away any of my sense of gaucherie), "There is a fountain in you. It will well up." That was not only the most encouraging thing that had ever been said to me; it was also like a kind of responsibility, a trust. I owe her such a lot.[900]

During the Vancouver Book Fair in 1961, an "Evening with Ethel Wilson" celebration was held. That night in her speech, Ethel Wilson praised *This Side Jordan*, calling it a warm, urgent, "and beautifully written novel of power and understanding."[901]

Margaret appreciated that encomium and, after leaving Vancouver, she treasured their subsequent correspondence. "Her letters, even when she was ill and mourning her husband's death, never failed to encourage me and to help me believe in myself. I owe her a great debt, which I can only repay by trying to encourage writers younger than myself, in whom I have the same kind of faith as she had in me."[902]

By September 1960, the Laurences' financial situation in Vancouver must have improved. Jack has fond memories of driving about in his large white Jaguar, although it was not brand new.[903] The Laurences also purchased a small vacation place on the western side of Point Roberts, in the State of Washington, for the sum of fourteen hundred and fifty dollars.[904] Point Roberts, a peninsula, belongs to the United States as the result of a rather anomalous historical boundary settlement; its latitude, however, actually places it between Victoria and Nanaimo (on Vancouver Island). Point Roberts, with an area of about ten square miles, was an attractive summer spot for some Vancouverites, but its permanent population was less than five hundred.[905] There is little about Point Roberts in Margaret's letters, but some of her relatives and neighbours recall her there. And it was at the Laurences' cottage at Point Roberts that Margaret Laurence wrote a good deal of *The Stone Angel*.[906]

One approach to Point Roberts by car would have taken Margaret across wide stretches of low-lying fields and active farms, with an open horizon reminiscent of a prairie vista. The Laurences' small lot, located on Park Lane, an unpaved road, was surrounded by large fir trees and cedars. Their neighbour's lot had the biggest Sitka Spruce on the point.[907] A path through the woods led Park Lane cottagers to Gulf Road, where there was a general store, a small post office, a liquor store, and a roadhouse, which had formerly been a cannery. The Laurences' cottage was surrounded by trees and set back from the road. Like many other summer places, it lacked running water and electricity. Jack did a lot of work on the cottage, putting on cedar shakes and doing interior restoration as well.[908] The most attractive feature of the cottage was a large split-granite fireplace with a raised hearth on the south corner of the west wall. The fireplace and other features of the site must have reminded Margaret of those magic childhood summers in Manitoba at her family's cottage amid the trees overlooking Clear Lake in Riding Mountain National Park.[909]

The Laurences sometimes went to Point Roberts as a family, but Margaret herself valued the simple cottage chiefly as a place where she might go from time to time in order to write. June Schulhof remembers seeing in the cottage a large paper kite of an owl that Margaret especially liked.[910] Helen Bazaluk and her husband, Pete, lived in a log cabin next door (no longer standing). Thinking that Margaret might be lonely, Helen made a point of watching for her to come out of the cabin to use the outhouse. Helen would then invite her in, but Margaret explained she was writing and made clear to Helen that she didn't want to be disturbed.[911]

Not only was the small, quiet community at Point Roberts conducive to writing, its rural environment held great interest. Around the peninsula there are wonderful tidal pools alive with small fish, crab, and purple starfish. Sea anemones, exposed at low tide, hang on the sides of immense barnacled rocks. From spring to late fall, the waters off Point Roberts were then bustling with seine boats, gill-netters, and reef-net boats. At night, when the boats were at anchor, the water, dotted with lights, "looked like a village on the sea." The coasts of Point Roberts to the west and south are situated on the cold waters of the Gulf of Georgia, but the eastern side faces Boundary Bay where there are sand dunes and a lovely beach. Sandbars stretch far out into the bay and the shallower warm water makes it attractive for swimming. Boundary Bay probably reminded Margaret of happier days on the coast at Accra and Tema in West Africa.

From the Laurences' cottage, Margaret could reach Boundary Bay by walking along the old Atlanta Packers' dirt road, which for years had been the approach to the cannery at Lily Point, located on the east side of the peninsula. As Margaret came nearer to the bay, she passed a very old cemetery on the right, with headstones bearing names such as Gudmundson, Hjalmarson, and Thordarson. Then, she would have entered a thickly wooded area for a short walk to the top of a high bluff, from which there are splendid views of Boundary Bay. Across the water to the east, even in summer, one can see the awesome, snow-capped peak of Mount Baker. The trail from the tall bluffs to the beach descends steeply, meandering under a canopy of mature maple trees. A person has to step over exposed roots and duck under fallen trees in order to reach the base of the cliff and what remains of the old APA cannery. There is a sense of solitude and peace at the APA site, from which no dwellings are visible and the beach follows a little natural bay.[912] It is that cannery at Lily Point which figures so significantly in *The Stone Angel*, a fact that Laurence was pleased to share with fellow writer and friend Silver Donald Cameron, who knew the area, having spent summers at Point Roberts during his youth.[913]

Driving back to Vancouver from Point Roberts, cars climb from the low-lying area near the sea to a much higher border checkpoint for Customs. Then the road descends steeply to the plain below, while in the distance to the northeast a ridge of black jagged mountain peaks scripts the horizon: Grouse Mountain, the brooding, inescapable presence over Vancouver. The geographical situation of that city is the very antithesis of the fog-free Manitoba prairie where blue skies open to the heavens and the distant horizon seems to stretch forever. The rugged geography and changing climate of Vancouver call forth enormously varied responses in individuals. Ethel Wilson and her husband owned a cabin on Bowen Island and she felt deeply attached to Vancouver and to the province of British Columbia. Friends of the Laurences, such as the Schulhofs, loved the area. June, who was born and raised in Ireland, enjoyed Vancouver's climate and found it familiar. Her husband, an Austrian, was attracted to its snow-covered mountains and the prospects for skiing. Both felt at home in Vancouver and "fell in love with the place."[914] That did not happen to Margaret Laurence.[915] She never felt comfortable in Vancouver, where the hovering dark mountains seemed to push the land into the mighty Pacific, and the unpredictable fog rolled in and out.[916] In Vancouver, Margaret did not hear Eliot's "mermaids singing, each to each." She found the oppressive aspects of the place too much in tune with her own worries and discouragement.

1961

In the autumn of 1960, Laurence informed her agent, Willis Wing, that she had completed nine short stories set in West Africa and asked him if they might be published as a collection.[917] His reply, which echoed Whit Burnett's earlier response, was not encouraging: "For the present it is true and is likely to remain so that the short story collection is not nearly as welcome nor as easy to publish with all success as is the novel."[918] That view, however, was not shared by Alan Maclean at Macmillan, London, who five years before had inaugurated their short-story annual, *Winter's Tales*. In his introduction to that volume, Maclean noted that, although collections of stories are generally commercially unprofitable to both author and publisher, nevertheless, approximately fifty collections of stories had been produced by British publishers in 1959.[919] Margaret Laurence was encouraged by Maclean's comments, despite her agent's reluctance. Her desire to have a collection of her stories published was further strengthened by the appearance of *Mrs. Golightly and Other Stories*, a collection by Ethel Wilson, and by favourable reviews of *Canadian Short Stories*, edited by Robert Weaver.

During January 1961, Margaret was paid twelve hundred and fifty dollars by the *Saturday Evening Post* for "Voices of Adamo." It was an astonishing jump from the fee of twenty-five dollars that *Prism* had paid for one of her stories only two years before.[920] Of course, such a large sum could only be paid by magazines that had a sizable circulation; certainly not by the smaller Canadian literary journals. At that time, the *Saturday Evening Post* regularly carried fiction by major writers and it was a milestone for Margaret Laurence to have her work appear there. Ethel Wilson was delighted to see Laurence's story published in the *Saturday Evening Post* and told her friends the Crawleys that Laurence was "a good writer who doesn't follow anyone's creative lead. . . . She is self-critical & not self-important."[921]

That January favourable reviews of *This Side Jordan* appeared in the *New York Herald Tribune* and in *The New Yorker*.[922] Such publicity in the United States was heartening, although at that moment Margaret was dealing with the challenges of writing another novel. She had recently reminded her agent that she had wasted an enormous amount of effort in writing sections of *This Side Jordan* that subsequently had to be discarded. She explained, "I am not a very speedy writer and I re-write a great deal." She then sketched out for him her ambitious literary plans: she intended to write a book chronicling her personal experiences in the British Somaliland Protectorate; complete a series of short stories; and work on one more novel set in West Africa: "If I can bring it off (and this is always a frightening question), it will, I think, be a better novel than the first."[923] Laurence did, in fact, embark on all three projects. As time passed, however, the new West African novel gave her considerable trouble and she decided to abandon it.[924]

By October 1961, she was struggling with a different sort of novel — one set in Canada. She had almost finished the first draft and told Adele, "although it needs a lot more work, I can see now the shape of it."[925] The novel that she had begun to set down was to become *The Stone Angel*, the first of Laurence's Manawaka books (1964) and a major literary accomplishment for her.

As she worked on the manuscript in 1961, however, she encountered many problems, some of which she described to Adele: "It's difficult, I find, to maintain any sort of faith in oneself. I haven't got an ounce of it myself, for all the way in which I write to you. Maybe I'm hoping to convince myself as well as you. I fluctuate between extremes re. this novel, & may yet become a manic-depressive."[926]

The letter reveals a good deal about a phenomenon that often beset Laurence, and, indeed, plagues many authors: when writers are struggling with a new book, they are unable to feel elated or even reassured by their previous successes and see only the abyss that the new work represents.

Letters between Laurence and her editors reviewed the issue of the novel's title. At first *Hagar* seemed to be agreed on, but after many letters back and forth Margaret changed it to *The Stone Angel*. That change resulted in an improvement in Macmillan's cover design. They had actually printed a provisional cover in black, pink, and white, which was then discarded.[927]

When Margaret later talked about the genesis of *The Stone Angel*, she often stated that the process had been fairly simple; she had written it in "a kind of single-minded burst of activity." Its central character, Hagar Shipley, seemed to tell her story directly to Laurence. However, that account is not supported by her contemporary correspondence. In letters written while she was wrestling with *The Stone Angel*, a very different picture emerges. She recounted many periods of difficulty and uncertainty. She anticipated pitfalls. She worried that *The Stone Angel* was written too simply and directly, in a style that was "perhaps almost archaic now." She felt that the book could be called "unsophisticated," but at the same time she realized that what she was trying to imply in the novel "isn't really simple at all." Margaret's struggles and anxieties are rampant in a seven-page, handwritten letter sent to Adele Wiseman early the same month. Reporting that she was "absorbed to a total degree by this damn novel," Margaret apologized for not keeping in touch and shared her profound uncertainties about her novel with Adele.

Laurence, however, did not mention those anxieties when she was later interviewed. After the *The Stone Angel* was finally completed, she seemed to recall its composition as something akin to automatic writing. That feeling was probably due more to the forcefulness of Hagar's character than to the accuracy of Laurence's memory. It may well be that when the breakthrough with *The Stone Angel* finally came, the release was powerful enough to overshadow all the earlier false starts and uncertainties, or it may be that, after spending months reshaping and editing *This Side Jordan*, Margaret Laurence's second novel indeed felt like a gift from the gods. With regard to *The Stone Angel*, she remembered the gift, not the struggle.

In a letter to Adele that autumn she brought up a significant point about her work: "Kind friends & acquaintances still say from time to time very peculiar things such as 'how does it feel to be a successful writer?' and I look at them oddly as though they were speaking to me in Hindustani. I feel I haven't really learned a thing about writing except that no one really knows what is good & what is bad. So you might as well write to please yourself & not worry about anything else."[928]

Here Laurence identifies the demon with which she was struggling. Writing to satisfy herself, trusting her own judgement about her work — that was the single most important thing she had to learn. In order to succeed with her writing, Margaret Laurence had to relinquish turning for literary approval to others: whether her agent, her editors, or her husband, Jack.

As she concluded that letter, Margaret tried to shift the focus away from her personal struggles and convey some family news to Adele: "I never seem to talk of the external world in my letters to you, possibly because I know very few people to whom I can talk about the interior battles, so you get it all. Sorry. Anyway, we are all quite well. The kids are fine."[929]

David was in Grade One and happy to be learning to read. Jocelyn, in Grade Four, was busy with her Brownie troop, piano lessons, and dancing. Laurence also offered a brief update on Jack and herself:

> Jack & I are having a lot of fun lately making wine from real grapes, with the help of an Italian friend. I'm still marking essays, doing about 4 book reviews a month, & this year (don't faint) I'm teaching Sunday School in the Unitarian Church. Sometimes I feel I have too much to do, but I guess I don't really. Jack finds his job very interesting still & always has too much to do, but in general we both feel quite happy here now, if it weren't for the very-present threat of fallout, bombs, etc. Please write etc.[930]

"The very-present threat" of nuclear fallout or nuclear bombs formed the background of Margaret's years in Vancouver. For her it remained a jarring fact of life after returning from completely different concerns in the Gold Coast on the eve of its independence from Great Britain. Margaret's worries about the danger of nuclear fallout, however, may not have been shared to the same degree then by Adele or other friends. For it was on the West Coast, particularly in places such as Vancouver, that proximity to nuclear test sites in the Pacific, Cold War threats of a nuclear "standoff" between the United States and the Soviet Union, as well as health hazards from the Hanford nuclear reactor in nearby Washington State combined to create in citizens a state of awareness and alarm that was much more immediate than in many other parts of North America.

In 1959, a film version of Nevil Shute's novel *On the Beach* (1957) had begun showing in cinemas. The grim plot focused on how the world ends after a nuclear war. That same year the "Women's Committee on Radiation Hazards" was formed in Vancouver. Members, particularly mothers, undertook to investigate and alert citizens to the hazards that could result from nuclear testing, particularly cancer and congenital or developmental defects in children.

Newspapers the following year did not allay people's fears, as summit talks between the U.S. President Eisenhower and Soviet Premier Nikita Khrushchev were "near collapse." The papers announced: "Nuclear War Seen If Arms Talks Fail"; "U.S. Blasts Rocket 9,000 miles"; "Russian Scientific Bases Drift In and Out of the Canadian Arctic" (supplied by air power). In British Columbia, the provincial secretary Wesley Black declared, "Every householder should build a basement bomb shelter." And the city of New Westminster, B.C. became the first in the Lower Mainland to provide a fallout shelter for civic government.

In the United States, the American artist Georgia O'Keeffe had a bomb shelter built into a hillside near her home in New Mexico. And in England there was an unprecedented turnout for a great sit-down protest in Trafalgar Square in September 1961. At one point, the renowned artist Augustus John, "an old man, who had been, and was, very ill . . . emerged from the National Gallery, walked into the Square and sat down."[931]

In some churches in British Columbia, members formed groups to express distress over the arms race and nuclear testing and to "promote better understanding between the people of the world." Those efforts gave rise to the "Voice of Women," an important group founded in Vancouver in 1960 after the collapse of the summit talks in Geneva, Switzerland. In Vancouver, members were now collecting babies' teeth to have them tested for Strontium 90. Margaret Laurence had friends who were active in Voice of Women, but it is not clear whether she joined the group then, although she was sympathetic to their concerns. Anxieties about the nuclear arms race are prominent in her novel *The Fire-Dwellers*, which is set in Vancouver.

Laurence was deeply committed to efforts which promoted world peace and said "no" to nuclear arms. Years later when she had moved to Ontario, she continued to be publicly outspoken about the arms race and the danger of a nuclear disaster.[932] By then she was very well-known, and her public statements warning of the dangers of the nuclear buildup have been described by the prominent educator Dr. Margaret Fulton as "courageous."[933]

While living in Vancouver, Margaret did collect money for the Red Cross one day a year. She related the following anecdote to some old friends. Once she had encountered an "elderly maiden who took me inside her gloomy Edwardian living room to show me her cannibal goldfish — as soon as another goldfish was put in the glass tank with it, the cannibal at once devoured its playmate. The old girl told me she had to quit putting in other fish, as they were too expensive and she could no longer afford it!"[934] The scene was not forgotten, however, and a much transformed version of it appears in Laurence's novel *The Fire-Dwellers*.[935]

In March 1961 the Laurences' friends June and Fred Schulhof returned to Vancouver. They had gone back to Ireland the previous July with the intention of staying, but soon changed their minds and decided to remain permanently in Canada. Upon their return, the Schulhofs were met at the airport by Jack, Margaret, and Gordon Elliott. Margaret and Jack offered to take the two older boys, while the Schulhofs with their younger children searched for a house. Mark and Stefan Schulhof stayed with the Laurences for about six weeks.[936] So, for a while, Margaret, like Stacey in *The Fire-Dwellers*, had the experience of being parent to four children. During those weeks, June Schulhof became aware that Margaret was trying to write and was very grateful that, under such circumstances,

Margaret had offered to take her two sons. As a consequence, June stopped by often in order to help Margaret with the laundry and household chores. In doing so, she became aware of how necessary writing was to Margaret's well-being. At last, the Schulhofs found a house about a block from Margaret and Jack in the Dunbar area and settled there, and the couples continued their friendship.

That spring, Margaret was delighted to hear that Adele Wiseman's plans for a trip to China had been finalized. In June, Adele sailed for the Far East from Brooklyn, New York, on board the *Demosthenes D*, a Greek ship registered in Monrovia.[937] A distinct difference was becoming apparent, however, between the two women in terms of publication. Although they continued to remain strongly supportive of each other's efforts, Adele's early success with *The Sacrifice* had not been followed by other publications, while Margaret's work was steadily growing in volume as well as number of acceptances.

During autumn 1961, Laurence went to Toronto to receive the Beta Sigma Phi award for the best "first" novel by a Canadian (*This Side Jordan*), given at the Canadian Authors' Association awards dinner. She was also awarded the President's Medal from the University of Western Ontario for the best Canadian short story of 1960 ("A Gourdful of Glory"). In addition, there was good news from *Prism*; they were ready to publish another of her stories, "The Tomorrow-Tamer."[938]

That autumn, Laurence and other Vancouverites rejoiced in the news that Ethel Wilson, Lawren Harris, and several others would receive the new "Canada Council Medals" and a monetary award of two thousand dollars each for making major contributions in the arts, humanities, or social sciences. The awards were presented on the opening day of the city of Vancouver's first book fair. Margaret probably attended in order to hear speeches by John Gray of Macmillan, Canada; Donald Stainsby, columnist for the *Vancouver Sun*; and her friend and award recipient, Ethel Wilson. Further recognition of the importance of literary contributions to the cultural life of Canada was emphasized during the book fair, which ran from November 10 to 18 and had a great deal of publicity in the local papers. A lengthy article in the *Vancouver Sun* featured photos of three Vancouver writers. There Margaret Laurence's picture appeared beside that of fellow Vancouver writer Roderick Haig-

Brown and the celebrated Ethel Wilson.[939] During the week, events were planned for a variety of locations and Laurence was scheduled to speak at the YWCA. Although there seems to be no written account of Laurence's response to the publicity, surely after her unceasing literary toil during the previous four years, she would have been thrilled to see her photo in the *Vancouver Sun* beside those of accomplished writers whom she admired.[940] Such public recognition of her literary accomplishment must have been a real surprise to Laurence. But was it enough to put her fears and anxieties to rest?

She persevered with the demanding schedule she had set for herself, and by the end of December 1961 had completed six of fifteen projected chapters of her travel memoir, *The Prophet's Camel Bell*, as well as the first draft of *The Stone Angel*. She made a significant decision, however, to put the draft of the novel aside so that later she could return to it with a fresh eye.[941]

About this time, Laurence learned of unacknowledged "borrowings" of her Somali translations by Danish writer John Bucholzer.[942] She was shocked to learn that his book, *The Horn of Africa*, contained sections from *A Tree for Poverty*, which he had "passed off as his own."[943] After obtaining a copy of his book, she was very annoyed to find it conveyed the impression that direct translations are rather easy — a person simply sits around the campfire and jots down notes. But Margaret was much more angry about the fact that Bucholzer had taken whole paragraphs and sections directly from her introduction to *A Tree for Poverty*, "and all my conclusions and ideas about Somali literature were presented as his own — and in my words!"[944] She contacted her agent, Willis Wing, giving him the details about Bucholzer's plagiarism. Although she did not intend to pursue the matter through legal channels, she "wanted to let Mr. Bucholzer know that I resented somewhat the fact that if I ever wrote a book on Somaliland and used material from my earlier essay on Somali poetry and folk-tales, it might appear that I was plagiarizing [him] when, in fact, I was quoting myself."[945]

Margaret's restrained letter to Willis Wing belies the fact that she was deeply upset and very angry. Four months later, she again referred to the plagiarism, telling Mr. Wing she had heard that several people in London who were involved in the study of African languages were also "most annoyed at John Bucholzer's unacknowledged borrowing of the material in *A Tree for Poverty*."[946]

His publisher sent back word that Bucholzer was currently in Tierra del Fuego and unavailable for comment. The matter was not entirely laid to rest, however. Twenty years later Laurence was reminded of the episode and wrote to her friend, the Canadian scholar Clara Thomas, summarizing what had happened and remarking that she would have liked to tell Karen Blixen, the Danish author whose pseudonym was Isak Dinesen, that the translations which she referred to in *Shadows in the Grass* "were not Bucholzer's, but mine, done with a hell of a lot of help from Somali friends."[947]

Four years later, while composing her memoirs, Laurence again became so distressed by the memory of Bucholzer's plagiarism that she filled one side of an audio tape (forty-five minutes) with comments about it. Joan Johnston, the friend who had transcribed the tapes during Laurence's final months, reports that Margaret later instructed her not to include those comments in the transcript and to erase the tape, which Joan did.[948]

The Vancouver Sun

During 1960-1961, Margaret contributed a number of book reviews to the *Vancouver Sun*. Although those reviews have not been discussed in biographies of Laurence, they are significant, and the challenge of writing them certainly contributed to her literary development. Less flippant and more reflective than her Winnipeg newspapers reviews (1947-1948), the *Vancouver Sun* reviews were written while Laurence was deeply engaged with her own fiction. The nagging anxiety that frequently surfaces in her letters during this period is absent from her reviews. In them her tone is self-assured, her analysis comprehensive and succinct. The reviews were not tossed off casually, but rather were the product of conscientious reflection and careful composition. In the columns allotted to her, Laurence used an enviable economy of words and precision of phrasing. The nineteen reviews that she wrote between May 1960 and March 1961 discussed works by Morley Callaghan, Brian

Moore, Mikhail Sholokhov, Graham Greene, and Marguerite Duras, among others.

Among those books, four were set in Africa. Laurence, referring to a novel about South Africa, made the acerbic remark: "No one could deny that the Voortrekkers were remarkable people. . . . But it would be interesting some day to read an historical novel of the same period written by a Zulu."[949] She criticized another novel in which the characters are secondary to the author's social and political agenda, and praised one in which the author explored "with striking honesty not only the South African situation but the mixed motives in the heart of every individual."[950]

Laurence herself frequently commented in letters and essays on the many paradoxes in the human condition. She understood that individuals may be complex, and her fictional characters often have very negative traits as well as admirable qualities. Working on the Somali tales early in her career had provided many opportunities for Margaret to examine the Somali use of paradox. She, herself, seemed to delight in the way situations can sometimes be reversed by the less fortunate, when, with ingenuity and good humour, they manage to thwart the plans of the powerful.

In her own fiction, Laurence displays great skill in creating distinctive speech patterns without relying on dialect, and her *Vancouver Sun* reviews show that she also admired that ability in other writers: "Mrs. Klapper is a memorable and entirely delightful character. The author never resorts to dialect and yet he achieves in her speech a startling audible quality. One can really hear her rich Brooklyn Jewish voice and can perceive directly her warmth, her need to be needed, the self-mockery that keeps her from self-pity."[951]

Laurence, unfazed by the fact that Conrad Richter had won the Pulitzer Prize in 1951, found little to praise in his novel *The Waters of Kronos* (1960). The central character, Donner, is "not well drawn" and is "much closer to Freud's Oedipus than to Sophocles." She concluded with the trenchant observation that readers who follow Donner's symbol-strewn ascent of the ancestral stairs toward the ultimate door, may feel there is really only "the same old Womb at The Top."[952]

The next month, with succinct imagery, she praised a novel that she found interesting, remarking, "This book is a light, dry, eidery brew that readers should find a refreshing change from the fiery shots of raw rum offered by many realistic novels."[953]

Laurence's considerable skill as a reviewer, which Ethel Wilson had remarked, is apparent in her review of Kern's *The Clown*, a novel that relates the story of a young Swiss clerk who runs away and joins the circus. "The greatest achievement of this epic novel in which the fate of nations is paralleled by that of the circus," noted Laurence, "[is] its insight into the soul of a clown. In his cruel and tender parodies on love and war, Hans [the clown] finds his only real existence. The ring is his world, in which he is both creator and created. It is his confessional, in which he is both priest and suppliant."[954] In concluding the review she wrote: "Kern's novel is a veritable circus itself, with all the color and diversity of the Big Top. In places as oddly stylized as a poster, it can also move with the swiftness and grace of a trapeze act. Sometimes there is an excess of brilliance, too many acts going on simultaneously. The reader leaves the show feeling impressed but slightly dazed."[955]

Would writing those reviews of contemporary novels for the *Vancouver Sun* have made Margaret Laurence more anxious about her own fiction, or would struggling with the work of others have served to strengthen her own writing? Perhaps the outcome was a bit of both. In 1961, she reviewed two novels which may well have had some impact on her own subsequent work.[956]

Laurence's review of *A Candle to Light the Sun* appeared in January 1961. It was a first novel by her friend and former college classmate, Patricia Blondal (née Jenkins). Pat, even as an undergraduate, had been as serious about writing as Peggy Wemyss. However, Pat had married during her last year at United College (the first in their class to wed). She and her husband later moved to Montreal. Pat had two children and a rosy future when she was stricken with cancer and died before her thirty-third birthday. *A Candle to Light the Sun* was published posthumously.

Laurence had read the manuscript of *A Candle to Light the Sun* during the previous summer, when it was sent to her from Jack McClelland. He was unaware that Margaret had known the author and asked her to assess it. Afterwards, Margaret wrote to Adele, remarking that Pat's novel "attempts such a lot — an overall picture of a small prairie town & all its people . . . a picture of one man's search for identity." Laurence speculated that had Pat lived, she would have made considerable revisions to the novel, nevertheless, she told Adele *A Candle to Light the Sun* was "a serious novel done with subtlety and great compassion."[957] In reviewing the novel, Laurence said:

> This novel's treatment of a Canadian prairie town is the best I have ever read. The book's scope is broad, covering the thirties and the harshness of the land in the dry years, and going on to chronicle the lives of the generations that grew up during the war. . . . With unusual perception the author shows us that the hiding of hearts in a small town, the concealed scandal and the tacit understanding that some things are not talked about — these are not mere hypocrisy. They are Mouse Bluffs' protection, the only way in which these people can live so close together and in such isolation.[958]

The next month Laurence commented on Mikhail Sholokhov's saga of South Russia, *Harvest on the Don*, which gives "an authentic picture of the collective farms of the thirties."[959] She noted that "a very odd thing happens" as the story unfolds. "A stupid and garrulous old Cossack begins upstaging all the other characters. . . . The real heart and real art of this novel lie in the character of an old man who has no political significance whatsoever."[960]

Did Sholokhov's portrait of the old Cossack, who is not a stereotypical elder uttering wise homespun philosophy, but rather "an old crackpot" who "brags" and "whines," unconsciously encourage her own emerging fictional portrait of Hagar in *The Stone Angel*? Did Patricia Blondal's bold treatment of the harsh and stifling realities of small-town prairie life encourage Laurence's approach to Manawaka? The answer to such questions lies hidden in the mystery of creativity and the many ways in which authors absorb ideas, situations, and characters, magically weaving them into the cloth of their own books. Both novels are quite different from Laurence's fiction, and it can only be conjectured whether and how reviewing those books might have affected or encouraged Laurence's own literary efforts.

At a later period in her life, she recounted in a letter to the writer Ernest Buckler that she had first read his book *The Mountain and the Valley* in Vancouver, after *This Side Jordan* had been published, and she recalled that his novel "both scared and heartened" her. "I was beginning to think seriously about how I could return (in the deepest ways — because physically I was living in Vancouver but hadn't yet returned home in my writing) to the background which was truly my own."[961] It is certainly possible that in some unconscious ways reading and reviewing so many important works of fiction at that time did influence the direction of Laurence's own literary development.

Laurence's reviews for the *Vancouver Sun* indicate, albeit indirectly, her own concerns as a novelist. No better summary of Margaret Laurence's goals as a writer can be made than her own remarks about Roger Vailland's novel *Fête*: "[*Fête's*] characters are revealed gradually, delicately, with the consummate skill of the true novelist. They impress not with what they do but with what they are. They come to life, and their presence leaves an echo in the mind."[962]

1962

Although Laurence's agent had been unable to find a market in North America for "The Rain Child," after Macmillan accepted that story, she suggested to him that her stories might stand "a better chance in England."[963] While awaiting his reply, however, pressing issues arose on the domestic front in January 1962. She and Jack were in the midst of serious and difficult discussions about whether or not Jack would seek engineering work abroad. He was not satisfied with his job in British Columbia and hankered to return to work in an underdeveloped country. Margaret summed up for Adele the problematic situation that was unfolding: "[Jack] just cannot find the same sort of satisfaction in work here, where he never really feels it matters whether the job is done or not. So I hope he is able to find the right sort of job somewhere else. Now, of course, the conditions are not as simple as they once could be — now we have to consider places where we can take the kids, and where there are schools. So we shall see."[964]

A few months later, although Jack had made inquires about an over-seas post, nothing seemed imminent, and Margaret was considering tak-ing a one-year librarian's course at the University of British Columbia. She thought it might prove interesting and also provide some additional income.[965] In early June, Jack was away again, having gone up to Balfour near Nelson "for the purpose of hauling the power cables out of the river. The cables that were part of the lines the Doukhobors blew up."[966]

On June 13, Margaret wrote two letters that shed light on the way things were developing for her. Although she had started several letters to Adele during the past month, she had not been able to finish them. This was not due to a lack of time or reluctance to write, she explained, rather it was the effect of taking diet pills. Her efforts to lose weight came at a price however:

> I am either in a manic or depressive condition all the time. In my manic phase, I concentrate on that great novel which I am writing, convinced that it will ulti-mately be deathless prose. In my depressive phase, I feel the novel is pure garbage, and I cannot even consider it worthwhile to sit down and write to friends, as I am suffering from both lung cancer and TB and will prob-ably not survive the night. However, I seem to be in an in-between place now, and not suffering from any lethal diseases, so I'll try to write now. No kidding — these diet pills really work. I have shed 15 lbs. and have set my goal for another 10. . . . The only trouble with these pills is that I smoke like a furnace the whole time, and seem unable to stop, and this really terrifies me. But all seemed worthwhile today when I went down-town and bought a summer dress — sheath style, the first time in several years that I have been able to wear this kind of dress.[967]

Margaret wrote much the same news to Gordon Elliott on the same day, mentioning her mood swings and the diet pills that were helping her to lose weight.[968] The situation that Margaret describes was hardly unique to her; in fact, it was rather typical for North American women in the 1960s, as Betty Friedan cogently remarked in *The Feminine Mystique.*[969]

In August Margaret reported that "everything was at sixes and sevens." She had abandoned "the old lady novel" (*The Stone Angel*) although she hoped to return to it one day if she could work out how to do it properly, "but right now I can see only that it is boring. This is the one thing that is not permitted. The whole thing really is very poor, and right now I feel I can only cut my losses and put it away. I feel intensely depressed about it, needless to say, especially as I wonder if I can write anything about this country [Canada]."[970] She was also distressed because she and Jack were at an impasse: "[We] have been trying to sort out what it was that each of us really wants to do in this life, and this appears a more complex thing than we thought it might be — he may be going abroad again, and I know that is right for him, but I wonder if I can become a memsahib once more? Anyway, we shall see. I may stay with the kids in England for a year, I don't know."[971]

In the summer of 1962, Margaret met the Barbadian writer George Lamming in Vancouver. His novels, focusing on the changes in West Indian society from the colonial period to the present, had won for him an international reputation. More recently, his achievements in fiction and poetry had been highlighted in an essay by Frank Collymore, which appeared in the *Tamarack Review*, along with a fine poem by Lamming ("The Swan") and an excerpt from his collected essays.[972] Laurence's West African novel, *This Side Jordan*, and several of her short stories set in the Gold Coast had received praise in Vancouver and London, and she would have been pleased to meet with Lamming, a fellow writer, who was an outspoken West Indian nationalist and supporter of trade unionism.

Although one of Laurence's biographers alleges that a romantic involvement with George Lamming was the reason why Margaret Laurence left Vancouver and separated from her husband, this claim has not been supported by sufficient evidence.[973] Furthermore, if Laurence had been feeling lonely and at loose ends when she met Lamming, her correspondence over several years shows that the decision to have a trial separation evolved over time and prior to her meeting with him. In fact, a stronger case could be made that Jack Laurence's dissatisfaction with his work in Canada, which may be clearly traced in a number of her letters, and his desire to find an engineering post in underdeveloped regions of the world, was a significant, divisive, and long-standing issue in the couple's marriage.[974]

In the summer of 1962, the needs of husband and wife in terms of what they perceived as their respective vocations were in direct conflict. While Jack's satisfaction with his work was diminishing, Margaret's success as a writer was increasing. She had received several fiction awards, in addition to important encouragement from her editors and recognition from the press. However, Jack's strong desire to leave Canada so that he could work in underdeveloped countries brought their future as a family into question. In overseas regions where Jack might find work as an irrigation engineer, it would be unheard of to find a local school that went beyond the most rudimentary sort of instruction, and that instruction would have been in the local language. Moreover, it was unthinkable that Western families stationed in those countries would send their children to such a school. Westerners always sent their children away to boarding schools.

As the weeks of summer passed and the implications of moving overseas were discussed at length, it was becoming painfully clear to Margaret that she could not go with Jack to East Pakistan [Bangladesh], a place where they and the children could expect tropical monsoons, floods, cyclones, and a variety of diseases.

Margaret Laurence was also aware that, once abroad, where years of tradition had forged the patterns of colonial life, she would, of course, be obliged to resume the position of a "memsahib" and fit into the colonial social situation. As the wife of a chief engineer, there could be no viable alternative for her. Moreover, if Jack returned, as he intended, to that sort of work, then as soon as an irrigation project was completed, he would naturally have to move to another location and another contract. As it turned out, moving from place to place did prove to be the trajectory of Jack's career. Between 1962 and 1969, Jack Laurence would move often. His engineering work took him to many far-flung places in addition to East Pakistan, among them Belize, Malawi, Swaziland, and once again Somalia.

In 1962, however, as Jack and Margaret tried to sort out their future as a couple, she realized that, with two young children, it would be difficult for the family to adapt over and over again to life in distant countries where the culture, language, and history were completely different. Moreover, there was a real health issue. If they resided with their children in places where malaria and other serious diseases were common, they would be remote from modern medical facilities and the children's health might well be jeopardized.

Margaret's concerns about Jocelyn and David's schooling and their health cannot be lightly dismissed. Her fears were based on her first-hand experience of crises in East and West Africa, where on many occasions she had seen children's health seriously compromised in a matter of hours. As far as school was concerned, the idea of sending her own children away to school was unthinkable to Margaret, who had been bereft of her parents by the age of nine. Moreover, she had not forgotten those Christmas seasons in the Gold Coast when a planeload of children would arrive from boarding schools in England to spend the holiday with their parents — and the unhappy departure of those children a few weeks later. In fact, health issues did arise years later when Jack Laurence was working in India. Both his second wife, Esther, and his brother, Bob, who had come out for a visit, contracted serious, chronic illnesses there.

In 1962, Margaret's second concern about living in underdeveloped regions related, of course, to her writing. After years of struggling to develop her literary talents, uprooting to distant countries would have felt very self-defeating. Although in theory a person may write anywhere, in reality a writer is often affected in major ways by a shift in physical location and all that may follow as a result of such a move. How long would it take for editors' letters and publishers' proofs to reach Margaret in places as remote as Pakistan or Uganda? If Margaret were again to accompany Jack abroad, her own work as a writer, "her vocation," would be seriously jeopardized.

Despite these urgent concerns, by the end of August 1962, it had become clear that Jack intended to accept an engineering post in East Pakistan and had to leave "fairly quickly."[975] His decision set in motion a chain of events that was to have an enormous impact on the lives of his family. It was agreed that Margaret and the children would spend a year in England. She had no idea how things would turn out there, but told Adele on August 29 that she had done a great deal of "intensive soul-searching" and, in an unusually revelatory phrase, mentioned that a "sense of despair" had diminished:

> All things which I have recently realized about myself, etc., now seem so obvious that I really wonder how I could have not seen them for so long. It takes me so painfully long to learn anything at all. But I feel free, or reasonably so, from the sense of despair that has been with me for some years now, so I don't really mind the slowness of growth. As far as I am concerned this will be the opportunity to terminate a kind of delayed adolescence, at the advanced age of 36, and it is really now or never. I feel now that it will work out both to my advantage and Jack's, if things go as we hope and trust.[976]

Within a month, Jack had completed plans to leave Vancouver on October 6. Margaret and the children were to leave for England the following week, stopping briefly in Winnipeg for a visit with the Wisemans, and in Toronto to see her publisher, Jack McClelland, but she could not spend too long in transit because she "[did not] want the children to be out of school any longer than is necessary."[977] Although Margaret referred to the pending separation as a one-year trial period, nonetheless, it involved an enormous wrench after fifteen years of married life with Jack.

She decided to apply to the Canada Council for a senior fellowship, but felt hesitant about asking for letters of recommendation because "one cannot, after all, guarantee results. This novel may turn out to be horrible."[978] She was anxious about producing a work that would measure up to such an award: "What if I do get the money and then goof somehow on that year in London?"[979] If the Canada Council fellowship did not come through, she planned to seek part-time work marking papers for a secondary school in London.

Although she had been "laid low with a terrible cold and flu," Margaret managed to complete the necessary arrangements for the journey. On October 12, she and the children were driven to the airport by her friend Mona. Laurence later said, "I was so tense I kept having horrible cramps in my legs and feet."[980] The departure from Vancouver was emotionally painful. Margaret felt "guilty and worried sick about what the separation might do" to the children, who were ten and seven.[981] As Mona drove them to the airport, it seemed things had come full circle — from their anxious arrival in 1957 to their anxious departure six years later. It is surprising but true that neither Mona, who was Margaret's oldest friend, nor any of the Laurences' Vancouver friends had any inkling that Jack had been dissatisfied with work there, nor did they suspect a trial separation might occur. Margaret and Jack were discreet about their personal lives and the lives of their children. That discretion would remain a constant throughout the years ahead.

When Margaret finally reached the check-in counter at the airport, their baggage was declared overweight for a transatlantic flight. The officials, nevertheless, permitted her to proceed to Winnipeg. There Margaret gave Adele some items to forward by mail, including "the only copy in existence of the manuscript *The Stone Angel.*" In her memoirs, Laurence says that the parcel took three months to reach London, and during that time she imagined it lost forever. That reminiscence is not supported by her correspondence, however. The manuscript of *The Stone Angel* actually arrived in about six weeks; but it must have seemed like an eternity to her:

> This was the novel for which I had separated from my husband and embarked on who knew what, uprooting and dragging along my two children, and I almost seemed to be trying to lose it. Guilt and fear can do strange things to the mind and the body. I questioned my right to write, even though I knew I had to do it. I had just wanted everything — husband, children, work. Was this too much?[982]

In *Dance on the Earth*, she then replies with insight to that rhetorical question: "Of course it wasn't, but the puritan conscience can be a fearsome thing and when, in a woman, it is combined with the need to create in a society that questions this need or ignores it, the results are self-inflicted wounds scarring the heart."[983]

As Margaret Laurence's sixth year in Vancouver came to a close, it marked the end of an intensely productive literary period in her life. Her departure for England also brought to a close an acutely painful personal period, during which she had struggled to stretch twenty-four-hour days to the limit. In fact, during the previous year, Margaret had found it necessary to consult a physician:

> Life became a little too hectic for me some time ago, and I was convinced I had a brain tumour or something, as I had a pounding headache the whole time, the various weird symptoms such as pins-and-needles in all legs and arms. The doctor told me it was "tension," so I gave up all book reviewing, essay marking and Sunday school [teaching]. Now I am beginning to feel almost human again. The thing was, I guess, that I had done the first draft of the novel and had then commenced work on the Somaliland book [*The Prophet's Camel Bell*], with no break at all.[984]

While the pace of such activities and her responsibilities as wife and mother may well have exhausted Laurence, it is important to ask why she decided to put away the first draft of *The Stone Angel* and immerse herself in working on another book. The answer resides in the complex background of that decision.

During the previous autumn (1961), Margaret had been totally absorbed in writing *The Stone Angel*, completing the first draft "in a kind of single-minded burst of activity, letting the thing go where it seemed to want to go." Looking back years later, she recalled sitting in their house in Vancouver, when suddenly she began to write: "An old woman had come into my mind. I suppose she had been there for a while, but all at once she became insistent."[985] The gestation of *The Stone Angel*, however, was not as effortless or immediate as her remarks seem to suggest. Laurence's description pertains more to feelings of release and exhilaration that accompanied her efforts than to the literal facts of the book's composition. The effort to write *The Stone Angel* had filled her with anxiety over a period of months. After informing Adele in October how rapidly and easily the first draft had been completed, she reported four months later that, after looking again at the manuscript, she had fallen into in a period of semi-depression. "The whole thing will have to be rewritten. . . . It is terrible. . . . Everything needs fixing."[986]

What accounts for this dramatic change in Margaret's sense of her novel? The shift from confidence to great uncertainty took place after she had shown the draft to Jack. He did not view it favourably. As a result, Margaret was thrust into a very difficult position, and her frustration with the first draft of *The Stone Angel* arose largely from the nagging realization that Jack, to whom Margaret customarily turned for comments about her fiction, did not take her writing as seriously as she did. He made it clear that he did not like *The Stone Angel*, while Margaret was enthusiastic about the novel and felt a growing attachment to Hagar, its central character. Nevertheless, she decided to revise the manuscript, and tried to accommodate Jack's suggestions. Adele had cautioned Margaret earlier about doing that. She considered it to be self-defeating behaviour and pointed that out when Margaret and Jack were still living in Africa. Adele thought that, by looking for Jack's approval of her writing and taking his criticism to heart, Margaret was leaving herself open to a growing resentment and further insecurity about her abilities as a writer.[987]

The very situation that Adele had warned against years before had now developed. The result was enormous tension. Margaret's pain and frustration are clear in her lines to Adele. She tries to explain: "It's difficult, I find, to maintain any sort of faith in oneself. I haven't got an ounce of it myself." As the letter continues, Margaret offers advice to Adele, but then pauses when she comes to understand that she is really having a conversation with herself. This is borne out, too, by the shifting pronoun references in that letter. Margaret states several objections to *The Stone Angel* and then sets down a reply to each. When her paragraph is rearranged in the following format, Margaret's dialogue with herself becomes much more obvious:

1. The novel is written simply and directly.
   "I am not clever enough to write it any other way."

2. The style is archaic.
    "I have a strong feeling for direct and simple writing."

3. The theme is not new.
    "What theme is new?"

4. The novel is unsophisticated.
    "What I am trying to imply in it isn't really simple at all."

5. It's too obvious.
    "Maybe it's not obvious enough?"

The letter then breaks off with the comment: "Well, this way lies madness."[988] Are Margaret's five statements replies to objections raised by Jack?[989] If so, that would account for her terrible emotional turmoil. As her lengthy letter to Adele continues, it is clear that Margaret is still speaking to herself when she asks rhetorically: "What can you do except go ahead & do it as you see it yourself, even if everyone else who ever sees it thinks it is perfectly horrible, or, even worse, boringly naive or just plain boring. I have brooded over this so much lately that it has got to stop."[990]

Here Margaret addresses the crux of her problem as she goes on to state that "getting to trust your own judgment and attempting honestly to write what you feel and not what you're supposed to feel" is essential.[991] This shift in her attitude toward her work was necessary if Margaret was to embrace the life and outlook of a professional writer. In working on *The Stone Angel*, she had come to understand that she must write the novel in a way that satisfied her as its author, and let go of her desire to seek the approval of Jack or of others. She realized that this was the only way to keep her sanity. At last in England she was able to achieve that attitude toward her work.

CHAPTER TEN

Uncertain Alchemy

Once it became clear that Jack was actually going to East Pakistan, Margaret had to face the issue of where she and the children might live. Remaining in Vancouver seemed out of the question. She had never really liked living there, and neither had her fellow writer Alice Munro. In fact, Munro once summed up her reaction to Vancouver during the 1950s this way: "It was much more boring [than Wingham was]. I have never even been able to do much with it fictionally because I hated it so much."[992] Although Laurence did use contemporary Vancouver as the setting for *The Fire-Dwellers*, she rarely mentioned the city in interviews. On one occasion, however, she admitted to another writer, Harold Horwood, that after the stimulation of living in Africa with its nationalists, poets, and drummers, Margaret had found living in Vancouver "like being tossed into a swamp," and added the comment, "life surely wasn't meant to be so boring!"[993]

Margaret rejected the idea of moving back to Winnipeg. It would have meant proximity to family as well as the likelihood of being frequently upbraided for not going overseas with her husband. As for locating to Toronto or Montreal, in the early 1960s neither city seemed to be viable as a residence when compared with the possibility of living

in England. Margaret and Jack had lived there for more than a year
before going to Somaliland, and had frequently returned to London
when Jack was on leave. England was a country that cherished its writers and London was familiar to her. In addition, she would be near her
British publisher, who had been very supportive of Margaret's writing.
As a youngster she had read Kipling's account of the ancient history of
England, *Puck of Pook's Hill*.[994] And like many collegians of her generation, Margaret also had read the English classics throughout her school
years.[995] During the Second World War, she had wept over the patriotic
poems in Alice Duer Miller's *The White Cliffs*, which proclaimed "that a
world without an England wouldn't be worth living in."[996] As Margaret
weighed the various options in terms of relocating, she also believed
that it would be advantageous for Jocelyn and David to attend school in
England. For both Margaret and the children, England seemed to be the
best temporary location.

Within a week of arriving in London, Margaret, with the help of a
friend from Winnipeg days, had found a furnished flat on Heath Hurst
Road in Hampstead. It was near Keats' Grove, "where stood the tree," she
noted, "under which the poet is said to have written 'Ode to a
Nightingale.'"[997] It was also very close to the area where she and Jack had
lived for several months in 1952 when Jocelyn was born. Margaret was
pleased and relieved that it was both affordable and in a part of the city
that she "knew best and liked the best."[998]

Other writers, such as Ernest Hemingway, Raymond Chandler, F.
Scott Fitzgerald, Norman Levine, and Mordecai Richler, had arrived in
England with a list of contacts and letters of introduction to other writers. That was not the case with Margaret Laurence. The fact that she was
able to manage initially was due in large part to the singular kindness of
her editors at Macmillan, Lovat Dickson and Alan Maclean, who recognized Laurence's talent, encouraged her writing, and gave advice and
moral support. Since she did not have a network of writer friends to
whom she could turn, and because she and Jack had now separated,
Margaret also was a bit embarrassed to look up some of their old friends.

Alone in London, Margaret rented the third and fourth floors at the
back of an old Victorian red-brick house. She and the children shared a
bath on the floor below with a business couple who went out to work

each day. In Margaret's flat the rooms were small but adequate. On one floor there was a bedroom, a living room, and a kitchen. Up a short flight of stairs were two small bedrooms for the children. From London, Margaret wrote back to Canada, "We seem to have landed on our feet, at least so far," and added this description of their new surroundings:[999]

> We are well situated — only a few minutes walk from Hampstead High Street and the tube station, 15 minutes easy walk to the school where the kids will be going (with no major roads for them to cross), a public library just around the corner (next door to Keats House), which is kept as a small museum. . . . Small shops and post office only a block away, and Hampstead Heath just at the end of the street, one minute from here. This last is a real marvel — I never imagined I'd be able to find a flat so close to the Heath. I can take the kids there, and they can run around and work off steam, David especially. There is even a Unitarian Church on the High Street.[1000]

All this seemed almost too good to be true. And in characteristic fashion Margaret could not help worrying about whether some awful problem would shortly appear. She also understood that her anxiety was connected to her Presbyterian background, and explained, "If something good happens to you, you will soon have to pay for it."[1001]

Her letters describing those first weeks in London are generally cheerful and optimistic. However, when she later looked back on that period, the picture was not quite so rosy.[1002] In a letter to Ernest Buckler, she reported that the flat was "ghastly," and she made many similiar remarks about it in an interview with Harold Horwood.[1003] Perhaps in her contemporary letters she had tried to put a brave face on the situation, which was not only wrenching emotionally, but very challenging on the domestic and practical front.

Margaret realized that, to Jocelyn and David, who were ten and seven, the move from Canada, the separation from their father, and the new surroundings in London would feel strange and disorienting. So she began "an evening ritual of cocoa in front of the fire after dinner, when she would tell them a serial story, 'very sensational and corny,' but it seemed to make them feel more at home."[1004] She was optimistic that, when the school term began on November 5, the children would make new friends and a good adjustment would follow. In the meantime she did a good bit of sightseeing with the children. "Every weekend, we used to take small tours. I was determined to show London to the children, so we tramped through the museums, we mastered the Tube, we walked up and down the millions of stairs at the Tower of London."[1005] One day, they visited the Science Museum, where David "was fascinated by all the models of old trains and boats."[1006] Margaret was pleased that she was able to find her way around London "so much better than any other city, even Vancouver, because the underground is so well marked."[1007]

Within a few weeks of their arrival in England, Margaret received several air letters from Jack and she informed their old friend Gordon Elliott that Jack was "tremendously busy already, caught up in all kinds of official complications, which was to be expected. He seems very happy to be there [East Pakistan]. It is certainly his kind of job. I wish it were mine."[1008]

Although as a parent and an emerging writer, Margaret could not imagine moving with Jack from one overseas post to another while he searched for satisfaction as an engineer, she was unable to shake off the nagging feeling that she was at fault; that she had let Jack down by not going abroad again with him. She also felt she had been a disappointment to him because she had found herself unable to be the kind of wife she thought Jack wanted. However, both husband and wife looked upon the move to London as a trial separation, which would give each of them the time and distance to sort out what it was they needed and wanted in life. In England, Margaret hoped to secure "a room of one's own" — one of the essentials identified by Virginia Woolf as necessary for a woman writer. If Margaret had any thoughts of a divorce, they were not foremost in her mind; such a step was virtually unthinkable at that time, and it certainly would have been a shock to both their families. Until Jack later requested a formal divorce in 1969, no one in either of their families had taken such a step.

Once settled in London, Margaret found Virginia Woolf's second prerequisite for a writer — sufficient income — much more difficult to achieve. She was surprised to learn that the cost of living had risen significantly since her last visit to England and everything now seemed very expensive. Although she was determined to be self-supporting, it soon became clear that it would be difficult to manage on the amount of money Jack and she had agreed upon.[1009] Margaret put a brave face on the situation and hoped that she might receive a Canada Council senior fellowship, although she conceded that this was unlikely. It is not clear whether Jack's salary made it impossible for him to send more money or whether Margaret's pride and guilt about not accompanying him to East Pakistan made it impossible for her to ask him for the additional financial support, which she and the children certainly needed. Margaret continued to frame her present situation in ways that made her feel guilty, and she seemed unable to accept the fact that, in large measure, it had been Jack's unwillingness to continue working in Canada that had precipitated these major changes.

Although her new domestic situation in London was challenging, Margaret's literary prospects were very encouraging. During the first month after her arrival, "The Rain Child" appeared in *Winter's Tales 8*, alongside stories by Doris Lessing, Edna O'Brien, Muriel Spark, and V.S. Pritchett. In addition, Margaret met during that time with several people at Macmillan, including Alan Maclean, the man she "had corresponded with the most." Maclean gave her the good news that Macmillan, London, would publish *The Prophet's Camel Bell* in spring 1963. And Margaret was particularly pleased that the firm had decided to bring out a collection of her West African stories, even though she then had to spend two weeks "madly typing them all out — 250 pages." She found the task quite boring since she had typed them many times before. The positive side of that effort, however, was the opportunity to cut "some of the fancier bits from a few of the stories." She thought "The Merchant of Heaven" had been overwritten and removed some of the "highflown phrases . . . that one thinks are so terrific at the moment of writing but lives to regret later."[1010]

The next month, Margaret sent George Woodcock, editor of *Canadian Literature*, a book review for the journal. In the accompanying letter she explained to him why she had left Vancouver:

The great difficulty with life at home, from a writer's point of view, seems to me to be the inevitable involvement with a relatively large number of activities — whether these are worthy causes or community responsibilities or friendships, each may be rewarding in itself but taken as a whole they seem to diminish one's time to a point where one can begin to feel a little desperate. It is the anonymity of London that appeals most to me, I think. I have a number of friends here, whom I see from time to time, but I can spend many more hours a week here in working at writing, without the guilty feeling at the back of my mind that I ought to be doing something else. I have begun to work again on the novel which I had done in rough draft [*The Stone Angel*]. I hope something may come of it — one never knows.[1011]

A few days before she wrote to Woodcock, the manuscript of *The Stone Angel*, which she had given Adele to mail in Winnipeg, arrived. As Margaret prepared to wrestle again with the text, she was surprised and pleased to realize the novel would require less rewriting than she had previously thought. In two significant letters to Adele, Margaret re-examined her earlier difficulties with *The Stone Angel*. Her excitement upon rereading the manuscript is almost palpable:

You know, the old lady comes across — I'm almost certain of it. And also — and this is the stunning surprise to me — all the things which I thought were there when I wrote it, everything that moves under the surface, as it were, seems to me to be actually there. *When Jack didn't see any of them, I was convinced for a long time that I had only deluded myself that they were there. But now I feel strongly that they are there, and that I wasn't wrong about the book* [emphasis added]. He felt at that time that I was not a novelist and that I should stick to short stories. I put the novel away and could not bring myself to look at it for a year. But now I feel, looking at it very soberly, and as objectively as possible, that it is done the way I wanted it to be done, and it says what I wanted it to say. It may not be everyone's cup of tea, but it is mine. Whether the publishers or anyone else likes it, I like it. I don't say it is tremendous stuff, for obviously it is not, but it is serious and it says something and at least one person in it seems to me to be alive in that indefinable way.[1012]

Margaret intended to continue working on *The Stone Angel* as soon as she finished typing up her African short stories.

As Margaret Laurence typed those stories in November 1962, a certain physical and emotional exhaustion made itself felt. She was still trying to get a telephone installed, and the tension from handling detailed arrangements for departing from Canada during the previous month, as well as the daunting tasks of getting settled with the children in England, had taken a toll. In addition, the implications and uncertainties of her new circumstances pressed upon her and she now had very mixed feelings about the situation:

> About half the time I feel pretty good about life, and can work hopefully, etc. The other half I feel depressed, miserable, lonely, bereft, empty, and just plain bloody awful, if you know what I mean. However, people do not die of this kind of affliction, luckily. Anyway, having discovered to my surprise that I am a survivor at heart, I do not despair. Also, I can't afford to drink a great deal, which is also a good thing. I can't afford to smoke, but I do, anyway.... I also walk miles — to and from school with the kids, to the shops, up to the Heath on weekends, etc.[1013]

In one sense, Margaret had indeed left her home, Canada, and her husband, Jack. No doubt the confusing feelings she was experiencing evoked those she had felt as a child after the deaths of her parents — loss, guilt, abandonment — typical responses, according to many psychologists, for a child who has experienced at an early age the death of parents.[1014] It is not surprising, then, that after parting from her country and her husband, Margaret Laurence began to deal fictionally with the material of her childhood. It was one way of managing her current situation. "The Sound of the Singing," a short story set in Manawaka, was accepted for publication (to appear the next year).[1015] Later she placed it as the opening story in *A Bird in the House*, a collection of eight linked short stories that centre on the coming of age of Vanessa MacLeod in Manawaka, a small Canadian prairie town.

By December 1962, Margaret was weighing the prospects of getting a job in London, but soon realized that she lacked the skills as well as the necessary "paper" qualifications for a good job. In addition, having a job would entail complicated and costly domestic arrangements. She also felt that might have a negative effect on the children and there would be difficulties finding the right person to look after them on school holidays. "So at the moment," she explained, "I have shelved this question, and am trying to settle down to do the only thing which I know something about, namely writing."[1016] She was reviewing some manuscripts for Macmillan, but the work was not very well paid and she could only hope they would be able to give her more work to supplement her income.

As the first Christmas without Jack approached, Margaret planned some special events with the children. They went to Harrods department store to see the toys; and with a small sum sent from a friend in Canada she was able to take the children out to lunch and then to a Walt Disney film, "In Search of the Castaways," based on a Jules Verne story and "full of wild and fantastic adventures." After the film they enjoyed tea and lots of French pastries at a special shop. The day's excursion ended at Trafalgar Square, where they watched the lighting of the Christmas tree and stayed for the carol singing.[1017]

During that harsh English winter, Margaret had been shaping *The Stone Angel* and typing the manuscript of *The Tomorrow-Tamer and Other Stories*, which was scheduled for publication in 1963. These stories set in the Gold Coast are very different from those that she subsequently included in *A Bird in the House*, and, therefore, merit some discussion here.

The Tomorrow-Tamer and Other Stories, was published when Africa was much in the news, as the European colonial powers withdrew and various countries "gained" their independence. The stories are set in a milieu of rapidly ending colonialism and the emerging political independence of many African nations. Each story stands as an independent unit and the characters and situations do not overlap as they do in *A Bird in the House*.

Although *The Tomorrow-Tamer* stories are not experimental in terms of form, Laurence excels in the evocation of place and the creation of character and incident. Her handling of this challenging material is noteworthy. She captures West African culture at the point at which traditional African customs, white colonialism, and encroaching modern technology meet, and she deals with events not in terms of ideologies or generalities, but as they are reflected in the lives of individuals. She describes the haunting beauty of West Africa and its terrors, both real and imagined. She presents British colonials stationed there — many of whom are attached to a mythical Gold Coast and blind to contemporary Ghana. She also presents Africans who must reconcile tribal customs with what they have learned in mission schools or abroad at British universities. She is even-handed in her treatment, depicting some Africans succumbing to materialism and greed. She shows the confusion caused by rapid change. As the West Africans try to cope with the country's shifting scene, their uncertain future looks both promising and frightening.

Laurence, in addition to having a keen ear and excellent powers of observation, did an enormous amount of background reading to broaden her understanding of Ashanti festivals and of West Africa's long history. That reading provided her with some ethnographic knowledge, without which an interpretation of Africa cannot be done responsibly. Margaret also had Ghanaian friends, such as Professor Ofosu-Appiah, with whom she discussed these matters.

It is significant that at the time of her death (thirty years after her first return to Canada) and after living in many different places, more than one hundred books dealing with African material still remained in her personal library. Those books are now at McMaster University. Some of them have extensive pencil notes and scoring by Laurence. Among the various titles are: *The Akan Doctrine of God*; *West African Folk Tales and Fables*; *West Coast Nutrition and Cookery;* and Meyerwitz's study *The Sacred State of Akan*. These titles represent a few of the many and diverse books that contributed to her understanding of West Africa and to her postcolonial perspective. Laurence endeavoured to be open-minded toward the complex ancient religious, social, and political cultures of the region.

In *The Tomorrow-Tamer* stories, one does not find demeaning descriptions of indigenous people. On the contrary, Laurence is harsh in dealing with her European characters. In an essay "Ten Years Sentences," she admits, "I was against colonialism" and states that her editor wanted changes in *This Side Jordan* (1960) because she had stereotyped Europeans. In that novel, Europeans are embittered, unhappy, and hostile toward Africa. Her white women are thin, jaundiced, and on the verge of a nervous breakdown. They also appear that way in many of the *The Tomorrow-Tamer* stories. Laurence was very critical of the "sahib type" and acknowledged, "I have never in my life felt such antipathy towards people anywhere as I felt towards those pompous and whining sahibs and memsahibs."[1018]

It is no surprise that Laurence thought herself different from the British colonialists who were in Africa on government business. She also saw herself as different from other Europeans who were there, whether missionaries or workers. She was, after all, a Canadian. But she soon came to understand that Africans made no such distinctions. They considered her as indistinguishable from all the other non-Africans. That was quite a lesson for the young writer.

In rendering African conversations, Laurence seems to reflect the actual situation: many West Africans were multilingual, and she shows them using "code switching," a bilingual strategy that takes place between standard English, with its authoritative connotation, and a type of pidgin that may be a transcript of the language as it was spoken, i.e., as a deviation from standard English. In *The Tomorrow-Tamer* the conversations of Africans are not rendered in a condescending fashion as they are in a good deal of colonialist literature. Laurence does not convey their speech as linguistically incompetent and by extension "racially" inferior. Her use of what might be called dialect is limited, and it mirrors the heteroglossia and complexity of West Africa. Her effort at verisimilitude in rendering English speech patterns as used by non-native speakers appears early in her writing — even in her high school and college fiction. But even at that early stage, Laurence's characters are portrayed with such respect that her attempt at replicating their speech patterns does not result in negative stereotyping.

In "The Rain Child," for example, a sixteen-year-old garden boy named Yindo is not an Ashanti, but a Dagomba from the North. In his own eyes, therefore, he was not only from another place, but from another world. At one point, nearly incoherent with terror, Yindo pleads with the school mistress: "I beg you. You not give me sack. I Dagomba man, madam. No got bruddah dis place." The use of dialect in this passage does not evoke arrogant condescension on the part of the Western reader, but rather elicits understanding and concern for the pain of another human being.

In *The Tomorrow-Tamer* stories, Laurence presents vignettes of nine major characters whose lives shed light on the situation in West Africa. Her approach and tone in dealing with this material is postcolonial rather than colonial.

In one story, Moki, who had come to the Gold Coast many years before with a trader's caravan, is elderly and partially blind. He now begs beside the women in the marketplace. He remembers the name of his village, but not of his country.

Then there is Danquah who runs the "Hail Mary" chop bar. He is a stranger to that place, having neither family nor tribe. An *isolato*, he is a puzzle to the village and will always remain an outsider.[1019]

One of Laurence's most poignant stories, "The Voices of Adamo," holds up a mirror to certain historically determined relationships of dominance and subordination under the British colonial regime. Adamo loses his family to the ravages of smallpox. Eventually, as a teenager, he is taken in by the British military and becomes a drummer in the regimental band. Adamo, however, cannot understand the discourse of other members of the band, because they are not of his tribe, nor can he understand the British bandmaster, Captain Fossey, who eventually receives orders to return to England. As a result of profound miscommunication, Captain Fossey is murdered by Adamo, the one African he had assumed had great personal loyalty to him.

Another serious miscommunication occurs in "A Fetish for Love." The story's perspective is entirely that of an Anglo-colonial woman, a do-gooder named Constance, who is the wife of an import-export merchant. Constance wants to "understand" Africa. But she understands neither her cook, Sunday, nor his wife, Love. And Constance's misguided effort to take their destiny into her own hands very nearly brings the younger African woman to catastrophe.

In "The Pure Diamond Man," Laurence successfully handles the type of situation that the critic Homi Bhabha has discussed as the mockery of the West by colonized people. The situation in the story is akin to "doing the police in different voices." In an hilarious scene, a gullible and ignorant Westerner is seeking an "authentic" African experience. He is roundly deceived by a local family, showing that the colonized can appropriate the terms of exchange.

"The Drummer of All the World" is narrated by Matthew, the son of a white missionary. It opens as follows: "My father thought he was bringing Salvation to Africa. I, on the other hand, no longer know what salvation is. I am not sure that it lies in the future. And I know now that it is not to be found in the past."

In childhood, Matthew's primary caretaker had been an African servant named Yaa. Matthew is the same age as her son, and Yaa had nursed both boys. Eventually, Matthew leaves to go abroad to university. He returns twice, each time expecting to find "the" Africa he had known and loved as a child, and expecting to resume his friendship with Yaa's son, Kwabena. But both young men have changed. The story unfolds with several flashbacks and covers a period of about twenty years; as a result the reader is introduced to the complexities of both a colonial and post-colonial world. The Western narrator mourns the loss of the old Africa, while his African counterpart is bitter because he has glimpsed a world that he can never enter. As Kwabena grows up, he puts aside thoughts of becoming a fetish priest, and wants instead to become a twentieth-century doctor. But for him to achieve that within the story's context is quite impossible. His disappointment and anger are palpable.

The final story in this collection "A Gourdful of Glory" is narrated from an African perspective. The central figure, Mammii Ama, is a market woman, one of a group of women whose activities, as Laurence realized, were very important to the West African economy. Here, Mammii Ama ekes out a meagre living by selling calabashes to other Africans, and waits with great excitement for the day when the Gold Coast, renamed Ghana, will become independent under the leadership of Premier Kwame Nkrumah. The first part of the story takes place before Ghanaian independence, and the last few pages take place in the days immediately following it.

Mammii Ama is presented with dignity, appreciation, and vitality. Here Laurence's rendering of local speech achieves a success that has built upon her early effort with college fiction. Laurence's work is significantly different from Europeans such as Elspeth Huxley and others, who did not appreciate African culture and whose judgmental attitudes presented Africans to the West as inferior, primitive, and in need of "paternal" intervention. Huxley's description of Accra and the market women in *Four Guineas: A Journey through West Africa* is frequently superficial and condescending.[1020] On the other hand, Margaret Laurence shows that, although Mammii Ama does not have a realistic idea of the consequences of independence, she does cope with the actual situation rather than the one she had imagined. Mammii Ama's disappointment does not overwhelm her, and she maintains her integrity as well as her position as a leader among the other market women by refusing to sell her pots as mere commodities to a white woman who has had a very patronizing exchange with her, an exchange in which she insulted Mammii Ama and tried to control the sale of the pot by offering far more than the asking price. Mammii Ama stands firm. She rejects the money and remains memorable as a leader of the market women. Having very little herself, she nevertheless shows compassion and generosity toward less-fortunate villagers. In the closing scene, she raises a calabash and chants a new verse to her song. The others caught the rhythm, and the faith, and the new words, and joined in the song. Then "Mammii Ama straightened her plump shoulders. Like a royal palm she stood, rooted in magnificence, spreading her arms like fronds, to shelter the generations."

While Margaret typed up these stories, she tried to make plans to celebrate Christmas. She intended to have a young couple and several Canadian women join the family for dinner. In a letter to Gordon Elliott, she reflected on the fact that in Vancouver she had begun drinking in order to feel better, now she notes that she has changed course. "I have gone on the wagon, at least for the time being. When I have people in for dinner, I have 1 glass of wine, but that is all. Otherwise, it is not being bought any more. This regime has lasted for 2 weeks, and although I cannot say I feel any better. . . . This step is long overdue, as you know." She explained that "when a person discovered they were drinking to drown their sorrows, it was time they quit. So I have quit. Let us hope it lasts."[1021] In later years, there would be times when Margaret again struggled with drinking, but that was in the privacy of her home, and the situation was known only to close friends and family.

On Boxing Day (celebrated in England on the day following Christmas), snow began to fall. It continued for days. London was unprepared for such a heavy snowfall and it seemed as if nothing could be done while "the snow hardened and froze. Sidewalks and streets became a rugged terrain of ice."[1022] As the cold period continued, electric service became intermittent and pipes froze throughout the city. In *Dance on the Earth* Laurence refers to the situation in understated terms, however:

> That winter was a severe one in England. . . . Cold and fog and snow. It was not a terribly pleasant time, particularly since the English are totally unprepared for large quantities of snow. People were skiing down Hampstead High Street. The electricity kept going off. . . . I was rewriting *The Stone Angel* and typing out the stories in *The Tomorrow-Tamer*, sometimes with hands nearly freezing, in between walking the kids to and from school because I was terrified they might get lost in the fog.[1023]

As a matter of fact, the winter of 1963 was the worst winter England had experienced in sixty years. It has been described in grim detail by the American writer Sylvia Plath in her essay "Snow Blitz."[1024] During December 1962, Sylvia Plath and her two children had moved back to London. They were living in a maisonette on Fitzroy Road in Hampstead, not far from where Margaret was living, although the two did not know each other. On February 11, Sylvia Plath, who was only thirty, committed suicide. Laurence read the account of Plath's death in the *Hampstead and Highgate Express*, and remarked later to Ernest Buckler:

I had never met her, and at that time I had not even read any of her poetry or her novel *The Bell Jar*. But I mourned her as though it had been myself who had died. I was luckier, that's all, and luckier just in the fact that my childhood had not damaged me as much as hers had done with her. I had been given some kind of on-going strength, from my stepmother (who was my mother's sister) and even from my much-hated grandfather.[1025]

At about this time, Margaret informed her agent that she had finished typing the manuscript of her novel (*The Stone Angel*) and planned to take two copies of it to Michael Horniman of A.P. Watt Agency, London, the next week.[1026] In March, the Canada Council turned down her application for a senior fellowship, and Margaret must have been disappointed, because the money would have alleviated some financial stress. However, she told a friend that she did not mind because, if she had received the award, she would have "felt indebted," and that would not be good "especially when it comes to writing."[1027] Exciting news, however, soon offset her disappointment about the fellowship. Macmillan had accepted *Hagar*. Both Lovat Dickson and Alan Maclean were enthusiastic about her novel, and Margaret was hopeful that her Canadian publisher, Jack McClelland, would also respond favourably.

Such affirmation of her talent by her publishers was very important to her. Over a number of years Margaret had served an apprenticeship as a writer, consistently putting in long hours at her craft. And her reluctance to keep moving with Jack to far-flung regions had led to a decision not to accompany him. That difficult decision was based on her needs as a writer as well as the needs of her children. Now she was able to look back upon her earlier struggles with several novels and a number of short stories as necessary stages in her journey towards becoming a writer.

Margaret Laurence had been discouraged, but not disheartened. She had continued, with ambition and great determination, to labour at the craft of writing, feeling that she had been given a talent and a concomitant responsibility to develop it. Her confidence in the vision and voice that had developed in her over the years was affirmed in a major way by

Macmillan's acceptance of *Hagar* (*The Stone Angel*). This marked a critical turning point in her life, a kind of epiphany that is made clear in a revealing letter that she wrote:

> I can't really explain how I feel about this novel . . . in some way it has restored my faith in myself and in the fact that my way of seeing is not so personal or private that it will not communicate something at least to some people. Also, I feel now that the African writing was not a kind of fluke, but was related to everything else, and the fact that I wrote for awhile about Africa and now do not want to do so is not important.[1028]

As the school term drew to its close in 1963, Margaret was looking forward to the arrival from Canada of Frances Bolton, the daughter of the Elliot and Kay Bolton.[1029] Because her father then worked for Air Canada, Frances was able to fly without charge to England. She had just graduated from college and was pleased with the opportunity to be in London during the summer as a "mother's helper." Her chief responsibility would be to look after Jocelyn and David, who were ten and seven, and take them out of the flat during the day so that Margaret could continue to work on the final stages of *The Stone Angel*.

She told Gordon Elliott that, although *The Stone Angel* would not appear until 1964, two other books were presently in process of being published: *The Prophet's Camel Bell* and *The Tomorrow-Tamer and Other Stories*. Laurence was now situated in England, but those books and *The Stone Angel*, the three that were soon to bring her acclaim, had been written in Vancouver, although she had worked on the final manuscripts in England. Her apprentice period clearly had come to an end. She was not to be known as a one-book author, but as a writer.

Margaret Laurence could never have imagined that, during the next decade, she would become one of the most highly regarded writers of her generation. She was to become known throughout Canada for her writing about the prairies (her Manawaka novels), and to be almost exclusively identified with them. That perception, however, does not do justice to the body of her work. The fictional world of Manawaka did not emerge overnight, nor was it simply Peggy Wemyss's hometown of Neepawa set down on paper. In fact, Laurence's Manawaka cycle came about as the fruition of many years of work, struggle, and dedication to her calling as a writer. Clearly she was gifted, but that did not make the process an easy one for her. Moreover, in those early years she had to struggle both with her own diffidence as well as with the enormous social and personal demands made on her as a young wife and mother during the 1950s and early 1960s.

Her abilities as a writer were challenged and rewarded during her years in Africa, which required of her both an immersion in a culture remarkably different from that of Canada, as well as a kind of detachment that involved both taking up and working from viewpoints not her own. Throughout those early years and beyond, she dedicated herself to her calling with an amazing tenacity, even stubbornness, and refused to compromise, despite setbacks and disappointments.

As a youngster, Peggy Wemyss had responded with excitement and interest to storytelling. It is no accident that, over millennia, storytelling has engaged and frequently transfixed hearers with its power and energy. But little did that prairie youngster realize that she would herself become a teller of tales. Margaret Laurence's first novel *This Side Jordan*, her travel memoir *The Prophet's Camel Bell*, and her remarkable and splendid translations of Somali literature in *A Tree for Poverty* are a significant part of her legacy as a writer and need to be placed beside her Manawaka fiction. The unfolding of Margaret Laurence's own early story — her literary apprenticeship and her emergence as a writer — makes the account of her literary beginnings as compelling and vivid a story as any in the world of her own fiction.

INTRODUCTION TO APPENDICES:
Three Stories by Margaret Laurence

In the autumn of 1962, Margaret Laurence and her two children arrived in England. It was the beginning of a trial separation for the couple, since her husband, Jack, had decided to leave Canada and accept an engineering post in East Pakistan. By that time, Margaret had published one novel set in Africa, *This Side Jordan*, and another small book, *A Tree for Poverty*. That book consisted of her translations of Somali tales and poems, the first into English of the literature of that ancient oral culture. She had also completed the manuscript of another novel, *The Stone Angel*, which needed some revisions and did not yet have a publisher.

For over a year, Margaret and the children lived in difficult circumstances in a London flat, but after Christmas, 1963, they were able to move to the village of Penn, near High Wycombe in Buckinghamshire. There, they lived in a large house (Elm Cottage) set on spacious grounds which she rented at first, and later was able to purchase, from Alan Maclean of Macmillan, London.

While living in England, Laurence worked steadily on another novel and managed to complete a number of short stories which she sent to John Cushman, who was then handling her work at a New York agency. Her correspondence with him provides titles for some of those stories, for example, "The Holy War of Mr. Feather," "The Lilac Tea," "The Commotion is Elsewhere," and "Mrs. Cathcart, In and Out of Purdah."

These appendices offers readers the opportunity to read the complete text of a previously unpublished story, "Mrs. Cathcart, In and Out of Purdah," as well as two relatively unknown stories by Margaret Laurence. Because she routinely destroyed earlier versions of her work, as well as material that was never published, readers have here the unusual opportunity of seeing examples of her short fiction apart from the well-known Manawaka stories in *A Bird in the House* or the collection of her African short stories, *The Tomorrow-Tamer and Other Stories*.

"Mrs. Cathcart, In and Out of Purdah," which was never published despite Cushman's enthusiasm for it, remained in the files of the agency. "A Queen in Thebes," a grim tale, which she called "almost a fable," was published in *Tamarack Review*, Summer 1964. Another story, "A Fable — For the Whaling Fleets," written almost twenty years later, appeared in *Whales: A Celebration*, an anthology compiled and edited by Greg Gatenby. An indication of this story's significance to Laurence lies in the fact that she decided to include it in the second part of her memoirs, *Dance on the Earth*.

These three stories shed light on the range of Laurence's talent in short fiction as well as science fiction. Readers may speculate about what other narrative styles Margaret Laurence might have developed along similar lines or in entirely new directions.

Mrs. Cathcart,
In and Out of Purdah

Although Margaret Laurence's agent, John Cushman, was enthusiastic about "Mrs. Cathcart, In and Out of Purdah," which she sent him in 1964, he was unable to place Laurence's story and it remained in his archives.[1030] Since very few documents or other materials relating to her unpublished works are extant, this story holds special interest.

In fashioning "Mrs. Cathcart, In and Out of Purdah," Laurence relied not only on reading and imagination, but also on her personal experience and observations. She had spent November 1963 in East Pakistan, where she joined her husband for a month. In a letter to the writer Ethel Wilson, Margaret described their holiday.[1031] Jack took leave from his engineering project and they traveled extensively, visiting the Chittagong hills region, Calcutta, Kaptai, and the province of Orissa on the Bay of Bengal where they saw the famous Black Pagoda of Konarak.[1032]

As both a traveler and a resident in British colonial territories, Laurence felt deep disquiet about the effects of imperialism. Some years later, when she came to write *The Prophet's Camel Bell*, a travel-memoir about her experiences in the British Somaliland Protectorate, she grappled with innumerable revisions of chapter 14, "The Imperialists." As she looked back on her experiences, she was not satisfied with her depiction of the British in that colonial setting, a theme she felt had been addressed many times by other writers. In addition, she had come to feel that the subject was now more or less obsolete due to the changed political situation in former British colonies. In "Mrs. Cathcart, In and Out of Purdah," however, Laurence offers a light touch on the serious topic of British colonials abroad.

In Laurence's story, Mrs. Cathcart, a widow of a British High Court Judge in India, relates to her friend Dorcas an incident from her younger married days there. Although the frame story takes place in London, the setting for the story that she relates is Chittagong, in East Pakistan (now Bangladesh), in the northeastern portion of the Indian subcontinent.

Mrs. Cathcart is a decisive, at times, impetuous woman who has managed, even as the wife of a High Court judge, to carve out a life for herself. The story deals with the question of purdah, the role of women, the possibility of forgiveness, and issues of local culture and custom in a colonial situation. Laurence's handling of these matters displays a wit and ironic playfulness that undergirds her more serious critique of the British enterprise.

Mrs. Cathcart, In and Out of Purdah

"Sitting one day in Chittagong," Mrs. Cathcart began, "I was dreaming of the ageing prince, my lover, who was at that moment, or so I supposed, translating his Icelandic sagas in his bedsitting room in Stepney."

This, I knew, was the famous Sven, who was unfortunately no longer with us.

"Was it Stepney?" I enquired tactlessly. "And was he, honestly, a prince?"

"Your sense of dramatic emphasis, dear child," Mrs. Cathcart replied coldly, "is certainly most limited. He could not have been more of a prince to me if he had been Hamlet himself. You exemplify quite strikingly the reasons why writers nowadays are so dull. No flights. Or else such peculiar ones, somehow lacking in enjoyment."

She looked at me with her misleadingly Roman stare like the marble head of some emperor. Then her severe features softened, and I thought I was probably in for an afternoon's recital of past flights.

"Get back to Chittagong," I suggested.

Mrs. Cathcart, her grey hair ringletted in uncertain but hopeful defiance of contemporary sleekness, poured us both another sherry. Despite her limited means as the widow of a civil servant, she never failed to have a sherry on hand. "Earnest beggars cannot be choosers, of course," Mrs. Cathcart used to say, "but for modified beggars like myself it is only too easy. If you can buy Cyprus for nine bob a bottle, why on earth buy British at six and six, so deadly sweet, even the dry, like turpentine and saccharine." I accepted the glass from her and we toasted silently the dead Icelandic poet, whose turbulent association with her had extended over a quarter century. Poets, I felt, were more comfortably loved when dead, and I would have been willing to bet money that Mrs. Cathcart shared this view, but loyally she would never have said.

"Yes, Chittagong," she mused. "Well, I was thinking of him, naturally, and pondering the fact that it would be seven months before my dear Cathcart went on leave, and I with him, and there was Sven, miserably situated, or so I hoped, lacking my presence, and there was I, breaking my mid-morning boredom with an orange squash on the verandah of Circuit House, where we stayed when the High Court was in session in that area, and there was Cathcart, bless him, dispensing justice up there in that vast red-painted tomb they called the Court House, not a bit of use, as everyone knew, but he was filled with duty and so on, so what could anyone do, dear child?"

"What happened," She would go on in a contemplative vein for hours unless some check were applied.

"It was a shrill and piercing voice," Mrs. Cathcart explained, "that drew me out of myself. I rose – summoned, as it were, and left the screened verandah. All was orderly there, you understand, bamboo furniture and corpulent cushions in decorous pastels, and a ceiling fan twirling around persistently as though to cool the air by an act of will. I walked out onto the road, where the glaze of the sun was quite beyond my describing – a steady and sombre sun, Dorcas, not as warm as we understand warmth but merely devitalizing, a power that turns even the really well-intentioned into dullards. I, dear child, was well-intentioned in those days. It was my affliction. I walked out into the sun and the red dusty road, and looked for the voice that had commanded me so peremptorily there."

"And it was — ?"

"How I hate to be hurried," Mrs. Cathcart complained, fanning herself with the Sunday Times, quite absurdly, for her Putney flat, encumbered with camel saddles, carved brass tables and innumerable silver filigree boxes, was almost sub-Arctic at this time of year. "If you would leave me alone, Dorcas, I would do this sort of thing much better."

"I'm sorry," I murmured falsely.

"Well, of course you are not sorry, dear child, and why should you be? You are thinking – the bloody old bitch, why does she not get on with it? The trouble is that we are all bound by the style of our contemporaries. Mine is more leisurely than yours. You will get ulcers, Dorcas, or perish in some flamboyant nervous breakdown, but all that is nonsense to me. With us, if we went mad it was done more politely. Your generation – contrary to popular belief – has the better morals, but we had the better manners. When I emerged onto the street that day, I perceived that the voice was the whine of a beggar woman."

"One of the many?"

"Yes – the many. I was always a liberal at heart, Dorcas, and like all liberals I had a rather squeamish stomach. She stood beside the gutter, as though she had been waiting for me, expressly for me. She was demanding alms in the name of Allah. Not in the name of herself, naturally. In the name of Allah, the Compassionate, the Merciful. I do not know why she would have affected me, suddenly, more powerfully than the beggars I saw every day. She was emaciated, I need hardly say. She seemed to have no outer shape, only the inner one of the bones. Her flesh was virtually non-existent, and her skin was draped rather loosely around her, as a piece of frail silk might be draped over a body and yet contrive to reveal every line of it. Her skin lay in just such a relationship to her skeleton. She was terribly crippled, and used one large and clumsy crutch. It did seem to me that the enormous quantity of massed bandage on her left leg was slightly exaggerated. For this, however, I could in no way blame her. I did not have the right, you understand, to blame her for anything. Even had she committed murder, I would have been forced to keep my silence. I was not like Cathcart, whose duty it was to judge, poor man. I stood facing this slight and grotesque bundle of rags and bones. It seemed incredible that she could be alive, breathing, feeling what kind of pain one did not dare think, or perhaps dulled by too much of it, and living now, for all we knew, in a semi-consciousness, drugged not by opium or hashish but by the slings and arrows of outrageous fortune."

"Outrageous is the exact word, isn't it?"

"Yes, and fortune too, something so arbitrary. Shakespeare knew everything. Everything."

"He wasn't referring to a Bengali beggar woman."

"Nonsense," Mrs. Cathcart said. "What makes you think he wasn't? To get on, however – one is caught in a peculiar situation in countries where beggars abound. There is really no use in giving alms at all, in one sense. It is only what you, with your more robust idiom, would call a spit in the ocean. Yet, on the other hand, persons can only be thought of in terms of one – one at a time. You have to begin with one. It is the only number which has any meaning. Or do we give alms solely to soothe ourselves even if only monetarily? I opened my handbag, which I habitually carried with me because of my husband's contention that all servants were light-fingered. I took out a few annas and gave them to her. I then found myself looking into her dark and absolutely impenetrable eyes, and unexpected words were issuing from my mouth. I was saying to her – *"Forgive me. Forgive me."*

Mrs. Cathcart poured herself a little more sherry. She swirled it gently around in her glass and then drank it in one long swallow, like a film cowboy in a saloon. She did this, I knew, to emphasize that she was a study in contrasts, and also, perhaps, because she feared my reaction to her confession, if that was what it was.

"I did not have the sense to say these words in English," she went on, "which the old woman would not have understood. No, no. Nothing but meaningful words for me. I spoke in Bengali, in which I was reasonably fluent in those days. Odd – I can scarcely remember a word of it now. This is not due to the onset of extreme age, as you might imagine, but to a desire to forget. I recalled as I spoke that I was the wife of a judge, and was expected to behave like a relatively superior type of memsahib. Nevertheless, there was I, standing in some sort of supplication before her."

"Did she know at all what you were asking?"

"I don't suppose so. She looked at me as though she thought I were suffering from sunstroke, and then she hobbled away, shrieking her thin bitter cry to other passers-by. I saw then that she did not forgive me, that she could not have done so, even if she had known what I wanted from her. I also saw that what I had asked her could never be asked, or perhaps only of God, if one had happened to have the gift of faith. A rickshaw was passing, and I hailed it. I hated taking these rickshaws, always because it pained me to see a man forced into the role of a beast of burden. But all I achieved by my fastidiousness was to deny work and therefore food to someone. One really cannot win, you see. The thing is overwhelming – there is no end to their dilemma and our own. That morning my need overcame my scruples. I instructed the rickshaw man to take me to the bazaar."

"Why?"

"I did not have the faintest idea why. Not everything can be explained, you know, Dorcas. The centre of the town was like a maze, a fantasy of wildly winding streets that seemed to shift and squirm like snake coils as one looked at them, and senile shacks that served as shops. Merchandise of all varieties was dancing around, displaying itself – saris of midnight blue or magenta or pure clear orange, silver bangles and necklaces, boots and soap, mangoes and bananas. Amid all this muddle the eternal hordes of people pushed their way past one another and past the bullock carts and shambling goats that cluttered up the entire place – you know the sort of thing."

"Yes."

"No, of course you don't. No one does, who hasn't been there. I wish you wouldn't agree with me for the sake of agreement. I instructed the rickshaw man to let me out, and then I walked. I was led quite literally by my footsteps and was perfectly certain that I would arrive somewhere. Then I was a sign above a doorway. It said in faded lilac lettering, *Mr. Abdul Kahliq Khan, Magician.* Instantly I entered, and although the dwelling was of a dilapidated nature on the outside and the door was shaky and half devoured by termites, I found myself standing in a cool and not unpleasant room. Two high-backed chairs and a table were the only furniture. A huge brass jar stood on the floor, filled with pink lilies. On one of the chairs sat Mr. Khan. He was dressed in evening dress of a not entirely new appearance, and on his head he wore a small solar topee, khaki in colour. He was a middleaged man, rather on the stout side, and his ample black moustache looked too villainous for his curiously soft-featured face and placid although definitely sad eyes.

"'Sit down, madam,' he said, most courteously. 'You wish to see my magic, of course?' I told him yes, that was why I had come. 'Splendid,' he said. 'Which trick would you like to see first? I am a well-qualified magician, madam. I have studied magic arts two years Lahore, two years Karachi, and one further year I was studying under teachership of internationally well-known Doctor Choudhury, Calcutta. For me, all things are possible. I am using, you see, arts of sleight-of-hand, arts of mesmerism, arts of hypnotism, and arts of illusion of every variety.' He then took out his equipment, which included packs of cards, ropes, a large handkerchief, four longish knives, a skull with the lower jaw missing and red wool pompoms in the eye-holes and nose. I sat patiently while he was performing. He pulled cards and rupee notes from the air, and did other tricks of the usual kind. Then, as though he knew all this had been merely a preliminary, he leaned across the table and said, 'What shall I make to disappear?' This gave me an exceedingly apprehensive feeling."

Mrs. Cathcart paused, and her eyes, catching mine, smiled.

"I not only thought, you see, Dorcas, that he would try to make me disappear. I thought he would succeed."

I could not imagine Mrs. Cathcart disappearing. I told her so, and she sighed.

"Well, no more could I," she admitted. "I was full of spiritual pride in those days. I begged him not to make me disappear, and he chortled, rather like gargling, in the depths of his throat. 'No, no, madam,' he said, shaking a finger at me, 'you will not get off that easily, never in this world.' I asked him then what I should do. I was filled with an unreasonable confidence that he would be able to tell me. 'Not yet,' he chided me gently. 'First you must tell me what you want me to make disappear.' Quite calmly, then, I told him about the beggar woman. He shook his head. 'I am well-qualified magician, madam, but for me this is not possible. You are troubling yourself without due cause. You have good heart, dear lady – what more do you want? Please pardon me, but your demand seems unreasonable to the extremity.' I asked him once more what I should do. Mr. Khan brooded for awhile, his forefinger laid flat along his nose. 'Must you do something?' he asked. I nodded. Then all at once his face brightened in revelation. 'You will assist understanding between our two peoples', he said. He sounded most relieved to have come up with an answer. Well, I ask you, Dorcas. I was a liberal at my heart, dear child, but I was not a dunce. I could scarcely see myself preaching to the Romans, under circumstances that would inevitably be ludicrous. I murmured as much to Mr. Khan. Again he chuckled. He seemed inordinately fond of laughing at odd moments, and I was rather put out, to tell you the truth. Then he spoke in a low and even confidential tone. 'You have forgotten, madam,' he said, 'that your Saint Paul gave himself the following name, containing great embarrassment and dignity. *The Fool of God.'* As he spoke, I sat silently, with my head lowered. I was, of course, infinitely surprised."

Mrs. Cathcart accepted a cigarette and puffed at it reflectively. She smoked a good deal, and her ring-laden fingers were stained with nicotine, but she never liked this to be noticed and always held a cigarette gingerly, as though she were unaccustomed.

"You must not suppse," she said, "that I was comparing myself to Saint Paul."

I laughed, thinking I would not put it past her. She laughed, too, and I seemed to hear in her voice an echo of Mr. Khan's ironic chortling.

"Well, perhaps you are right," she said. "Spiritual pride again. How one longs to save. And in the end, you have not done too badly if you have managed to save even a fragment of yourself. However, when I looked up, I discovered what it was that Mr. Khan had finally made to disappear."

"What?"

"Himself," Mrs. Cathcart said triumphantly. "He had quite vanished. I left the place then and returned to my apartment at Circuit House. On the way back I remembered I had asked a number of other European women, mainly wives of the judiciary, in for tea that afternoon, it being my turn to do so. I had missed lunch, but I was just in time to bathe and dress before my guests arrived."

"The tea parties were a duty?" I asked.

"Oh, largely, yes," Mrs. Cathcart replied, and yet I have to admit that there was always a portion of me which did not at all mind holding court. This was what alarmed me, Dorcas, as you can well imagine. The conversation, however, was usually confined to the misdeeds of servants, or the morals of various members of the European community not at the moment present, so one was not keenly stimulated, as it were."

"In fact, it was boring as hell."

"Hell," Mrs. Cathcart remakred, "would almost certainly not be quite that boring. Or – yes – perhaps you are right, and that is hell. Everyone speaking, but soundlessly, if you see what I mean, as though through some unsuitable medium such as water, and what emerges into the listeners' ears is merely a few small fish-bubbles of sound. That afternoon we had with us the wife of the Chief Justice. Phoebe Mortimer. She was a doer. An extremely progressive woman."

I lifted my eyebrows questioningly, not sure what definition Mrs. Cathcart gave to 'progressive'.

"I mean," she explained, "that she knew herself to be in complete possession of the truth, and was most generous in her desire to share this spiritual wealth with others. At that time, she was especially concerned with the question of purdah."

"Purdah?"

"Yes, dear child. The local populace was largely Muslim, and their women were covered from head to toe in voluminous garments, usually black, with the merest slit for the eyes. Some of the wives of professional men were beginning to emerge, but slowly and with enormous hesitance. Phoebe was explaining to the assembled company that afternoon that progress would be impeded indefinitely unless the women of the country could be persuaded to abandon these tent-like disguises and take their rightful place and so on. All very true, in one way, of course."

"But —?"

"Well, yes. I did suggest that it might not be such a simple matter, but Phoebe tended to insist and naturally everyone else agreed with her. 'The men here will never grant equality until the women demand it,' she said. 'It is precisely the same as it was with the suffragettes in England, except that the Bengalis do not have the same intelligence and sheer drive. I am afraid these women will never demand anything. So essential to make them see they must, but very discouraging, as they are so sheeplike and not overly bright.' Well, Dorcas, I was in an awkward spot, as you will appreciate. Because of course I did believe in the equality of women, and all that, but – oh, difficult to say. I was recalling Mr. Khan and everything, and I felt quite despondent. I was not an entirely calm person in those days. *The Fool of God.* I could not forget the magician's words."

Mrs. Cathcart sighed and accepted another cigarette. "A week went by. I then invited for tea the same group of people, including the strong-charactered Phoebe, who really did intimidate me, rather."

"You?"

"I," Mrs. Cathcart said, smiling. "There – you see, Dorcas? One can be a broken reed without everyone else's being aware of it, as one feels they must be. I wish you would remember in your less elated moments."

"I will," I promised.

"No, you won't," she contradicted. "One never does. In any event, the ladies gathered, and tea was brought, and everything was amicable. Phoebe was holding forth with her accustomed lucidity on the necessity of European wives not closeting themselves in their compounds in slovenly fashion (true, true, thus far, all true, Dorcas!) but going forth and telling Bengali women how to lead emancipated lives, and as we all know, the hand that rocks the cradle may yet rule the world, etcetera. I excused myself and went into my bedroom. After a short while I returned. I was, you might say, in a drastically altered state. I had changed."

"How so?" My impatience was verging on annoyance. Mrs. Cathcart knew it and treasured it. She smiled distantly, loving every moment, and I marvelled, even as I was nearly ready to throttle her.

"I was wearing a cotton skirt, dear child," she said, "a light leaf-green cotton patterned rather fetchingly with golden spiderwebs. I was bare from the waist up."

"You don't mean it?"

"Indeed. I had in those days, I may say, breasts that were not unattractive. Not large, but distinct and – not unattractive. I walked slowly into the gathering of women. A silence, as I had anticipated, fell. It crossed my mind at that instant that I was an exhibitionist, nothing less and certainly nothing more. But I had chosen. I could not turn back. Phoebe, in particular, was looking at me wide-eyed, as one would at someone who has suddenly taken leave of her senses. 'I have come out of purdah,' I said. 'This, for us, must be comparable to their dropping the veil. There is nothing actually wrong in revealing one's breasts, is there? But I have to tell you that I feel – although we are all women – somewhat shy, and would really prefer to be clad.'"

"Well, bless you," I said impulsively.

"Bless me nothing," Mrs. Cathcart retorted. "At that precise moment the front door opened and in walked my husband Claude, accompanied by Trevelyn Mortimer the Chief Justice, and four other members of the judiciary. I need hardly say, Dorcas, that they remained frozen in their tracks. I looked at them with considerable dismay. 'Please do not misunderstand me,' I said clearly and with deliberation. 'I was seeking only to demonstrate that Muslim women might possibly have the same feelings against the discarding of *purdah* as we do towards – ah –' I could say no more. What was there to say? I folded my arms inadequately across my exposed bosom and stood there, waiting to be in some fashion released. Then Claude spoke. He was, Dorcas, invariably able to take command of a situation. Within himself he was an excessively reserved man, but no one would ever have guessed it. He had a more convincing poise than anyone I have ever known – perhaps that is why I married him. He did not become angry, at least not visibly. He merely said, 'I think we can take it that you have registered your point of view, Felicity. You may now go and clothe yourself.'"

"And did you?"

"Ah yes," Mrs. Cathcart said. "I departed with all the nervous haste of a tropical cockroach. I did not appear again until everyone had gone."

"Was your husband really angry?"

"Yes, dear child, he was livid, as a matter of fact. I said to him, 'Claude, I was only trying to discover the truth.' And he said – with complete justification in his terms, Dorcas – 'If one were to attempt that at every waking moment, the entire civilized world would crumble. One must consider not only what is true, Felicity, but what is suitable.' By this time I was becoming worked up, and was also ready to cloak my embarrassment with anger. 'You need not misinterpret me,' I said to him. 'I am no Lady Godiva.; He looked at me very coldly. 'That may quite well be so,' he replied, 'but I should prefer, nonetheless, that you never grew your hair too long, Felicity – it might prove too tempting as an only garment.'"

"What was the upshot?"

"Oh, quite the wrong one, ethically," Mrs. Cathcart said. "Claude decided I had gone round the bend, as people sometimes do in such places. He sent me home six months before him, for a rest. I had sought expiation for my lack of suffering, Dorcas, and that was what I got instead – a gift I did not deserve."

"You found Sven, though?"

"I found him," Mrs. Cathcart said, a trifle grimly, "in the arms of a female Bulgarian artist of dubious character."

"Whom you despatched speedily, no doubt?"

"I would not say speedily," Mrs. Cathcart replied. "It took me the better part of a fortnight."

I laughed. "What do you take as the meaning of the whole thing?"

"Meaning?" she said. "You remind me of myself, some years ago. I almost wish I had not told you. I did not intend to impart meaning to you, Dorcas. I wanted only to entertain you, and to hold you here with me for awhile, because I am not over-blessed with company these days."

Then Mrs. Cathcart emptied the last of the Cyprus sherry into our glasses, dividing it evenly.

"Come, dear child," she said. "Let us drink to justice."

APPENDIX B

A Fable — For the Whaling Fleets

"A Fable — For the Whaling Fleets" was written in August 1981 in response to a request from Greg Gatenby, who was then compiling an anthology of whale and dolphin art, poetry, prose, and fiction, in order to raise funds to donate to the Greenpeace Foundation for its program to save whales.[1033]

Laurence's fable was published in *Whales: A Celebration*, edited by Gatenby (Toronto: Prentice Hall/Lester & Orpen Denys, 1983). It was later set to music by Dr. Jack Behrens of the Glenn Gould School of Music of the Royal Conservatory of Music, Toronto. First performed by *Trillium Plus* on March 31, 1985 at the London (Ontario) Regional Art Gallery with author Margaret Laurence as narrator, it was later revised and issued on a CD, *Water Music*, which also includes works by John Cage and Erik Satie.[1034]

Although "A Fable — For the Whaling Fleets" has not attracted the attention of Laurence critics or scholars, its importance lies in showing another side of Laurence's literary imagination. In this fable, the position of the animal world (whales) and that of the human world is reversed, and leads to an unexpected ending.

As the scholar Matthew Hodgart points out, fables are stories in which the non-human behaves like the human, and a simple moral point is made.[1035] Although fables descend from folk-tales, their written literary manifestation achieved a high degree of acclaim in works by, among others, La Fontaine in the seventeenth century, and James Thurber in the twentieth century. Although Margaret Laurence is not known as a satirist, she worked intensively with fables while fashioning her English translations of Somali and Arabic tales in *A Tree for Poverty* (1954), and throughout her literary career showed a penchant for paradoxes and reversals.

A Fable – For the Whaling Fleets

Imagine the sky creatures descending to our earth. They are very different from humankind. We have known of their existence, although we cannot truly conceive of the realms in which they live. Sometimes a tiny thing has fallen to earth violently, lifeless when we found it, like a lost bird with wings broken and useless. But the sky creatures are not birds. They are extremely intelligent beings. Their brains, although not as large as ours, have been developed for complex and subtle use. They bear their young live from the mothers' bodies, as humans do, and nourish them from the breast. Although they live in the highest heights, we breathe the same air. Like us, they have language, and like humankind they have music and song. They care for their young, love them and teach them in the ways of their species. But when they loom low over our lands in their strong air vessels, they hunt humanity with the death sticks. At first there are only a few of them, then more and more. There are fewer and fewer human beings. The sky creatures make use of the dead bodies of our children, of our hunted young women and young men, of our elders. The flesh of our dead children is eaten by the sky creatures and their slaves. The fat from the bodies of our loved children gives oil which is used by the sky creatures in various ways – much of it goes to make unguents and creams for their vanity. They do not need to hunt humans in order to survive. They continue to slaughter us out of greed. Some of their number believe the slaying is wrong. Some of them sing their songs to us, and we in return answer with our own songs. Perhaps we will never be able to speak in our human languages to those who speak the sky creatures' languages. But song is communication, respectful touch and trust are ways of knowing. Too many of them, however, do not think in this manner, do not have these feelings. Too many of them hear the sounds and songs of humanity but do not sense the meanings. Too many do not see our beauty as beauty, our music as music, our language as language, our thoughts as thoughts, for we are different from the sky creatures. Our songs are lost to their ears, and soon may be lost even to our own earth, when the last of humankind is hunted and slain and consumed. If that terrifying time should come, then our love, our mirth, our knowledge, our joy in life, will disappear forever, and God will mourn, for the holy spirit that created the sky creatures and gave them the possibility of the knowledge of love, also created us with the same possibilities, we who are the earthlings, humankind.

APPENDIX C
A Queen in Thebes

Margaret Laurence's short story "A Queen in Thebes" was published in *Tamarack Review* (1964).[1036] Set in a world destroyed by nuclear catastrophe, the story addresses several themes that appear later in her novel *The Fire-Dwellers,* where Stacey, the anxious and fearful central character, lives in a world threatened by nuclear annihilation. Laurence referred to "A Queen in Thebes," as "a kind of horror story" and called it "one of the bleakest stories" she had ever written.

This story is unique in the Laurence canon. It holds special significance, moreover, because the archives contain incisive comments about it that she made in a letter responding to a request for permission to include "A Queen in Thebes" in a Science Fiction module planned for a correspondence course under the auspices of the Ontario Ministry of Education.[1037] Her response offers a rare opportunity to read Laurence's extended remarks about one of her short stories.

In 1981, Laurence made the following comments in a letter to Fred Farr who had sought permission to use "A Queen in Thebes":

> The story suggests that people still may struggle towards humanity.... But it also suggests that survival as human beings is virtually impossible in total isolation, without other people, without human society.

> In effect, it is a fantasy look at a post-nuclear world, and an extremely bleak look, in which two isolated humans have been cut off forever from the society of humankind.
>
> If there is a message, and I guess there is, it is that terrifying and awful and flawed though our human society is, we must try to better it, not destroy it.

The reference in the title is to Queen Jocasta, the wife of Oedipus in the ancient Greek play by Sophocles, *Oedipus Rex*. Laurence, however, intended the reference to be ironic. She wrote: "The queen in this post-nuclear 'Thebes' is queen of nothing; her son suffers no remorse; they have both become less aware of the human condition than the Greeks of thousands of years ago were. The woman has been so deeply damaged by the loss of her husband, her world, everything, and by the experience of bringing up her son alone in a world devoid of other humans (as far as she is able to discover), that she ultimately loses her grip on her own identity and even loses her memory of her own name (which may or may not have been Jocasta)."

The relationships between the characters, which shift over time, as well as the descriptions of their world are suggestive of the point that Laurence wished to make, namely, "that survival as human beings is virtually impossible in total isolation, without other people, without human society." Writing about this story twenty years after it had been published, Laurence noted that although in her fiction she had dealt with a multiplicity of themes and war had come into all her Manawaka books, "the terrible tragedies of World Wars I and II," she subsequently decided to take action not only through fiction, but "as a citizen" in an effort to address the issues of a nuclear threat and the devastation caused by war. She served then on the boards of Ploughshares and Energy Probe, contributed newspaper articles, and delivered an important and oft quoted academic lecture, "My Final Hour" at Trent University.[1038]

A Queen in Thebes

Fear of a war was not what had taken them to the cottage in the mountains. Everyone had feared war for so long that it seemed it might never happen after all. Nerves cannot be kept on edge year in and year out without making the possibility of devastation seem impossible in the face of the continuing realities – the newspapers delivered each day to the door, the passing of seasons, the favourite TV serials which would, everyone somehow felt, continue in spite of the fires of hell or the Day of Judgement. No, they had simply gone to the mountains because it would be good to get the baby out of the stifling city for the summer, into the cooler air and the quiet. It was a long way for her husband to drive for the weekends, but he said he did not mind, and later in the summer he would be getting his two weeks' holiday. Her husband had built the cottage the year they were married. It was only a shack, really, and it was not close to any settlement or town. They had to bring in all their supplies, and they decided to have the tinned goods sent in all at once, by truck, enough to last the summer, so her husband would not have to both-er with much shopping when he came up on the weekends. Although it was isolated, it was a place they both loved. The lake was nearby, azure, and alive with fishes, and the pine and tama-rack brushed their low-sweeping boughs against the windows as the night wind stirred them. Her husband spent a day in getting enough firewood for a week, making certain everything was all right.

"You don't mind being alone here with Rex?" he said. "If any-thing happens, you can always walk down the hill to Benson's Garage, and phone me."

She was afraid, but she did not say so. He went back to the city then. The day after he left, the sky turned to fire, as though the sun had exploded.

The city was a long way off, down on the plains, too far for the death to reach here, but she saw it like the disintegrating sun, the light like no other light, a dark illumination and not the health which we associate with light. Then the dust cloud formed like the shape of a giant and poisonous toadstool, and she knew the thing had come which everyone had feared. She herself had feared it until it no longer seemed real, and now it had come. She did not scream or cry, after the first unbelieving cry. She hid her eyes, lest the sight damage them. She ran into the cottage and sat quite still. It grew dark, and the baby was crying. She fed him, picking him up with small stiff movements of her hands. Then she put him into his bed and he went to sleep. She did not think at all of the cloud or the light of the death, or of how it would be this moment in what had been the city. She was waiting for her husband to arrive.

In the morning, she looked out and saw the sun rising. The fire of it glowed red and quiet in the sky. For an instant she gazed at it in panic. Then she drew the curtains across the windows so the light would not infect her or the baby. Everything was all right, she calmed herself. It was only that she had never been away from people before, although she was twenty years old. Either her family or her husband had always been with her. He will soon come, she told herself. She fed the baby. Then she took out her purse mirror and combed her hair, so she would look nice when her husband arrived.

She lived this way for some days, going outside the shack only at night. Then one morning she knew the sun did not threaten her. She walked out in the daylight, although she still could not look directly at the sun. When she looked beyond the forest, in the direction of the far-off city, she remembered the death. She ran back to the shack and took the baby in her arms. She rocked him there, and for the first time she cried and could not stop. She mourned wordlessly, and when her tears were done and the violence of the pain had momentarily spent itself, she thought of herself and the baby. She set out, carrying the child, to find people.

When she reached the foot of the mountain, she found no one at Benson's Garage. The place had been deserted. The money was gone from the till, but otherwise everything had been left as it was.

The people must have felt that they were not far enough away, thinking of the dust that could enter them in the air they breathed, rotting the blood and bone. They must have fled to some more distant and uncontaminated place. She wondered dully if they had found such a place, or if they had only run into other deaths, other polluted places, other cities shattered and lying like hulked shadows of the earth. She became afraid of the air now herself, and because she felt safer on the mountains, she wanted to start back. But she thought of the telephone, and an unreasoning hope possessed her. She was certain her husband was still somewhere and that she would be granted the miracle of his voice. She lifted the receiver and dialled. There was no response. She tried again and again, but there was no sound. She replaced the phone carefully, as though it mattered. Then she took the baby and began walking up the hill.

She knew she had to find people. In the days that followed, she walked long distances through the forest, marking her way so she would not get lost. She walked down the hill on every side, through the heavy bracken and the snarled bushes, until her legs and arms were bleeding with the small incisions of thorns and branches, and her arms ached with the fatigue of carrying the child, for she would not leave him alone in the shack. But in all her treks she found no one. At night she did not cry. She lay sleepless, her eyes open, listening to owls and wind, trying to believe what had happened.

The leaves of the poplar were turning a clear yellow, and she knew it was autumn. She looked with sudden terror at the tins of food on the shelves, and saw they were almost gone. She picked berries and cooked them on the wood stove, wondering how long they would keep. She had fished only to provide her daily needs, but now she caught as many fish as she could. She slit and cleaned them, and laid them out in the sun to dry. One afternoon she found a black bear from the forest, feeding on the outspread fish. She had no gun. At that moment she was not afraid of the animal. She could think only of the sun-dried fish, hers, the food she had caught. She seized a stick and flew at the bear. The creature, taken by surprise, looked at her with shaggy menace. Then it lumbered off into the green ferns and the underbrush.

Each evening now, when the child was asleep, she lighted one of the remaining candles for only a few minutes and looked at herself in the mirror. She saw her long brownish blond hair and her thin tanned face and eyes she hardly knew as hers. Sometimes she wondered if her husband would recognize her when he arrived. Then she would remember, and would pick up the child and hold him tightly, and speak his name.

"Rex – it's all right. We're going to be all right."

The baby, wakened by her tears, would be frightened, and then she would be sufficiently occupied in quieting him. Sometimes, after she had looked in the mirror, she would not recall what had happened. She would go to bed comforted by the thought of her husband's arrival and would sleep without dreaming of the human shadows which she had long ago heard were etched on stone, their grotesque immortality.

Only when the first snow fell did she really believe that her husband was dead. She wanted and needed to die then, too, but she could not bring herself to kill her son and she could not leave him alone, so she was condemned to life.

The winter went on and on, and she thought they would not live until spring. The snow was banked high around the shack, and in the forest the hollows were filled with white, a trap to her unsure feet. She stumbled and fell, gathering firewood, and her axe severed the leather of the old boots which had been her husband's, cutting deeply into her ankle. She bound the wound clumsily, not expecting it to heal. It did heal, but the muscle had been affected and she walked with difficulty for a long time. She and the child were always cold and usually hungry. The thought uppermost in her mind was that she had to keep the fire going. She became obsessed with the gathering of wood, and would go out and drag the spruce branches back, even when the pile of boughs outside the shack was still high.

She prayed for help to come, but none came. Gradually she stopped praying. She did not curse God, nor feel she had been deserted by Him. She simply forgot. God seemed related to what had once been and was no more. The room in her mind where the prayers had dwelt became vacant and uninhabited.

The thing she loved most was the sound of the child's voice. What she missed most now was not her husband's protective presence, nor his warmth, but the sound of human voices. The child was learning to talk, and soon they would be able to speak together, as people do. This thought heartened her.

When she looked in the mirror now, she saw how bony and drawn her face had become, but the wide eyes were harder than before, and an alertness lurked in them. Her hearing was becoming keener. She could hear the deer that approached the cabin at night, and she would look out at them, but although she tried making traps, she caught only an occasional jack-rabbit. Once, seeing the deer, their bodies heavy with meat, she took the axe and they vanished into the night forest where she dared not follow.

The dried fish were almost gone. She lived in a semi-conscious state, drugged by exhaustion and hunger. Even her despair had lost its edge and was only a dulled apprehension of hopelessness. One day she threw the bones of a rabbit out into the snow, and for a moment sank down beside them, summoning strength to walk back into the cabin. A flock of sparrows landed on the snow beside her and began to explore the gnawed bones. She remembered dimly having once put out bread crumbs for the birds in winter. Delicately, hardly realizing she was doing it, her hands moved with a swiftness she had not known she possessed. She reached out and seized. When she drew back her hands, she had a live sparrow in each. She throttled them between thumb and forefinger, and began to tear off the feathers even before the small wings had stopped palpitating. Stolidly, feeling nothing, she cooked the birds and ate them. Then she vomited, and frightened the child with the way she cried afterwards. But the next time, when she caught birds and felt the life ebbing away between her fingers, she did not vomit or cry.

When the days began to lengthen, and spring came, she did not know whether it mattered that she and Rex were still alive. She could not think ahead. When the pain took possession of her heart, she still believed that she did not care whether they lived or died. Yet every day she gathered the firewood and foraged for some kind of food, and nothing was loathsome to her now, if her teeth and stomach could turn it into one more day of life.

She had kept only an approximate accounting of seasons, but one day she realized that Rex must be nearly six years old. She was much stronger than she had been – how weak and stupid she had been in the early days, after the Change – but now the boy was almost as strong as she. He was better at trapping rabbits and birds, and when he went to the lake, he never came back without fish. He would lie for hours on the shore, watching where the fish surfaced and which reedy places in the shallows were most likely to contain them. His eyes were better than hers, and his ears, and he had discovered for himself how to walk through the forest noiselessly, without allowing the ferns and bracken to snap under his feet.

At first she had tried to teach him things from that other world – how to read and how to pray. But he only laughed, and after a while she laughed, too, seeing how little use it was to them. She taught him instead what she had learned here – always to keep the fire going, always to gather wood, how to uproot dandelions and how to find the giant slugs where they concealed themselves on the underside of fallen logs. Then, gradually and imperceptibly, the boy began to teach her.

He was standing in the doorway now, and across his shoulders was a young deer with its throat slit.

"Rex – where? How?" They did not speak together tenderly and at length, as she once imagined they would. Their days were too driven by the immediate matters of food, and in the evenings they wanted only to sleep. They spoke briefly, abruptly, exchanging only what was necessary.

The boy grinned. "I ran after it, and then I used my knife. You never tried. Why?"

"I tried," she said. She turned away. The boy was laughing softly to himself as he took the animal outside and began to skin it. She looked out the doorway at him as he squatted beside the deer, his face frowning in concentration as he tried to decide how to do something he had not done before. He took the skin off badly, and grew furious, and hacked at the slain animal with his knife. They ate meat that night, though, and that was what counted. But for the first time she felt a fear not of the many things that there were to fear outside, but of something inside the dwelling, something unknown. When the boy was sleeping, she took out her mirror and looked. I am strong, she thought. We can live. I have made this possible. But her own eyes seemed unfamiliar to her, and she looked at the image in the glass as though it were separate from herself.

The years were no longer years but seasons — the season of warmth and growth, when the green forest provided deer and the lake swarmed with fish; the season of coolness and ripening, when the berries reddened on the bushes; the season of snow and penetrating chill, when the greatest fear was that the fire might die. But when, after all the seasons of care, the fire did die, it happened in spring, when the melting snow drenched into the shack one night through the weakening timbers of the roof. She had left the iron lid off the old stove so it would draw better, for the wood was not quite dry. It was her fault that the fire had died, and both of them knew it. Rex was almost as tall as she was, now, and he grasped her wrist in his intensely strong hand and led her to see.

"You have killed the fire. Now what will we do? You are stupid, stupid, stupid!"

She looked at his other hand, which was clenched, and wondered if she dared draw away from his grip. Then some deep pride straightened her. She pried at the noose-like fingers which held her wrist, and she used her fingernails like talons. He let go and gazed his rage at her. Then he dropped his eyes. He was not yet full grown.

"What will we do?" he repeated.

She then saw that he was waiting for her to tell him, and she laughed — but silently, for she could not risk his hearing. She put her hands gently on his shoulders and stroked the pliant sun-browned skin until he turned to her and put his head against her in a gesture of need and surrender. Then, quickly, he jerked away, and stood facing her, his eyes bold and self-contained once more.

"I have tried to strike fire from stone," she said. "We must try again."

They did try, but the sparks were too light and fleeting, and the shreds of birch bark never caught fire. They ate their meat raw that summer, and when the evenings lengthened into the cool of autumn, they shivered under the deer hides that were their blankets.

Rex became ill on meat that had spoiled. They had both been sick before, many times, but never as badly as this. He vomited until his stomach was empty, and still he could not stop retching. She gave him water and sat beside him. There was nothing else she could do. The cabin was almost a wreck now, for although they had tried to repair it, they lacked sufficient tools, and Rex was not old enough yet to invent new and untried ways of building. They hardly moved outside for many days, and in this period the shack's mustiness and disrepair came to her consciousness as never before, and she looked with fear at the feeble timbers and the buckling walls, thinking of the winter. One night, when Rex's fever was at its height, and he lay silently, contracted with pain, she tried to think back to the distant times before the Change. She had forgotten her husband. But she remembered that some words used to be spoken, something powerful when everything else had failed.

"I should – pray," she said.

He opened his eyes. "Pray?"

She felt then, in some remote and dusty room of her mind, that she had not imparted to him something which was his due. There was always too much to do. She was too tired to talk much in the evenings.

"We used to speak of God," she said. "All life comes from God. Something great and powerful, greater than we are. When many people lived, they used to say these things."

The boy looked at her vacantly, not comprehending. Later, however, he asked her again, and she attempted once more to tell him.

"All life comes from God ..." but she no longer understood this very well herself and could not express it.

Gradually the illness left, and Rex grew strong again. One day he came back to the shack and told her he had found a cave in the side of a cliff.

"It will be better for the winter," he said.

She knew he was right. They moved everything they had, the knives and axe, the worn utensils, the tattered blankets, the deer hides. When she left the shack she cried, and the boy looked at her in astonishment.

Late that summer there was a severe storm, and the lightning descended to earth all around them, gashes of white light streaking the sky and tearing apart the darkness. She crouched on the cave floor and hid her eyes, as she always did in the presence of a sudden violence of light. Her fear was mingled with a sorrow whose roots she could no longer clearly trace. The boy knelt beside her and put his hands on her hair, and spoke to her, not roughly but quietly. He was afraid of the lightning, too, for he had learned her fear. But he was less afraid than she. He had no memory, not even her dim and confused ones, of any other life.

When the storm was over, they saw that the lightning had set the forest ablaze, a long way off, on the crest of the hill beyond their territory. The boy went off by himself. He was away for several days and nights, but when he returned he was carrying a smouldering pine torch. Their fire came to life again, and as it flared up in the circle of stones on the floor of the dark cave, the boy made an involuntary movement, as though compelled by something beyond his own decision. He raised his hands and bowed his head. Then, as though feeling that this was not enough, he knelt on the rock of the cave floor. He looked up and saw her standing immobile beside him, and his eyes became angry. With a sharp downward motion of his hand, he signalled what she was to do.

Slowly, doubtfully, and then as she stared at him at last unresisting, she went down onto her knees beside the circle of stones that contained the live fire. Together they knelt before the god.

One day she looked at Rex and saw he was much taller than she. He killed deer now mainly with his spear, and unless it was an exceptionally dry summer when the deer moved away in search of grazing, they were always well supplied with meat. The boy's hair grew down around his shoulders, but he lopped it off with his knife when it grew too long, for it got in his way when he was not hunting. The hair was growing now on his face, but he did not bother to cut this. Age had no meaning for them, but she tried to count, as they counted the dried fish and strips of dried venison for the winter. The boy would be fifteen, perhaps, or sixteen.

She told him, without knowing in advance that she was going to say it, that the time had come for them to try once more to find the people. They thought of them as The People, those who perhaps lived somewhere beyond the mountain. She believed in their existence, but Rex believed only occasionally.

"There are no people," he said now.

"Yes," she said. "We must try."

"Why?" he asked.

She did not reply. She could only repeat the same words, over and over. "We must try." Rex shrugged.

"You go, then."

So she went alone, walking through the forest, descending into gullies where the loose shale slid under her feet, drinking face down from mountain streams, trapping squirrel and rabbit when she could. For many days and nights she travelled, but she did not find the people. Once she came to some dwellings, a few houses with weeds grown into the doorways, but they were deserted except for the mice and rats which eyed her, unblinking, from the corners of the dusty floors. Finally she knew she could not travel far enough. She was not any longer certain, herself, that the people really existed. She turned and started back.

When she reached the mountain once more, and entered the cave, Rex looked different, or else her time away from him had enabled her to see him differently.

"You are back," he said, with neither gladness nor regret.

But that evening in front of the fire, she saw he really had changed. He knelt as before, but more hastily, more casually, as though it were not quite so important as it had been. He saw her questioning eyes.

"I was wrong," he explained.

"Wrong?" she was bewildered.

He indicated the fire. "This one is small. There is – something else."

He did not say anything more. He turned away and went to sleep. He wakened her at dawn and told her to come outside the cave. He pointed to the sun, which was appearing now over the lake, a red globe in the pale sky of morning.

"Our fire comes from there. The voices told me when you were not here. I was alone, and I could hear them. They were waiting for you to go away. You do not hear the voices. Only I can hear them, when I am alone."

He spoke almost pityingly, and with a certainty she had not heard before. She wanted to cry out against what he said, but she did not know why, nor what she could say to him.

"Look ..." he said. "You look."

He knew she could not look directly at the sun. She feared, always, that the sight would damage her. The man grinned and turned his face to the sky.

"I can look," he said. "I can look at God. The fire comes from there. He does as He wishes. If He is pleased, then all things will go well. If He is angry, then we will suffer."

He went into the cave and brought forth the liver and heart of the deer he had killed the evening before. He laid these on a raised slab of stone. He brought a pine brand and made a fire underneath the entrails. Then he knelt, not as he had inside the cave, but prostrating himself, forehead to the earth in obeisance.

"Shall I kneel?" she asked him.

"Yes," he said. "But you are not to touch this stone and this fire and this meat. That is for me to do."

She obeyed. There was nothing else she could do. When he had gone to the lake to fish, she went to the corner of the cave where the cooking pots were piled. She had dug a niche into the rock, and here her secret possession lay. She took out the bundle of dried leaves, unfolded them carefully, and held the mirror in her hands. She looked into it for a long time. It calmed her, as though it were a focus for the scattered fragments of herself. Dream and daylight hovered in uncertain balance within her, always. Only when she looked in the mirror did she momentarily know she really existed.

"What is that?" The man's voice was harsh. She glanced up and quickly tried to conceal what she held in her hands. She had never allowed him to see her looking at herself. He had never seen the mirror. He had seen his own image in the quivering lakewater, but never the sharp, painful, and yet oddly reassuring picture she had of her own cruel and gentle eyes.

"It is nothing," she told him.

He took hold of her hand and forced it open. He looked at the shining object. His face was puzzled, but only for an instant. He glanced out the cave entrance to the sky and the mid-morning sun. Then he hurled the mirror from his hand, and it shattered against the rock of the cave walls. After that, he hit her, again and again and again.

"You are unclean!" he cried.

She knew then he was afraid of her, too. They were afraid of each other.

The season went by, and she kept no account of time. Generally she was content. She sat crosslegged now on the wide ledge outside the cave entrance. She was scraping a deer hide with the bone blade Rex had made. He had discovered, on one of his longer trips, a place where the people used to live and where pieces of iron lay rusting, and he had brought some back and fashioned spearheads and knives and an axe. But these were kept for his use, for he needed them more in hunting than she did in scraping the hides and making them into clothes. It was slow work, this, but she did not mind. The sun of late spring warmed her, and the raw trilling of frogs from the lake made her feel glad, for this was a good time of year, with hunger gone. The fish and game were plentiful, and the roots and leaves of the dandelions were succulent and tender.

The pointed shadow of the altar stone on the rock ledge told her that he would soon be back from the forest. She must prepare food, for he would be hungry when he returned. He did not like to be kept waiting. That was as it should be. A man was hungry after hunting.

But still she sat in the sunshine, drowsing over her work. Then the insinuating voice began, humming its tune inside her, and she blinked and shook her head as though to shake the whispered song away, for when it came to her she felt threatened and unsafe and she did not want to listen. Rex said the voices came only to him. But she heard this voice occasionally, unknown to him, in the deep quietness of the morning, when the birds were suddenly still, or in the wind that brushed through the forest at night. She did not recall when the voice had begun. She did not have a name for herself, as Rex did, and although it was enough to be what she was, in some way the voice was connected with the name she had once held, the name which had been shattered somewhere, some-time, like lakewater when a stone is thrown into it. She never understood what the voice was saying to her, with its jingling music, a monotonous chanting from a long way off and yet close to her as her blood. The words, familiar in form but totally unfamiliar in meaning, were like the dry and twisted shells she found on the shore of the lake, objects that had once contained live creatures, but very long ago, so that no trace of flesh remained. The voice echoed again now, hurting and frightening her.

"Lavender's blue, dilly dilly, lavender's green,
When you are king, dilly dilly, I shall be queen."

She half shut her eyes, and listened intently, but still she could not understand and could only feel troubled by something untouchable, some mystery that remained just beyond her grasp.

Then, inside the cave, one of the children began crying, and she went to give comfort.

PERMISSIONS

NOTES

1. Budge Wilson, interview by author, Halifax, 19 July 1991. Additional informa-
    tion about this period in Margaret Laurence's life came from interviews with
    Joan Johnston and with one of the nurses at the hospital, as well as from com-
    ments in Laurence's memoirs *Dance on the Earth*. (Toronto: McClelland &
    Stewart, 1974). Hereafter *Dance*.

2. ML, *Journals*. MS: McMaster University. In July 1986, a party to celebrate
    Margaret Laurence's birthday was held in Peterborough at the home of Joan
    and Glen Johnston. Not long after her birthday, Margaret had to be hospital-
    ized and was subsequently diagnosed with terminal cancer. She kept a journal,
    in several notebooks, from her sixtieth birthday until she was no longer able to
    continue writing in it during the winter of 1986.

3. Joan Johnston, interview by author, Peterborough, Ontario, 8 June 1994.

4. ML, *Journal #4*, McMaster University Archives.

5. The entries in her journal make clear that Margaret's decision was not easy and
    that, in addition to her own soul-searching, she had consulted several clergy
    during the months of her final illness.

6. ML to Will Ready, 19 August 1979, in J.A.Wainwright, *A Very Large Soul:
    Selected Letters from Margaret Laurence to Canadian Writers*. (Dunvegan,
    Ontario: Cormorant Press, 1995), 165-66.

7. *Dance*, 29.

8. See obituary notice for Robert Wemyss, *Neepawa Press*, 15 January 1935, 4.

9. *Dance*, 31.

10. Photo given to the Margaret Laurence Home in Neepawa by Jean Kerr
    Williams, who received it from a daughter of Elmer Ivey, manager of the Royal
    Bank and sponsor of the dance.

11. It was built in 1906. Two of Verna's older sisters participated in the recital.
    Margaret (Maggie) read a "Sketch of the Life of Beethoven" that she had writ-
    ten, and Ruby, the oldest girl, read "The Interpreter of Music" by Perry.

12. According to the program, Mason and Rich pianos, one of which had been sent
    up from Winnipeg, were used for the recital, held in the evening of 10 May 1907.

York University Archives and Special Collections, Margaret Laurence Fonds.

13.   In 1992, the piano that had belonged to Margaret Laurence's mother, Verna, was donated to the Margaret Laurence Home in Neepawa from the estate of Ruth Faryon (who had been a next-door neighbour of Bob and Verna on Vivian Street).

14.   The paper also reported that she showed "musicianly" qualities of a high order and received great applause. See *Heritage: History of the Town of Neepawa and District as Told and Recorded by Its People.* (Neepawa, Manitoba: History Book Committee, 1983), 268. Hereafter *Heritage.*

15.   Bob and Verna's bungalow was not, as James King states in his biography of Laurence, on the wrong side of town. *The Life of Margaret Laurence.* (Toronto: Alfred A. Knopf, 1997), 13. See *Heritage* and Dorothy Coutts, letter to author, 19 October 1998. Letters to Donez Xiques are in the author's collection, unless a specific archive is indicated.

16.   *Dance*, 34.

17.   *Dance*, 40.

18.   *Dance*, 38-40.

19.   See *Heritage*, 86-87.

20.   According to Professor John Coutts, the citizens of Neepawa were very much aware of social status. The self-sufficient side of the town's economy may have made them more self-absorbed than they might have been if the basis of the town's economy had been less stable. Professor John W. Coutts letter to author, 2 September 1992.

21.   Jean Kerr Williams, interview by author, Ottawa, 17 September 1992.

22.   *Dance*, 25.

23.   It would have been very rare for a town to have a public library during those years of the Depression. One of Peggy's teachers, Mildred Musgrove, recalls that, when she first went to teach at the high school in Neepawa during the Depression, "the school did not even have a set of encyclopedias. The library shelves were empty." (Mildred Musgrove, interview by author, Boissevain, Manitoba, 29 September 1991).

24.   *Dance*, 41.

25.   *Dance*, 49.

26.   *Dance*, 49.

27.   *Dance*, 39-40. At the time of his death in 1935, Bob Wemyss was president of the Neepawa Horticultural Society.

28.   As Margaret Laurence's literary reputation grew, she was approached by Professor William B. Ready of McMaster University, who offered to purchase her papers for McMaster's archives. He also informed her that his mother had played tennis with her father, Bob, during the 1920s. That prairie connection was important to Margaret, and she always felt close to Will Ready and his wife, Bess. Later, through the intercession of Professor Clara Thomas, the York University Archives and Special Collections became a major repository for letters and documents pertaining to Margaret Laurence.

29.   *Dance*, 33-34.

30.   Jean Kerr Williams letter to author, 12 January 1993. Here she refers to the period when Peggy was a preschooler.

31.   Mona Spratt Meredith, interview by author, Vancouver, 13 October 1992. Dorothy Coutts, who had to share a room with her siblings until she was a teenager, remarks that the Wemyss's "small, cozy home was like a dream house,"

and adds, "I have to admit that I was envious of Peggy's beautiful bedroom in the half-storey of their cottage." Dorothy Coutts Shields, letter to author, 2 September 1992.

32. Dorothy Coutts Shields, telephone conversation with author, 14 November 1992.

33. Dorothy Coutts Shields, letter to author, 2 September 1992.

34. See interviews conducted by Greta Coger with Phyllis Ralph #3, and with Virginia Shore #1. Typescripts provided to author, January 1992, by Greta Coger, who subsequently deposited the interviews in the archives at the University of Winnipeg.

35. Dorothy Coutts Shields, letter to author, 2 September 1992.

36. Donnalu Wigmore, "Margaret Laurence: The Woman behind the Writing." Interview by Wigmore, *Chatelaine* (February 1971): 28-29; 52-54.

37. *The Diviners*. Toronto: McClelland & Stewart, 1974, 11. Hereafter *Diviners*.

38. Rev. John Speers, interview by author, Barrie, Ontario, 10 September 1994. The poet Dorothy Livesay, who also grew up in Winnipeg, describes going out to the snowy countryside with her younger sister and their father in search of the first crocuses. See "A Prairie Sampler," *Mosaic* 3 (Spring 1970): 85-92.

39. See *The Canvasback on a Prairie Marsh* by Albert H. Hochbaum (Harrisburg, Pa.: Stackpole Press, 1959). I am indebted to Professor Norman Seymour for sharing with me his experience of the Manitoba prairie, gleaned from many years of observing and researching waterfowl there, particularly in the area of the Delta Marsh. Even at the close of the twentieth century, the Winnipeg airport shut down from time to time because of the numbers of migrating birds in the area. I am grateful, also, to Ivan Traill, former principal of NCI, for several conversations about flora and fauna in the area. He related that Oak Hammock Marsh, not far from Winnipeg, had approximately one million geese on the water there during migration in 2003.

40. Dorothy Coutts Shields, letter to author, 2 September 1992.

41. He had been born in May 1933.

42. *Dance*, 52.

43. In Neepawa, Bobby's adoption was common knowledge, and as an adult Margaret Laurence told a number of friends that her brother, Bob, had been adopted. Her reticence about mentioning Bobby's adoption in her memoirs (*Dance on the Earth*) can be understood better in the light of comments addressed to her brother in her private journal (10 October 1986, unpublished), McMaster University Archives and Special Collections, Margaret Laurence Collection. In that section of her journal, Margaret is mourning Bob's recent death and the fact that he had not lived to see what she had written about their Mum. The passage is written as though Margaret were speaking directly to him.

44. In the summer of 1948 the leasehold on that property, which was then jointly held by Bertha Simpson (widow of Stuart) and her sister-in-law Margaret C. Wemyss (widow of Bob), was transferred to a couple from North Dakota.

45. Riding Mountain National Park, brochure, undated, 4.

46. See "The Shack," *Heart of a Stranger*. (Toronto: McClelland & Stewart, 1976), 187-91. Hereafter cited as *Heart*. A detailed map of the area and information about the lot and the cottage (which has been significantly altered structurally) were sent to the author from the present owner of the site, 17 February 1998.

47. "The Shack," *Heart*, 187-91.

48. The beautiful trees in Neepawa are one of the glories of the town, especially in autumn. Their presence is due, in part, to the foresight of the town fathers who planted fourteen hundred trees in Neepawa in 1902. Until the last decades of

the twentieth century, when Dutch Elm disease struck, the Neepawa elms were among the most beautiful trees in that town.

49.   Laurence's names for these homes of her childhood are used throughout.

50.   The rose window, which was removed from the house by a subsequent owner, was later donated to the Margaret Laurence Home in Neepawa.

51.   Perhaps it is merely a coincidence, but in the *The Stone Angel*, Hagar's father bears the same surname (Currie) as the editor of *The Works of Horace*, which were on the shelf in Grandfather Wemyss's library. John Wemyss's signature and the name of his school appears on the flyleaf of a one-volume edition of *The Works of Horace* that was donated to the Margaret Laurence Home in Neepawa. On the volume's title page, the name Joseph Currie appears, and the book's inside cover is filled with marks made by a young child (Joseph Currie, *The Works of Horace, with English Notes* (London: Charles Griffin and Company, n.d.).

52.   See also Laurence's notes on the Wemyss family, York University Archives and Special Collections, Margaret Laurence Fonds.

53.   Their children were: Robert (Margaret Laurence's father), Jack, and Norma.

54.   Dorothy Batchelor Brown, telephone conversation with author, 15 March 1999.

55.   "Where the World Began," *Heart*, 213-19. Bert Batchelor was kind to the children of Neepawa, and there are many stories about his warm-heartedness. In those days bicycles were considered expensive, and Peggy's first real bicycle came from him. Many years later, when Peggy (then Margaret Laurence) and her children were living at Elm Cottage in Buckinghamshire, the Batchelors made a point of stopping by after visiting his birthplace in Old Romney, where his father had been a shepherd.

56.   *Dance*, 55.

57.   "Upon a Midnight Clear," *Heart*, 192-99.

58.   *Dance*, 55.

59.   She made reference to this china in "Jericho's Brick Battlements," *A Bird in the House*. (Toronto: McClelland & Stewart, 1970). Hereafter cited as *Bird in the House*.

60.   These details about Christmas are from Margaret Laurence's essay "Upon a Midnight Clear," *Heart*, 192-99, and from her memoirs.

61.   Jennie Maud Little, Diary, 13 January 1935, University of Manitoba Archives.

62.   "For five days he had been ill with pneumonia and although the case was serious, it was not thought he was in great danger. Shortly before his passing, his condition became grave and he failed to recover from the attack."(*Neepawa Press*, 15 January 1935, 4). Jack Pink, who then lived in Neepawa, also recalls the death of his aunt that winter when "there was a terrible plague of pneumonia." (Jack Pink, interview by author, Nova Scotia, 11 September 1992).

    On the day of Robert Wemyss's death, the roads were badly drifted and the bus for Brandon had to turn back because it could not get through. (Jennie Maud Little, Diary, 13 January 1935, University of Manitoba Archives). During the winter, however, burials did take place in Neepawa. Graves were dug by hand under a sort of tent, and a heater was used to thaw the ground. (Doug White, Neepawa funeral director, telephone conversation with author, 5 February 1998).

63.   *Dance*, 56.

64.   Ibid., 25.

65.   Ibid., 24.

66.   Ibid.

67.   Ibid., 56.

68.   Margaret Laurence gives her age as nine in several interviews as well as her memoirs, but she was actually only eight and a half at the time of her father's death.

69.   *Dance*, 41-42.

70.   Ibid., 58. The Neepawa phone directory lists them at Vivian Street in December 1935. This accords with Laurence's memory as set down in *Dance on the Earth*.

71.   Jennie Maud Little, Diary, January 1936, University of Manitoba Archives.

72.   *Dance*, 58.

73.   Ibid., 61.

74.   Eileen Graham Goodrich, interview by author, Neepawa, 10 September 1991. She was there and identified the teacher as Gwen Saunders.

75.   *Dance*, 58-59.

76.   *Heritage*, 1983, erroneously reports that Jane Bailey Simpson died in 1937 (705), although Laurence correctly cites 1936. The date of 1936 was confirmed by Doug White, telephone conversation with author, 5 February 1998. The funeral service from the Simpson residence was conducted by Rev. Cook, with internment in Riverside Cemetery.

77.   *Dance*, 69.

78.   Grandfather's Simpson's home was sold while she was at university, and Laurence says that, although she never again went inside it, nevertheless the "Big House" always remained for her "a part of my emotional luggage." *Dance*, 101.

79.   This is the opening sentence of "Baa Baa, Black Sheep," Kipling's heart-wrenching fictional account of his youth in England, following his early childhood in India.

80.   *Dance*, 63.

81.   ML, *Journal #4*, McMaster University Archives. In several interviews Margaret Laurence minimized Simpson's harshness and referred instead to the "many hardships" that her grandfather must have endured in his youth. She referred to him in 1973 as "a pioneer, one of the Selkirk settlers." She mentioned the "remarkable" fact that he had walked from Winnipeg to Portage La Prairie. Even today, while gazing at the expanse of the Manitoba prairie, one cannot help thinking about the ancestors whose labour over the years transformed that immense landscape.

82.   The driver was Wes McAmmond. He would have remembered quite clearly the visit to the cottage, since he was familiar with the area and used to date Ruth Faryon, a teacher who lived next door to the Wemyss family on Vivian Street.

83.   "Road to the Isles," *Heart*, 145-57.

84.   Ibid.

85.   Ibid.

86.   Laurence refers to her maternal uncle as follows: "Stuart, the eldest of the family, smart, handsome Stuart, who wanted to be a lawyer but who instead ultimately went into the undertaking business with his father." *Dance*, 27.

87.   *Dance*, 46. Two of John Simpson's other daughters, Ruby and Velma, became nurses, a position he also considered acceptable for women.

88.   *Neepawa Press*, 11 January 1935.

89.   Eileen Graham Goodrich, interview by author, Neepawa, 10 September 1991. Her father was the workman. Other interviewees in Neepawa related anecdotes that underscored the fact that John Simpson was a hard man with an unyielding disposition. He was known for tough business deals.

90.   The Beautiful Plains Museum in Neepawa, now housed in the former CNR railway station, has many photos and artifacts from various periods in the history of the town and district.

91.   *Dance*, 69.

92.   "Where the World Began" in *Heart*, 213-19.

93.   Ibid.

94.   See John Metcalf, *Sixteen by Twelve: Short Stories by Canadian Writers.* (Toronto: McGraw Hill Ryerson, 1970), 71-73.

95.   ML to Lorna Nelson, 4 May 1983. Archives, Margaret Laurence Home, Neepawa, Manitoba.

96.   Page references to *A Bird in the House* are from the New Canadian Library edition, no.96, paperback, published by McClelland & Stewart, 1987. The pagination is identical to the hardcover edition published by Alfred A. Knopf, New York, 1970.

      A sophisticated and thoughtful analysis of these stories and an overview of the critical literature up to 1992 may be found in Jon Kertzer, *That House in Manawaka: Margaret Laurence's* A Bird in the House. (Toronto: ECW Press, 1992).

97.   In a letter to Silver Donald Cameron, a fellow writer, Laurence expressed great annoyance over the fact that Vanessa's surname, MacLeod, had been misspelled as "McCloud," in *A Reader's Guide to the Canadian Novel*, edited by John Moss. (Toronto: McClelland & Stewart, 1981). The letter also shows Laurence's wonderful sense of humour, a side of her personality which often came into play when she wrote to or was with old friends such as Clara Thomas, Timothy Findley and Bill Whitehead, or Donald Cameron (ML to Donald Cameron, 1982, Cameron Archives, University College of Cape Breton). Cameron and his wife, Ann, had come to know Margaret in England in the 1960s, and in writing to him about the *Guide*, she facetiously provided some background material "For Scholars and the Like":

> McCloud: Not properly a clan in itself, the McCloud family has been from time immemorial a sept of the Clan Macdonald of Sleat. Because of the largely illiterate nature of the McClouds, they have tended to spell the clan name as "Sleet."

> Pipe Music: I Wandered Lonely as A McCloud.
> War Cry: Stormy Weather!
> Plant Badge: Daffodil.
> Motto: What be the Forecast?
> Crest Badge: A daffodil, proper, argent, vert, gules and rampant, upon a cloud, unlikely.

98.   ML to Lorna Nelson, 4 May 1983. Archives, Margaret Laurence Home, Neepawa, Manitoba.

99.   "A Place to Stand On," *Heart*, 13.

100.   Ibid.

101.   Helen Porter, interview with author, Toronto, 29 September 2002.

102.   These stories were written over a period of years. Most of them were published separately after *The Stone Angel* appeared in 1964.

103.   *Bird in the House*, 133.

104.   Ibid. All quotations in this paragraph are from "Horses of the Night."

105.   Ibid., 48.

106.   Ibid., 16. "The Sound of the Singing."

107.   Ibid.
108.   Ibid.
109.   Ibid., 162-63.
110.   Ibid., 15.
111.   Geraldine Jewsbury, as quoted by Kathy Chamberlain, "A 'Creative Adventure': Jane Welsh Carlyle's 'Simple Story.'" *The Carlyles at Home and Abroad*, edited by David R. Sorensen and Rodger L. Tarr. (Aldershot, England: Ashgate Press, 2004), 231. I am grateful to Professor Chamberlain for bringing this article to my attention.
112.   *Bird in the House*, 78.
113.   Ibid., 55.
114.   Ibid., 12.
115.   Ibid., 22.
116.   Ibid., 81.
117.   Ibid., 39.
118.   Ibid., 78.
119.   Ibid., 103.
120.   Ibid., 107.
121.   Ibid., 144.
122.   Ibid., 108.
123.   *Dance*, 55-56. Such behaviour is typical in a young child after the death of a parent.
124.   Ibid., 55.
125.   Some examples of events that are contrary to the facts in Peggy's own life: Vanessa's mother does not die, Peggy's mother did. Vanessa's father is a doctor, Peggy's was a lawyer. Vanessa's brother is born into the family, Peggy's brother was adopted.
126.   "September" by Helen Hunt Jackson.
127.   Wes McAmmond, interviews by author, Winnipeg, 12 and 17 September 1991. During two long interviews, McAmmond spontaneously recited a number of poems from his teaching days and showed rollbooks and photos of former students, including some of Peggy Wemyss.
128.   *Dance*, 71. This description by Laurence was shaped from two accounts of McAmmond's influence, one in *Dance* (71) and the other in a letter to Lorna Nelson, 4 May 1983. Archives, the Margaret Laurence Home, Neepawa. This description was supported by Jack Pink, who also had McAmmond as a teacher. (Jack Pink to author, 9 September 2000).
129.   ML to Lorna Nelson, 4 May 1983. Archives, Margaret Laurence Home, Neepawa.
130.   Wes McAmmond, interviews by author, Winnipeg, 12 and 17 September 1991.
131.   Ibid.
132.   Mildred Musgrove, interview by author, Boissevain, Manitoba, 29 September 1991.
133.   Former playmates Jean Kerr, Dorothy Coutts, and Mona Spratt recall the books in Peggy's home on Vivian Street and later in Grandfather Simpson's house.
134.   The writers Nellie McClung and Alice Munro, for example, relate a similar situation in their youth.
135.   The yearly membership fee was approximately three dollars. Later, due to the efforts of this core group, a public library for the town was approved by the province.
136.   Wes McAmmond, interviews by author, Winnipeg, 12 and 17 September 1991.

137.   Ibid.

138.   *Dance*, 71.

139.   *Dance*, 71-72. Leona Thwaites, interview by author, Neepawa, 1993. She came from the same region as the Bailey family, and gave this author a map of the Bailey farm. See also Laurence's poignant poem "For Lorne" (1976), in which she uses a verbal play on his given name, Lorne, and the word "forlorn." *Dance*, 257-62.

140.   *Dance*, 72.

141.   Jennie Maud Little, diary, 12 September 1939, University of Manitoba Archives.

142.   Mona Spratt, interview by author, Vancouver, 28 November 1994. Additional information comes from Jennie Maud Little's diary, University of Manitoba Archives.

143.   *Dance*, 74.

144.   "Books that Mattered to Me" in *Margaret Laurence: An Appreciation*, edited by Christl Verduyn (Peterborough, Ontario: Broadview Press, 1988), 239-41. Here Laurence comments at length about books that she had read during her youth. Her remarks were initially given as a talk to the Friends of the Bata Library, Trent University (*Friends' Bulletin*, No.4, 1981).

145.   Lucy Maud Montgomery, *Emily of New Moon* (Toronto: McClelland-Bantam Inc., Seal Books, 1983), 17.

146.   See "Books that Mattered to Me," 239-41.

147.   *Emily of New Moon*, 41.

148.   *Winnipeg Free Press*, 16 November 1940.

149.   The *Winnipeg Free Press* published Purdy's poem "Sum," and made reference to other poems of his, "Canada's Answer" and "Mountains and Departures." Later it published an early poem of Purdy's about Kipling. None of these poems seems to have been published elsewhere. A selection of his later correspondence with Laurence was published in 1993: *Margaret Laurence — Al Purdy: A Friendship in Letters*, ably edited and with a comprehensive introduction by John Lennox (Toronto: McClelland & Stewart, 1993). An outstanding study of Al Purdy's poetry by the scholar Sam Solecki was published in 1999: *The Last Canadian Poet: An Essay on Al Purdy* (Toronto: University of Toronto Press, 1999).

150.   This is evident in the column "With the Editor." The editor's name was Polly Evans, but it is not clear whether that was a pseudonym. The page actually seems to have been the work of more than one editor, although the name "Polly Evans" is the only one that appears at this time.

151.   *Winnipeg Free Press*, 22 February 1941.

152.   R.H. Grenville was then a frequent younger contributor to the page; *Winnipeg Free Press*, 22 March 1941.

153.   Ibid.

154.   Contribution from Elma Machan of Flin Flon.

155.   *Winnipeg Free Press*, 5 July 1941.

156.   *Winnipeg Free Press*, 23 March 1940.

157.   This work was by Elma R. Machan.

158.   Dance, 74.

159.   *Dance*, 73.

160.   In her memoirs, Laurence describes how she managed to get her submission typed, but she mistakenly dates the event as occurring when she was twelve or thirteen (*Dance*, 73). It actually occurred during the summer of 1940, when she had turned fourteen.

161.   This information about Peggy's high-school years comes from archival research, from over a dozen interviews conducted by the author, as well as from contemporary accounts and information in the high-school newspaper, *Annals of the Black and Gold*, in the *Neepawa Press*, and in *Heritage: A History of the Town of Neepawa*. As a result, it has been possible to fill in some gaps in Laurence's account of those years in her memoirs and to provide further details about this important period in her life.

162.   Jack Pink, interview by author, New Glasgow, Nova Scotia, 11 September 1992, and Jean Kerr Williams, interview by author, Ottawa, 17 September 1992.

163.   Mildred Musgrove, interview by author, Boissevain, Manitoba, 29 September 1991.

164.   Connie Offen Sword, interview by author, Toronto, 6 October 1992.

165.   Jack Pink, interview by author, New Glasgow, Nova Scotia, 11 September 1992, and Jack Pink, letter to author, 16 September 2000.

166.   The NCI paper, *Annals of the Black and Gold*, provides many details about Neepawa Collegiate Institute during Peggy's four years there. The paper was unpaginated, however, and did not have volume numbers. Typically there were three issues each year, but some issues of the paper may be missing from the collections at the Margaret Laurence Home and at the Neepawa Public Library. It is possible that some issues have not been preserved or that, in a given year, fewer than three issues were published.

167.   *Winnipeg Free Press*, 28 September, 1940, 6.

168.   She signed it Jean Margaret Wemyss. In *Dance on the Earth*, Laurence mistakenly refers to her story as "The Pillars of the Nation." In an interview with Laurence, William French states that "The Pillars of the Nation" was composed when Margaret was ten (*Globe and Mail*, 25 April 1970, 6). The *Winnipeg Free Press*, however, states that her story was called "The Land of Our Fathers." Peggy was then age fourteen, not ten. Perhaps "The Pillars of the Nation" was an earlier effort, but it seems more likely and would be characteristic that Margaret Laurence so identified with her fictional creation that she remembered Vanessa's story as factually her own. On the other hand, it is possible that Laurence wished to prevent her juvenile effort from being discovered, and hence deliberately obscured the reference.

169.   That does not seem to have happened, however.

170.   Connie Offen Sword, interview by author, Toronto, 6 October 1992.

171.   It is signed JMW. Peggy Wemyss was identified as the author by Dorothy Coutts Shields, a neighbour of Peggy's and the sister of John Coutts, who was then editor of the *Annals of the Black and Gold*. Mrs. Shields forwarded a copy of that issue to this author.

172.   Part II was published the following week, on 25 January 1941.

173.   The editors removed a few words in order to save space and made suggestions about a line of dialogue.

174.   *Dance*, 74.

175.   ML to Lorna Nelson, 4 May 1983. Archives, Margaret Laurence Home, Neepawa, and Connie Offen Sword, interview by author. Toronto, 6 October 1992.

176.   John Bell, interview by author, Lakefield, 16 February 1994.

177.   *Winnipeg Free Press*, 19 April, 1941.

178.   *AB&G*, June 1941. This abbreviation of the high-school paper will be used hereafter.

179.   *AB&G*, October 1941. The paper also praised Peggy for her war-time salvage activities.

180.   The history of the Elementary Flying Training School at Neepawa is somewhat complicated. Initially begun as an RAF training site, the school was turned over to the RCAF in 1943 and was known as No.26 EFTS, RCAF. By March 1944, all RAF personnel had been transferred away and replaced by RCAF etc. The base changed names and hands over the several years of its operation, until it closed in 1945.

      The history of the EFTS is chronicled in the following books: *Five Decades of Flying: The History of the Moncton Flying Club*, edited by Roger Mills.(Moncton, New Brunswick: Moncton Flying Club, 1979); *A History of No.35 EFTS, RAF Neepawa*, edited by F/Lt. G.J. Billing and Miss Audrey HumphreyNeepawa, Manitoba: with the permission and under the authority of Mr. J.W. Humphrey, Manager. This book has no pagination. T

181.   Jean Kerr Williams, interview by author, Ottawa, 17 September 1992.

182.   Connie Offen Sword, interview by author, Toronto, 13 June 1993. See also *AB&G*, 1941.

183.   This poem by Peggy has not been previously noted, and only one other poem by her ("Song for Spring, 1944 / Canada") seems to have been published in *AB&G*.

184.   Margaret Laurence spoke with affection of these books many years later with her friends Kate and Kim Krenz who lived in Lakefield. The Krenzes, interview by author, Lakefield, 19 June 1994. See also her essay "Books that Mattered to Me," in *Margaret Laurence: An Appreciation*, 239-49.

185.   Lord Birkenhead, *Rudyard Kipling* (New York: Random House Inc., 1978), 245. *A Choice of Kipling's Verse*, edited by T.S. Eliot (London: Faber and Faber, 1941) included "If," 273-74.

186.   *AB&G*, Christmas issue, 1941.

187.   *AB&G*, Christmas issue 1941, unpaginated. See "Foreign Events."

188.   *The Canadians at War, 1939-45*, vol.2 (Canada: Readers' Digest Canada Ltd., 1969), 123. See also Margaret Laurence's references to Hong Kong in *Dance*, 31, 83-84.

189.   "A History of No.35 EFTS, RAF: Neepawa, Manitoba" by J.W. Humphrey in *Heritage*, 122–124.

190.   *AB&G*, Christmas 1941.

191.   The date of "Goodwill Towards Men" is erroneously given as December 1944 rather than 1941 as cited in *Embryo Words: Margaret Laurence's Early Writings*, edited by Nora Foster Stovel (Edmonton: Juvenilia Press, 1997), 57.

192.   The title appears in capital letters in *AB&G*.

193.   The impact of the base on the town was enormous. In the weeks that followed, all sorts of jobs became available to Manitoba civilians. The town's economy also received a substantial boost from the young airmen in their brass-buttoned blue uniforms, who arrived every six weeks, and from services required by the RAF staff as well as the civilians who worked at the base.

194.   Mona Spratt Meredith remembers that dances at the base were chiefly for adults. When girls of her age went there or to the base at Carberry, they were taken by bus and carefully chaperoned.

195.   The quotation is from the Stan Rogers song "The Field behind the Plow."

196.   Today there is a Commonwealth Air Training Plan Museum in Brandon, Manitoba. "The museum is dedicated to the preservation of the history of the

British Commonwealth Air Training Plan." It also maintains a Web site: /www.airmuseum.ca/

197. *AB&G*, Graduation issue, 1942.

198. Gene Walz, e-mail to author, 16 November 2004.

199. Marjorie Osborn English, interview by author, London, Ontario, 17 June 1993. The students signed their note. Many years later, Margaret Laurence recalled this teacher in a letter to the writer Budge Wilson. Laurence commented favourably on Wilson's multi-layered story "The Metaphor," which deals with a girl and her teacher. Laurence wrote: "It speaks to all our lives, to the time when we might have conveyed love and did not, and then it was too late. Perhaps, too, some thanks for the times when we have indeed conveyed that love before it was too late."

Margaret Laurence also told Budge Wilson that she hoped "The Metaphor" might prompt someone to write to an old teacher, and mentioned her own "great debt of gratitude" to Miss Mildred Musgrove, her high-school teacher of English. Laurence expressed gratitude that she had been able to thank Miss Musgrove publicly over the years. (ML to Budge Wilson, 22 September 1983. Budge Wilson Fonds, Dalhousie University Archives).

200. ML to Budge Wilson, 22 September 1983, Budge Wilson Fonds, Dalhousie University Archives.

201. *Five Decades of Flying*, 56.

202. With the new management the school's name also changed. See Cecil and Maureen Pittman, "Elementary Flying Training School, Neepawa, Manitoba: #35 RAF 1941-43, #26 RCAF 1943-44." *Heritage*, 121-25

203. *Dance*, 83. Laurence on many occasions emphasized the impact that Dieppe had on her. The tenor of her concern is also reflected decades later in her 1980 Convocation address at York University ("A Message to the Inheritors"), and in a slightly rewritten version of that address (typed MS., York University Archives and Special Collections, Margaret Laurence Fonds).

> My world had emerged two years earlier from a six-year peri-
> od of world war. Most of us had lost a member of our family,
> or friends and school-mates. These were the young men of my
> generation who died on the beaches at Dieppe or in France
> and Italy in the final stages of the European war, or in North
> Africa or Hong Kong, or in the ruins of their shot-down planes
> or torpedoed ships. Some of them were the boys from my
> town and surrounding towns, the kids I'd grown up with, sev-
> eral years older that I was. When *Dieppe happened, in 1942*,
> [emphasis added] and so many of them were killed or spent
> the rest of the war in prison camps, I was 16 years old. That
> was when I first realized — really realized — what war meant.
> It meant that many of the people you had known were dead,
> dead at a very young age, and had died horribly.

204. *Dance*, 84.

205. ML to Paul Hiebert, 15 February 1983, University of Manitoba Archives. As an undergraduate, she had known Hiebert, who was then a member of the faculty at the University of Manitoba.

206. *Dance*, 84. Principal Ray was also the class teacher for Grade Twelve.

207.   *AB&G*, Graduation issue, 1944.

208.   Mildred Musgrove, interview by author, Boissevain, 29 September 1991.

209.   ML to Lorna Nelson, 4 May 1983, Archives, Margaret Laurence Home, Neepawa. Margaret Laurence gave a copy of her first novel, *This Side Jordan*, to Mildred Musgrove and inscribed it "with sincere appreciation for all the help and encouragement you gave me when I needed it most" (Mildred Musgrove, photocopy to author).

210.   *AB&G*, Graduation Issue 1942, 1.

211.   *Dance*, 63.

212.   Mona Spratt Meredith, interview by author, Vancouver, 13 October 1992.

213.   *Dance*, 85.

214.   Ibid.

215.   *Dance*, 58, 69, 85.

216.   See interviews by author with Musgrove, Osborn, Offen, Spratt, and Alguire.

217.   *Dance*, 76.

218.   *Dance*, 77. Laurence used almost the same phrasing in a letter to Lorna Nelson (4 May 1983). "Browning's incredible dramatic monologues probably did influence me greatly, in a fascination with the portrayal of a human individual." Archives, Margaret Laurence Home, Neepawa.

219.   ML to Lorna Nelson, 4 May 1983, Archives, Margaret Laurence Home, Neepawa. Laurence also noted that the bible given her by Grandmother Simpson was the only book she owned that went back further in her life, and was more marked and referred to than *The Pocket Book of Verse*.

220.   John W. Coutts, letter to author, 2 September 1992.

221.   Evelyn Vivian, telephone conversation with author, 17 May 1998. Wes McAmmond, interviews by author, Winnipeg, 12 and 17 September 1991.

222.   *Dance*, 79.

223.   *Dance*, 78. The indoor rink had been built in 1935.

224.   Jack Pink, interview by author, Nova Scotia, 11 September 1992.

225.   "Where the World Began," *Heart*, 214.

226.   See *Heritage*. The citizens' helpfulness and good relationship with the base is detailed in *A History of No.35 EFTS., RAF*.

227.   Alice Dalquist received highest academic honours for Grade Eleven.

228.   Contrary to statements by previous biographers (cf. King, 42, Powers, *Alien Heart: The Life and Work of Margaret Laurence*, Winnipeg, University of Manitoba Press, 2003, 40), neither Peggy nor Mona Spratt wrote the "I.M. Nosey" column. It was written by Dorothy Coutts, who made this clear in a letter: "Peggy was the editor of the school paper in 1943 and, in her modesty, refused to allow a write-up of her award. Under the supervision and secrecy of the teacher-advisor for the school paper, Mildred Musgrove, I [Dorothy Coutts] wrote a 'gossip column' entitled 'Here and There' for each issue. Even Peggy didn't know who wrote the column. Since she wouldn't allow an article about her achievement, this column was utilized to pass on her well-deserved accolades." Dorothy Coutts, letter to author, 2 September 1992.

229.   *AB&G*. The particulars of this contemporary description are supported by various articles in the school paper during the previous months which mention that Peggy and her close friends, Louise Alguire, Margie Crawford, and Mona Spratt were busy as convenors of several NCI committees as well as with various other tasks on behalf of the war effort.

230.   In published interviews, Margaret Laurence rarely referred to this summer job,

although she mentions it briefly in *Dance on the Earth*. However, when she visited Neepawa in 1975, Laurence did share some memories of her work as a reporter
and editor for the district news (*Neepawa Press*, 9 October 1975). See also ML to
Lorna Nelson, 25 August 1975. Archives, Margaret Laurence Home, Neepawa.

231. "Through high school and college I thought I would be a journalist, and
indeed I did become one, at least for a year." (*Dance*, 74). Peggy's desk was still
at the *Press* in 1991; the staff claimed that the cigarette burns attested to its having been "Margaret Laurence's" desk.

232. The War Savings Committee under Louise Alguire also exceeded by 600 per-
cent its stated quota for the sale of war savings stamps and bonds. Such success
obviously involved many people both at school and in the community.

233. *Annals of the Black and Gold* had these comments about the orchestra: "We
have another star volunteer who is an old stand-by, having joined the orchestra three years ago. This is none other than our busy editor, Peggy Wemyss."
Margie Crawford also belonged, as did Louise Alguire, who was a fine pianist.

234. *AB&G*, Fall, 1943. This was also the graduation issue for the previous year's class.

235. *AB&G*, graduation issue, 1943.

236. *AB&G*, Christmas issue, 1943.

237. *Dance*, 89.

238. "None of the boys I had ever gone to school with would have given poetry the
time of day." *Dance*, 86.

239. *Dance*, 87.

240. *Dance*, 87.

241. *Dance*, 86.

242. *Dance*, 86-88.

243. *Dance*, 86.

244. *Dance*, 88.

245. A photograph of cadets and officers was included in the No.26, *EFTS Year
Book*.

246. *AB&G*, 1944.

247. This sonnet seems to be the only poem by Peggy that was published in the school
paper after "Scholar's 'If'" appeared when she was in Grade Nine (1939). "Song for
Spring, 1944 \ Canada" was reprinted, however, in Gladys Taylor's essay, "Laurence
of Manitoba," *Canadian Author and Bookman* 42 (Winter 1966): 4-7. But twenty
years later, when Margaret Laurence received a letter from Remi Bouchard, an
accomplished musician and composer who had settled in Neepawa, requesting
permission to set that sonnet to music, she refused. Laurence's reply to him was
uncharacteristically harsh. She said in part: "I am honoured that you would like
to set some words of mine to music, and I must refuse, very adamantly. The poem
to which you are referring ["Song for Spring"] was written by me when I was a
young, young person, and it is a very amateurish poem and I do not wish it to be
broadcast in any way now. I do wish that before that childish poem had been read
[at a town gathering], someone had asked my permission. . . . I do not wish that
poem to be read or circulated or in any way made public now or ever." (Remi
Bouchard, interview by author, Neepawa, 27 October 1997. That letter, ML to
Bouchard, 11 April 1985, may now be found in the Société historique de Saint-
Boniface Archives, Fonds Remi Bouchard, Saint-Boniface, Manitoba.

The vehemence of Laurence's reply is puzzling. It may be attributed to the
frustration she was then experiencing about her own writing and to health
problems which plagued her in 1985-1986, or it could be that the poem was

connected to her youthful romance with Derek and the pain of that may have remained with her, brought to the surface by Bouchard's request.

During her college years, a number of her poems were published in college papers such as *Vox* and *The Manitoban*. Over the years Margaret Laurence continued to write poetry, chiefly occasional pieces intended for her children, dear friends, or relatives. She selected nine poems for inclusion in her memoirs.

248.   *Alberta Poetry Year Book*, 1943-1944, Twelfth Year (Edmonton, Alberta: Canadian Authors' Association, Edmonton Branch).

249.   Ibid.

250.   *Winnipeg Free Press*, Saturday magazine section (4 December 1943): 9.

251.   *Dance*, 89.

252.   Laurence makes clear that her stepmother did not sell the family Limoges china in order to raise money for her college education. See Coles notebook and three pages entitled "The Manawaka Limoges," York University Archives and Special Collections, Margaret Laurence Fonds. ML 89-039, box 14.

253.   I am indebted for background about this period in Laurence's life to the following works: *One University: A History of the University of Manitoba, 1877-1952* by W.L. Morton (Toronto: McClelland & Stewart, 1956); *The University of Winnipeg: Commemorative Journal, 1888-1988*, ed. A.G. Bedford et. al. (Winnipeg: University of Winnipeg, 1988); *The University of Winnipeg: A History of the Founding Colleges* by A.G. Bedford, (Toronto and Buffalo: University of Toronto Press for the University of Winnipeg, 1976); *Turning the World Upside Down: A Memoir* by Lois [Freeman] Wilson (Toronto: Doubleday Canada Ltd., 1989); *Reading from Left to Right: One Man's Political History* by H.S. Ferns (Toronto, Buffalo, London: University of Toronto Press, 1983); *Red Tory Blues: A Political Memoir* by Heath MacQuarrie (Toronto, Buffalo, London: University of Toronto Press, 1992).

254.   Morton, *One University*, 17.

255.   Wilson, *Turning the World Upside* Down, 14.

256.   The University of Manitoba, on the other hand, did have sororities and fraternities.

257.   Dorothie Neil Lindquist, interview with author, Toronto, 8 February 1992.

258.   Helen Warkentin Stanley, interview by author, Shediac Bridge, New Brunswick, 21 July 1996.

259.   Her letter was published in *Annals of the Black and Gold*, "From the Mail Box," December 1944.

260.   Dorothie Neil Lindquist, interview with author, Toronto, 8 February 1992.

261.   Ibid.

262.   *AB&G*, "From the Mail Box," December 1944.

263.   Peggy's friends, Patricia Jenkins and Mary Turnbull, also used male pseudonyms.

264.   See *The Tools of War: 1939-45* (Canada: The Readers' Digest Association Ltd.), 71. Laurence also mentions that pseudonym in an interview with Michael Malegus and Melissa Steele (*The Manitoban Literary Supplement*, 1985, 13). The presence in Neepawa of the Elementary Flying Training School (EFTS) would have made Peggy aware of this powerful plane. During Peggy's first semester at college, *Vox* carried an essay about the pilot of a Lancaster bomber: "Phineas Student Goes to War" (November 1944). An angry anti-war poem "The Children of Europe: A Pastoral" also appeared in that issue.

265.   *Dance*, 96. Ludwig did not actually leave the precincts of the University of Manitoba until March 1946. He was in the Winnipeg area and writing dur-

ing those two years (Jack Ludwig, telephone conversation with author, 2 March 1994).

266.   Details pertaining to this may be found in an unpublished essay by Laurence Wall that was part of his course work for History 236, spring 1975, University of Manitoba (typescript given to author by Wall); See also Barry Broadfoot *Six War Years: Memories of Canadians at Home and Abroad* (Toronto: Doubleday Canada Ltd., 1974).

267.   Shlomo Ben Adam reports that, after debate and discussion in the Manitoba Legislature in 1944, the public learned that: "a specific quota, or 'numerus clausus,' was in effect. Every applicant [to the Medical College] was required to state his father's racial origin and religion, and the forms were sorted into separate lists accordingly. Of the sixty-four available places, fifty-one or fifty-two were reserved for Anglo-Saxon and other preferred candidates, and three or four for women. Four or five places were assigned to Jews and four or five to other 'ethnics.' When a category was filled, no further admission could be made, regardless of the candidate's merit." See "The Unlikely Warrior," in *The Worst of Times, the Best of Times,* edited by Harry and Mildred Gutkind (Markham, Ontario: Fitzhenry and Whiteside, 1987), 181. The Gutkinds also note that "the quota system for Jews and East Europeans was in full force," 73, 203.

268.   Dorothy Beales, a classmate at United, wrote to Stanley Knowles about the discriminatory nature of the quota system and received a four-page letter from him in reply (Dorothy Beales Wyman, interview by author, Mississauga, Ontario, 13 January 1994).

        The SCM was very active at United College. The students were aware of the massive destruction that resulted during the Second World War, and had profound questions about traditional religious teaching. The SCM was a place where those issues could be shared, debated etc. See also Wilson, *Turning the World Upside Down,* 15.

269.   Lois Freeman and Peggy moved in very different circles while at college. Decades later, when Margaret Laurence was living in Ontario, she resumed contact with Lois, who had become an ordained minister in the United Church. Wilson subsequently became the first woman moderator of the United Church in Canada. From the late 1970s until Margaret's death in 1987, the two women were in frequent contact. (Lois Freeman Wilson, telephone conversation with author, 3 January 1992).

270.   Charles Forsyth, telephone conversation with author, 9 December 1996.

271.   Lois Freeman Wilson, telephone conversation with author, 3 January 1992.

272.   In the aftermath of the Depression and the war years, the province gave very little financial support to the colleges.

273.   *Dance,* 95.

274.   Alan Hockin, interview by author, Toronto, 9 January 1992; A.G. Bedford, interview by author, Winnipeg, 16 October 1996; and John Speers, interview by author, Barrie, Ontario, 10 September 1994. The papers of Arthur Phelps are now archived at the University of Manitoba, where they may yield further information about this period. It is hoped that a biography of Arthur Phelps may be published in the not-too-distant future.

275.   Peggy devoted her column "It's in the Air" (*Winnipeg Citizen,* 18 August 1948, 4) to comments about Arthur Phelps, who at that time was broadcasting a series "Books and Things" on the CBC. In it she also mentions his previous series: "This Canada" and "These United States," as well as his class at United College.

276. Dorothy Beales Wyman, interview by author, Mississauga, Ontario, 13 January 1994.

277. Alan Hockin, interview by author, Toronto, 9 January 1992.

278. "It's in the Air," *Winnipeg Citizen*, 18 August 1948.

279. Ibid.

280. When Laurence recounted this in her memoirs, she did not mention Phelps's complimentary remarks (which Alan Hockin had related to her when he later met her in Toronto). Hockin offered this explanation for Laurence's omission of the compliment: "She was not one to brag." (Alan Hockin, interview by author, Toronto, 9 January 1992).

281. Galloway, "Our Myths: Our Selves." *Indirections 2 (Winter 1977)*: 33-42. See also *Vox*, XVII, no. 2 Graduation 1945, 3-4.

282. Ann Phelps Hamilton (daughter of Arthur Phelps) relates that her parents hoped that the club would also provide an opportunity for students, who often came from small prairie towns, to feel comfortable in social settings which they might not previously have experienced. (Ann Phelps Hamilton, interview by author, Toronto, 17 October 1991).

283. *Dance*, 94.

284. Peterson received her doctorate from the University of Minnesota. At one meeting they discussed Somerset Maugham's recent novel, *The Razor's Edge*, Although Peggy continued to attend the English Club meetings after Phelps's departure, for her, things were not quite the same without him.

285. Doris Peterson Franklin, telephone conversation with author, 16 December 1996.

286. When Peggy was an undergraduate, T.S. Eliot's work also was taught by Doris Peterson and other members of United College's English department. (Max Cohn, interview by author, Montreal, 12 February 1997). See also course outline and notes of Peggy's classmate Patricia (Jenkins) Blondal. University of British Columbia, Blondal Papers.

    Professor Roy Daniells, who had been a member of the English department at the University of Manitoba, also admired and taught the work of T.S. Eliot. Daniells, however, left Winnipeg in 1946 to take up a position at the University of British Columbia. There is no evidence that Peggy enrolled in Daniells's class at the Fort Garry campus during her first two years of college. She does not refer to him among the many professors from her college years whom she does mention in *Dance on the Earth*, and nothing on her transcript indicates that she was in his class, although she was in contact with him many years later when she lived in British Columbia.

287. Stirling Lyon later became premier of Manitoba. Heath MacQuarrie had a long career in public service, retiring as the senior senator from Prince Edward Island, and Lyall Powers, whom Laurence says she always considered as an older brother (ML. Journal, MS. McMaster University), became distinguished as a professor of English literature at the University of Michigan. He also wrote a biography of Laurence, *Alien Heart.*

288. A.G. Bedford, interviews by author, Winnipeg, 16 October 1996. Bedford later joined the faculty at the University of Winnipeg (formerly United College). Heath MacQuarrie, interview by author, Victoria by the Sea, Prince Edward Island, 11 July 1995.

289. Helen Warkentin Stanley, interview by author, Shediac Bridge, New Brunswick, 21 July 1996.

290.   Madge Hetherington Allen, interview by author, Toronto, 9 January 1992. After graduation, Madge went to Toronto, where she earned a Master's degree in Social Work.

291.   Ibid.

292.   Additional details about this will be found here in Chapter Nine.

293.   See ML to Professor Laurie Ricou, 12 October 1973. He included excerpts from her letter in his biographical entry for Patricia Jenkins Blondal in the *Dictionary of Literary Biography: Canadian Writers 1920-1959*, Second Series, 88. (Detroit, Michigan: Gale Research Inc., 1989): 29-32.

       In her senior year, Patricia Jenkins married Harold Blondal from Deep River, Ontario, and after that she and Peggy did not see as much of one another. After graduation, both Pat and Peggy wrote for Winnipeg newspapers.

294.   Margaret Laurence, preface to *The Collected Plays of Gwen Pharis Ringwood*. (Ottawa: Borealis Press, 1982), xi. See also Robert Kroetsch, "A Conversation with Margaret Laurence," in *A Place to Stand On: Essays by and about Margaret Laurence*, edited by George Woodcock (Edmonton: NeWest Press, 1983), 46-55.

295.   Robert Kroetsch, "A Conversation with Margaret Laurence," in *A Place to Stand On: Essays by and about Margaret Laurence*, edited by George Woodcock (Edmonton: NeWest Press, 1983), 54.

296.   *Vox* XVIII, no.3, Graduation 1945, 8.

297.   "Margaret Laurence and Nuclear War," CBC broadcast, 1985, 9 min. National Archives, Ottawa.

298.   See David Jay Bercuson, *Confrontation at Winnipeg: Labour, Industrial Relations and the General Strike*. (Toronto: McGill-Queen's University Press, 1974).

299.   *Dance*, 91. Founded in Canada in the 1930s, the CCF was a political party based on democratic socialist ideals.

300.   Ann Phelps Hamilton, interview by author, Toronto, 17 October 1991.

301.   Convocation address to Emmanuel College, Victoria University, University of Toronto, 6 May 1982. In Woodcock, *A Place to Stand On* , 56-60.

302.   ML to Paul Hiebert, 15 February 1983. Hiebert Collection, University of Manitoba Archives.

303.   Wilson, *Turning the World Upside Down*, 237.

304.   Joyce Friesen, telephone conversation with author, 9 February 1997.

305.   *The Manitoban*, 1 October 1946.

306.   Alan Hockin, interview by author, Toronto, 9 January 1992.

307.   Margaret Laurence, "Tribute to Malcolm Ross." MS.York University Archives and Special Collections, Margaret Laurence Fonds. Ross is warmly remembered by many Canadians as an inspiring teacher, thoughtful literary critic, and an enthusiastic founding editor of the New Canadian Library series issued by McClelland & Stewart under the aegis of its publisher Jack McClelland.

308.   John Speers, interview by author, Barrie, Ontario, 10 September 1994.

309.   Ibid.

310.   Ross pointed out that his lectures had been further developed and refined at Queen's University, Kingston, although many of the ideas in that book had been part of his seminar when Margaret Laurence [Peggy Wemyss] was in his class (Malcolm Ross to author, 2 August 1994). Professor Ross subsequently became very involved with Canadian literature, about which he said, "'I am not preaching nationalism in the old European meaning of the word, rather I am trying to define a community which opens into the community of man." *The Impossible Sum of Our Traditions*. (Toronto: McClelland & Stewart, 1986), 11.

311.   John Fraser, "An Afternoon, an Institution, a Revelation." York University Archives and Special Collection, Margaret Laurence Fonds.

312.   John Speers, interview by author, Barrie, Ontario, 10 September 1994.

313.   Ibid.

314.   Although both young women studied with Professor Ross, it does not seem that they met in his class. When Peggy took Ross's seminar during 1946-1947, Adele was in her second year at the University of Manitoba. It is doubtful that they were enrolled in his seminar at the same time. Moreover, neither of them has referred to that as a joint experience.

315.   As quoted by David Staines, introduction to *The Impossible Sum of Our Traditions*, 10-11. Dean Roland Penner, a former student of Malcolm Ross, refers to him as a "tremendously great teacher of English and an English scholar," adding the caveat "and I don't use the term great, lightly. Malcolm Ross stimulated *all* of us." Dean Roland Penner, interview by author, Winnipeg, 5 October 1992.

316.   Not to be confused with Dean Carl Hallstead of the Collegiate Division of United College. Robert Halstead hailed from Pennsylvania and had done graduate work at Cornell University, as had Malcolm Ross.

317.   Anne Halstead, telephone conversation with author, 5 October 1992.

318.   ML letters to Robert Halstead (January 1965, April 1965, July 1965, January 1966). Halstead Archives, University of Winnipeg.

319.   Professor Daniell's letter as well as a modernist poem by Malcolm Ross appeared in *The Manitoban*, 24 November 1946.

New Day
by Malcolm Ross

The whispering before the door
    ceased
as the bell began in the chapel
and the young hill came in
    at the window
Morning birds darkened the room
their throats and their wings about me
There was no time for a proper adieu
to the tall cool orange glass at my
    elbow.

320.   For Laurence's comments on the internment of Japanese Canadians, see *Dance*, 81. Further information about that period may be found in Ken Adachi, *The Enemy That Never Was: A History of the Japanese Canadians*. (Toronto: McClelland & Stewart, 1976).

321.   For a history of the Roslyn Road community and the life and thought of Watson Thomson, see Michael Welton's excellent, comprehensive study "To Be and Build the Glorious World": The Educational Thought and Practice of Watson Thomson, 1899-1946." (Unpublished Ph.D. dissertation, University of British Columbia, 1983), referred to hereafter as "To Be and Build," and Watson Thomson's autobiography *Turning into Tomorrow* (New York: The Philosophical Library, 1966).

322.   Welton, "To Be and Build," 308.

323.   Ibid., ii.

324.   Ibid., 311.

325.   Professor Doris Peterson, telephone interview with author, 4 January 1997. Peterson herself was renting that apartment from Professor Meredith Thompson and she sublet it to Mary and Peggy.

326.   See Laurence's comments in Wainwright, *A Very Large Soul*, 17-18.

327.   The poem does not seem to have been published in Laurence's lifetime. The text, which is in the York University archives, has been discussed by Margaret A. Wigmore, who published it in *Prairie Fire* 20, no.2 (Summer 1999): 100-109, along with an essay on its significance, "North Main Car: A Context," 110-13. The poem was also included in *Colors of Speech*, selections from Laurence's early writing, edited and with an introduction by Nora Foster Stovel (Edmonton: Juvenilia Press, 2000).

328.   See, for example, Harry and Mildred Gutkind, eds. *The Worst of Times, The Best of Times* (Markham, Ontario: Fitzhenry and Whiteside, 1987); Birk Sproxton and G.N. Louise Jonasson, eds., *Winnipeg in Fiction: 125 Years of English-Language Writing*, a special issue of *Prairie Fire* 20, no.2 (Summer 1999).

329.   *Dance*, 108.

330.   Mary Turnbull Mindess, interview by author, Winnipeg, 3 December 1991.

331.   A copy of the invitation to this party was sent to this author by the former Jeannette Grosney, who had also worked at the *Winnipeg Citizen* and was a friend of Mary Turnbull.

332.   *Dance*, 102.

333.   Walking upstairs in her grandparents' house, the thought "I have to be a writer" came to her "with enormous strength." Laurence reports the idea "appalled and frightened [her]." *Dance*, 74.

334.   Welton, "To Be and Build," 312. See also, ML to AW, 2 January 1954.

335.   Kay Bolton, interview by author, Montreal, February 1997; and Michael Welton, interview by author, Halifax, 20 July 1994. Welton had previously interviewed Kay Bolton when he was researching his study of Watson Thomson ("To Be and Build a Glorious World").

336.   Else Fry Laurence puts the date at 1939, but she may have attended in 1940, as well, according to records for the school. See also, Elsie Laurence, letter to Michael Welton ("To Be and Build," 158).

337.   Elsie Fry Laurence, letter to Michael Welton. ("To Be and Build," 158).

338.   Information about the Roslyn Road community was gathered from interviews with Kay Bolton, Mary (Mrs. Watson) Thomson, Michael Welton, Leone Wilcox, and Harry Penny. Welton and Penny have written extensively on Watson Thomson and his intentional community.

339.   Author interviews with Mona Spratt, Vancouver, 13 October 1992; Enid Rutland, Ottawa, 13 February 1997; John Speers, Ontario, 10 September 1994.

340.   *Dance*, 86-87.

341.   Other members of Jack Laurence's family said that their father seemed to resent the fact that his wife wrote, and they reported that he actually destroyed or insisted that Elsie destroy some of her writing, despite the fact that, when he was out of work, a little income from his wife's writing provided much-needed financial assistance to the family.

342.   *Dance*, 91.

343.   See Arthur L. Phelps, *Canadian Writers*. (Toronto: McClelland & Stewart, 1951).

The distinguished Canadian historian, Arthur M. Lower, was a good friend of Arthur Phelps. The manuscript of Lower's unpublished biographical essay about Phelps is at Queen's University, Kingston, Ontario, Arthur M. Lower Fonds.

344.   A.G. Bedford, interview by author, Winnipeg, 16 October 1996.

345.   Ibid.

346.   John Speers quoted these lines from Wordsworth's *The Prelude*, Book xi, during an interview by the author, Barrie, Ontario, 10 September, 1994.

347.   Because the archival holdings of *Vox* and *The Manitoban* may not be complete, it is possible that other poems may have appeared in issues that have not been archived.

348.   The poems are: "Thought," 13 October 1944, 3; "The Imperishable," 17 October 1944, 3; and "Bus-Ride at Night," 20 October 1944, 3; "Pagan Point — Wasagaming — Approaching Night," *The Manitoban*, 3 November 1944, 3. This was signed JMW. It seems, however, that her first appearance in a college literary journal was "Fallen King," a rather short piece of fiction.

349.   She signed herself as follows: JMW (her initials), J.M. Wemyss, Margaret Jean Wemyss, or Jean Margaret Wemyss (her full name). The single exception occurs in *Vox* XVIII: 3 where "Peggy Weymss" [sic] appears. This concern about an appropriate "literary" signature is not untypical with aspiring writers.

350.   A copy of the poem was given to this author by Mildred Musgrove, who taught Peggy at Neepawa Collegiate Institute.

351.   *The Manitoban*, 3 November 1944, 3. This was signed JMW.

352.   The only reference to this poem seems to be in her moving essay, "An Open Letter to the Mother of Joe Bass." "Heart, 200-203. Her essay, which was occasioned by the race riots in the U.S.A., has received little, if any, attention from biographers and critics.

353.   United College's yearbook write-up (1947) comments on Peggy's fondness for Jeffers's poetry.

354.   This poem appeared in *The Manitoban*, 9 October 1945, not November.

355.   These are simply titled "Poems."

356.   "Song of the Race of Ulysses" and "Bread Hath He" were published in *Vox* XX, no. 2 (March 1947), not March of 1944, as stated in Stovel, *Embryo Words*, when, in fact, Peggy was still in high school).

357.   See *Vox* XX, no.3 (December 1947). MacQuarrie's valedictory remarks are reminiscent of those in editorials by Herb Ray, Peggy's principal at NCI.

358.   I am indebted to the Nova Scotia poet and historian Sandra L. Barry for her comments about Margaret Laurence's poetry.

359.   Author interviews with Roland Penner, John Speers, Jack Ludwig, and A.G. Bedford. Adele Wiseman also remarked that, when she first knew Peggy, she thought of her primarily as a poet.

360.   "Fallen King," mentioned previously, is less significant in terms of her efforts with short fiction.

361.   "Letter to Bob Sorfleet," 13 November 1978, in *Journal of Canadian Fiction*, 27 (1980): 52–53. The visit to Carman was also commented on by Madge Hetherington Allen, interview by author, Toronto, 9 January 1992.

362.   Ibid.

363.   Ibid.

364.   ML, "Letter to Bob Sorfleet."

365.   *Vox* XX, no.2 (March 1947): 5-8.

366.   *Tamarack Review* 32 (Summer 1964).

367. For more information about the *Winnipeg Citizen*, see publications by Harry Ferns; Kenneth Goldstein; and Noelle Boughton.
368. John Marshall, interview by author, Toronto, 16 December 1991.
369. It seems misleading to suggest that Louise and Mona did not attend because of disagreements with Peggy. Cf. King, 48.
370. When Peggy Wemyss began working for this paper in May 1947, it was called the *Western Tribune*, abbreviated hereafter as *TWT*. The name on the masthead changed to *The Westerner* during June 1947 (*TW*).
371. She realized, however, that some of the staff were members of the Communist Party and recalled their idealism with respect (*Dance*, 107). See also ML to Al Purdy, 23 October 1967. *Selected Letters of Margaret Laurence and Adele Wiseman*. Edited by John Lennox and Ruth Panofsky. (Toronto: University of Toronto Press, 1997), 61. Hereafter Lennox and Panofsky.

There are hundreds of letters between Margaret Laurence and Adele Wiseman in the archives at York University, Ontario. These letters were unpublished at the time of this author's research there. In 1997, however, a selection from this correspondence was published in an important volume, *Selected Letters of Margaret Laurence and Adele Wiseman*, edited with an excellent introductory essay and extensive notes by John Lennox and Ruth Panofsky (University of Toronto Press, 1997). For ease of reference for others, I have, therefore, cited that volume when a particular letter can be found there.
372. For a more detailed account of her newspaper columns, see Donez Xiques, "Early Influences: Laurence's Newspaper Career," in *Challenging Territory*, edited by Chris Riegel. (Edmonton: The University of Alberta Press, 1997), 187- 210.
373. Jean Cole, a writer and friend from the Peterborough/Lakefield area of Ontario, reports that Margaret did talk about her journalism days with Alf, Jean's husband, who was a writer and journalist. Jean Cole, interview by author, Lakefield, 7 June 1994.
374. *TWT*, May 3, 1947.
375. *TW*, 30 August 1947.
376. *TW*, 6 September 1947.
377. Adele Wiseman, interview by author, Toronto, 9 November 1991.
378. *TW*, 13 September 1947.
379. See Chapter II, "The Nuisance Grounds," *The Diviners*, 124-32.
380. *TW*, 11 October 1947.
381. The history of this unique newspaper has been chronicled in Master's theses by Kenneth Goldstein,"The *Winnipeg Citizen*: A History and Analysis of the World's first Co-operative-owned Daily Newspaper." Ryerson Polytechnical Institute (1966), and by Noelle Boughton. "The Fall of the *Winnipeg Citizen*." Carleton University (1978). See also H.S. Crowe, "The *Winnipeg Citizen*: First Co-op Newspaper " *The Canadian Forum*, XXVII (March 1948): 273-74; and Professor Harry S. Ferns *Reading from Left to Right: One Man's Political History* (Toronto: University of Toronto Press, 1983). During the early days of the paper, one of Ferns's talented former history students, Jeannette Grosney '46, gave important direction to the running of the paper's first office (Ferns, 238-39).
382. Kenneth Goldstein, interview by author, Winnipeg, 1 October 1991. He recalls that Laurence mentioned that working on the labour beat was "just wild."
383. For details about the staff, see Goldstein.
384. *Dance*, 107. By 1949 Peggy Laurence was no longer writing for this paper and

there are no articles with her byline in the *Winnipeg Citizen* during that year.

385.   Anne Ross, interview by author, Winnipeg, 30 September 1991; and Shirley Lev Sharzer, interview by author, Ottawa, 24 October 1991.

386.   Professor J.C. Woodbury, telephone conversation with author, 3 May 1993; and Shirley Sharzer, interview by author, Ottawa, 24 October 1991.

387.   "In the Air" was limited to two columns, but the length of the columns varied. This feature appeared six days a week from the paper's inception in March 1948 to mid-July 1948. As the result of an acute shortage of newsprint during the postwar period, however, the number of pages was subsequently reduced, and Peggy Laurence's column then appeared only once a week rather than daily.

388.   *TW*, 2 August 1947.

389.   *TW*, 2 August 1947.

390.   *TW*, 2 August 1947. In 1962, however, Margaret Laurence favourably reviewed W.O. Mitchell's novel *Jake and the Kid* in *Canadian Literature* 11 (1962): 68-70.

391.   *WC*, 24 May 1948.

392.   *WC*, 17 April 1948.

393.   Kenneth Goldstein, interview by author, Winnipeg, 1 October 1991.

394.   *WC*, 3 April and 7 June, 1948.

395.   *WC*, 7 June 1948.

396.   *WC*, 9 April 1948.

397.   In 1948, CKSB reached every French community in the province of Manitoba. There were fifty-two communities within the station's primary coverage area, which extended as far as Kenora in Ontario.

398.   *WC*, 5 April 1948.

399.   *WC*, 25 March 1948.

400.   *WC*, 15 April 1948.

401.   *WC*, 6 May 1948.

402.   *WC*, 4 March 1948.

403.   *WC*, 2 March 1948.

404.   *WC*, 11 May 1948.

405.   *WC*, 11 May 1948.

406.   *WC*, 6 April 1948. See also Peggy's columns on 7 and 8 April, 3 May, and 13 July 1948. Adele Wiseman, in a column for *The Westerner* in July 1947, called attention to a brief that had been presented to the Commons Radio Committee. It alleged that Canada was nothing but a "dumping ground for American talent," and that the cost of "piping in" American programs was so little that advertisers preferred to do that rather than use Canadian talent. The brief demanded, among other things, that some sort of tariff be established to protect Canadian talent (*TW*, 12 July 1947).

407.   *TWT*, 3 May 1947.

408.   *WC*, 15 September 1948.

409.   *WC*, 12 May 1948.

410.   *WC*, 22 April 1948.

411.   *WC*, 6 April 1948.

412.   *WC*, 19 May 1948.

413.   *WC*, 28 May 1948.

414.   *WC*, 27 May 1948.

415.   *WC*, 8 June 1948.

416.   *WC*, 8 June 1948.

417.   *WC*, 17 March 1948.

418.   *WC*, 22 March 1948.

419.   *Dance*, 108. Some sense of the distinctive character of Winnipeg's North End during that period is conveyed in Gutkind, *The Worst of Times, The Best of Times* (Markham, Ontario: Fitzhenry and Whiteside, 1987), as well as in Adele Wiseman's *Memoirs of a Book Molesting Childhood and Other Essays* (Toronto: Oxford University Press, 1987), and the paintings of A.J. Paquette, a number of which are reproduced in his book, *Markings: Scenes and Recollections of Winnipeg's North End* (Winnipeg: Loch & Mayberry, 1995).

420.   Anne Ross, interview by author, Winnipeg, 30 September 1991.

421.   Ibid.

422.   Decades later, after Anne Ross had become executive director of the Mount Carmel Clinic in Winnipeg, she called upon her experiences at the clinic to write *Pregnant and Alone* (Toronto: McClelland & Stewart, 1978), and turned to Margaret for advice about her manuscript, which Laurence willingly gave.

423.   Anne Ross, interview by author, Winnipeg, 30 September 1991.

424.   *Dance*, 108. Given Peggy's penchant for writing, it is possible that she wrote for an in-house publication or newsletter at the YWCA.

425.   *Dance*, 107.

426.   Kenneth Goldstein, interview by author, Winnipeg, 1 October 1991.

427.   Ferns, *Reading from Left to Right*, 251.

428.   Roland Penner, interview by author, Winnipeg, 5 October 1992; Anne Ross, interview by author, Winnipeg, 30 September 1991. See also *Dance*, 107-108.

429.   *WC*, 22 September 1948. In addition to her regular column, "In the Air," Peggy Wemyss/Laurence probably wrote a number of unsigned articles while on staff at *The Westerner* and the *Winnipeg Citizen*.

430.   "The Greater Evil," *Toronto Life*, September 1984. Laurence included this essay in the second part of her memoirs, *Dance on the Earth*, 265-74.

431.   Harold Horwood, "Unforgettable Margaret Laurence," *Reader`s Digest* (April 1988): 107-11.

432.   *The Prophet's Camel Bell*, paperback edition (Toronto: McClelland & Stewart, 1963, rpt. 1988), with afterword by Clara Thomas, 11. References throughout are to this edition, since it is widely available; abbreviated hereafter as *PCB*.

433.   *PCB*, 14.

434.   ML to Adele and the Wiseman family, 24 November 1949. York University Archives and Special Collections, Margaret Laurence Fonds.

435.   Jack Laurence to AW, 16 July 1950. The Eliot passage is from "The Love Song of J. Alfred Prufrock."

436.   ML to AW, 16 July 1950. York University Archives and Special Collections, Margaret Laurence Fonds.

437.   ML to AW, 28 January 1950 in Lennox and Panofsky, 34-37.

438.   Ibid.

439.   ML to the Wiseman family, 1 January 1950. York University Archives and Special Collections, Margaret Laurence Fonds.

440.   This quotation and the details are from Laurence's review of *Radclyffe Hall at the Well of Loneliness*, a biography written by Lovat Dickson, Margaret's former editor, at Macmillan, London. *Globe and Mail* (30 August 1975): 28-29.

441.   Roland Penner, interview by author, Winnipeg, 5 October 1992.

442.   Helen Warkentin Stanley, interview by author, Shediac Bridge. New Brunswick,

21 July 1996. Helen and Peggy had been roommates during their first two years at United College.

443. Joyce Friesen, telephone conversation with author, 9 February 1997.

444. The poem contains echoes of Robinson Jeffers, a poet whom she had admired when she was an undergraduate. Laurence wrote an essay about Jeffers that appeared in *Vox* XX, 2 (March 1947), 5-8.

445. Laurence mentions these poems in a letter to Adele, 28 January 1950. Lennox and Panofsky, 34.

446. ML to the Wiseman Family, 17 November 1950. York University Archives and Special Collections, Margaret Laurence Fonds.

447. *PCB*, 12.

448. Peggy referred to John Ruskin's remarks on the subject (ML to AW, 27 December 1950), Lennox and Panofsky, 44.

449. All quotations in this paragraph are from ML to AW, 27 December 1950. Lennox and Panofsky, 43.

450. *PCB*, 13.

451. ML to AW, 27 December 1950. Lennox and Panofsky, 46-47.

452. In a letter to Clara Thomas, Margaret Laurence clarified the origin of the reference to the stone angel and offered details about the Staglieno cemetery in Italy and the stone angel there. (See York University, Archives and Special Collections, Clara Thomas Fonds). Although there is a large stone angel in the cemetery at Neepawa, which townspeople have "claimed" as the angel referred to in that novel, Laurence has given no support for that assumption, which probably arose from an understandable desire by some townspeople to equate many of the places in Margaret's hometown with the fictional town of Manawaka.

453. *PCB*, 15.

454. Sixteen years later Margaret Laurence returned to Port Said on assignment for *Holiday*. The resulting essay, "Captain Pilot Shawkat and Kipling's Ghost," was published in *Heart of a Stranger*, 109-129.

455. *PCB*, 24.

456. Ibid., 23.

457. Ibid., 20.

458. ML to AW, 12 February 1951. Lennox and Panofsky, 48.

459. See Margaret Castagno, *Historical Dictionary of Somalia* (Metuchen, NewJersey: The Scarecrow Press, 1975). This work, initiated by Alphonso A. Castagno, was completed by his widow and remains very helpful in explaining aspects of life in Somaliland during this period.

460. During the very hot season, the colonials preferred Sheikh to Hargeisa, even though it involved a round-trip journey of two days.

461. All quotations in this paragraph are from ML to AW, 12 February 1951. Lennox and Panofsky, 47-51.

462. Ibid.

463. Ibid.

464. Ibid.

465. *PCB*, 57.

466. ML to AW, 19 February 1951. York University Archives and Special Collections, Margaret Laurence Fonds.

467. ML to AW, 29 March 1951, airletter #1. York University Archives and Special Collections, Margaret Laurence Fonds.

468. ML to B.W. Andrzejewski, 9 November 1951. York University, Archives and

Special Collections, Margaret Laurence Fonds.

469. *PCB*, 59.

470. "Lost in the Storm," Radio Letter #2. March 1954. MS. Elizabeth Long Papers, University of Waterloo Archives.

471. *PCB*, 77.

472. See "Lost in the Storm." Radio Letter #2, March 1954. MS. Elizabeth Long Papers, University of Waterloo Archives. See also *PCB*, 77-78.

473. C.J. Martin to author, 22 April 1989. In the Protectorate he was then known as "Bob" Martin.

474. *PCB*, 228. After he retired to England, Philip Shirley wrote to Margaret Laurence about *The Prophet's Camel Bell*. He praised her analysis and remarked that he did not think she had been hard on some of the colonialists. Then, he made an important distinction, namely that it was not so much the Colonial attitude as such, but it was the attitude of a section of society which is always "'objectionable,' but whose 'small talk' is more unfair and stupid in such countries. We have 'memsahibs' in our village [in England] who have never been much further than Norwich." Philip Shirley to Margaret Laurence, 3 October 1963. Trent University Archives.

475. *Heart*, 54.

476. "Lost in the Storm." Radio Letter #2, March 1954. MS. University of Waterloo Archives, Elizabeth Long papers.

477. *PCB*, 87.

478. Ibid., 88-89.

479. Ibid., 89.

480. Ibid., 94.

481. Laurence also recounts this in her unpublished Journal, 18 August 1986, MS. McMaster University Archives.

482. *PCB*, 71.

482. Ibid., 96.

484. Sheila Andrzejewski, e-mail to the author, 23 November 2004.

485. ML to AW, 22 December 1952. York University Archives and Special Collections, Margaret Laurence Fonds.

486. T.S. Eliot, *Four Quartets*, "Burnt Norton," II.

487. *PCB*, 96.

488. Ibid., 96

489. ML to AW, 12 February 1951. Lennox and Panofsky, 51.

490. J.W.C. Kirk published an English grammar of the Somali language in 1905, but it was neither complete nor current. Kirk's book was in Laurence's library at the time of her death. Chris Bell had also worked on a grammar when he was director of the government school in Sheikh.

491. Margaret Laurence in her letters referred to him as Goosh, and his wife, Sheila, states that he was never called Bogumil. His countrymen referred to him as Bogus, and he anglicized the spelling to Goosh. Sheila Andrzejewski, e-mail to author, 26 February 2001.

492. His poems were praised by Czeslaw Milosz, the distinguished Polish author and Nobel Laureate (Shelia Andrzejewski, letter to author, 1 August 1995). Goosh's wife pointed out that her husband's poems, which are in Polish, have such nuance and verbal play that they are very difficult to translate into English. She noted, moreover, that the complexity and subtlety of Goosh's poems are very different from the traditional Somali poems that he translated.

493.   See obituaries: "A Wise Scholar in Somalia," by Anita Suleman Adam, the *Guardian*, 14 December 1994; "Professor B.W. Andrzejewski," by I.M. Lewis, the *Independent*, 6 December 1994; and "Professor Bogumil Witalis Andrzejewski" by Martin Orwin, *Bulletin of the School of Oriental and African Studies*, University of London, vol. LIX, Part I, 1996.

494.   Anita Suleman Adam, "A Wise Scholar in Somalia." *Guardian*, 14 December 1994.

495.   After completing his doctoral studies, B.W. (Goosh) Andrzejewski returned to Somalia on many other occasions and was held in high esteem by the people of Somalia.

496.   B.W. Andrzejewski to author, 11 April 1989.

497.   Ibid.

498.   ML to B.W.Andrzejewski, 12 May 1962. York University, Archives and Special Collections, Margaret Laurence Fonds.

499.   Sheila Andrzejewski, e-mail to the author, 17 April 2001.

500.   In due course, when Professor Andrzejewski had the opportunity to refine his notes and supplement his field work with additional analysis back in England, he published many books and articles on the subject. In the years that followed he became recognized world-wide as an authority on the subject.

501.   ML to AW, 2 May 1951. Lennox and Panofsky, 52.

502.   T.S. Eliot, "What the Thunder Said," in *The Wasteland*, Section V, lines 331-33, 336.

503.   ML to AW, 2 May 1951. Lennox and Panofsky, 51.

504.   C.J. Martin letter to author, 22 April 1989.

505.   In his youth, Musa Haji Ismail Galaal had been a nomadic pastoralist. Later he became a teacher and subsequently engaged in linguistic and literary research at the Department of Education at Sheikh. He also spent three years at the School of Oriental and African Studies, University of London. After returning to Somalia, which by then had become an independent country, Musa Galaal was recognized as a national authority on the Somali language.

506.   B.W. Andrzejewski clarified this point in a letter to the author, 24 November 1991.

507.   *PCB*, 113.

508.   B.W. Andrzejewski letter to author, 24 November 1991.

509.   The Transcription Centre, London, under the directorship of Professor Dennis Duerden, amassed a tape library of discussions, talks, and interviews, originally produced for broadcast over various radio networks in Africa. Most of that material is now archived in the United States, at the Harry Ransom Research Center, University of Texas (Austin) and at the University of Indiana.

510.   *A Tree for Poverty: Somali Poetry and Prose* (Shannon, Ireland: Irish University Press and Mc Master University Library, 1970), 36. (This reprint is a photolithographic facsimile of the first edition and unabridged even to the extent of retaining original printer's imprint). Hereafter *Tree*.

511.   *PCB*, 94.

512.   Although Peggy used the spelling, "gabei" in *A Tree for Poverty*, she later adopted "gabay" in *The Prophet's Camel Bell*. The latter had become the accepted spelling by then, and for that reason has been used throughout this book.

513.   ML to AW, 4 September 1951. Lennox and Panofsky, 63.

514.   Introduction to *Tree*, 4.

515.   Ibid.

516.   *PCB*, 106. For a more detailed discussion of the challenge which these poems presented for Laurence, see Xiques "Margaret Laurence's Somali Translations," *Canadian Literature* 135 (Winter 1992): 33-48.

517. These two versions appear in Xiques, "Margaret Laurence's Somali Translations," 46.

518. *PCB*, 248.

519. ML to AW, 15 June 1951. Lennox and Panofsky, 55.

520. C.J. Martin letter to author, 28 March 1990.

521. In that book see especially Chapters 6 and 7. In the "Acknowledgements" to *A Tree for Poverty*, Margaret Laurence thanks by name all those who gave her assistance with the translations.

522. ML to AW, 2 May 1951. Lennox and Panofsky, 52. All information in this paragraph is taken from this letter.

523. ML to B.W. Andrzejewski, 9 November 1951. York University Archives and Special Collections, Margaret Laurence Fonds. Unfortunately, Hersi Jama did lose the use of that hand.

524. Ibid. Some of this information is also in *PCB*, 174-75.

525. All quotations in this paragraph are from *PCB*, 117.

526. ML to B.W.Andrzejewski, 21 July 1951. York University Archives and Special Collections, Margaret Laurence Fonds.

527. King, 84-85. Margaret Laurence describes the journey to Djibouti and Zeilah in her contemporary letters and in *The Prophet's Camel Bell* (118-133). After the hazards and challenges that she and Jack endured as they tried to reach Djibouti in time to meet the shipment of tractors, Laurence describes the place and its inhabitants in great detail, referring to it as the "shabby Paris of the Gulf of Aden." Although they sometimes went out to dinner and a nightclub, that was expected of an engineer and his wife. It was also a respite from the day's harsh labours and intense heat. Margaret Laurence concluded her comments about that trip with the statement: "We were as glad to leave Djibouti as we had been to arrive . . . . Djibouti — may we never see you again." *PCB*, 133.

528. ML to AW, 4 September 1951. Lennox and Panofsky, 60.

529. ML to Elsie and John Laurence, 14 August 1951.

530. *PCB*, 106.

531. ML to Elsie and John Laurence, 14 August 1951.

532. ML to B.W.Andrzejewski, 9 November 1951.York University Archives and Special Collections, Margaret Laurence Fonds.

533. Tim Howells, telephone conversation with author, 16 May 1990.

534. R.W. Turnbull letter to author, 15 July 1989. After leaving the Protectorate, Rob Turnbull became a veterinarian. While in the Protectorate he had worked with Edward Peck, who is "Ernest" in *The Prophet's Camel Bell*.

535. Tim Howells, telephone conversation with author, 16 May 1990.

536. In a letter to B.W. Andrzejewski, 9 November 1951, Peggy mentions several people in the colonial service whom she and Jack liked and with whom they did enjoy socializing. York University Archives and Special Collections, Margaret Laurence Fonds.

537. Michael Wilson to letter author, 6 January 1992. Wilson's impressive character is described by Laurence in a telling anecdote in *The Prophet's Camel Bell*, where she changed his name to "Matthew," pp.40-44.

538. Michael Wilson later joined the UNO and went to Uganda and Afghanistan for about sixteen years. Over the years, he and Peggy exchanged many letters (Michael Wilson, letter to author, 6 January 1992).

539. ML to B.W.Andrzejewski, 9 November 1951. York University Archives and

Special Collections, Margaret Laurence Fonds.

540.   ML to AW, 4 September 1951, Airletter #3. York University Archives and Special Collections, Margaret Laurence Fonds.

541.   Ibid.

542.   Ibid.

543.   Margaret Laurence makes that clear in a letter to Goosh Andrzejewski and his wife, Sheila (9 November 1951). York University, Archives and Special Collections, Margaret Laurence Fonds.

544.   ML to AW, 30 January 1952. Lennox and Panofsky, 72.

545.   Ibid.

546.   ML to Whit Burnett, 5 November 1951. Princeton University, *Story* archives, box 112.

547.   As quoted in Ludwig. "You Always Go Home Again," *Mosaic* 3 (Spring 1970), 107-11.

548.   Ludwig, 193.

549.   There may be some correspondence between Philip Shirley, (E.P.S. Shirley, CMG, OBE) and Peggy between 1952 and1954 in the Colonial Archives at the Public Records Office in England. But it is unlikely that any trace remains in Somalia, since the government buildings in Mogadishu were destroyed by artillery barrage in the 1990s. Shirley's son, William, thought their correspondence was no longer extant (William Shirley, letter to author, 26 March 1990).

550.   ML to AW, 30 January 1952. Lennox and Panofsky, 71.

551.   Ibid.

552.   ML to B.W. Andrzejewski, 22 April 1952. York University, Archives and Special Collections, Margaret Laurence Fonds.

553.   *PCB*, 247.

554.   C.J. Martin, letter to author, 27 April 1989.

555.   *PCB*, 245.

556.   Ibid.

557.   Philip Shirley to ML, 3 October 1963, Trent University Archives.

558.   Ann Phelps Hamilton, interview by author, 17 October 1991.

559.   For a more nuanced depiction of expatriate life in another part of Africa, one may read Doris Lessing's novels and volume one of her autobiography, *Under My Skin*. For Margaret Laurence's comments on memsahibs, see *PCB*, 16, 25, 88; and Chapter 14, "The Imperialists."

560.   Michael Wilson, letter to author, 6 January 1992.

561.   Margaret Laurence, preface to the facsimile edition of *A Tree for Poverty* (Shannon, Ireland: Irish University Press and McMaster University Library, Hamilton, Ontario, 1970), v. This Irish University Press reprint is a photolithographic facsimile of the first edition, published in 1954, in Nairobi, through arrangements made then by the government of the British Somaliland Protectorate.

562.   B.W.Andrzejewski letter to author, 18 March 1989.

563.   Laurence herself distinguishes between translations and paraphrases of the tales. Professor Andrzejewski reported that he "never checked any of her prose narratives in detail and they are not translations but rather 'tales retold,' in which the principal fidelity applies only to the themes but not to the actual wording." B.W. Andrzejewski letter to author, 24 November 1991. For further discussion and details about *A Tree for Poverty*, see Fiona Sparrow's excellent and comprehensive study, *Into Africa with Margaret Laurence* (Toronto: ECW

Press, 1992) and Xiques "Margaret Laurence's Somali Translations," *Canadian Literature* 135 (October 1992).

564. Among Somalis in the years that followed, the *belwo* became a much-longer love poem, the *heello*. For further details on fascinating forms of Somali oral poetry see B.W. Andrzejewski and I.M. Lewis, *Somali Poetry: An Introduction* (Oxford: Clarendon Press, 1964) and more recent articles cited by Fiona Sparrow.

565. *Heart*, 81.

566. Ibid., 50.

567. Ibid., 79.

568. *Somaliland Journal* 1.3 (December 1956): 138-41. Margaret Laurence's name appears in this issue amongst members of The Somaliland Society (65). Only three issues of the *Somaliland Journal* were published — "in December of the years 1954, 1955, and 1956. Both the Society and the Journal just faded away at the time of Independence." (John Lawrie, letter to author, 28 January 1993).

569. See Tree, 17, and *PCB*, Chapter 9.

570. *Tree*, 17. Margaret Laurence is very precise about this in her introduction to *A Tree for Poverty*, where she explains that the stories are of two types: "those translated directly from the Somali and those paraphrased. The former were translated literally for me by Musa Haji Ismail Galaal and B.W. Andrzejewski, and I have taken these literal translations and tried to put them into English which would convey as much as possible of the dramatic effect of the original. The latter type of story was obtained in a very different way." Those tales were told to her partly in Somali, but mainly in English. "They are, therefore, not exact translations but paraphrases of the stories I heard."

571. It appears in *PCB*, 218-23.

572. ML to B.W. Andrzejewski, 9 November 1951. York University Archives and Special Collections, Margaret Laurence Fonds.

573. Ibid.

574. *Tree*, 37.

575. Ian Serraillier, letter to author, 20 February 1990. Letter and BBC tape in author's collection.

576. C.J. Martin interview by author, Christchurch, Dorset, England, 3 May 1990.

577. *Somaliland Journal* 1:1. 52 (December 1954). Public Records Office, Kew, England.

578. *War Somali Sidihi*, 23 October 1954. This was a fortnightly newssheet produced in the Department of Information in Hargeisa, beginning in 1953. Public Records Office, Kew, England.

579. B.W. Andrzejewski letter to author, 18 March 1989.

580. In a letter to Adele, Peggy said she had finished translating a lot of Somali poems and stories, but she was not sure what to do with them and doubted that they would appeal to a publisher. "Still," she noted, "it was interesting work and I'm not sorry I did it." (ML to AW, 30 January 1952). Lennox and Panofsky, 72.

581. See John Buchholzer, *The Horn of Africa: Travels in British Somaliland*, translated from the Danish by Maurice Michael, especially Chapters 12 and 13. I discovered Bucholzer's book and his appropriation of Laurence's work while browsing in a bookshop. His plagiarism of her translations was subsequently confirmed by letters in the Margaret Laurence Fonds at York University and by my interviews.

582. ML to AW, 15 June 1951. Lennox and Panofsky, 54.

583. Ibid.

584.   Ibid. While Peggy was growing up, there remained a good deal of prejudice in Neepawa against Ukrainians (whom they also referred to as Galicians) and other Eastern Europeans.

585.   ML to AW, 15 June 1951. Lennox and Panofsky, 54.

586.   *Rachel, Rachel* was the first film directed by the American actor Paul Newman. It starred his wife, Joanne Woodward. *Life* magazine featured the film on the cover of its October 18, 1968, issue and carried an article about it.

587.   ML to AW, 30 January 1952. Lennox and Panofsky, 72.

588.   Some Somali tales are not unlike stories of the trickster in Canadian Native literature.

589.   William J. Keith, "'Uncertain Flowering': An Overlooked Short Story by Margaret Laurence," *Canadian Literature* 112 (1987): 202-5.

590.   Since Somaliland was celebrating the anniversary of its independence from colonial powers, the government was not eager to invite Westerners back to its celebrations. Peggy was invited because of her English translation of Somali tales and poems, *A Tree for Poverty*.

591.   The American edition had a different title: *New Wind in a Dry Land* (New York: Alfred A. Knopf, 1964).

592.   *Dance*, 140.

593.   *Dance*, 141.

594.   ML to Gabrielle Roy, 15 February 1976, Fonds Gabrielle Roy, National Archives, Ottawa. See also *Dance*, 142. This letter, written in 1976, gives an indication of the impact that fictional characters could have in shaping Laurence's approach to situations that she faced in her own life. A very fine collection of the letters between these two writers is now available to the general public: *Intimate Strangers: The Letters between Margaret Laurence and Gabrielle Roy*, edited by Paul G. Socken (Winnipeg: University of Manitoba Press, 2004).

595.   *Dance*, 142.

596.   Jack Laurence, interview by author, Vancouver, 23 October 1992.

597.   *Dance*, 142.

598.   Ibid., 143.

599.   Ibid.

600.   Ibid.

601.   ML to AW, 12 March 1955. York University Archives and Special Collections, Margaret Laurence Fonds.

602.   ML to AW, 1 December 1952. Lennox and Panofsky, 75.

603.   Ibid.

604.   *Heart*, 33.

605.   ML to AW, 26 October 1953. York University Archives and Special Collections, Margaret Laurence Fonds.

606.   Ibid.

607.   Lawrence Henry Yaw Ofosu-Appiah (1920-1990) was one of the first African lecturers at the University of Ghana. He also became the first African master of Akuafo Hall, built in 1957. Professor Ofosu-Appiah edited the first two volumes of the *Encyclopaedia Africana*, wrote several books, including *People in Bondage: African Slavery in the Modern World*, and translated Homer's *Odyssey* into Twi, one of the major languages of Ghana.

608.   *Heart*, 33.

609.   Mrs. Ofosu-Appiah, telephone interview with the author, 12 February 2001.

610.   In *Dance on the Earth* Laurence mistakenly identifies Ofosu-Appiah's college as

Achimista (153). James King, following Laurence, also makes that identification (115). However, the college was actually Achimota, located in Achimista. Known for its rigorous standards, Achimota College later became part of the University of Ghana.

611.   ML to AW, 16 January 1953. York University Archives and Special Collections, Margaret Laurence Fonds.

612.   ML to AW, 16 February 1953. Lennox and Panofsky, 79.

613.   ML to Burnett, 5 November 1951. Further details about the publication of Margaret Laurence's first story may be found in Xiques, "New Light on Margaret Laurence's First African Short Story," *Canadian Notes and Queries* 42 (1990).

614.   Whit Burnett to ML, 19 July 1952, Princeton University Library, *Story* archives.

615.   Quotation from the jacket of *The Story of "Story Magazine"* by Jay Neugeboren.

616.   ML to AW, 16 February 1953. Lennox and Panofsky, 79.

617.   Whit Burnett to ML, 12 February 1953, in *Story* archives, Princeton University. On the other hand, Laurence's letters to Adele Wiseman present a different picture and make clear that she had been struggling rather unsuccessfully with one or two novels for a long period of time. No doubt Peggy decided those efforts were best left unmentioned in her letter to Burnett.

618.   More complete details about this appear in W.J. Keith, "'Uncertain Flowering': An Overlooked Short Story . . ." and in Xiques, "New Light on Margaret Laurence's First African Short Story."

619.   "The" was omitted from the published title.

620.   *Prism* 1 (September 1959).

621.   The section, which appears in both works, is found in *Story* 4: 16-18 and in *The Prophet's Camel Bell*, 60-61.

622.   "The Young and the Old" by William Peden is a review of *Story: The Magazine of the Short Story in Book Form*. Number 4. Edited by Whit Burnett and Hallie Burnett. (New York: A.A. Wyn, Inc. Publishers, 1953). In it, Peden states that several new writers, including Margaret Laurence, have stories that are "first-rate." Undated clipping, York University Archives and Special Collections, Margaret Laurence Fonds. The clipping is signed by her at the top (J.M. Laurence) and dated Accra, 1954.

623.   ML to AW, 16 January 1953. York University Archives and Special Collections, Margaret Laurence Fonds.

624.   Ibid.

625.   ML to AW, 16 February 1953. Lennox and Panofsky, 79.

626.   ML to AW, 20 July 1953. York University Archives and Special Collections, Margaret Laurence Fonds.

627.   ML to AW, 16 February 1953. Lennox and Panofsky, 79.

628.   Kay Bolton, interview by author, Montreal, 12 February 1997. Her husband, Eliot, had officiated at the wedding of Watson and Mary Thomson. Kay and Eliot had lived at the Roslyn Road house for several years, but they were not related to Jack Laurence, although James King states that Frances, their daughter, was a cousin to Jack (192).

629.   ML to AW, 8 June 1953. Lennox and Panofsky, 82.

630.   Ibid.

631.   Ibid.

632.   Ibid.

633.   ML to AW, 20 July 1953. York University Archives and Special Collections, Margaret Laurence Fonds.

634.   Ibid.

635.   Ibid.

636.   *Dance*, 17.

637.   ML to AW, 19 September 1953. York University Archives and Special Collections, Margaret Laurence Fonds.

638.   Ibid.

639.   ML to AW, 27 November 1953. While the content of these scripts is clearly Peggy's, the style is not typical. She states that Elizabeth Long of the CBC did edit them, but it remains unclear as to whether Laurence also edited them for the purposes of broadcasting. If she did, that would also account for the distinct differences between the way the same content is presented in *PCB* and in the archived scripts.

640.   ML to AW, 26 October 1953. York University Archives and Special Collections, Margaret Laurence Fonds.

641.   Ibid.

642.   Ibid., 19 September 1953.

643.   Ibid., 2 January 1954.

644.   Ibid., 14 December 1953. Lennox and Panofsky, 84.

645.   Ibid.

646.   Wiseman's review appeared in *Queen's Quarterly* 62 (Winter 1956): 610-11.

647.   ML to AW, 4 September 1951. Lennox and Panofsky, 57. Laurence's translation of that *belwo* also appears in *Tree*, 48.

648.   ML to AW, 7 April 1954. Lennox and Panofsky, 87. Here Laurence mentions her letter to Professor Malcolm Ross.

649.   Ibid.

650.   ML to AW, 8 June 1953. Lennox and Panofsky, 82.

651.   ML to AW, 26 October 1953 and 27 November 1953. York University Archives and Special Collections, Margaret Laurence Fonds.

652.   Ibid., 27 November 1953.

653.   Ibid., 26 October 1953.

654.   Ibid., 2 January 1954.

655.   Ibid., 19 February 1954.

656.   Ibid., 10 March 1954.

657.   Ibid., 19 February 1954.

658.   Ibid., 2 January 1954.

659.   This project involved Aluminum Ltd. of Canada and the British Aluminum Company in Great Britain. The findings of Commander Jackson's commission were published in three volumes in 1956.

660.   Jack Laurence, interview by author, 23 October 1992.

661.   Clara Thomas notes that Margaret Laurence typed the first draft of Ward's *Faith and Freedom*. See "Morning Yet on Creation Day: A Study of *This Side Jordan*," in *A Place to Stand On: Essays by and about Margaret Laurence*, edited by George Woodcock (Edmonton: NeWest Press, 1983), 93-105.

662.   *Faith and Freedom*, 4-5. In 1961, Barbara Ward delivered the first Massey Lectures in Canada. These were broadcast by the CBC and later published as *Rich Nations, Poor Nations*. Laurence, who was then living in Canada, may well have heard them. Twenty years later, Margaret Laurence again referred to Barbara Ward in her Convocation Address to Emmanuel College, Victoria

University, University of Toronto, 6 May 1982. She said: "The late Dr. Barbara Ward, the great economist, in one of her books put forward the thesis that if the world's economy could be geared less towards arms production and more towards helping people, it would be possible for everyone in the world to have enough fresh water." See Laurence, "A Statement of Faith" in Woodcock, 15-19.

663.   Jack Laurence, interview by author, 23 October 1992.

664.   ML to AW, 19 February 1954. Although this is Margaret's account, there seems to be no reason to question it, since she was writing to a close friend. In addition, Sheila Andrzejewski remembers that, when she knew the Laurences, both in the British Somaliland Protectorate and later in England, with one exception she had not seen either Jack or Margaret drink too much. Sheila Andrzejewski, e-mail to author, 14 November 2000.

665.   ML to AW, 19 February 1954. York University Archives and Special Collections, Margaret Laurence Fonds.

666.   Ibid.

667.   Ibid., 10 March 1954.

668.   Ibid.

669.   ML to AW, 7 April 1954. Lennox and Panofsky, 87.

670.   John Simpson died in 1953, one month before his ninety-seventh birthday. When Margaret was interviewed many years later, she admitted: "I hated him for a long time even after his death." But she also noted that she had subsequently acquired "a kind of respect and admiration for him. He walked from Winnipeg to Portage La Prairie, you know, as a pioneer. That was really remarkable." Interview with William French, *Globe and Mail*, 25 April 1970, 6.

Circumstances had made it necessary for Marg Wemyss to sell the Big House on First Avenue. She then moved with her elderly father back to the Little House. After John Simpson's death, she sold the Little House and moved to British Columbia, where she joined her sister, Ruby.

671.   Dance, 110.

672.   ML to AW, 20 September 1954. York University Archives and Special Collections, Margaret Laurence Fonds.

673.   Ibid.

674.   Ibid., 29 March 1955.

675.   Ibid., 20 September 1954.

676.   Ibid.

677.   Rawlplugs (Peg's spelling here has been regularized).

678.   *PCB*, 247-48. The original typescript of *A Tree for Poverty* was presented to the Somaliland Society by the Chief Secretary to the government. See the *Somaliland Journal* 1.1 (1954): 62.

679.   ML to AW, 15 November 1954. York University Archives and Special Collections, Margaret Laurence Fonds.

680.   Ibid.

681.   Ibid., 31 December 1954.

682.   Ibid.

683.   Ibid.

684.   Ibid.

685.   Ibid.

686.   Ibid., 12 March 1955.

687.   Ibid.

688.   Ibid.

689.   Ibid., 29 March 1955.

690.   Barbara Ward (Baroness Jackson) Papers, Georgetown University Archives and Special Collections, Box 1, 11.

691.   *This Side Jordan* (Toronto: McClelland & Stewart, 1960, reprinted 1989, New Canadian Library), 121-22. This edition will be used throughout.

692.   Barbara Ward, 26 June 1955. Barbara Ward (Baroness Jackson) Papers, Georgetown University Archives and Special Collections, Box 1.

693.   ML to AW, 20 June 1955. Lennox and Panofsky, 89.

694.   ML to AW, 29 March 1955. York University Archives and Special Collections, Margaret Laurence Fonds.

695.   ML to AW, 20 June 1955. Lennox and Panofsky, 89.

696.   Ibid.

697.   *Dance*, 150-51.

698.   *Dance*, 150.

699.   *Dance*, 149.

700.   Ibid.

701.   Ibid., 149-50.

702.   Ibid., 150.

703.   Ibid., 152.

704.   Ibid.

705.   Ibid.

706.   Ibid., 110. It is clear from this passage that Aunt Ruby, not Mum, had broken her wrist.

707.   Ibid.

708.   Ibid., 110-112.

709.   Ibid., 112.

710.   Toward the end of her life, Margaret Laurence had the same sort of response when a very dear friend, Evelyn Robinson, her next-door neighbour for many years in Lakefield, died. Although Evelyn's husband asked Margaret to say a few words at the memorial service for his wife, she preferred to write a tribute to Evelyn. Earl Robinson recalls that Margaret had come into their house twice on the day that his wife had died: "Margaret didn't say anything. Later she returned with something she had written. It was a tribute. Afterwards it was printed in the Lakefield paper." That Margaret could not then speak directly to Evelyn's husband, but needed to put her thoughts on paper, was partially the result of her shyness and partially due to her great respect for the written word and the fact she felt more comfortable writing her deepest feelings than speaking them.

711.   ML to AW, 27 January 1956. York University Archives and Special Collections, Margaret Laurence Fonds.

712.   Ibid.

713.   Ibid., 3 April 1956.

714.   Ibid.

715.   Ibid., 28 May 1956.

716.   Ibid. These are significant remarks that bear, in fact, on a major problem that Margaret Laurence later encountered when trying to write a novel after *The Diviners* had been published. She attempted then to deal fictionally with those persons and groups who had declared *The Diviners* to be reprehensible (despite the fact that many of them had never read it). It was extremely difficult for Laurence to arrive at the necessary critical distance, nor was she able to

summon, as she so often had done before, a deep sympathy and understanding of her characters. The basis for the novel was to have been her own experience with the book-banners in the Peterborough area. Having been so profoundly wounded by their attacks, she was unable to position herself to write about that, although to do so would have been in accord with the way she had dealt with hurt and misunderstanding in the past.

717.   ML to AW, 3 April 1956.York University Archives and Special Collections, Margaret Laurence Fonds.

718.   Ibid., 28 May 1956.

719.   Ibid.

720.   ML to AW, 10 July 1956. Lennox and Panofsky, 91.

721.   Ibid.

722.   Ibid.

723.   Ibid.

724.   Klein, Carole. *Doris Lessing: A Biography* (New York: Carroll & Graf, 2000), 74-86.

725.   ML to AW, 23 July 1956. Lennox and Panofsky, 94.

726.   Ibid.

727.   *Dance*, 152.

728.   At the time of Margaret Laurence's death in 1987, more than a hundred books pertaining to Africa, including works by R.S. Rattray, E.L.R. Meyerowitz, and J.B. Danquah, remained in her personal library. They were subsequently acquired by McMaster University, Hamilton, Ontario.

729.   ML to AW, 23 July 1956. Lennox and Panofsky, 94.

730.   Ibid.

731.   Alice Munro, telephone interview with author, 21 May 1993.

732.   ML to AW, 10 July 1956. Lennox and Panofsky, 91.

733.   ML to AW, 31 July 1956. York University Archives and Special Collections, Margaret Laurence Fonds.

734.   Ibid.

735.   Ibid.

736.   ML to AW, 31 July 1956. Airletter #2. York University Archives and Special Collections, Margaret Laurence Fonds. Peggy added a p.s. to the letter: "The story is *not* autobiographical."

737.   Ibid.

738.   ML to AW, 4 December 1956. York University Archives and Special Collections, Margaret Laurence Fonds.

739.   Ibid.

740.   Ibid.

741.   "In East and in West Africa I saw children who were desperately ill with malaria. My own two children had malaria, as babies, in Ghana. They were fortunate. They had medical help. . . . But I remember as though it were yesterday — and it was in fact nearly thirty years ago — my own sense of helplessness and anguish. How many parents in malarial areas, now as then mourn their children killed by a disease that could have been eradicated years ago?" Laurence, "A Statement of Faith," in Woodcock, 56-60.

742.   ML to AW, 4 December 1956. York University Archives and Special Collections, Margaret Laurence Fonds.

743.   Ibid., 26 November 1956.

744.   Ibid., 14 December 1956.

745.   *Dance*, 113. See also ML to AW, 26 November 1956 and 4 December 1956. York University Archives and Special Collections, Margaret Laurence Fonds.

746.   1952 is the date of Amos Tutuola's *The Palm-Wine Drinkard*, and 1966 the date of Achebe's *A Man of the People* and Ekwensi's *Iska*. Due to the efforts of Professor Nora Foster Stovel, Margaret Laurence's study of Nigerian writers, *Long Drums and Cannons*, was reissued by the University of Alberta Press in 2001. Edited with an introduction by Stovel, it also has a foreword by Professor Doug Killam, as well as the previously unpublished text of a talk that Laurence gave in 1969, "Tribalism as Us vs. Them," and an essay by Abdul-Rasheed Na'Allah "Nigerian Literature Then and Now." Since Laurence's work had become difficult to obtain, this new edition is an important contribution to the field.

747.   Laurence's African books were subsequently acquired by McMaster University Library, where they became part of the library's general collection. Other books in her library, principally ones dealing with Canada and Canadians, went to Trent University.

748.   Kay Bolton, telephone conversation with author, 6 September 1994.

749.   Mona Spratt Meredith, interview by author, Vancouver, 28 November 1994.

750.   *Dance*,113.

751.   *Vancouver Sun*, 19 February 1957.

752.   "Letter to Bob Sorfleet." Some years later, however, Laurence did publish another science-fiction story, "Fable for the Whaling Fleets," in *Whales: A Celebration*, edited by Greg Gatenby (Boston and Toronto: Little Brown and Co. 1983), 89. Laurence also included that story in *Dance on the Earth*.

753.   ML to AW, 18 February 1957. York University Archives and Special Collections, Margaret Laurence Fonds.

754.   *Dance*, 113.

755.   Ibid., 114-15.

756.   Ibid., 115.

757.   Ibid., 117.

758.   Elsie's first novel was published in 1916 under the pseudonym Christine Field. After her marriage, however, her creative efforts focused chiefly on poetry and short magazine pieces, which, as a busy housewife and mother, she could complete more easily than a novel. The income from Elsie's writing augmented her husband's rather modest salary. In her later years she did publish another novel, *Bright Wings* (1964).

759.   *Dance*, 115.

760.   ML to AW, 17 March 1957. Lennox and Panofsky, 100.

761.   Ibid.

762.   Ibid.

763.   Ibid.

764.   "Let My Voice Live" was signed: "by Meg — A Canadian living in England," and appeared on 9 January 1950. Peg mentioned the poem's publication to Adele later that same month and was pleased that appropriate photographs had appeared with it. She also submitted a poem about the Italian peasants' revolt to the *Canadian Tribune*, but she was not sure whether the *Tribune* planned to publish it. The poem has not been traced and seems not to have been published.

765.   ML to AW, 17 March 1957. Lennox and Panofsky, 100.

766.   Ibid.

767.   See ML to AW, 12 June 1957. York University Archives and Special Collections, Margaret Laurence Fonds.

768. Ibid.

769. Ibid.

770. Ibid. Wiseman held a Guggenheim Fellowship and was living in New York City at that time.

771. ML to AW, 1 December 1957. Lennox and Panofsky, 102.

772. *Dance*, 115.

773. ML to AW, 1 December 1957. Lennox and Panofsky, 102.

774. Ibid.

775. Ibid.

776. ML to AW, 19 February 1958. York University Archives and Special Collections, Margaret Laurence Fonds.

777. Since Laurence's letter to Adele (14 August 1958) gives her address as 3556 W. 21 St. Vancouver, it is reasonable to suppose their move occurred before Jack left in May for Fort St. John.

778. ML to AW, 14 August 1958. Lennox and Panofsky, 104.

779. Ibid.

780. Ibid.

781. Ibid.

782. Ibid.

783. Elliott had done graduate work in history at Harvard, was widely read, and enjoyed discussing literature and language with Margaret. He also became a close friend of Jack's, visiting often and enjoying with the Laurences a group of mutual friends. Jack and Gordon Elliott enjoyed going to the movies and discussing current issues. Years later, when Jack and his second wife, Esther, returned to live in Vancouver, Gordon resumed his friendship with Jack and grew to know Esther too.

784. ML to AW, 28 February 1959. York University Archives and Special Collections, Margaret Laurence Fonds.

785. Laurence told Adele that Michael Wilson, a friend from Somali days (or his brother John), had shown the translations to a person he knew at Macmillan. (ML to AW, 28 February 1959. York University Archives and Special Collections, Margaret Laurence Fonds).

786. Ruth May also represented the prominent Vancouver writer Ethel Wilson.

787. ML to AW, 28 February 1959. York University Archives and Special Collections, Margaret Laurence Fonds.

788. Ibid.

789. Ibid.

790. ML to AW, 13 May 1959. Lennox and Panofsky, 106.

791. Ibid.

792. Ibid.

793. Prior to publication, she had to revise the story for their editors.

794. ML to AW, 13 May 1959. Lennox and Panofsky, 106.

795. *Prism* 1.1 (September 1959).

796. ML to Al Purdy, 24 May 1969, in *Margaret Laurence — Al Purdy: A Friendship in Letters* (Toronto: McClelland & Stewart, 1993), 138.

797. The gloomy letter that was burned in August is mentioned in ML to AW, 10 September 1959. Lennox and Panofsky, 110.

798. Ibid.

799. Ibid.

800. Ibid.

801. Ibid.
802. Reprinted in Kourany, Janet, James P. Sterba, and Rosemarie Tong, eds. *Feminist Philosophies* (Englewood Cliffs, N.J.: Prentice Hall, 1992), 185-96.
803. ML to AW, 10 September 1959. Lennox and Panofsky, 110.
804. Ibid.
805. See, "IN TRIBUTE: Margaret Laurence" by Jack McClelland, *Quill & Quire*, February 1987, 9.
806. ML to AW, 10 September 1959. Lennox and Panofsky, 110.
807. "Uncertain Flowering" in *Story* (1954); "Drummer of All the World" in *Queen's Quarterly* (1956); "The Merchant of Heaven," in *Prism* (1959); and the translations, *A Tree for Poverty* (1954).
808. Although that was the second-highest sum received by a contributor, Peggy probably did not know that. See *Prism* archives, University of British Columbia.
809. Michael Holroyd, letter to author, 20 February 1997.
810. Judging from the archival evidence, Laurence seems to have replied to Dickson on the same day that she received his letter.
811. It went into a second printing in August 1958 (Macmillan, Canada, and St. Martin's Press, New York). Several years before that, sections of the novel had been submitted to the *Maclean's* short-story contest. Alice Munro later tried unsuccessfully to have Hutchison's novel reprinted in the New Canadian Library series. Information from interviews and correspondence with Margaret Hutchison and her niece, J.M. Deplissey, and correspondence between Hutchison and Ruth May, her agent.
812. William McConnell, interviews by author, Vancouver, 19 and 22 November 1995.
813. William McConnell, letter to author, 7 February 1994. Neilson single-handedly constructed a peeled-log chalet and planned later to make a number of smaller dispersed cabins for individual work and privacy.
814. Margaret Hutchison, interview by author, Vancouver, 24 October 1992.
815. Margaret Hutchison, interview by author, Vancouver, 24 October 1992.
816. Although Ruth May was also Ethel Wilson's agent, it is unlikely that Laurence, who had not yet met Wilson, was aware of that.
817. Margaret Hutchison, interview by author, Vancouver, 24 October 1992.
818. Laurence also requested that this dedication appear in the paperback edition of the book. Some of the letters between Nadine Asante and Margaret Laurence are now archived at York University Archives and Special Collections, Margaret Laurence Collection.
819. Fred and June Schulhof, interview by author, 20 October 1992.
820. Ibid.
821. Eva and René Temple, interview by author, Vancouver, 22 October 1992.
822. Ibid. All quotations in this paragraph are from that interview.
823. Ibid.
824. *Dance*, 219. Margaret Hutchison, Mary and Watson Thomson, Nadine Asante, and Earle Birney and his wife were among the members of Hewett's congregation at that time.
825. Dr. Phillip Hewett, telephone conversation with author, January 1994.
826. Unitarian Membership book, p. 68, signatures #448 and #449.
827. Noreen Foster, telephone conversation with author, January 1994.
828. Noreen Foster also recognized the cadences of the King James Bible in Margaret's remarks.

829.   Noreen Foster, telephone conversation with author, 17 January 1994.

830.   *Dance*, 219.

831.   Ibid., 220.

832.   ML to Helen Lucas, 3 May 1978. Copies of several letters from Margaret Laurence were given to the author by Helen Lucas, who subsequently gave them to York University Archives and Special Collections, Margaret Laurence Collection.

833.   Noreen Foster described the scene in some detail to the author.

834.   Nonie Lyon, interview by author, Peterborough, Ontario, 9 June 1994. In letters to several correspondents, Margaret recounted the story of how a copy was returned to her.

835.   Inscription to Helen Lucas from Margaret Laurence; see also *Dance*, 220. Lucas planned to set forth a visual presentation of five aspects of the nativity story: 1) the love and affection between Mary and Joseph; 2) Mary as pregnant; 3) Joseph involved with and holding Jesus; 4) both Mary and Joseph actively engaged with their son as he grows; 5) the connections among all living things. (Helen Lucas, letter to author, 17 March 1994.)

836.   ML to Phillip Hewett, 20 September 1980. Trent University Archives.

837.   Ibid.

838.   Her memoir, *Dance on the Earth*, edited by her daughter, Jocelyn, was published posthumously in 1989.

839.   Only in 1963, however, did Margaret insist that old friends also drop Peggy and refer to her as Margaret. (See ML to Gordon Elliott, 29 April 1963, and ML to Adele Wiseman, 17 August 1963). Her neighbour June Schulhof had encouraged Peggy to resume her full name, Margaret, which she advised would be more professional than Peggy. (June Schulhof, interview by author, Vancouver, 20 October 1992).

840.   The photographer was Peter Esterhazy.

841.   Alan Maclean, *Winter's Tales* 6, introduction, (New York: St. Martin's Press, 1960), v.

842.   Stainsby's concerns about the state of book reviewing in Canadian newspapers are apparent in his essay "The Press and Literature," in *Canadian Literature* 10 (Autumn 1961): 62-65.

843.   ML to AW, 6 May 1960. Lennox and Panofsky, 114.

844.   *Prism* 1:3 (Spring 1960). The check was for twenty-five dollars.

845.   Margaret repeated his comment in a subsequent letter to Jack McClelland, noting that the phrase seemed rather like saying "moderately dead." (ML to McClelland, 13 May 1960). Although the St. Martin's reader later apologized for his bluntness, Margaret remembered that remark for many years, and made specific reference to it in 1969 at the beginning of her personal essay "Ten Years' Sentences."

846.   ML to McClelland, 13 May 1960. McClelland & Stewart Archives, McMaster University Archives and Special Collections.

847.   She provides details of these changes on 13 May 1960 in two letters: one to Jack McClelland, McClelland & Stewart Archives, McMaster University Archives and Special Collections, the other to Lovat Dickson, Macmillan archives, Basingstoke, England. This collection is now deposited in the British Museum Library.

848.   Jack McClelland to ML, 17 May 1960. McClelland & Stewart Archives, McMaster University Archives and Special Collections. McClelland also made some humorous comments which would have put Margaret at ease.

849. McClelland to ML, 18 May 1960. McClelland & Stewart Archives, McMaster University Archives and Special Collections.

850. It appeared as the opening piece in *Tamarack Review* 17 (Autumn 1960): 5-20.

851. *Prism* 2.1 (Autumn 1960): 61.

852. ML to Lovat Dickson, 29 October 1960. His full name was Horatio Lovat Dickson. Margaret Laurence referred to him as "Rache," as did his friends, but in the interests of clarity I have retained the more formal Lovat Dickson. Macmillan archives, Basingstoke, England

853. See ML to Maclean, 29 October 1960. Macmillan archives, Basingstoke, England; and ML to Willis Wing, 4 November 1960. Curtis Brown Collection, Columbia University Archives and Special Collections, Box 245.

854. Blair Fuller, then fiction editor, had lived in Ghana. See comments in ML to Willis K. Wing, 4 November 1960. Curtis Brown Collection, Columbia University Archives and Special Collections, Box 245.

855. ML to McClelland, 26 September 1960. McClelland & Stewart Archives, McMaster University Archives and Special Collections.

856. McClelland to Willis Wing, 18 October 1960. Curtis Brown Archives, Columbia University Archives and Special Collections, Box 245.

857. Ibid.

858. See Laurence's letters to Alan Maclean and also to Adele Wiseman, 29 October 1960 (York University Archives and Special Collections, Margaret Laurence Fonds). A few days later she wrote to her agent, Willis Wing:

> As far as the new novel is concerned, I am trying to summon sufficient courage to begin writing it. . . . I have the novel planned in rough, but of course have no way of knowing how long it will take to write. I hope it will not take as long as the first. I am not a very speedy writer, and I re-write a great deal. However, with the first novel I wasted an enormous amount of effort in writing sections that subsequently had to be discarded. I am hoping that this new effort will be better organized from the beginning. If I can bring it off (and this is always a frightening question) it will, I think, be a better novel than the first.
>
> P.S. Perhaps I should explain that I do not intend to keep on writing about Africa indefinitely, nor do I want to spin out this material too far. I want to do one more novel set in West Africa, and the short stories which I mentioned, and that will be all. I have also had in mind for some years a possible book of personal experiences [this became *The Prophet's Camel Bell*] during a rather fantastic couple of years which we spent in the desert of British Somaliland in East Africa, but I don't know when I will get around to tackling this project, if ever.

ML to Willis Wing, 4 November 1960. Curtis Brown Archives, Columbia University Archives and Special Collections, Box 245.

859. ML to AW, 29 October 1960. York University Archives and Special Collections, Margaret Laurence Fonds.

860. ML to AW, 4 November 1960. York University Archives and Special Collections, Margaret Laurence Fonds. Laurence's novel was praised by Mary Renault, "On

Understanding Africa" *Saturday Review* (10 December 1960): 23-24. Laurence's photo did not appear on the cover.

861. ML to McClelland, 4 November 1960. McClelland & Stewart Archives, McMaster University Archives. Her letter to Willis Kingsley Wing was indeed written the same day; ML to Willis Wing, 4 November 1960. Curtis Brown Archives, Columbia University, Box 245.

862. ML to McClelland, 4 November 1960. McClelland & Stewart Archives, McMaster University Archives and Special Collections.

863. McClelland to ML, 9 November 1960. McClelland & Stewart Archives, McMaster University Archives and Special Collections.

864. ML to McClelland, 4 November 1960. McClelland & Stewart Archives, McMaster University Archives and Special Collections.

865. This is probably a reference to Octave Mannoni, whose work *Prospero and Caliban* (Ann Arbor, Michigan: University of Michigan Press, 1990, from reprint of 1950) she had read with great interest after returning from Africa.

866. ML to McClelland, 16 November 1960. McClelland & Stewart Archives, McMaster University Archives and Special Collections.

867. *Canadian Literature* 8 (Spring 1961): 62-63.

868. *Saturday Review*, 10 December 1960.

869. McClelland to ML, 29 November 1960. McClelland & Stewart Archives, McMaster University Archives and Special Collections.

870. ML to McClelland, 4 December 1960.

871. Gerda Charles, "New Novels," *New Statesman* (19 November 1960), 60, no.1549: 800-02.

872. ML to Alan Maclean, 16 November 1960. Macmillan Archives, Basingstoke, England. This collection is now deposited in the British Museum Library.

873. ML to Alan Maclean, 5 December 1960. Macmillan Archives, Basingstoke, England. Years later when Margaret was living in England, she was invited to dinner at Alan and Robin Maclean's home. There she met Muriel Spark. Maclean recalls, however, that it was an evening when Margaret was rather overcome with shyness (Alan Maclean, interview with author, 9 May 1990).

874. ML to AW, 3 December 1960. Lennox and Panofsky, 123.

875. *Saturday Evening Post*, 3 June 1961. "The Perfume Sea" first appeared in *Winter'sTales* 6 (1960) along with short stories by nine other authors. Laurence later included "The Perfume Sea" in her collection, *The Tomorrow-Tamer and Other Stories*. The *Saturday Evening Post* also reprinted this story in its anthology: *The Saturday Evening Post Stories* (New York: Doubleday, 1962).

876. ML to McClelland, 4 December 1960. McClelland & Stewart Archives, McMaster University Archives and Special Collections.

877. This is a reference to the photo of Margaret which, despite her explicit instructions to the contrary, Macmillan had used for the dust jacket.

878. Alan Crawley, an influential member of the writing community in Vancouver, was the founder of *Contemporary Verse*, a leading Canadian poetry quarterly during the 1940s and 1950s. He and his wife were close friends of Ethel Wilson.

879. Ethel Wilson to Alan and Jean Crawley, 28 December 1960, in *Ethel Wilson: Stories, Essays and Letters*, edited by David Stouck. (Vancouver: University of British Columbia Press, 1987), 216. Wallace Wilson gave *This Side Jordan* to his wife, Ethel, for Christmas 1960.

880. *Prism* 1: 3 (Spring 1960).

881. See, for example, Henry Kreisel, "The African Stories of Margaret Laurence."

882. The chapbooks were titled: *XII Poems* (1929) and *Rearguard and Other Poems* (1944). Elsie Fry Laurence's second novel, *Bright Wings*, was published in 1964. "The Phoenix," an apocalyptic short story, grew out of her alarm over the prospect of a nuclear conflagration. It was broadcast on the CBC and then published in *Stories with John Drainie*, edited by John Drainie (Toronto: The Ryerson Press, 1963), 92-98.

883. This was related by several members of Elsie's family.

884. Alice Munro, telephone conversation with author, 21 May 1993.

885. Munro already had several publications to her credit. Robert Weaver also had published some of her short stories. Over the years Weaver became a friend and literary adviser to Munro, encouraging her talent.

886. Alice Munro, telephone conversation with author, 21 May 1993.

887. Ibid.

888. *Prism* 1:2 (Spring 1960): Wilson, 69; Haig-Brown, 72; McConnell, 71.

889. William McConnell, interview with author, Vancouver, 19 and 21 November 1995.

890. William McConnell, letter to author, 7 February 1994.

891. Ibid.

892. William McConnell, interview with author, Vancouver, 19 and 21 November 1995.

893. See Stouck's excellent biography, *Ethel Wilson: A Critical Biography* (Toronto: University of Toronto Press, 2003), 115-18, and his *Major Canadian Authors: A Critical Introduction to Canadian Literature in English*. Second edition, revised and expanded. (Lincoln, Nebraska: University of Nebraska, 1988), 81.

894. This side of Ethel Wilson also is captured by David Stouck, in the collection of her letters, essays, and stories that he edited. Although Ethel Wilson was born in South Africa, she and her father had left there when she was a small child, after the death of her young mother.

895. William McConnell, interview with author, Vancouver, 19 and 20 November, 1995.

896. Joyce Marshall, "Ethel Wilson," *Brick* 35 (Spring 1989): 32-36.

897. David Stouck reprints nine of those letters in *Ethel Wilson: Stories, Essays and Letters*. Other letters may have been destroyed since Wilson died in a nursing home at an advanced age and had moved several times after the death of her husband.

898. Margaret Laurence, "A Friend's Tribute to Ethel Wilson," *Vancouver Sun*, 24 January 1981.

899. Alan Twigg, *For Openers: Conversations with 24 Canadian Writers* (Madiera Park, B.C.: Harbour Press, 1981), 261-71.

900. ML to Beverly Mitchell, 13 April 1977. In Beverly Mitchell, *Ethel Wilson* (Toronto: ECW Press, n.d.) In a letter to Adele Wiseman, Margaret once wrote, "Had tea with Ethel Wilson the other day. She is terrific. A lady, in the best, wisest and most gracious sense. I was very impressed by her, and felt one would not dare say anything one didn't quite mean, for she would spot it at once." (ML to AW, 22 January 1961; Lennox and Panofsky, 127).

901. Ethel Wilson Collection, University of British Columbia Archives. Box 10.

902. Margaret Laurence, "A Friend's Tribute to Ethel Wilson." *Vancouver Sun*, 24 January 1981.

903. Jack Laurence, interview with author, Vancouver, 23 October 1992.

904. They purchased the place from James Anderson and, in October 1965, sold it to a man from New Westminster, British Columbia. Their signatures on those sale papers were notarized in High Wycombe, England, on 23 October 1965. (Deeds on file at the Public Records Office, Whatcom County, Washington, U.S.A.). Although the Laurences were to enjoy their cottage at Point Roberts for a relatively short time, it had great importance for Margaret as a writer.

905. Richard E. Clark, *Point Roberts, U.S.A.: The History of a Canadian Enclave.* (Bellingham, WA: Textype Publishing, 1980). The area was even more accessible by car after the opening of the Deas Island Tunnel in July 1959 (later renamed the George Massey Tunnel).

906. See ML to Alfred Knopf, 1 February 1964. Knopf Archives, Harry Ransom Humanities Research Center, Austin, Texas.

907. Neil and Doreen Coen, telephone conversation with author, August 1996.

908. ML to AW, 5 September 1961. Lennox and Panofsky, 134.

909. When Margaret Laurence decided in the 1970s to buy a cottage on the Otonabee River near Lakefield, Ontario, her choice of location may well have been influenced by memories of these previous summer dwellings, where she had had time to write and to enjoy nature.

910. June Schulhof, interview with author, Vancouver, 20 October 1992. June also recalls that Margaret spent time at Point Roberts early in the summer of 1962, working hard on a manuscript (probably *The Stone Angel*).

911. Pete Bazaluk, telephone conversation with author, 18 August 1996.

912. During a visit to Point Roberts in November 1995, the author met several local residents who were very helpful. I am particularly grateful to Jim Julius, realtor, whose family have long been residents of Point Roberts, and to Pauli DeHaan, lifelong Point Roberts resident and an active member of the Point Roberts Historical Society, both of whom shared valuable information with me and knew the area at the time the Laurences had a cottage there.

913. Other sites have been suggested for the cannery, but the site itself was Lily Point, as Laurence remarked in a taped interview with Donald Cameron. See the University College of Cape Breton, Donald Cameron Fonds, Sydney, Nova Scotia.

914. June and Fred Schulhof, interview with author, Vancouver, 20 October 1992.

915. Alan Twigg, *Vancouver and Its Writers.* (Madeira Park, B.C.: Harbour Publishing, 1986), 33-34.

916. Robin Laurence, interview with author, Vancouver, 20 October 1992.

917. Four had been published, and another was to appear in *Winter's Tales 6.*

918. Willis Wing to ML, 22 November 1960. Curtis Brown Archives, Columbia University Archives and Special Collections, Box 245.

919. *Winter's Tales 1* (1955): 1.

920. The editors planned to call the story "The Voices of the Distant Drum." However, when it appeared in the *Saturday Evening Post* (5 May 1962), it was entitled "The Spell of the Distant Drum."

921. Ethel Wilson to Crawleys, 28 June 1961. University of British Columbia Archives and Special Collections, Ethel Wilson Collection.

922. On January 7 and January 8, respectively. The *Canadian Forum* carried a lengthy, favourable review of *This Side Jordan* by Henry Kreisel (April 1961).

923. ML to Willis Wing, 4 November 1960. Curtis Brown Archives. Columbia University Archives and Special Collections, Box 245.

924. She explained to Adele, "I feel I don't know enough about Africa to do it." ML to AW, 1 February 1961.York University Archives and Special Collections, Margaret Laurence Fonds.

925. Ibid., 8 October 1961.

926. Ibid.

927. Many letters flew back and forth from publishers to Laurence over the question of the novel's title. Alfred A. Knopf Archives, Harry Ransom Humanities Research Center, University of Texas, Austin.

928. ML to AW, 8 October 1961. Lennox and Panofsky, 138.

929. Ibid.

930. Ibid. Gordon Elliott, along with Lino Magagna, who had come to Canada from Italy and been an older student in Gordon's class, were the central figures in the wine-making experiments. Lennox and Panofsky, 138.

931. As quoted in Michael Holroyd, *Augustus John: A Biography* (New York: Holt, Rinehart, Winston, 1974), 577.

932. See Patricia Morley, *Margaret Laurence: The Long Journey Home* (Montreal and Kingston: McGill-Queen's University Press, rev.1992), 155-58.

933. Margaret Fulton, telephone interview with author, 20 January 1994. Professor Fulton is a distinguished member of the academic community, who served two terms as the first laywoman and non-Catholic president of Mount St. Vincent University in Nova Scotia.

934. ML to Goosh and Shelia Andrzejewski, 12 May 1962. York University Archives and Special Collections, Margaret Laurence Fonds.

935. *The Fire-Dwellers.* (Toronto: McClelland & Stewart, 1969), chapter 7.

936. June and Fred Schulhof, interview with author, Vancouver, 20 October 1992.

937. Douglas Barnaby (crew member on the voyage), letter to author, 17 March 1998.

938. "The Tomorrow-Tamer" was published in *Prism* 3:1 (Fall 1961), but was erroneously listed in the table of contents as "The Tomorrow-maker." That issue of *Prism* also included Robert Kroetsch's first published poem "Letter to a Friend's Wife," and Gwendolyn MacEwen's "first professional publication," a poem entitled "Yesterday's Horsemen."

939. *Vancouver Sun*, 9 and 10 November 1961.

940. Ibid.

941. ML to W. Wing, 29 December 1961. Curtis Brown Archives, Columbia University Archives and Special Collections, Box 245.

942. It is clear that Buchholzer did go to Somalia. He hunted game there and took many photos. Although much in his book is not taken from Laurence, nevertheless there are many passages in which he simply took material directly from *A Tree for Poverty*. In other instances, he is content to paraphrase Laurence, but he does this so closely that the reader one can clearly see Laurence's style and comments in Buchholzer's prose.

943. She had come across references to *The Horn of Africa* in *Shadows in the Grass* by Isak Dinesen, pseudonym of the Danish writer, Karen Blixen.

944. ML to AW, 5 September 1961. Lennox and Panofsky, 134.

945. ML to W. Wing, 8 January 1962. Curtis Brown Archives, Columbia University Archives and Special Collections, Box 245.

946. ML to W. Wing, 8 May 1962. Professor Goosh Andrzejewski had written to inform Margaret of the reactions of other scholars to Buchholzer's plagiarism.

947. ML to Clara Thomas, 17 February 1982. York University Archives and Special Collections, Clara Thomas Fonds.

948.   Joan Johnston, telephone conversation with author, 16 January 1994.

949.   *Vancouver Sun*, 24 December 1960.

950.   Ibid., 18 June 1960.

951.   Ibid., 27 August 1960.

952.   Ibid., 2 July 1960.

953.   Ibid., 27 August 1960.

954.   Laurence's review is concise, but nuanced.

955.   *Vancouver Sun*, 22 October 1960.

956.   This cannot be proven, but the juxtaposition may be significant.

957.   ML to AW, 21 July 1960. Lennox and Panofsky, 120.

958.   *Vancouver Sun*, 21 January 1961.

959.   Ibid., 11 February 1961.

960.   Ibid.

961.   ML to Buckler, 30 August 1974, as quoted in Wainwright, *A Very Large Soul*, 26.

962.   *Vancouver Sun*, 11 March 1961.

963.   He also returned "A Fetish for Love" and told her that further stories about Africa would be difficult to place because of the market. W. Wing to ML, 16 January 1962. Curtis Brown Archives, Columbia University Archives and Special Collections, Box 245.

964.   ML to AW, 13 January 1962. York University Archives and Special Collections, Margaret Laurence Fonds.

965.   Ibid., 13 June 1962.

966.   ML to Gordon Elliott, 13 June 1962. McMaster University Archives and Special Collections.

967.   ML to AW, 13 June 1962. York University Archives and Special Collections, Margaret Laurence Fonds.

968.   ML to G. Elliott, 13 June 1962. McMaster University Archives and Special Collections.

969.   Betty Friedan, *The Feminine Mystique* (New York: Viking Paperback, 1963).

970.   ML to AW, 5 August 1962. Lennox and Panofsky, 141.

971.   See ML to Gordon Elliott, 17 August 1962. McMaster University Archives and Special Collections.

972.   *Tamarack Review* 14 (Winter 1960).

973.   James King, 168-69, 418-19.

974.   See particularly her letter to Adele Wiseman, 13 January 1962. York University Archives and Special Collections, Margaret Laurence Fonds.

975.   ML to AW, 29 August 1962. Lennox and Panofsky, 148.

976.   Ibid.

977.   ML to AW, 22 September 1962. York University Archives and Special Collections, Margaret Laurence Fonds.

978.   ML to G. Elliott, 29 September 1962. McMaster University Archives and Special Collections.

979.   ML to AW, 29 September 1962. York University Archives and Special Collections, Margaret Laurence Fonds.

980.   *Dance*, 159.

981.   Ibid., 158.

982.   Ibid.,159-60.

983.   Ibid., 160.

984.   ML to AW, 17 March 1962. York University Archives and Special Collections, Margaret Laurence Fonds.

985.   *Dance*, 155. It is not uncommon for writers to describe sudden inspiration and the experience of writing as though they were taking dictation.

986.   ML to AW, 13 January 1962, York University Archives and Special Collections, Margaret Laurence Fonds. In fact, her attitude toward the novel fluctuated wildly, as her letters during that period show. In March, for example, when she mentioned that Jack was making tentative inquiries about overseas jobs, she also stated that "The novel is a complete mess. It will have to be entirely rewritten. Maybe it's not even worth re-writing, although I still feel I like the character." ML to AW, 17 March 1962. York University Archives and Special Collections, Margaret Laurence Fonds.

987.   AW to ML, 20 August 1962. Lennox and Panofsky, 145.

988.   ML to AW, 8 October 1961. Lennox and Panofsky, 138.

989.   The flaws in the novel that had been pointed out to her were probably raised by Jack, since correspondence with her editors and with Adele does not indicate that such concerns originated with them.

990.   ML to AW, 8 October 1961. York University Archives and Special Collections, Margaret Laurence Fonds.

991.   Ibid.

992.   As quoted in Thomas Tausky's "Biocritical Essay," which opens the first Calgary inventory of *The Alice Munro Papers, First Accession,* edited by Apollonia Steele and Jean F. Tener. (Calgary: University of Calgary Press, 1986), xl. Munro did use Vancouver later in her fiction.

993.   Margaret Laurence, interview by Harold Horwood, "Unforgettable Margaret Laurence."

994.   *Dance*, 85.

995.   See "Books That Mattered to Me," in *Margaret Laurence: An Appreciation,* 239-49.

996.   *Dance*, 85.

997.   Ibid., 160.

998.   ML to Gordon Elliott, 1 November 1962. McMaster University Archives and Special Collections.

999.   Ibid.

1000.   Ibid.

1001.   Ibid.

1002.   They moved to Elm Cottage in Buckinghamshire after celebrating Christmas 1963 in their London flat.

1003.   See ML to Buckler, 30 August 1974, in J.A. Wainwright, *A Very Large Soul,* 26-29, and Harold Horwood, "Unforgettable Margaret Laurence." 107-11.

1004.   ML to G. Elliott, 1 November 1962. McMaster University Archives and Special Collections.

1005.   *Dance*, 162.

1006.   ML to G. Elliott, 25 November 1962. McMaster University Archives and Special Collections.

1007.   Ibid., 1 November 1962.

1008.   Ibid.

1009.   *Dance*, 161.

1010.   ML to G. Elliott, 25 November 1962. McMaster University Archives and Special Collections.

1011.   ML to G. Woodcock, 29 November 1962. York University Archives and Special Collections, Margaret Laurence Fonds.

1012.   ML to AW, 11 December 1962. York University Archives and Special Collections, Margaret Laurence Fonds.

1013.   ML to G. Elliott, 25 November 1962. McMaster University Archives and Special Collections.

1014.   Among the many works that deal with loss of parents in childhood are: Maxine Harris, *The Loss that Is Forever: The Lifelong Impact of the Early Death of a Mother or Father* (New York: A Plume Book, Penguin Book, 1996) and Hope Edelman, *Motherless Daughters: The Legacy of Loss* (New York: A Delta Book, Bantam Doubleday Dell, 1974).

1015.   It was published later in *Winter's Tales 9*, 1963.

1016.   ML to G. Elliott, 10 March 1963. McMaster University Archives and Special Collections.

1017.   Ibid., 17 December 1962.

1018.   *PCB*, 228.

1019.   Laurence's choice of the name Danquah is interesting in this context. Dr. J.B. Danquah was one of the most important political figures of that era.

1020.   Compare, for example, Huxley's depiction of the mores, climate, and market women in her chapter "The Gold Coast" with Laurence's descriptions of those places and people in *The Tomorrow-Tamer*, especially in "A Gourdful of Glory."

1021.   ML to G. Elliott, 17 December 1962. McMaster University Archives and Special Collections. See also ML to AW, 11 December 1962. York University Archives and Special Collections, Margaret Laurence Fonds.

1022.   Sylvia Plath "Snow Blitz: Essay 1963," in *Johnny Panic and the Bible of Dreams: Short Stories, Prose and Diary Excerpts* (New York, Harper & Row, 1977), 28.

1023.   *Dance*, 161-62.

1024.   In Plath, *Johnny Panic and the Bible of Dreams*, 27-35.

1025.   ML to E. Buckler, 30 August 1974, as quoted in Wainwright, 26-29.

1026.   ML to Willis Wing, 9 February 1963. Curtis Brown Collection, Columbia University Archives and Special Collections.

1027.   ML to G. Elliott, 10 March 1963. McMaster University Archives and Special Collections.

1028.   Ibid.

1029.   Although James King states that Bolton was Jack's cousin, this is not the case. Frances (née Bolton) Jones, telephone conversation with author, 2 October 1994. See also ML to AW, 12 June 1963. York University Archives and Special Collections, Margaret Laurence Fonds.

1030.   John Cushman Associates, Rare Book and Manuscript Library, Columbia University Box 127, Series 3.

1031.   ML to Ethel Wilson, 23 January 1964. University of British Columbia Library, the Wilson Papers.

1032.   Ibid. She also raised the possibility of an article for *Holiday* with John Cushman. See ML to John Cushman, Curtis Brown Papers, Rare Book and Manuscript Library, Columbia University Box 245.

1033.   Greg Gatenby, letter to ML (York University Archives and Special Collections, Margaret Laurence Fonds, August 6, 1981 and August 24, 1981).

1034.   The CD *Water Music* containing "A Fable for the Whaling Fleets" with narration by Margaret Laurence is presently available from The Canadian Music Centre Distribution Service, Toronto.

1035.   Michael Hodgart, *Satire* (London: World University Library, 1969), 171-76.

1036.   (No. 32 Summer 1964), 25-37. It was reprinted a decade later in an anthology edited by A.J. M. Smith, *The Canadian Century: English Canadian Writing Since Confederation* (Toronto: Gage, 1973).

1037.   See Fred C. Farr, letter to ML (11 November 1981), and ML to Fred C. Farr, (2 December 1981),York University Archives and Special Collections, Margaret Laurence Fonds. All quotations by Margaret Laurence are taken from her letter to Farr.

1038.   This was reprinted in *Margaret Laurence: An Appreciation*, edited by Christl Verduyn (Peterborough, Ontario: Broadview Press and the *Journal of Canadian Studies*, 1988). Laurence's lecture was originally presented to the Trent Philosophy Society, March 29, 1983. It was also published in *Canadian Literature*, (no.100, Spring 1984).

SELECTED BIBLIOGRAPHY

Andrzejewski, B.W. "Poetry and Camels in Somalia: Reflections on *Suugaanta Geela*, in IUFAHA-MU, 17. 2 (Spring,1989): 157-63.

_____. "Somali Literature" in *Literatures in African Languages*. Cambridge: Cambridge Univesity Press, 1985.

Andrzejewski, B.W. and I.M. Lewis, eds. *Somali Poetry: An Introduction*. Oxford: Clarendon Press, 1964.

Bedford, A.G. *The University of Winnipeg: A History of the Founding Colleges*. Toronto: The University of Toronto Press, 1976.

Castagno, Margaret. *Historical Dictionary of Somalia*. Metuchen, N.J.: The Scarecrow Press, 1975.

Clark, Richard. E. *Point Roberts, USA.: The History of a Canadian Enclave*. Bellingham, WA.: Textype Publishing, 1980.

Coger, Greta McCormick, ed. *New Perspectives on Margaret Laurence*. Westport: Greenwood Press, 1996.

Ferns, H.S. *Reading from Left to Right: One Man's Political History*. Toronto: Buffalo, London: University of Toronto Press, 1983.

Gibson, Graeme. *Eleven Canadian Novelists*, interviews. Toronto: House of Anansi Press, 1973.

Gunars, Kristjana. *Crossing the River: Essays in Honour of Margaret Laurence*. Winnipeg, Turnstone Press, 1988.

Horwood, Harold. "Unforgettable Margaret Laurence." *Reader's Digest* (April 1988): 7-11.

Heritage: History of the Town of Neepawa and District as Told and Recorded by its People. Neepawa, Manitoba: History Book Committee, 1983.

Kerzer, Jon. *"That House in Manawaka": Margaret Laurence's A Bird in the House.* Toronto: ECW Press, 1992

King, James. *The Life of Margaret Laurence.* Toronto: Alfred A. Knopf, Canada. 1997.

Laurence, Margaret. *A Bird in the House* New Canadian Library edition, no. 96, paperback, published by McClelland & Stewart, 1987. The pagination is identical to the hardcover edition published by Alfred A. Knopf, New York, 1970.

_____. *A Tree for Poverty: Somali Poetry and Prose.* Shannon: Irish University Press and McMaster University Library Press, 1970. This is a photolithographic facsimile of the first edition, published in Nairobi, 1954.

_____. *Dance on the Earth: A Memoir.* Toronto: McClelland & Stewart. 1989.
_____. *The Diviners.* Toronto: McClelland & Stewart, 1974.

_____. *Heart of a Stranger.* Toronto: McClelland & Stewart, 1976.

_____. *Journal.* Margaret Laurence Collection. McMaster University Library Archives.

_____. "Letter to Bob Sorfleet," 13 November 1978, in *Journal of Canadian Fiction,* 27 (1980): 52–53.

_____. *The Prophet's Camel Bell.* Toronto: McClelland & Stewart, 1963. Reprint with an afterword by Clara Thomas, Toronto: McClelland & Stewart, New Canadian Library, 1988.

_____. *This Side Jordan.* Toronto: McClelland & Stewart, 1960. Reprint, Toronto: McClelland & Stewart, New Canadian Library, 1989.

Lennox, John, ed. *Margaret Laurence — Al Purdy: A Friendship in Letters.* Toronto: McClelland & Stewart, 1993.

Lennox, John and Ruth Panofsky, eds. *The Selected Letters* of *Margaret Laurence and Adele Wiseman.* Toronto: The University of Toronto Press, 1997.

Little, Jennie Maud. Diary. University of Manitoba Archives.

Metcalf, John. *Sixteen by Twelve: Short Stories by Canadian Writers.* Toronto: McGraw Hill Ryerson, 1970.

Morley, Patricia. *The Long Journey Home.* Montreal and Kingston: McGill-Queens University Press, revised edition, 1991.

New, William H., ed. *Margaret Laurence: the Writer and Her Critics*. Toronto: McGraw Hill Ryerson, 1977.

Nicolson, Colin, ed. *Critical Approaches to the Fiction of Margaret Laurence*. Vancouver: The University of British Columbia Press, 1990.

Phelps, Arthur L. *Canadian Writers*. Toronto: McClelland & Stewart, 1951.

Powers, Lyall. *Alien Heart: The Life and Work of Margaret Laurence*. Manitoba: The University of Manitoba Press, 2003.

Riegel, Christian, ed. *Challenging Territory: The Writing of Margaret Laurence*. Edmonton: The University of Alberta Press, 1997.

Sparrow, Fiona. *Into Africa with Margaret Laurence*. Toronto: ECW Press, 1992.

Sproxton, Birk and G.N. Louise Jonasson, eds. *Winnipeg in Fiction: 125 Years of English-Language Writing*, special issue of *Prairie Fire* 20 no. 2 (Summer 1999).

Thomson, Watson. *Turning Into Tomorrow*. New York: The Philosophical Library, 1966.

Staines, David, ed. *Margaret Laurence: Critical Reflections*. Ottawa: University of Ottawa Press, 2001.

Stouck, David, ed. *Ethel Wilson: Stories, Essays, and Letters*. Vancouver: University of British Columbia Press, 1987.

_____. *Ethel Wilson: A Critical Biography*. Toronto: Univesity of Toronto Press, 2003.

Stovel, Nora Foster, ed. *Embryo Words: Margaret Laurence's Early Writings*. Edmonton: Juvenilia Press, 1997.

Taylor, Gladys. "Laurence of Manitoba," *Canadian Author and Bookman,* 42 (Winter 1966): 4-7.

Thomas, Clara. *Margaret Laurence*. Toronto: McClelland & Stewart, Canadian Writers Series, no.3, 1969.

_____. *The Manawaka World of Margaret Laurence*. Toronto: McClelland & Stewart, 1975.

Twigg. Alan. *Vancouver and its Writers: A Guide to Vancouver's Literary Landmarks*. Madeira Park, British Columbia: Harbour Publishing, 1986.

_____. *For Openers: Conversations with 24 Canadian Writers*. Madeira Park, British Columbia: Harbour Publishing, 1981.

Verduyn, Christl, ed. *Margaret Laurence: An Appreciation*. Peterborough, Ontario: Broadview Press, 1988.

Wainwright, J.A., ed. *A Very Large Soul: Selected Letters from Margaret Laurence to Canadian Writers*. Dunvegan, Ontario: Cormorant Press, 1995.

Warwick, Susan. *Margaret Laurence: An Annotated Bibliography*. Toronto: ECW Press, 1979.

Welton, Michael. "To Be and Build the Glorious World": The Educational Thought and Practice of Watson Thomson, 1899-1946." Ph.D. diss., University of British Columbia, 1983.

Wigmore, Donnalu, "Margaret Laurence: The Woman behind the Writing." Interview, *Chatelaine* (February 1971): 28-29; 52-54.

Wigmore, Margaret. "'North Main Car': A Context." *Prairie Fire* 20, no.2 (Summer 1999): 100-9.

Wilson, Lois. *Turning the World Upside Down: A Memoir*. Toronto: Doubleday Canada Ltd., 1989.

Wiseman, Adele. *Memoirs of a Book Molesting Childhood and Other Essays*. Toronto: Oxford University Press, 1987.

Woodcock, George, ed. *A Place to Stand on: Essays by and about Margaret Laurence*. Edmonton: NeWest Press, 1983.

Xiques, Donez. "Margaret Laurence's Somali Translations." *Canadian Literature* 135 (Winter 1992), 33-48.

_____. "New Light on Margaret Laurence's First African Short Story." *Canadian Notes and Queries* 42 (Spring 1990): 14-21.

INDEX